CHARLOTTE BRONTË AND HER CIRCLE

Charlotte Brontë
(Mrs Arthur Bell Nicholls)
From the portrait by George Richmond in the possession of Mr A. B. Nicholls

CHARLOTTE BRONTË

AND HER CIRCLE

BY

CLEMENT K. SHORTER

GREENWOOD PRESS, PUBLISHERS
WESTPORT, CONNECTICUT

AAC 3519

Originally published in 1896
by Dodd, Mead and Company

First Greenwood Reprinting 1970

SBN 8371-2811-0

PREFACE.

It is claimed for the following book of some five hundred pages that the larger part of it is an addition of entirely new material to the romantic story of the Brontës. For this result, but very small credit is due to me; and my very hearty acknowledgments must be made, in the first place, to the Rev. Arthur Bell Nicholls, for whose generous surrender of personal inclination I must ever be grateful. It has been with extreme unwillingness that Mr. Nicholls has broken the silence of forty years, and he would not even now have consented to the publication of certain letters concerning his marriage, had he not been aware that these letters were already privately printed and in the hands of not less than eight or ten people. To Miss Ellen Nussey of Gomersall, I have also to render thanks for having placed the many letters in her possession at my disposal, and for having furnished a great deal of interesting information. Without the letters from Charlotte Brontë to Mr. W. S. Williams, which were kindly lent to me by his son and daughter, Mr. and Mrs. Baumer Williams, my book would have been the poorer. Sir Wemyss Reid, Mr. J. J. Stead, of Heckmondwike, Mr. Butler Wood, of Bradford, Mr. W. W. Yates, of Dewsbury, Mr. Erskine Stuart, Mr. Buxton Forman, and Mr. Thomas J. Wise are among the many Brontë specialists who have helped me with advice or with the loan of material. Mr. Wise, in particular, has lent me many valuable manuscripts. Finally, I have to thank my friend Dr. Robertson Nicoll for the kindly pressure which has practically compelled me to prepare this little volume amid a multitude of journalistic duties.

CLEMENT K. SHORTER.

198 STRAND, LONDON,
    September 1st, 1896.

CONTENTS.

CHARLOTTE BRONTË AND HER CIRCLE

A BRONTË CHRONOLOGY

CHARLOTTE BRONTË AND HER CIRCLE

A BRONTË CHRONOLOGY

PRELIMINARY.

MRS. GASKELL.

In the whole of English biographical literature there is no book that can compare in wide-spread interest with the 'Life of Charlotte Brontë' by Mrs. Gaskell. It has held a position of singular popularity for forty years; and while biography after biography has come and gone, it still commands a place side by side with Boswell's 'Johnson' and Lockhart's 'Scott.' As far as mere readers are concerned, it may indeed claim its hundreds as against the tens of intrinsically more important rivals. There are obvious reasons for this success. Mrs. Gaskell was herself a popular novelist, who commanded a very wide audience, and 'Cranford,' at least, has taken a place among the classics of our literature. She brought to bear upon the biography of Charlotte Brontë all those literary gifts which had made the charm of her seven volumes of romance. And these gifts were employed upon a romance of real life, not less fascinating than anything which imagination could have furnished. Charlotte Brontë's success as an author turned the eyes of the world upon her. Thackeray had sent her his 'Vanity Fair' before he knew her name or sex. The precious volume lies before me —

with the grateful regards of W. M. Thackeray.

July 18. 1848.

And Thackeray did not send many inscribed copies of his books even to successful authors. Speculation concerning

1

the author of 'Jane Eyre' was sufficiently rife during those
seven sad years of literary renown to make a biography
imperative when death came to Charlotte Brontë in 1855.
All the world had heard something of the three marvellous
sisters, daughters of a poor parson in Yorkshire, going one
after another to their death with such melancholy swiftness,
but leaving — two of them, at least — imperishable work behind them. The old blind father and the bereaved husband
read the confused eulogy and criticism, sometimes with a
sad pleasure at the praise, oftener with a sadder pain at
the grotesque inaccuracy. Small wonder that it became
impressed upon Mr. Brontë's mind that an authoritative
biography was desirable. His son-in-law, Mr. Arthur Bell
Nicholls, who lived with him in the Haworth parsonage
during the six weary years which succeeded Mrs. Nicholls's
death, was not so readily won to the unveiling of his
wife's inner life; and although we, who read Mrs. Gaskell's
'Memoir,' have every reason to be thankful for Mr. Brontë's
decision, peace of mind would undoubtedly have been more
assured to Charlotte Brontë's surviving relatives had the
most rigid silence been maintained. The book, when it
appeared in 1857, gave infinite pain to a number of people,
including Mr. Brontë and Mr. Nicholls; and Mrs. Gaskell's
subsequent experiences had the effect of persuading her that
all biographical literature was intolerable and undesirable.
She would seem to have given instructions that no biography of herself should be written; and now that thirty
years have passed since her death we have no substantial
record of one of the most fascinating women of her age.
The loss to literature has been forcibly brought home to
the present writer, who has in his possession a bundle of
letters written by Mrs. Gaskell to numerous friends of
Charlotte Brontë during the progress of the biography.
They serve, all of them, to impress one with the singular
charm of the woman, her humanity and breadth of sympathy.

2

They make us think better of Mrs. Gaskell, as Thackeray's letters to Mrs. Brookfield make us think better of the author of 'Vanity Fair.'

Apart from these letters, a journey in the footsteps, as it were, of Mrs. Gaskell, reveals to us the remarkable conscientiousness with which she set about her task. It would have been possible, with so much fame behind her, to have secured an equal success, and certainly an equal pecuniary reward, had she merely written a brief monograph with such material as was voluntarily placed in her hands. Mrs. Gaskell possessed a higher ideal of a biographer's duties. She spared no pains to find out the facts; she visited every spot associated with the name of Charlotte Brontë — Thornton, Haworth, Cowan Bridge, Birstall, Brussels — and she wrote countless letters to the friends of Charlotte Brontë's earlier days.

But why, it may be asked, was Mrs. Gaskell selected as biographer? The choice was made by Mr. Brontë, and not, as has been suggested, by some outside influence. When Mr. Brontë had once decided that there should be an authoritative biography — and he alone was active in the matter — there could be but little doubt upon whom the task would fall. Among all the friends whom fame had brought to Charlotte, Mrs. Gaskell stood prominent for her literary gifts and her large-hearted sympathy. She had made the acquaintance of Miss Brontë when the latter was on a visit to Sir James Kay Shuttleworth, in 1850; and a letter from Charlotte to her father, and others to Mr. W. S. Williams, indicate the beginning of a friendship which was to leave so permanent a record in literary history : —

TO W. S. WILLIAMS.

'NOVEMBER 20, 1849.

'MY DEAR SIR, — You said that if I wished for any copies of "Shirley" to be sent to individuals I was to name the parties.

CHARLOTTE BRONTË

I have thought of one person to whom I should much like a copy to be offered — Harriet Martineau. For her character — as revealed in her works — I have a lively admiration, a deep esteem. Will you inclose with the volume the accompanying note?

'The letter you forwarded this morning was from Mrs. Gaskell, authoress of "Mary Barton;" she said I was not to answer it, but I cannot help doing so. The note brought the tears to my eyes. She is a good, she is a great woman. Proud am I that I can touch a chord of sympathy in souls so noble. In Mrs. Gaskell's nature it mournfully pleases me to fancy a remote affinity to my sister Emily. In Miss Martineau's mind I have always felt the same, though there are wide differences. Both these ladies are above me — certainly far my superiors in attainments and experience. I think I could look up to them if I knew them. — I am, dear sir, yours sincerely,

'C. Brontë.'

TO W. S. WILLIAMS.

'November 29, 1849.

'Dear Sir, — I inclose two notes for postage. The note you sent yesterday was from Harriet Martineau; its contents were more than gratifying. I ought to be thankful, and I trust I am, for such testimonies of sympathy from the first order of minds. When Mrs. Gaskell tells me she shall keep my works as a treasure for her daughters, and when Harriet Martineau testifies affectionate approbation, I feel the sting taken from the strictures of another class of critics. My resolution of seclusion withholds me from communicating further with these ladies at present, but I now know how they are inclined to me — I know how my writings have affected their wise and pure minds. The knowledge is present support and, perhaps, may be future armour.

'I trust Mrs. Williams's health and, consequently, your spirits are by this time quite restored. If all be well, perhaps I shall see you next week. — Yours sincerely,

'C. Brontë.'

TO W. S. WILLIAMS.

'JANUARY 1, 1850.

' MY DEAR SIR, — May I beg that a copy of " Wuthering Heights " may be sent to Mrs. Gaskell ; her present address is 3 Sussex Place, Regent's Park. She has just sent me the " Moorland Cottage." I felt disappointed about the publication of that book, having hoped it would be offered to Smith, Elder & Co. ; but it seems she had no alternative, as it was Mr. Chapman himself who asked her to write a Christmas book. On my return home yesterday I found two packets from Cornhill directed in two well-known hands waiting for me. You are all very, very good.

' I trust to have derived benefit from my visit to Miss Martineau. A visit more interesting I certainly never paid. If self-sustaining strength can be acquired from example, I ought to have got good. But my nature is not hers ; I could not make it so though I were to submit it seventy times seven to the furnace of affliction, and discipline it for an age under the hammer and anvil of toil and self-sacrifice. Perhaps if I was like her I should not admire her so much as I do. She is somewhat absolute, though quite unconsciously so ; but she is likewise kind, with an affection at once abrupt and constant, whose sincerity you cannot doubt. It was delightful to sit near her in the evenings and hear her converse, myself mute. She speaks with what seems to me a wonderful fluency and eloquence. Her animal spirits are as unflagging as her intellectual powers. I was glad to find her health excellent. I believe neither solitude nor loss of friends would break her down. I saw some faults in her, but somehow I liked them for the sake of her good points. It gave me no pain to feel insignificant, mentally and corporeally, in comparison with her.

' Trusting that you and yours are well, and sincerely wishing you all a happy new year, — I am, my dear sir, yours sincerely,

'C. BRONTË.'

TO REV. P. BRONTË.

' THE BRIERY, WINDERMERE, August 10, 1850.

' DEAR PAPA, — I reached this place yesterday evening at eight o'clock, after a safe though rather tedious journey. I had to change carriages three times and to wait an hour and a half at Lancaster. Sir James came to meet me at the station; both he and Lady Shuttleworth gave me a very kind reception. This place is exquisitely beautiful, though the weather is cloudy, misty, and stormy; but the sun bursts out occasionally and shows the hills and the lake. Mrs. Gaskell is coming here this evening, and one or two other people. Miss Martineau, I am sorry to say, I shall not see, as she is already gone from home for the autumn.

'Be kind enough to write by return of post and tell me how you are getting on and how you are. Give my kind regards to Tabby and Martha, and — Believe me, dear papa, your affectionate daughter, C. BRONTË.'

And this is how she writes to a friend from Haworth, on her return, after that first meeting: —

'Lady Shuttleworth never got out, being confined to the house with a cold; but fortunately there was Mrs. Gaskell, the authoress of "Mary Barton," who came to the Briery the day after me. I was truly glad of her companionship. She is a woman of the most genuine talent, of cheerful, pleasing, and cordial manners, and, I believe, of a kind and good heart.'

TO W. S. WILLIAMS.

'SEPTEMBER 20, 1850.

'MY DEAR SIR, — I herewith send you a very roughly written copy of what I have to say about my sisters. When you have read it you can better judge whether the word "Notice" or "Memoir" is the most appropriate. I think the former. Memoir seems to me to express a more circumstantial and different sort of account. My aim is to give a just idea of their identity, not to write any narration of their simple, uneventful lives. I depend on you for faithfully pointing out whatever may strike you as faulty. I could not write it in the conventional form — *that* I found impossible.

'It gives me real pleasure to hear of your son's success. I trust he may persevere and go on improving, and give his parents cause for satisfaction and honest pride.

'I am truly pleased, too, to learn that Miss Kavanagh has managed so well with Mr. Colburn. Her position seems to me one deserving of all sympathy. I often think of her. Will her novel soon be published? Somehow I expect it to be interesting.

'I certainly did hope that Mrs. Gaskell would offer her next work to Smith & Elder. She and I had some conversation about publishers — a comparison of our literary experiences was made. She seemed much struck with the differences between hers and mine, though I did not enter into details or tell her all. Unless I greatly mistake, she and you and Mr. Smith would get on well together; but one does not know what causes there may be to prevent her from doing as she would wish in such a case. I think Mr. Smith will not object to my occasionally sending her any of the Cornhill books that she may like to see. I have already taken the liberty of lending her Wordsworth's "Prelude," as she was saying how much she wished to have the opportunity of reading it.

'I do not tack remembrances to Mrs. Williams and your daughters and Miss Kavanagh to all my letters, because that makes an empty form of what should be a sincere wish, but I trust this mark of courtesy and regard, though rarely expressed, is always understood. — Believe me, yours sincerely,

'C. Brontë.'

Miss Brontë twice visited Mrs. Gaskell in her Manchester home, first in 1851 and afterwards in 1853, and concerning this latter visit we have the following letter : —

TO MRS. GASKELL, MANCHESTER.

'HAWORTH, April 14, 1853.

'MY DEAR MRS. GASKELL, — Would it suit you if I were to come next Thursday, the 21st?

'If that day tallies with your convenience, and if my father continues as well as he is now, I know of no engagement on my part which need compel me longer to defer the pleasure of seeing you.

'I should arrive by the train which reaches Manchester at 7 o'clock P. M. That, I think, would be about your tea-time, and, of course, I should dine before leaving home. I always like evening for an arrival; it seems more cosy and pleasant than coming in about the busy middle of the day. I think if I stay a week that will be a very long visit; it will give you time to get well tired of me.

'Remember me very kindly to Mr. Gaskell and Marianna. As to Mesdames Flossy and Julia, those venerable ladies are requested beforehand to make due allowance for the awe with which they will be sure to impress a diffident admirer. I am sorry I shall not see Meta. — Believe me, my dear Mrs. Gaskell, yours affectionately and sincerely, C. BRONTË.'

In the autumn of 1853 Mrs. Gaskell returned Charlotte Brontë's visit at Haworth. She was not, however, at Charlotte's wedding in Haworth Church.[1]

TO MISS WOOLER.

'HAWORTH, September 8.

'MY DEAR MISS WOOLER, — Your letter was truly kind, and made me warmly wish to join you. My prospects, however, of being able to leave home continue very unsettled. I am expecting Mrs. Gaskell next week or the week after, the day being yet undetermined. She was to have come in June, but then my severe attack of influenza rendered it impossible that I should receive or entertain her. Since that time she has been absent on the Continent with her husband and two eldest girls; and just before I received yours I had a letter from her volunteering a visit at a vague date, which I requested her to fix as soon as possible. My father has been much better during the last three or four days.

'When I know anything certain I will write to you again.— Believe me, my dear Miss Wooler, yours respectfully and affectionately, C. BRONTË.'

[1] Although so stated by Professor A. W. Ward in the "Dictionary of National Biography," vol. xxi.

But the friendship, which commenced so late in Charlotte Brontë's life, never reached the stage of downright intimacy. Of this there is abundant evidence in the biography; and Mrs. Gaskell was forced to rely upon the correspondence of older friends of Charlotte's. Mr. George Smith, the head of the firm of Smith and Elder, furnished some twenty letters. Mr. W. S. Williams, to whom is due the credit of 'discovering' the author of 'Jane Eyre,' lent others; and another member of Messrs. Smith and Elder's staff, Mr. James Taylor, furnished half-a-dozen more; but the best help came from another quarter.

Of the two schoolfellows with whom Charlotte Brontë regularly corresponded from childhood till death, Mary Taylor and Ellen Nussey, the former had destroyed every letter; and thus it came about that by far the larger part of the correspondence in Mrs. Gaskell's biography was addressed to Miss Ellen Nussey, now as 'My dearest Nell,' now simply as 'E.' The unpublished correspondence in my hands, which refers to the biography, opens with a letter from Mrs. Gaskell to Miss Nussey, dated July 6th, 1855. It relates how, in accordance with a request from Mr. Brontë, she had undertaken to write the work, and had been over to Haworth. There she had made the acquaintance of Mr. Nicholls for the first time. She told Mr. Brontë how much she felt the difficulty of the task she had undertaken. Nevertheless, she sincerely desired to make his daughter's character known to all who took deep interest in her writings. Both Mr. Brontë and Mr. Nicholls agreed to help to the utmost, although Mrs. Gaskell was struck by the fact that it was Mr. Nicholls, and not Mr. Brontë, who was more intellectually alive to the attraction which such a book would have for the public. His feelings were opposed to any biography at all; but he had yielded to Mr. Brontë's 'impetuous wish,' and he brought down all the materials he could find, in the shape of about a dozen letters. Mr. Nicholls, moreover, told Mrs. Gaskell that Miss Nussey was the person of all others to apply to; that she had been the friend of his wife ever since Charlotte was fifteen, and that he was writing to Miss Nussey to beg her to let Mrs. Gaskell see some of the correspondence.

But here is Mr. Nicholls's actual letter, unearthed after forty years, as well as earlier letters from and to Miss Nussey, which would seem to indicate a suggestion upon the part of 'E' that some attempt should be made to furnish a biography of her friend — if only to set at rest, once and for all, the speculations of the gossiping community with whom Charlotte Brontë's personality was still shrouded in mystery; and indeed it is clear from these letters that it is to Miss Nussey that we really owe Mrs. Gaskell's participation in the matter: —

TO REV. A. B. NICHOLLS.

'BROOKROYD, June 6, 1855.

'DEAR MR. NICHOLLS, — I have been much hurt and pained by the perusal of an article in "Sharpe" for this month, entitled "A Few Words about 'Jane Eyre.'" You will be certain to see the article, and I am sure both you and Mr. Brontë will feel acutely the misrepresentations and the malignant spirit which characterises it. Will you suffer the article to pass current without any refutations? The writer merits the contempt of silence, but there will be readers and believers. Shall such be left to imbibe a tissue of malignant falsehoods, or shall an attempt be made to do justice to one who so highly deserved justice, whose very name those who best knew her but speak with reverence and affection. Should not her aged father be defended from the reproach the writer coarsely attempts to bring upon him?

'I wish Mrs. Gaskell, who is every way capable, would undertake a reply, and would give a sound castigation to the writer. Her personal acquaintance with Haworth, the Parsonage, and its inmates, fits her for the task, and if on other

10

subjects she lacked information I would gladly supply her with
facts sufficient to set aside much that is asserted, if you yourself
are not provided with all the information that is needed on the
subjects produced. Will you ask Mrs. Gaskell to undertake
this just and honourable defence? I think she would do it
gladly. She valued dear Charlotte, and such an act of friendship, performed with her ability and power, could only add to
the laurels she has already won. I hope you and Mr. Brontë
are well. My kind regards to both. — Believe me, yours
sincerely,   E. Nussey.'

TO MISS ELLEN NUSSEY.

'Haworth, June 11, 1855.

'Dear Miss Nussey, — We had not seen the article in "Sharpe,"
and very possibly should not, if you had not directed our
attention to it. We ordered a copy, and have now read the
"Few Words about 'Jane Eyre.'" The writer has certainly made
many mistakes, but apparently not from any unkind motive, as
he professes to be an admirer of Charlotte's works, pays a just
tribute to her genius, and in common with thousands deplores
her untimely death. His design seems rather to be to gratify
the curiosity of the multitude in reference to one who had
made such a sensation in the literary world. But even if the
article had been of a less harmless character, we should not
have felt inclined to take any notice of it, as by doing so we
should have given it an importance which it would not otherwise have obtained. Charlotte herself would have acted thus ;
and her character stands too high to be injured by the statements in a magazine of small circulation and little influence —
statements which the writer prefaces with the remark that
he does not vouch for their accuracy. The many laudatory
notices of Charlotte and her works which appeared since her
death may well make us indifferent to the detractions of a
few envious or malignant persons, as there ever will be
such.

'The remarks respecting Mr. Brontë excited in him only
amusement — indeed, I have not seen him laugh as much for

some months as he did while I was reading the article to him. We are both well in health, but lonely and desolate.

'Mr. Brontë unites with me in kind regards. — Yours sincerely, A. B. NICHOLLS.'

TO MISS ELLEN NUSSEY.

'HAWORTH, July 24, 1855.

'DEAR MISS NUSSEY, — Some other erroneous notices of Charlotte having appeared, Mr. Brontë has deemed it advisable that some authentic statement should be put forth. He has therefore adopted your suggestion and applied to Mrs. Gaskell, who has undertaken to write a life of Charlotte. Mrs. Gaskell came over yesterday and spent a few hours with us. The greatest difficulty seems to be in obtaining materials to show the development of Charlotte's character. For this reason Mrs. Gaskell is anxious to see her letters, especially those of any early date. I think I understood you to say that you had some; if so, we should feel obliged by your letting us have any that you may think proper, not for publication, but merely to give the writer an insight into her mode of thought. Of course they will be returned after a little time.

'I confess that the course most consonant with my own feelings would be to take no steps in the matter, but I do not think it right to offer any opposition to Mr. Brontë's wishes.

'We have the same object in view, but should differ in our mode of proceeding. Mr. Brontë has not been very well. Excitement on Sunday (our Rush-bearing) and Mrs. Gaskell's visit yesterday have been rather much for him. — Believe me, sincerely yours, A. B. NICHOLLS.'

Mrs. Gaskell, however, wanted to make Miss Nussey's acquaintance, and asked if she might visit her; and added that she would also like to see Miss Wooler, Charlotte's schoolmistress, if that lady were still alive. To this letter Miss Nussey made the following reply : —

AND HER CIRCLE

TO MRS. GASKELL, Manchester.

'Ilkley, July 26, 1855.

'My dear Madam, — Owing to my absence from home your
letter has only just reached me. I had not heard of Mr.
Brontë's request, but I am most heartily glad that he has
made it. A letter from Mr. Nicholls was forwarded along
with yours, which I opened first, and was thus prepared for
your communication, the subject of which is of the deepest
interest to me. I will do everything in my power to aid the
righteous work you have undertaken, but I feel my powers
very limited, and apprehend that you may experience some
disappointment that I cannot contribute more largely the information which you desire. I possess a great many letters (for
I have destroyed but a small portion of the correspondence),
but I fear the early letters are not such as to unfold the
character of the writer except in a few points. You perhaps
may discover more than is apparent to me. You will read
them with a purpose — I perused them only with interests of
affection. I will immediately look over the correspondence, and
I promise to let you see all that I can confide to your friendly
custody. I regret that my absence from home should have
made it impossible for me to have the pleasure of seeing you
at Brookroyd at the time you propose. I am engaged to stay
here till Monday week, and shall be happy to see you any day
you name after that date, or if more convenient to you to come
Friday or Saturday in next week, I will gladly return in time
to give you the meeting. I am staying with our schoolmistress,
Miss Wooler, in this place. I wish her very much to give me
leave to ask you here, but she does not yield to my wishes;
it would have been pleasanter to me to talk with you among
these hills than sitting in my home and thinking of one who
had so often been present there. — I am, my dear madam, yours
sincerely,   Ellen Nussey.'

Mrs. Gaskell and Miss Nussey met, and the friendship
which ensued was closed only by death; and indeed one

13

of the most beautiful letters in the collection in my hands
is one signed ' Meta Gaskell,' and dated January 22, 1866.
It tells in detail, with infinite tenderness and pathos, of
her mother's last moments.[1] That, however, was ten years
later than the period with which we are concerned. In
1856 Mrs. Gaskell was energetically engaged upon a biography of her friend which should lack nothing of thorough-
ness, as she hoped. She claimed to have visited the scenes
of all the incidents in Charlotte's life, ' the two little pieces
of private governess-ship excepted.' She went one day
with Mr. Smith to the Chapter Coffee House, where the
sisters first stayed in London. Another day she is in
Yorkshire, where she makes the acquaintance of Miss
Wooler, which permitted, as she said, 'a more friendly
manner of writing towards Charlotte Brontë's old schoolmistress.' Again she is in Brussels, where Madame Héger
refused to see her, although M. Héger was kind and
communicative, 'and very much indeed I both like and
respect him.' Her countless questions were exceedingly
interesting. They covered many pages of note-paper.
'Did Branwell Brontë know of the publication of " Jane
Eyre," ' she asks, 'and how did he receive the news ? ' Mrs.
Gaskell was persuaded in her own mind that he had never
known of its publication, and we shall presently see that
she was right. Charlotte had distinctly informed her, she
said, that Branwell was not in a fit condition at the time to
be told. ' Where did the girls get the books which they
read so continually ? Did Emily accompany Charlotte as a
pupil when the latter went as a teacher to Roe Head ?
Why did not Branwell go to the Royal Academy in London
to learn painting ? Did Emily ever go out as a governess ?
What were Emily's religious opinions ? Did *she* ever make
friends ? ' Such were the questions which came quick and

[1] ' Mama's last days,' it runs, ' had been full of loving thought and tender
help for others. She was so sweet and dear and noble beyond words.'

fast to Miss Nussey, and Miss Nussey fortunately kept her replies.

TO MRS. GASKELL, MANCHESTER.

'BROOKROYD, October 22, 1856.

'MY DEAR MRS. GASKELL, — If you go to London pray try what may be done with regard to a portrait of dear Charlotte. It would greatly enhance the value and interest of the memoir, and be such a satisfaction to people to see something that would settle their ideas of the personal appearance of the dear departed one. It has been a surprise to every stranger, I think, that she was so gentle and lady-like to look upon.

'Emily Brontë went to Roe Head as pupil when Charlotte went as teacher; she stayed there but two months; she never settled, and was ill from nothing but home-sickness. Anne took her place and remained about two years. Emily was a teacher for one six months in a ladies' school in Halifax or the neighbourhood. I do not know whether it was conduct or want of finances that prevented Branwell from going to the Royal Academy. Probably there were impediments of both kinds.

'I am afraid if you give me my name I shall feel a prominence in the book that I altogether shrink from. My very last wish would be to appear in the book more than is absolutely necessary. If it were possible, I would choose not to be known at all. It is my friend only that I care to see and recognise, though your framing and setting of the picture will very greatly enhance its value. — I am, my dear Mrs. Gaskell, yours very sincerely,   ELLEN NUSSEY.'

The book was published in two volumes, under the title of 'The Life of Charlotte Brontë,' in the spring of 1857. At first all was well. Mr. Brontë's earliest acknowledgment of the book was one of approbation. Sir James Shuttleworth expressed the hope that Mr. Nicholls would 'rejoice that his wife would be known as a Christian heroine who could bear her cross with the firmness of a martyr saint.' Canon

Kingsley wrote a charming letter to Mrs. Gaskell, published in his ' Life,' and more than once reprinted since.

' Let me renew our long interrupted acquaintance,' he writes from St. Leonards, under date May 14th, 1857, ' by complimenting you on poor Miss Brontë's " Life." You have had a delicate and a great work to do, and you have done it admirably. Be sure that the book will do good. It will shame literary people into some stronger belief that a simple, virtuous, practical home life is consistent with high imaginative genius ; and it will shame, too, the prudery of a not over cleanly though carefully white-washed age, into believing that purity is now (as in all ages till now) quite compatible with the knowledge of evil. I confess that the book has made me ashamed of myself. " Jane Eyre " I hardly looked into, very seldom reading a work of fiction — yours, indeed, and Thackeray's, are the only ones I care to open. " Shirley " disgusted me at the opening, and I gave up the writer and her books with a notion that she was a person who liked coarseness. How I misjudged her ! and how thankful I am that I never put a word of my misconceptions into print, or recorded my misjudgments of one who is a whole heaven above me.

' Well have you done your work, and given us the picture of a valiant woman made perfect by suffering. I shall now read carefully and lovingly every word she has written, especially those poems, which ought not to have fallen dead as they did, and which seem to be (from a review in the current " Fraser ") of remarkable strength and purity.'

It was a short-lived triumph, however, and Mrs. Gaskell soon found herself, as she expressed it, ' in a veritable hornet's nest.' Mr. Brontë, to begin with, did not care for the references to himself and the suggestion that he had treated his wife unkindly. Mrs. Gaskell had associated him with numerous eccentricities and ebullitions of temper, which during his later years he always asserted, and undoubtedly with perfect truth, were, at the best, the fabrications of a dismissed servant. Mr. Nicholls had also his grievance. There was just a suspicion implied that he had not been quite the most sympathetic of husbands. The suspicion was absolutely ill-founded, and arose from Mr. Nicholls's intense shyness. But neither Mr. Brontë nor Mr. Nicholls gave Mrs. Gaskell much trouble. They, at any rate, were silent. Trouble, however, came from many quarters. Yorkshire people resented the air of patronage with which, as it seemed to them, a good Lancashire lady had taken their county in hand. They were not quite the backward savages, they retorted, which some of Mrs. Gaskell's descriptions in the beginning of her book would seem to suggest. Between Lancashire and Yorkshire there is always a suspicion of jealousy. It was intensified for the moment by these sombre pictures of 'this lawless, yet not unkindly population.'[1] A son-in-law of Mr. Redhead wrote to deny the account of that clergyman's association with Haworth. 'He gives another as true, in which I don't see any great difference.' Miss Martineau wrote sheet after sheet explanatory of her relations with Charlotte Brontë. 'Two separate householders in London *each* declares that the first interview between Miss Brontë and Miss Martineau took place at *her* house.' In one passage Mrs. Gaskell had spoken of wasteful young servants, and the young servants in question came upon Mr. Brontë for the following testimonial : —

'HAWORTH, August 17, 1857.

'I beg leave to state to all whom it may concern, that Nancy and Sarah Garrs, during the time they were in my service, were kind to my children, and honest, and not wasteful, but suffi-

[1] 'Some of the West Ridingers are very angry and declare they are half-a-century in civilisation before some of the Lancashire folk, and that this neighbourhood is a paradise compared with some districts not far from Manchester.' — Ellen Nussey to Mrs. Gaskell, April 16th, 1859.

ciently careful in regard to food, and all other articles committed
to their charge. P. Brontë, A.B.,
'*Incumbent of Haworth, Yorkshire.*'

Three whole pages were devoted to the dramatic recital
of a scandal at Haworth, and this entirely disappears from
the third edition. A casual reference to a girl who had
been seduced, and had found a friend in Miss Brontë, gave
further trouble. 'I have altered the word "seduced" to
"betrayed,"' writes Mrs. Gaskell to Martha Brown, 'and
I hope that this will satisfy the unhappy girl's friends.'
But all these were small matters compared with the Cowan
Bridge controversy and the threatened legal proceedings
over Branwell Brontë's suggested love affairs. Mrs. Gaskell
defended the description in 'Jane Eyre' of Cowan Bridge
with peculiar vigour. Mr. Carus Wilson, the Brocklehurst
of 'Jane Eyre' and his friends were furious. They threatened
an action. There were letters in the 'Times' and letters in the
'Daily News.' Mr. Nicholls broke silence — the only time in
the forty years that he has done so — with two admirable
letters to the 'Halifax Guardian.' The Cowan Bridge controversy was a drawn battle, in spite of numerous and glowing testimonials to the virtues of Mr. Carus Wilson. Most
people who know anything of the average private schools
of half a century ago are satisfied that Charlotte Brontë's
description was substantially correct. 'I want to show you
many letters,' writes Mrs. Gaskell, 'most of them praising
the character of our dear friend as she deserves, and from
people whose opinion she would have cared for, such as the
Duke of Argyll, Kingsley, Greig, etc. Many abusing me.
I should think seven or eight of this kind from the Carus
Wilson clique.'

The Branwell matter was more serious. Here Mrs. Gaskell
had, indeed, shown a singular recklessness. The lady referred
to by Branwell was Mrs. Robinson, the wife of the Rev.
Edmund Robinson of Thorp Green, and afterwards Lady

18

Scott. Anne Brontë was governess in her family for two years, and Branwell tutor to the son for a few months. Branwell, under the influence of opium, made certain statements about his relations with Mrs. Robinson which have been effectually disproved, although they were implicitly believed by the Brontë girls, who, womanlike, were naturally ready to regard a woman as the ruin of a beloved brother. The recklessness of Mrs. Gaskell in accepting such inadequate testimony can be explained only on the assumption that she had a novelist's satisfaction in the romance which the ' bad woman ' theory supplied. She wasted a considerable amount of rhetoric upon it. ' When the fatal attack came on,' she says, ' his pockets were found filled with old letters from the woman to whom he was attached. He died ! she lives still — in May Fair. I see her name in county papers, as one of those who patronise the Christmas balls ; and I hear of her in London drawing-rooms ' — and so on. There were no love-letters found in Branwell Brontë's pockets.[1] When Mrs. Gaskell's husband came post-haste to Haworth to ask for proofs of Mrs. Robinson's complicity in Branwell's downfall, none were obtainable. I am assured by Mr. Leslie Stephen that his father, Sir James Stephen, was employed at the time to make careful inquiry, and that he and other eminent lawyers came to the conclusion that it was one long tissue of lies or hallucinations. The subject is sufficiently sordid, and indeed almost redundant in any biography of the Brontës ; but it is of moment, because Charlotte Brontë and her sisters were so thoroughly persuaded that a woman was at the bottom of their brother's ruin ; and this belief Charlotte impressed upon all the friends who were nearest and dearest to her. Her letters at the time of her brother's

---

[1] To this bold statement (*i. e.* that love-letters were found in Branwell's pockets) Martha Brown gave to me a flat contradiction, declaring that she was employed in the sick room at the time, and had personal knowledge that not one letter, nor a vestige of one, from the lady in question, was so found. Leyland, ' The Brontë Family,' vol. ii. p. 284.

death are full of censure of the supposed wickedness of another. It was a cruel infamy that the word of this wretched boy should have been so powerful for mischief. Here, at any rate, Mrs. Gaskell did not show the caution which a masculine biographer, less prone to take literally a man's accounts of his amours, would undoubtedly have displayed.

Yet, when all is said, Mrs. Gaskell had done her work thoroughly and well. Lockhart's 'Scott' and Froude's 'Carlyle' are examples of great biographies which called for abundant censure upon their publication; yet both these books will live as classics of their kind. To be interesting, it is perhaps indispensable that the biographer should be indiscreet, and certainly the Branwell incident — a matter of two or three pages — is the only part of Mrs. Gaskell's biography in which indiscretion becomes indefensible. And for this she suffered cruelly. 'I did so try to tell the truth,' she said to a friend, 'and I believe *now* I hit as near to the truth as any one could do.' 'I weighed every line with my whole power and heart,' she said on another occasion, ' so that every line should go to its great purpose of making *her* known and valued, as one who had gone through such a terrible life with a brave and faithful heart.' And that clearly Mrs. Gaskell succeeded in doing. It is quite certain that Charlotte Brontë would not stand on so splendid a pedestal to-day but for the single-minded devotion of her accomplished biographer.

It has sometimes been implied that the portrait drawn by Mrs. Gaskell was far too sombre, that there are passages in Charlotte's letters which show that ofttimes her heart was merry and her life sufficiently cheerful. That there were long periods of gaiety for all the three sisters, surely no one ever doubted. To few people, fortunately, is it given to have lives wholly without happiness. And yet, when this is acknowledged, how can one say that the

picture was too gloomy? Taken as a whole, the life of
Charlotte Brontë was among the saddest in literature. At
a miserable school, where she herself was unhappy, she saw
her two elder sisters stricken down and carried home to die.
In her home was the narrowest poverty. She had, in the
years when that was most essential, no mother's care; and
perhaps there was a somewhat too rigid disciplinarian in
the aunt who took the mother's place. Her second school
brought her, indeed, two kind friends; but her shyness
made that school-life in itself a prolonged tragedy. Of the
two experiences as a private governess I shall have more
to say. They were periods of torture to her sensitive nature.
The ambition of the three girls to start a school on their
own account failed ignominiously. The suppressed vitality
of childhood and early womanhood made Charlotte unable
to enter with sympathy and toleration into the life of a
foreign city, and Brussels was for her a further disaster.
Then within two years, just as literary fame was bringing
its consolation for the trials of the past, she saw her two
beloved sisters taken from her. And, finally, when at last
a good man won her love, there were left to her only nine
months of happy married life. 'I am not going to die.
We have been so happy.' These words to her husband on
her death-bed are not the least piteously sad in her tragic
story. That her life was a tragedy, was the opinion of the
woman friend with whom on the intellectual side she had
most in common. Miss Mary Taylor wrote to Mrs. Gaskell
the following letter from New Zealand upon receipt of the
'Life':—

'WELLINGTON, July 30, 1857.

'MY DEAR MRS. GASKELL, — I am unaccountably in receipt by
post of two vols. containing the Life of C. Brontë. I have
pleasure in attributing this compliment to you; I beg, therefore, to thank you for them. The book is a perfect success, in
giving a true picture of a melancholy life, and you have prac-

tically answered my puzzle as to how you would give an account of her, not being at liberty to give a true description of those around. Though not so gloomy as the truth, it is perhaps as much so as people will accept without calling it exaggerated, and feeling the desire to doubt and contradict it. I have seen two reviews of it. One of them sums it up as "a life of poverty and self-suppression," the other has nothing to the purpose at all. Neither of them seems to think it a strange or wrong state of things that a woman of first-rate talents, industry, and integrity should live all her life in a walking nightmare of " poverty and self-suppression." I doubt whether any of them will.

'It must upset most people's notions of beauty to be told that the portrait at the beginning is that of an ugly woman.[1] I do not altogether like the idea of publishing a flattered likeness. I had rather the mouth and eyes had been nearer together, and shown the veritable square face and large disproportionate nose.

'I had the impression that Cartwright's mill was burnt in 1820 not in 1812. You give much too favourable an account of the black-coated and Tory savages that kept the people down, and provoked excesses in those days. Old Robertson said he " would wade to the knees in blood rather than the then state of things should be altered,"— a state including Corn law, Test law, and a host of other oppressions.

'Once more I thank you for the book — the first copy, I believe, that arrived in New Zealand. — Sincerely yours,

'MARY TAYLOR.'

And in another letter, written a little later (28th January, 1858), Miss Mary Taylor writes to Miss Ellen Nussey in similar strain : —

'Your account of Mrs. Gaskell's book was very interesting,' she says. 'She seems a hasty, impulsive person, and the needful

---

[1] Mrs. Gaskell had described Charlotte Brontë's features as 'plain, large, and ill-set,' and had written of her 'crooked mouth and large nose' — while acknowledging the beauty of hair and eyes.

drawing back after her warmth gives her an inconsistent look. Yet I doubt not her book will be of great use. You must be aware that many strange notions as to the kind of person Charlotte really was will be done away with by a knowledge of the true facts of her life. I have heard imperfectly of farther printing on the subject. As to the mutilated edition that is to come, I am sorry for it. Libellous or not, the first edition was all true, and except the declamation all, in my opinion, useful to be published. Of course I don't know how far necessity may make Mrs. Gaskell give them up. You know one dare not always say the world moves.'

We who do know the whole story in fullest detail will understand that it was desirable to 'mutilate' the book, and that, indeed, truth did in some measure require it. But with these letters of Mary Taylor's before us, let us not hear again that the story of Charlotte Brontë's life was not, in its main features, accurately and adequately told by her gifted biographer.

Why then, I am naturally asked, add one further book to the Brontë biographical literature? The reply is, I hope, sufficient. Forty years have gone by, and they have been years of growing interest in the subject. In the year 1895 ten thousand people visited the Brontë Museum at Haworth. Interesting books have been written, notably Sir Wemyss Reid's 'Monograph' and Mr. Leyland's 'Brontë Family,' but they have gone out of print. Many new facts have come to light, and many details, moreover, which were too trivial in 1857 are of sufficient importance to-day; and many facts which were rightly suppressed then may honestly and honourably be given to the public at an interval of nearly half a century. Added to all this, fortune has been kind to me.

Some three or four years ago Miss Ellen Nussey placed in my hands a printed volume of some 400 pages, which bore no publisher's name, but contained upon its title-page the statement that it was 'The Story of Charlotte Brontë's Life, as told through her Letters.' These are the Letters — 370 in number — which Miss Nussey had lent to Mrs. Gaskell and to Sir Wemyss Reid. Of these letters Mrs. Gaskell published about 100, and Sir Wemyss Reid added as many more as he considered circumstances justified twenty years back. It was explained to me that the volume had been privately printed under a misconception, and that only some dozen copies were extant. Miss Nussey asked me if I would write something around what might remain of the unpublished letters, and if I saw my way to do anything which would add to the public appreciation of the friend who from early childhood until now has been the most absorbing interest of her life. A careful study of the volume made it perfectly clear that there were still some letters which might with advantage be added to the Brontë story. At the same time arose the possibility of a veto being placed upon their publication. An examination of Charlotte Brontë's will, which was proved at York by her husband in 1855, suggested an easy way out of the difficulty. I made up my mind to try and see Mr. Nicholls. I had heard of his disinclination to be in any way associated with the controversy which had gathered round his wife for all these years; but I wrote to him, nevertheless, and received a cordial invitation to visit him in his Irish home.

It was exactly forty years to a day after Charlotte died — March 31st, 1895 — when I alighted at the station in a quiet little town in the centre of Ireland, to receive the cordial handclasp of the man into whose keeping Charlotte Brontë had given her life. It was one of many visits, and the beginning of an interesting correspondence. Mr. Nicholls placed all the papers in his possession in my hands. They were more varied and more abundant than I could possibly have anticipated. They included MSS. of childhood, of which so much has been said, and stories of adult life, one fragment indeed being later than the ' Emma ' which

appeared in the 'Cornhill Magazine' for 1856, with a note
by Thackeray. Here were the letters Charlotte Brontë had
written to her brother and to her sisters during her second
sojourn in Brussels — to 'Dear Branwell' and 'Dear E. J.,'
as she calls Emily — letters even to handle will give a
thrill to the Brontë enthusiast. Here also were the love-
letters of Maria Branwell to her lover Patrick Brontë, which
are referred to in Mrs. Gaskell's biography, but have never
hitherto been printed.

'The four small scraps of Emily and Anne's manuscript,'
writes Mr. Nicholls, 'I found in the small box I send you;
the others I found in the bottom of a cupboard tied up in
a newspaper, where they had lain for nearly thirty years,
and where, had it not been for your visit, they must have
remained during my lifetime, and most likely afterwards
have been destroyed.'

Some slight extracts from Brontë's letters in 'Macmillan's
Magazine,' signed 'E. Baumer Williams,' brought me into
communication with a gifted daughter of Mr. W. S. Williams.
Mrs. Williams and her husband generously placed the whole
series of these letters of Charlotte Brontë to their father at
my disposal. It was of some of these letters that Mrs.
Gaskell wrote in enthusiastic terms when she had read
them, and she was only permitted to see a few. Then I
have to thank Mr. Joshua Taylor, the nephew of Miss
Mary Taylor, for permission to publish his aunt's letters.
Mr. James Taylor, again, who wanted to marry Charlotte
Brontë, and who died twenty years afterwards in Bombay,
left behind him a bundle of letters which I found in the
possession of a relative in the north of London.[1] I dis-
covered through a letter addressed to Miss Nussey that the
'Brussels friend' referred to by Mrs. Gaskell was a Miss
Laetitia Wheelwright, and I determined to write to all the

[1] Mrs. Lawry of Muswell Hill, to whose courtesy in placing these and other
papers at my disposal I am greatly indebted.

Wheelwrights in the London Directory. My first effort succeeded, and *the* Miss Wheelwright kindly lent me all the letters that she had preserved. It is scarcely possible that time will reveal many more unpublished letters from the author of 'Jane Eyre.' Several of those already in print are forgeries, and I have actually seen a letter addressed from Paris, a city which Miss Brontë never visited. I have the assurance of Dr. Héger of Brussels that Miss Brontë's correspondence with his father no longer exists. In any case one may safely send forth this little book with the certainty that it is a fairly complete collection of Charlotte Brontë's correspondence, and that it is altogether a valuable revelation of a singularly interesting personality. Steps will be taken henceforth, it may be added, to vindicate Mr. Nicholls's rights in whatever may still remain of his wife's unpublished correspondence.

CHAPTER I.

PATRICK BRONTË AND MARIA HIS WIFE.

IT would seem quite clear to any careful investigator that
the Reverend Patrick Brontë, Incumbent of Haworth, and
the father of three famous daughters, was a much maligned
man.   We talk of the fierce light which beats upon a throne,
but what is that compared to the fierce light which beats
upon any man of some measure of individuality who is destined to live out his life in the quiet of a country village
— in the very centre, as it were, of 'personal talk' and
gossip not always kindly to the stranger within the gate.
The view of Mr. Brontë, presented by Mrs. Gaskell in the
early editions of her biography of Charlotte Brontë, is that
of a severe, ill-tempered, and distinctly disagreeable character.   It is the picture of a man who disliked the vanities
of life so intensely, that the new shoes of his children and
the silk dress of his wife were not spared by him in sudden
gusts of passion.   A stern old ruffian, one is inclined to consider him.   His pistol-shooting rings picturesquely, but not
agreeably, through Mrs. Gaskell's memoirs.   It has been
already explained in more than one quarter that this was
not the real Patrick Brontë, and that much of the unfavourable gossip was due to the chatter of a dismissed servant,
retailed to Mrs. Gaskell on one of her missions of inquiry
in the neighbourhood.   The stories of the burnt shoes and
the mutilated dress have been relegated to the realm of
myth, and the pistol-shooting may now be acknowledged

as a harmless pastime not more iniquitous than the golfing
or angling of a latter-day clergyman. It is certain, were
the matter of much interest to-day, that Mr. Brontë was
fond of the use of firearms. The present Incumbent of
Haworth will point out to you, on the old tower of
Haworth Church, the marks of pistol bullets, which he is
assured were made by Mr. Brontë. I have myself handled
both the gun and the pistol — this latter a very ornamental
weapon, by the way, manufactured at Bradford — which Mr.
Brontë possessed during the later years of his life. From
both he had obtained much innocent amusement; but his
son-in-law, Mr. Nicholls, who, at a distance of forty years
still cherishes a reverent and enthusiastic affection for old
Mr. Brontë, informs me that the bullet marks upon Haworth
Church were the irresponsible frolic of a rather juvenile
curate — Mr. Smith. All this is trivial enough in any case,
and one turns very readily to more important factors in the
life of the father of the Brontës. Patrick Brontë was born
at Ahaderg, County Down, in Ireland, on St. Patrick's Day,
March 17, 1777. He was one of the ten children of Hugh
Brunty, farmer, and his nine brothers and sisters seem all of
them to have spent their lives in their Irish home, to have
married and been given in marriage, and to have gone to
their graves in peace. Patrick alone had ambition, and, one
must add, the opportune friend, without whom ambition
counts for little in the great struggle of life. At sixteen he
was a kind of village schoolmaster, or assistant schoolmaster,
and at twenty-five, stirred thereto by the vicar of his parish,
Mr. Tighe, he was on his way from Ireland to St. John's
College, Cambridge. It was in 1802 that Patrick Brontë
went to Cambridge, and entered his name in the college
books. There, indeed, we find the name, not of Patrick
Brontë, but of Patrick Branty,[1] and this brings us to an

[1] 'Patrick Branty' is written in another handwriting in the list of admissions
at St. John's College, Cambridge. Dr. J. A. Erskine Stuart, who has a valuable

interesting point as to the origin of the name. In the register of his birth his name is entered, as are the births of his brothers and sisters, as ' Brunty ' and ' Bruntee '; and it can scarcely be doubted that, as Dr. Douglas Hyde has pointed out, the original name was O'Prunty.[1] The Irish, at the beginning of the century, were well-nigh as primitive in some matters as were the English of a century earlier; and one is not surprised to see variations in the spelling of the Brontë name — it being in the case of his brothers and sisters occasionally spelt ' Brontee.' To me it is perfectly clear that for the change of name Lord Nelson was responsible, and that the dukedom of Brontë, which was conferred upon the great sailor in 1799, suggested the more ornamental surname. There were no Irish Brontës in existence before Nelson became Duke of Brontë; but all Patrick's brothers and sisters, with whom, it must be remembered, he was on terms of correspondence his whole life long, gradually, with a true Celtic sense of the picturesqueness of the thing, seized upon the more attractive surname. For this theory there is, of course, not one scrap of evidence; we only know that the register of Patrick's native parish gives us Brunty, and that his signature through his successive curacies is Brontë.

From Cambridge, after taking orders in 1806, Mr. Brontë moved to a curacy at Weatherfield in Essex; and Mr. Augustine Birrell has told us, with that singular literary charm of his, how the good-looking Irish curate made successful love to a young parishioner — Miss Mary Burder.

note on the subject in an article on ' The Brontë Nomenclature ' (Brontë Society's Publication, Pt. III.), has found the name as Brunty, Bruntee, Bronty, and Branty — but never in Patrick Brontë's handwriting. There is, however, no signature of Mr. Brontë's extant prior to 1799.

[1] 'I translated this' (*i. e.* an Irish romance) 'from a manuscript in my possession made by one Patrick O'Prunty, an ancestor probably of Charlotte Brontë, in 1763.' 'The Story of Early Gaelic Literature,' p. 49. By Douglas Hyde, LL.D. T. Fisher Unwin, 1895.

Mary Burder would have married him, it seems, but for an obdurate uncle and guardian. She was spirited away from the neighbourhood, and the lovers never met again. There are doubtful points in Mr. Birrell's story. Mary Burder, as the wife of a Nonconformist minister, died in 1866, in her seventy-seventh year. This lady, from whom doubtless either directly or indirectly the tradition was obtained, may have amplified and exaggerated a very innocent flirtation. One would like further evidence for the statement that when Mr. Brontë lost his wife in 1821, he asked his old sweetheart, Mary Burder, to become the mother of his six children, and that she answered 'no.' In any case, Mr. Brontë left Weatherfield in 1809 for a curacy at Dewsbury, and Dewsbury gossip also had much to say concerning the flirtations of its Irish curate. His next curacy, however, which was obtained in 1811, by a removal to Hartshead, near Huddersfield, brought flirtation for Mr. Brontë to a speedy end. In 1812, when thirty-three years of age, he married Miss Maria Branwell, of Penzance. Miss Branwell had only a few months before left her Cornish home for a visit to an uncle in Yorkshire. This uncle was a Mr. John Fennell, a clergyman of the Church of England, who had been a Methodist minister. To Methodism, indeed, the Cornish Branwells would seem to have been devoted at one time or another, for I have seen a copy of the 'Imitation' inscribed 'M. Branwell, July 1807,' with the following title-page : —

AN EXTRACT OF THE CHRISTIAN'S PATTERN : OR, A TREATISE ON THE IMITATION OF CHRIST. WRITTEN IN LATIN BY THOMAS À KEMPIS. ABRIDGED AND PUBLISHED IN ENGLISH BY JOHN WESLEY, M.A., LONDON. PRINTED AT THE CONFERENCE OFFICE, NORTH GREEN, FINSBURY SQUARE. G. STORY, AGENT. SOLD BY G. WHITFIELD, CITY ROAD. 1803. PRICE BOUND 1s.

The book was evidently brought by Mrs. Brontë from Penzance, and given by her to her husband or left among her effects. The poor little woman had been in her grave for five or six years when it came into the hands of one of her daughters, as we learn from Charlotte's handwriting on the fly-leaf : —

'C. Brontë's book. This book was given to me in July 1826. It is not certainly known who is the author, but it is generally supposed that Thomas à Kempis is. I saw a reward of £10,000 offered in the " Leeds Mercury " to any one who could find out for a certainty who is the author.'

The conjunction of the names of John Wesley, Maria Branwell, and Charlotte Brontë surely gives this little volume, 'price bound 1s.,' a singular interest !

But here I must refer to the letters which Maria Branwell wrote to her lover during the brief courtship. Mrs. Gaskell, it will be remembered, makes but one extract from this correspondence, which was handed to her by Mr. Brontë as part of the material for her memoir. Long years before, the little packet had been taken from Mr. Brontë's desk, for we find Charlotte writing to a friend on February 16th, 1850 : —

'A few days since, a little incident happened which curiously touched me. Papa put into my hands a little packet of letters and papers, telling me that they were mamma's, and that I might read them. I did read them, in a frame of mind I cannot describe. The papers were yellow with time, all having been written before I was born. It was strange now to peruse, for the first time, the records of a mind whence my own sprang; and most strange, and at once sad and sweet, to find that mind of a truly fine, pure, and elevated order. They were written to papa before they were married. There is a rectitude, a refinement, a constancy, a modesty, a sense, a gentleness about them indescribable. I wish she had lived, and that I had known her.'

CHARLOTTE BRONTË

Yet another forty years or so and the little packet is in my possession. Handling with a full sense of their sacredness, these letters, written more than eighty years ago by a good woman to her lover, one is tempted to hope that there is no breach of the privacy which should, even in our day, guide certain sides of life, in publishing the correspondence in its completeness. With the letters I find a little MS., which is also of pathetic interest. It is entitled 'The Advantages of Poverty in Religious Concerns, and it is endorsed in the handwriting of Mr. Brontë, written, doubtless, many years afterwards : —

'The above was written by my dear wife, and is for insertion in one of the periodical publications. Keep it as a memorial of her.'

There is no reason to suppose that the MS. was ever published ; there is no reason why any editor should have wished to publish it. It abounds in the obvious. At the same time, one notes that from both father and mother alike Charlotte Brontë and her sisters inherited some measure of the literary faculty. It is nothing to say that not one line of the father's or mother's would have been preserved had it not been for their gifted children. It is sufficient that the zest for writing was there, and that the intense passion for handling a pen, which seems to have been singularly strong in Charlotte Brontë, must have come to a great extent from a similar passion alike in father and mother. Mr. Brontë, indeed, may be counted a prolific author. He published, in all, four books, three pamphlets, and two sermons. Of his books, two were in verse and two in prose. 'Cottage Poems' was published in 1811 ; 'The Rural Minstrel' in 1812, the year of his marriage; 'The Cottage in the Wood' in 1815 ; and 'The Maid of Killarney' in 1818. After his wife's death he published no more books. Reading over these old-fashioned volumes now, one admits that they possess but little distinction. It has been pointed out, indeed, that

32

one of the strongest lines in 'Jane Eyre'—'To the finest fibre of my nature, sir,'—is culled from Mr. Brontë's verse. It is the one line of his that will live. Like his daughter Charlotte, Mr. Brontë is more interesting in his prose than in his poetry. 'The Cottage in the Wood; or, the Art of Becoming Rich and Happy,' is a kind of religious novel — a spiritual 'Pamela,' in which the reprobate pursuer of an innocent girl ultimately becomes converted and marries her. 'The Maid of Killarney; or, Albion and Flora' is more interesting. Under the guise of a story it has something to say on many questions of importance. We know now why Charlotte never learnt to dance until she went to Brussels, and why children's games were unknown to her, for here are many mild diatribes against dancing and card-playing. The British Constitution and the British and Foreign Bible Society receive a considerable amount of criticism. But in spite of this didactic weakness there are one or two pieces of really picturesque writing, notably a description of an Irish wake, and a forcible account of the defence of a house against some Whiteboys. It is true enough that the books are merely of interest to collectors and that they live only by virtue of Patrick Brontë's remarkable children. But many a prolific writer of the day passes muster as a genius among his contemporaries upon as small a talent; and Mr. Brontë does not seem to have given himself any airs as an author. Thirty years were to elapse before there were to be any more books from this family of writers; but 'Jane Eyre' owes something, we may be sure, to 'The Maid of Killarney.'

Mr. Brontë, as I have said, married Maria Branwell in 1812. She was in her twenty-ninth year, and was one of five children — one son and four daughters — the father of whom, Mr. Thomas Branwell, had died in 1809. By a curious coincidence, another sister, Charlotte, was married in Penzance on the same day — the 18th of December

CHARLOTTE BRONTË

1812.[1] Before me are a bundle of samplers, worked by three of these Branwell sisters. Maria Branwell 'ended her sampler' April the 15th, 1791, and it is inscribed with the text, *Flee from sin as from a serpent, for if thou comest too near to it, it will bite thee. The teeth thereof are as the teeth of a lion to slay the souls of men.* Another sampler is by Elizabeth Branwell; another by Margaret, and another by Anne. These, some miniatures, and the book and papers to which I have referred, are all that remain to us as a memento of Mrs. Brontë, apart from the children that she bore to her husband. The miniatures, which are in the possession of Miss Branwell, of Penzance, are of Mr. and Mrs. Thomas Branwell — Charlotte Brontë's maternal grandfather and grandmother — and of Mrs. Brontë and her sister Elizabeth Branwell as children.

To return, however, to our bundle of love-letters. Comment is needless, if indeed comment or elucidation were possible at this distance of time.

TO REV. PATRICK BRONTË, A.B., HARTSHEAD.

'WOOD HOUSE GROVE, August 26, 1812.

'MY DEAR FRIEND, — This address is sufficient to convince you

[1] Mrs. Gaskell says Dec. 29th ; but Miss Charlotte Branwell of Penzance writes to me as follows: — 'My Aunt Maria Branwell, after the death of her parents, went to Yorkshire on a visit to her relatives, where she met the Rev. Patrick Brontë. They soon became engaged to be married. Jane Fennell was previously engaged to the Rev. William Morgan. And when the time arrived for their marriage, Mr. Fennell said he should have to give his daughter and niece away, and if so, he could not marry them ; so it was arranged that Mr. Morgan should marry Mr. Brontë and Maria Branwell, and afterwards Mr. Brontë should perform the same kindly office towards Mr. Morgan and Jane Fennell. So the bridegrooms married each other and the brides acted as bridesmaids to each other. My father and mother, Joseph and Charlotte Branwell, were married at Madron, which was then the parish church of Penzance, on the same day and hour. Perhaps a similar case never happened before or since : two sisters and four first cousins being united in holy matrimony at one and the same time. And they were all happy marriages. Mr. Brontë was perhaps peculiar, but I have always heard my own dear mother say that he was devotedly fond of his wife, and she of him. These marriages were solemnised on the 18th of December, 1812.'

34

that I not only permit, but approve of yours to me — I do indeed consider you as my *friend;* yet, when I consider how short a time I have had the pleasure of knowing you, I start at my own rashness, my heart fails, and did I not think that you would be disappointed and grieved at it, I believe I should be ready to spare myself the task of writing. Do not think that I am so wavering as to repent of what I have already said. No, believe me, this will never be the case, unless you give me cause for it. You need not fear that you have been mistaken in my character. If I know anything of myself, I am incapable of making an ungenerous return to the smallest degree of kindness, much less to you whose attentions and conduct have been so particularly obliging. I will frankly confess that your behaviour and what I have seen and heard of your character has excited my warmest esteem and regard, and be assured you shall never have cause to repent of any confidence you may think proper to place in me, and that it will always be my endeavour to deserve the good opinion which you have formed, although human weakness may in some instances cause me to fall short. In giving you these assurances I do not depend upon my own strength, but I look to Him who has been my unerring guide through life, and in whose continued protection and assistance I confidently trust.

'I thought on you much on Sunday, and feared you would not escape the rain. I hope you do not feel any bad effects from it? My cousin wrote you on Monday and expects this afternoon to be favoured with an answer. Your letter has caused me some foolish embarrassment, tho' in pity to my feelings they have been very sparing of their raillery.

'I will now candidly answer your questions. The *politeness of others* can never make me forget your kind attentions, neither can I *walk our accustomed rounds* without thinking on you, and, why should I be ashamed to add, wishing for your presence. If you knew what were my feelings whilst writing this you would pity me. I wish to write the truth and give you satisfaction, yet fear to go too far, and exceed the bounds of propriety. But whatever I may say or write I will *never deceive* you, or *exceed the truth.* If you think I have not placed the *utmost confidence* in you, consider

my situation, and ask yourself if I have not confided in you sufficiently, perhaps too much. I am very sorry that you will not have
this till after to-morrow, but it was out of my power to write sooner.
I rely on your goodness to pardon everything in this which may
appear either too free or too stiff, and beg that you will consider
me as a warm and faithful friend.

'My uncle, aunt, and cousin unite in kind regards.

'I must now conclude with again declaring myself to be yours
sincerely,   MARIA BRANWELL.'

TO REV. PATRICK BRONTË, A.B., HARTSHEAD.

'WOOD HOUSE GROVE, September 5, 1812.

'MY DEAREST FRIEND, — I have just received your affectionate
and very welcome letter, and although I shall not be able to send
this until Monday, yet I cannot deny myself the pleasure of writing a few lines this evening, no longer considering it a task, but
a pleasure, next to that of reading yours. I had the pleasure of
hearing from Mr. Fennell, who was at Bradford on Thursday afternoon, that you had rested there all night. Had you proceeded, I
am sure the walk would have been too much for you, such excessive fatigue, often repeated, must injure the strongest constitution.
I am rejoiced to find that our forebodings were without cause. I
had yesterday a letter from a very dear friend of mine, and had
the satisfaction to learn by it that all at home are well. I feel
with you the unspeakable obligations I am under to a merciful
Providence — my heart swells with gratitude, and I feel an earnest
desire that I may be enabled to make some suitable return to
the Author of all my blessings. In general, I think I am
enabled to cast my care upon Him, and then I experience a calm
and peaceful serenity of mind which few things can destroy. In
all my addresses to the throne of grace I never ask a blessing for
myself but I beg the same for you, and considering the important station which you are called to fill, my prayers are propor-
tionately fervent that you may be favoured with all the gifts and
graces requisite for such a calling. O my dear friend, let us pray
much that we may live lives holy and useful to each other and all
around us !

'*Monday morn.* — My cousin and I were yesterday at Coverley church, where we heard Mr. Watman preach a very excellent sermon from "learn of Me, for I am meek and lowly of heart." He displayed the character of our Saviour in a most affecting and amiable light. I scarcely ever felt more charmed with his excellencies, more grateful for his condescension, or more abased at my own unworthiness; but I lament that my heart is so little retentive of those pleasing and profitable impressions.

'I pitied you in your solitude, and felt sorry that it was not in my power to enliven it. Have you not been too hasty in informing your friends of a certain event? Why did you not leave them to guess a little longer? I shrink from the idea of its being known to every body. I do, indeed, *sometimes* think of you, but I will not say how often, lest I raise your vanity; and we sometimes talk of you and the doctor. But I believe I should seldom mention your name myself were it not now and then introduced by my cousin. I have never mentioned a word of what is past to any body. Had I thought this necessary I should have requested you to do it. But I think there is no need, as by some means or other they seem to have a pretty correct notion how matters stand betwixt us; and as their hints, etc., meet with no contradiction from me, my silence passes for confirmation. Mr. Fennell has not neglected to give me some serious and encouraging advice, and my aunt takes frequent opportunities of dropping little sentences which I may turn to some advantage. I have long had reason to know that the present state of things would give pleasure to all parties. Your ludicrous account of the scene at the Hermitage was highly diverting, we laughed heartily at it; but I fear it will not produce all that compassion in Miss Fennell's breast which you seem to wish. I will now tell you what I was thinking about and doing at the time you mention. I was then toiling up the hill with Jane and Mrs. Clapham to take our tea at Mr. Tatham's, thinking on the evening when I first took the same walk with you, and on the change which had taken place in my circumstances and views since then — not wholly without a wish that I had your arm to assist me, and your conversation to shorten the walk. Indeed, all our walks have now an insipidity in them which I never thought they would have possessed. When I work, if I wish to get *forward* I may be glad that you are at a distance. Jane begs me to assure you of her kind regards. Mr. Morgan is expected to be here this evening. I must assume a bold and steady countenance to meet his attacks!

'I have now written a pretty long letter without reserve or caution, and if all the sentiments of my heart are not laid open to you, believe me it is not because I wish them to be concealed, for I hope there is nothing there that would give you pain or displeasure. My most sincere and earnest wishes are for your happiness and welfare, for this includes my own. Pray much for me that I may be made a blessing and not a hindrance to you. Let me not interrupt your studies nor intrude on that time which ought to be dedicated to better purposes. Forgive my freedom, my dearest friend, and rest assured that you are and ever will be dear to   MARIA BRANWELL.

'Write very soon.'

TO REV. PATRICK BRONTË, A.B., HAPTSHEAD.

'WOOD HOUSE GROVE, September 11, 1812.

'MY DEAREST FRIEND, — Having spent the day yesterday at Miry Shay, a place near Bradford, I had not got your letter till my return in the evening, and consequently have only a short time this morning to write if I send it by this post. You surely do not think you *trouble* me by writing? No, I think I may venture to say if such were your opinion you would *trouble* me no more. Be assured, your letters are and I hope always will be received with extreme pleasure and read with delight. May our Gracious Father mercifully grant the fulfilment of your prayers. Whilst we depend entirely on Him for happiness, and receive each other and all our blessings as from His hands, what can harm us or make us miserable? Nothing temporal or spiritual.

'Jane had a note from Mr. Morgan last evening, and she desires me to tell you that the Methodists' service in church hours is to commence next Sunday week. You may expect frowns and hard words from her when you make your appearance here again, for,

AND HER CIRCLE

if you recollect, she gave you a note to carry to the Doctor, and
he has never received it. What have you done with it? If you
can give a good account of it you may come to see us as soon as
you please and be sure of a hearty welcome from all parties.
Next Wednesday we have some thoughts, if the weather be fine,
of going to Kirkstall Abbey once more, and I suppose your presence will not make the walk less agreeable to any of us.

' The old man is come and waits for my letter. In expectation
of seeing you on Monday or Tuesday next, — I remain, yours
faithfully and affectionately, M. B.'

TO REV. PATRICK BRONTË, A.B., Hartshead.[1]

'Wood House Grove, September 18, 1812.

' How readily do I comply with my dear Mr. B.'s request! You
see, you have only to express your wishes and as far as my power
extends I hesitate not to fulfil them. My heart tells me that it
will always be my pride and pleasure to contribute to your happiness, nor do I fear that this will ever be inconsistent with my
duty as a Christian. My esteem for you and my confidence in
you is so great, that I firmly believe you will never exact anything
from me which I could not conscientiously perform. I shall in
future look to you for assistance and instruction whenever I may
need them, and hope you will never withhold from me any advice
or caution you may see necessary.

['For some years I have been perfectly my own mistress, subject to no *control* whatever — so far from it, that my sisters who
are many years older than myself, and even my dear mother,
used to consult me in every case of importance, and scarcely ever
doubted the propriety of my opinions and actions. Perhaps you
will be ready to accuse me of vanity in mentioning this, but you
must consider that I do not *boast* of it, I have many times felt it
a disadvantage; and although, I thank God, it never led me into
error, yet in circumstances of perplexity and doubt, I have deeply
felt the want of a guide and instructor.]

' At such times I have seen and felt the necessity of supernatu-

[1] The passage in brackets is quoted by Mrs. Gaskell.

39

ral aid, and by fervent applications to a throne of grace I have experienced that my heavenly Father is able and willing to supply the place of every earthly friend. I shall now no longer feel this want, this sense of helpless weakness, for I believe a kind Providence has intended that I shall find in you every earthly friend united; nor do I fear to trust myself under your protection, or shrink from your control. It is pleasant to be subject to those we love, especially when they never exert their authority but for the good of the subject. How few would write in this way! But I do not fear that *you* will make a bad use of it. You tell me to write my thoughts, and thus as they occur I freely let my pen run away with them.

' *Sat. morn.* — I do not know whether you dare show your face here again or not after the blunder you have committed. When we got to the house on Thursday evening, even before we were within the doors, we found that Mr. and Mrs. Bedford had been there, and that they had requested you to mention their intention of coming — a single hint of which you never gave! Poor I too came in for a share in the hard words which were bestowed upon you, for they all agreed that I was the cause of it. Mr. Fennell said you were certainly *mazed,* and talked of sending you to York, etc. And even I begin to think that *this,* together with the *note,* bears some marks of *insanity!* However, I shall suspend my judgment until I hear what excuse you can make for yourself, I suppose you will be quite ready to make one of some kind or another.

' Yesterday I performed a difficult and yet a pleasing task in writing to my sisters. I thought I never should accomplish the end for which the letter was designed; but after a good deal of perambulation I gave them to understand the nature of my engagement with you, with the motives and inducements which led me to form such an engagement, and that in consequence of it I should not see them again so soon as I had intended. I concluded by expressing a hope that they would not be less pleased with the information than were my friends here. I think they will not suspect me to have made a wrong step, their partiality for me is so great. And their affection for me will lead them to rejoice in my welfare, even though it should diminish somewhat of their own. I shall think the time tedious till I hear from you, and must beg you will write as soon as possible. Pardon me, my dear friend, if I again caution you against giving way to a weakness of which I have heard you complain. When you find your heart oppressed and your thoughts too much engrossed by one subject, let prayer be your refuge — this you no doubt know by experience to be a sure remedy, and a relief from every care and error. Oh, that we had more of the spirit of prayer! I feel that I need it much.

'Breakfast-time is near, I must bid you farewell for the time, but rest assured you will always share in the prayers and heart of your own   MARIA.

'Mr. Fennell has crossed my letter to my sisters. With his usual goodness he has supplied my *deficiencies*, and spoken of me in terms of commendation of which I wish I were more worthy. Your character he has likewise displayed in the most favourable light; and I am sure they will not fail to love and esteem you though unknown.

'All here unite in kind regards. Adieu.'

TO REV. PATRICK BRONTË, A.B., HARTSHEAD.

'WOOD HOUSE GROVE, September 23, 1812.

'MY DEAREST FRIEND, — Accept of my warmest thanks for your kind affectionate letter, in which you have rated mine so highly that I really blush to read my own praises. Pray that God would enable me to deserve all the kindness you manifest towards me, and to act consistently with the good opinion you entertain of me — then I shall indeed be a helpmeet for you, and to be this shall at all times be the care and study of my future life. We have had to-day a large party of the Bradford folks — the Rands, Fawcets, Dobsons, etc. My thoughts often strayed from the company, and I would have gladly left them to follow my present employment. To write to and receive letters from my friends were always among my chief enjoyments, but none ever gave me so much pleasure as those which I receive from and write to my

41

newly adopted friend. I am by no means sorry you have given up all thought of the house you mentioned. With my cousin's help I have made known your plans to my uncle and aunt. Mr. Fennell immediately coincided with that which respects your present abode, and observed that it had occurred to him before, but that he had not had an opportunity of mentioning it to you. My aunt did not fall in with it so readily, but her objections did not appear to me to be very weighty. For my own part, I feel all the force of your arguments in favour of it, and the objections are so trifling that they can scarcely be called objections. My cousin is of the same opinion. Indeed, you have such a method of considering and digesting a plan before you make it known to your friends, that you run very little risque of incurring their disapprobations, or of having your schemes frustrated. I greatly admire your talents this way — may they never be perverted by being used in a bad cause! And whilst they are exerted for good purposes, may they prove irresistible! If I may judge from your letter, this middle scheme is what would please you best, so that if there should arise no new objection to it, perhaps it will prove the best you can adopt. However, there is yet sufficient time to consider it further. I trust in this and every other circumstance you will be guided by the wisdom that cometh from above — a portion of which I doubt not has guided you hitherto. A belief of this, added to the complete satisfaction with which I read your reasonings on the subject, made me a ready convert to your opinions. I hope nothing will occur to induce you to change your intention of spending the next week at Bradford. Depend on it you shall have letter for letter; but may we not hope to see you here during that time, surely you will not think the way more tedious than usual? I have not heard any particulars respecting the church since you were at Bradford. Mr. Rawson is now there, but Mr. Hardy and his brother are absent, and I understand nothing decisive can be accomplished without them. Jane expects to hear something more to-morrow. Perhaps ere this reaches you, you will have received some intelligence respecting it from Mr. Morgan. If you have no other apology to make for your blunders than that which you have given me, you must not expect to be excused, for I have not mentioned it to any one, so that however it may clear your character in my opinion it is not likely to influence any other person. Little, very little, will induce me to cover your faults with a veil of charity. I already feel a kind of participation in all that concerns you. All praises and censures bestowed on you must equally affect me. Your joys and sorrows must be mine. Thus shall the one be increased and the other diminished. While this is the case we shall, I hope, always find "life's cares" to be "comforts." And may we feel every trial and distress, for such must be our lot at times, bind us nearer to God and to each other! My heart earnestly joins in your comprehensive prayers. I trust they will unitedly ascend to a throne of grace, and through the Redeemer's merits procure for us peace and happiness here and a life of eternal felicity hereafter. Oh, what sacred pleasure there is in the idea of spending an eternity together in perfect and uninterrupted bliss! This should encourage us to the utmost exertion and fortitude. But whilst I write my own words condemn me — I am ashamed of my own indolence and backwardness to duty. May I be more careful, watchful, and active than I have ever yet been!

'My uncle, aunt, and Jane request me to send their kind regards, and they will be happy to see you any time next week whenever you can conveniently come down from Bradford. Let me hear from you soon — I shall expect a letter on Monday. Farewell, my dearest friend. That you may be happy in yourself and very useful to all around you is the daily earnest prayer of yours truly, MARIA BRANWELL.'

TO REV. PATRICK BRONTË, A.B., HARTSHEAD.

'WOOD HOUSE GROVE, October 3, 1812.

'How could my dear friend so cruelly disappoint me? Had he known how much I had set my heart on having a letter this afternoon, and how greatly I felt the disappointment when the bag arrived and I found there was nothing for me, I am sure he would not have permitted a little matter to hinder him. But whatever was the reason of your not writing, I cannot believe it to have been neglect or unkindness, therefore I do not in the least blame you, I only beg that in future you will judge of my feelings by your own, and if possible never let me expect a letter without receiving one. You know in my last which I sent you at Bradford I said it would not be in my power to write the next day, but begged I might be favoured with hearing from you on Saturday, and you will not wonder that I hoped you would have complied with this request. It has just occurred to my mind that it is possible this note was not received, if so, you have felt disappointed likewise ; but I think this is not very probable, as the old man is particularly careful, and I never heard of his losing anything committed to his care. The note which I allude to was written on Thursday morning, and you should have received it before you left Bradford. I forget what its contents were, but I know it was written in haste and concluded abruptly. Mr. Fennell talks of visiting Mr. Morgan to-morrow. I cannot lose the opportunity of sending this to the office by him as you will then have it a day sooner, and if you have been daily expecting to hear from me, twenty-four hours are of some importance. I really am concerned to find that this, what many would deem trifling incident, has so much disturbed my mind. I fear I should not have slept in peace to-night if I had been deprived of this opportunity of relieving my mind by scribbling to you, and now I lament that you cannot possibly receive this till Monday. May I hope that there is now some intelligence on the way to me ? or must my patience be tried till I see you on Wednesday? But what nonsense am I writing? Surely after this you can have no doubt that you possess all my heart. Two months ago I could not possibly have believed that you would ever engross so much of my thoughts and affections, and far less could I have thought that I should be so forward as to tell you so. I believe I must forbid you to come here again unless you can assure me that you will not steal any more of my regard. Enough of this ; I must bring my pen to order, for if I were to suffer myself to revise what I have written I should be tempted to throw it in the fire, but I have determined that

you shall see my whole heart. I have not yet informed you that
I received your serio-comic note on Thursday afternoon, for which
accept my thanks.

'My cousin desires me to say that she expects a long poem on
her birthday, when she attains the important age of twenty-one.
Mr. Fennell joins with us in requesting that you will not fail to be
here on Wednesday, as it is decided that on Thursday we are to go
to the Abbey if the weather, etc., permits.

'*Sunday morning.* — I am not sure if I do right in adding a few
lines to-day, but knowing that it will give you pleasure I wish to
finish that you may have it to-morrow. I will just say that
if my feeble prayers can aught avail, you will find your labours
this day both pleasant and profitable, as they concern your own
soul and the souls of those to whom you preach. I trust
in your hours of retirement you will not forget to pray for
me. I assure you I need every assistance to help me forward ; I feel that my heart is more ready to attach itself to
earth than heaven. I sometimes think there never was a
mind so dull and inactive as mine is with regard to spiritual
things.

'I must not forget to thank you for the pamphlets and tracts
which you sent us from Bradford. I hope we shall make good
use of them. I must now take my leave. I believe I need
scarcely assure you that I am yours truly and very affectionately,

'MARIA BRANWELL.'

TO REV. PATRICK BRONTË, A.B., HARTSHEAD.

'WOOD HOUSE GROVE, October 21, 1812.

'With the sincerest pleasure do I retire from company to
converse with him whom I love beyond all others. Could my
beloved friend see my heart he would then be convinced that
the affection I bear him is not at all inferior to that which
he feels for me — indeed I sometimes think that in truth
and constancy it excels. But do not think from this that I
entertain any suspicions of your sincerity — no, I firmly believe
you to be sincere and generous, and doubt not in the least
that you feel all you express. In return, I entreat that you

will do me the justice to believe that you have not only a *very large portion* of my *affection* and *esteem*, but *all* that I am capable of feeling, and from henceforth measure my feelings by your own. Unless my love for you were very great how could I so contentedly give up my home and all my friends — a home I loved so much that I have often thought nothing could bribe me to renounce it for any great length of time together, and friends with whom I have been so long accustomed to share all the vicissitudes of joy and sorrow? Yet these have lost their weight, and though I cannot always think of them without a sigh, yet the anticipation of sharing with you all the pleasures and pains, the cares and anxieties of life, of contributing to your comfort and becoming the companion of your pilgrimage, is more delightful to me than any other prospect which this world can possibly present. I expected to have heard from you on Saturday last, and can scarcely refrain from thinking you unkind to keep me in suspense two whole days longer than was necessary, but it is well that my patience should be some-times tried, or I might entirely lose it, and this would be a loss indeed! Lately I have experienced a considerable increase of hopes and fears, which tend to destroy the calm uniformity of my life. These are not unwelcome, as they enable me to discover more of the evils and errors of my heart, and discovering them I hope through grace to be enabled to correct and amend them. I am sorry to say that my cousin has had a very serious cold, but to-day I think she is better; her cough seems less, and I hope we shall be able to come to Bradford on Sat-urday afternoon, where we intend to stop till Tuesday. You may be sure we shall not soon think of taking such another journey as the last. I look forward with pleasure to Monday, when I hope to meet with you, for as we are no *longer twain* separation is painful, and to meet must ever be attended with joy.

'*Thursday morning.* — I intended to have finished this before breakfast, but unfortunately slept an hour too long. I am every moment in expectation of the old man's arrival. I hope my cousin is still better to-day; she requests me to say that she is much obliged to you for your kind inquiries and the concern you express for her recovery. I take all possible care of her, but yesterday she was naughty enough to venture into the yard without her bonnet! As you do not say anything of going to Leeds I conclude you have not been. We shall most probably hear from the Dr. this afternoon. I am much pleased to hear of his success at Bierly! O that you may both be zealous and successful in your efforts for the salvation of souls, and may your own lives be holy, and your hearts greatly blessed while you are engaged in administering to the good of others! I should have been very glad to have had it in my power to lessen your fatigue and cheer your spirits by my exertions on Monday last. I will hope that this pleasure is still reserved for me. In general, I feel a calm confidence in the providential care and continued mercy of God, and when I consider his past deliverances and past favours I am led to wonder and adore. A sense of my small returns of love and gratitude to him often abases me and makes me think I am little better than those who profess no religion. Pray for me, my dear friend, and rest assured that you possess a very, very large portion of the prayers, thoughts, and heart of yours truly,

'M. BRANWELL.

'Mr. Fennell requests Mr. Bedford to call on the man who has had orders to make blankets for the Grove and desire him to send them as soon as possible. Mr. Fennell will be greatly obliged to Mr. Bedford if he will take this trouble.'

TO REV. PATRICK BRONTË, A.B., HARTSHEAD.

'WOOD HOUSE GROVE, November 18, 1812.

'MY DEAR SAUCY PAT, — Now don't you think you deserve this epithet far more than I do that which you have given me? I really know not what to make of the beginning of your last, the winds, waves, and rocks almost stunned me. I thought you were giving me the account of some terrible dream, or that you had had a presentiment of the fate of my poor box, having no idea that your lively imagination could make so much of the slight reproof conveyed in my last. What will you say when you get a *real, downright scolding?* Since you show such a readiness to

47

atone for your offences after receiving a mild rebuke, I am inclined to hope you will seldom deserve a severe one. I accept with pleasure your atonement, and send you a free and full forgiveness. But I cannot allow that your affection is more deeply rooted than mine. However, we will dispute no more about this, but rather embrace every opportunity to prove its sincerity and strength by acting in every respect as friends and fellow-pilgrims travelling the same road, actuated by the same motives, and having in view the same end. I think if our lives are spared twenty years hence I shall then pray for you with the same, if not greater, fervour and delight that I do now. I am pleased that you are so fully convinced of my candour, for to know that you suspected me of a deficiency in this virtue would grieve and mortify me beyond expression. I do not derive any merit from the possession of it, for in me it is constitutional. Yet I think where it is possessed it will rarely exist alone, and when it is wanted there is reason to doubt the existence of almost every other virtue. As to the other qualities which your partiality attributes to me, although I rejoice to know that I stand so high in your good opinion, yet I blush to think in how small a degree I possess them. But it shall be the pleasing study of my future life to gain such an increase of grace and wisdom as shall enable me to act up to your highest expectations and prove to you a helpmeet. I firmly believe the Almighty has set us apart for each other; may we, by earnest, frequent prayer, and every possible exertion, endeavour to fulfil His will in all things ! I do not, cannot, doubt your love, and here I freely declare I love you above all the world besides. I feel very, very grateful to the great Author of all our mercies for His unspeakable love and condescension towards us, and desire " to show forth my gratitude not only with my lips, but by my life and conversation." I indulge a hope that our mutual prayers will be answered, and that our intimacy will tend much to promote our temporal and eternal interest.

['I suppose you never expected to be much the richer for me, but I am sorry to inform you that I am still poorer than I thought myself. I mentioned having sent for my books, clothes, etc. On Saturday evening about the time you were writing the description of your imaginary shipwreck, I was reading and feeling the effects of a real one, having then received a letter from my sister giving me an account of the vessel in which she had sent my box being stranded on the coast of Devonshire, in consequence of which the box was dashed to pieces with the violence of the sea, and all my little property, with the exception of a very few articles, swallowed up in the mighty deep. If this should not prove the prelude to something worse, I shall think little of it, as it is the first disastrous circumstance which has occurred since I left my home],[1] and having be n so highly favoured it would be highly ungrateful in me were I to suffer this to dwell much on my mind.

'Mr. Morgan was here yesterday, indeed he only left this morning. He mentioned having written to invite you to Bierly on Sunday next, and if you complied with his request it is likely that we shall see you both here on Sunday evening. As we intend going to Leeds next week, we should be happy if you would accompany us on Monday or Tuesday. I mention this by desire of Miss Fennell, who begs to be remembered affectionately to you. Notwithstanding Mr. Fennell's complaints and threats, I doubt not but he will give you a cordial reception whenever you think fit to make your appearance at the Grove. Which you may likewise be assured of receiving from your ever truly affectionate,

'MARIA.

'Both the doctor and his lady very much wish to know what kind of address we make use of in our letters to each other. I think they would scarcely hit on *this ! !* '

TO REV. PATRICK BRONTË, A.B., HARTSHEAD.

'WOOD HOUSE GROVE, December 5, 1812.

'MY DEAREST FRIEND,— So you *thought* that *perhaps* I *might* expect to hear from you. As the case was so doubtful, and you

---

[1] The passage in brackets is quoted, not quite accurately, by Mrs. Gaskell.

49

were in such great haste, you might as well have deferred writing a few days longer, for you seem to suppose it is a matter of perfect indifference to me whether I hear from you or not. I believe I once requested you to judge of my feelings by your own — am I to think that *you* are thus indifferent? I feel very unwilling to entertain such an opinion, and am grieved that you should suspect me of such a cold, heartless attachment. But I am too serious on the subject; I only meant to rally you a little on the beginning of your last, and to tell you that I fancied there was a coolness in it which none of your former letters had contained. If this fancy was groundless, forgive me for having indulged it, and let it serve to convince you of the sincerity and warmth of my affection. Real love is ever apt to suspect that it meets not with an equal return; you must not wonder then that my fears are sometimes excited. My pride cannot bear the idea of a diminution of your attachment, or to think that it is stronger on my side than on yours. But I must not permit my pen so fully to disclose the feelings of my heart, nor will I tell you whether I am pleased or not at the thought of seeing you on the appointed day.

'Miss Fennell desires her kind regards, and, with her father, is extremely obliged to you for the trouble you have taken about the carpet, and has no doubt but it will give full satisfaction. They think there will be no occasion for the green cloth.

'We intend to set about making the cakes here next week, but as the fifteen or twenty persons whom you mention live probably somewhere in your neighbourhood, I think it will be most convenient for Mrs. B. to make a small one for the purpose of distributing there, which will save us the difficulty of sending so far.

'You may depend on my learning my lessons as rapidly as they are given me. I am already tolerably perfect in the A B C, etc. I am much obliged to you for the pretty little hymn which I have already got by heart, but cannot promise to sing it scientifically, though I will endeavour to gain a little more assurance.

'Since I began this Jane put into my hands Lord Lyttleton's
"Advice to a Lady." When I read those lines, " Be never cool
reserve with passion joined, with caution choose, but then be fondly
kind, etc." my heart smote me for having in some cases used too
much reserve towards you. Do you think you have any cause to
complain of me? If you do let me know it. For were it in
my power to prevent it, I would in no instance occasion you the
least pain or uneasiness. I am certain no one ever loved you with
an affection more pure, constant, tender, and ardent than that
which I feel. Surely this is not saying too much ; it is the truth,
and I trust you are worthy to know it. I long to improve in
every religious and moral quality, that I may be a help, and if
possible an ornament to you. Oh, let us pray much for wisdom
and grace to fill our appointed stations with propriety, that we
may enjoy satisfaction in our own souls, edify others, and bring
glory to the name of Him who has so wonderfully preserved, blessed,
and brought us together.

'If there is anything in the commencement of this which looks
like pettishness, forgive it; my mind is now completely divested of
every feeling of the kind, although I own I am sometimes too apt
to be overcome by this disposition.

'Let me have the pleasure of hearing from you again as soon as
convenient. This writing is uncommonly bad, but I too am in
haste.

'Adieu, my dearest.— I am your affectionate and sincere
'MARIA.'

Mr. Brontë was at Hartshead, where he married, for five
years, and there his two eldest children, Maria and Elizabeth,
were born. He then moved to Thornton, near Bradford,
where Charlotte was born on the 21st of April 1816, Branwell in 1817, Emily in 1818, and Anne in 1819. In 1820
the family removed to the parsonage of Haworth, and in
1821 the poor mother was dead. A year or two later Miss
Elizabeth Branwell came from Penzance to act as a mother
to her orphaned nephew and nieces. There is no reason to
accept the theory that Miss Branwell was quite as formid-

able or offensive a personage as the Mrs. Read in 'Jane
Eyre.' That she was a somewhat rigid and not over demon-
strative woman, we may take for granted. The one letter to
her of any importance that I have seen — it is printed in
Mrs. Gaskell's life — was the attempt of Charlotte to obtain
her co-operation in the projected visit to a Brussels school.
Miss Branwell provided the money readily enough it would
seem, and one cannot doubt that in her later years she was
on the best of terms with her nieces. There may have
been too much discipline in childhood, but discipline which
would now be considered too severe was common enough at
the beginning of the century. The children, we may be sure,
were left abundantly alone. The writing they accomplished
in their early years would sufficiently demonstrate that.
Miss Branwell died in 1842; and from her will, which I
give elsewhere, it will be seen that she behaved very justly
to her three nieces.

The reception by Mr. Brontë of his children's literary
successes has been very pleasantly recorded by ·Charlotte.
He was proud of his daughters, and delighted with their
fame. He seems to have had no small share of their affection. Charlotte loved and esteemed him. There are hundreds of her letters, in many of which are severe and indeed
unprintable things about this or that individual; but of her
father these letters contain not one single harsh word. She
wrote to him regularly when absent. Not only did he secure
the affection of his daughter, but the people most intimately
associated with him next to his own children gave him a life-
long affection and regard. Martha Brown, the servant who
lived with him until his death, always insisted that her old
master had been grievously wronged, and that a kinder,
more generous, and in every way more worthy man had never
lived. Nancy Garrs, another servant, always spoke of Mr.
Brontë as 'the kindest man who ever drew breath,' and as
a good and affectionate father. Forty years have gone by

since Charlotte Brontë died; and thirty-six years have flown since Mr. Nicholls left the deathbed of his wife's father; but through all that period he has retained the most kindly memories of one with whom his life was intimately associated for sixteen years, with whom at one crisis of his life, as we shall see, he had a serious difference, but whom he ever believed to have been an entirely honourable and upright man.

A lady visitor to Haworth in December 1860 did not, it is true, carry away quite so friendly an impression. 'I have been to see old Mr. Brontë,' she writes, 'and have spent about an hour with him. He is completely confined to his bed, but talks hopefully of leaving it again when the summer comes round. I am afraid that it will not be leaving it as he plans, poor old man! He is touchingly softened by illness; but still talks in his pompous way, and mingles moral remarks and somewhat stale sentiments with his conversation on ordinary subjects.' This is severe, but after all it was a literary woman who wrote it. On the whole we may safely assume, with the evidence before us, that Mr. Brontë was a thoroughly upright and honourable man who came manfully through a somewhat severe life battle. That is how his daughters thought of him, and we cannot do better than think with them.[1]

[1] The following letter indicates Mr. Brontë's independence of spirit. It was written after Charlotte's death:

'HAWORTH, NR. KEIGHLEY, January 16, 1858.

'SIR,— Your letter which I have received this morning gives both to Mr. Nicholls and me great uneasiness. It would seem that application has been made to the Duke of Devonshire for money to aid the subscription in reference to the expense of apparatus for heating our church and schools. This has been done without our knowledge, and most assuredly, had we known it, would have met with our strongest opposition. We have no claim on the Duke. His Grace honour'd us with a visit, in token of his respect for the memory of the dead, and his liberality and munificence are well and widely known; and the mercenary, taking an unfair advantage of these circumstances, have taken a step which both Mr. Nicholls and I utterly regret and condemn. In answer to your query, I may state that the whole expense for both the schools and church

CHARLOTTE BRONTË

Mr. Brontë died on June 7, 1861, and his funeral in Haworth Church is described in the 'Bradford Review' of the following week:—

'Great numbers of people had collected in the churchyard, and a few minutes before noon the corpse was brought out through the eastern gate of the garden leading into the churchyard. The Rev. Dr. Burnet, Vicar of Bradford, read the funeral service, and led the way into the church, and the following clergymen were the bearers of the coffin: The Rev. Dr. Cartman of Skipton; Rev. Mr. Sowden of Hebden Bridge; the Incumbents of Cullingworth, Oakworth, Morton, Oxenhope, and St. John's Ingrow. The chief mourners were the Rev. Arthur Bell Nicholls, son-in-law of the deceased; Martha Brown, the housekeeper; and her sister, Mrs. Brown; and Mrs. Wainwright. There were several gentlemen followed the corpse whom we did not know. All the shops in Haworth were closed, and the people filled every pew, and the aisles in the church, and many shed tears during the impressive reading of the service for the burial of the dead, by the vicar. The body of Mr. Brontë was laid within the altar rails, by the side of his daughter Charlotte. He is the last that can be interred inside of Haworth Church. On the coffin was this inscription: "Patrick Brontë, died June 7th, 1861, aged 84 years."'

His will, which was proved at Wakefield, left the bulk of his property, as was natural, to the son-in-law who had faithfully served and tended him for the six years which succeeded Charlotte Brontë's death.

is about one hundred pounds; and that after what has been and may be subscribed, there may fifty pounds remain as a debt. But this may, and ought, to be raised by the inhabitants, in the next year after the depression of trade shall, it is hoped, have passed away. I have written to His Grace on the subject.— I remain, sir, your obedient servant,   P. BRONTË.

'SIR JOSEPH PAXTON, BART.,
   'Hardwick Hall,
      'Chesterfield.'

AND HER CIRCLE

*Extracted from the Principal Registry of the Probate Divorce
and Admiralty Division of the High Court of Justice.*

Being of sound mind and judgment, in the name of God the Father,
Son, and Holy Ghost, I, PATRICK BRONTË, B. A., Incumbent of
Haworth, in the Parish of Bradford and county of York, make
this my last Will and Testament : I leave forty pounds to be equally
divided amongst all my brothers and sisters to whom I gave considerable sums in times past ; And I direct the same sum of forty pounds
to be sent for distribution to Mr. Hugh Brontë, Ballinasceaugh, near
Loughbrickland, Ireland ; I leave thirty pounds to my servant,
Martha Brown, as a token of regard for long and faithful services
to me and my children ; To my beloved and esteemed son-in-law, the
Rev. Arthur Bell Nicholls, B.A., I leave and bequeath the residue
of my personal estate of every description which I shall be possessed
of at my death for his own absolute benefit ; And I make him my
sole executor ; And I revoke all former and other Wills, in witness
whereof I, the said PATRICK BRONTË, have to this my last Will,
contained in this sheet of paper, set my hand this twentieth day of
June, one thousand eight hundred and fifty-five.
PATRICK BRONTË. — Signed and acknowledged by the said
PATRICK BRONTË as his Will in the presence of us present at the
same time, and who in his presence and in the presence of each
other have hereunto subscribed our names as witnesses : JOSEPH
REDMAN, ELIZA BROWN.

The Irish relatives are not forgotten, and indeed this
will gives the most direct evidence of the fact that for the
sixty years that he had been absent from his native land
he had always kept his own country, or at least his relatives in County Down, sufficiently in mind.

CHAPTER II.

CHILDHOOD.

EIGHTY years have passed over Thornton since that village had the honour of becoming the birthplace of Charlotte Brontë. The visitor of to-day will find the Bell Chapel, in which Mr. Brontë officiated, a mere ruin, and the font in which his children were baptized ruthlessly exposed to the winds of heaven.[1] The house in which Patrick Brontë resided is now a butcher's shop, and indeed little, one imagines, remains the same. But within the new church one may still overhaul the registers, and find, with but little trouble, a record of the baptism of the Brontë children. There, amid the names of the rough and rude peasantry of the neighbourhood, we find the accompanying entries,[2] differing from their neighbours only by the fact that Mr. Morgan or Mr. Fennell came to the help of their relatives and officiated in place of Mr. Brontë. Mr. Brontë, it will be observed, had already received his appointment to Haworth when Anne was baptized.

There were, it is well known, two elder children, Maria and Elizabeth, born at Hartshead, and doomed to die speedily at Haworth. A vague memory of Maria lives in the Helen Burns of 'Jane Eyre,' but the only tangible records of the pair, as far as I am able to ascertain, are a couple of samplers, of the kind which Mrs. Brontë and her sisters had worked at Penzance a generation earlier.

[1] The vicar, the Rev. J. Jolly, assures me, as these pages are passing through the press, that he is now moving it into the new church.
[2] See opposite page.

'Maria Brontë finished this Sampler on the 16th of May at the age of eight years'

one of them tells us, and the other :

'Elizabeth Brontë finished this Sampler the 27th of July at the age of seven years.'

Maria died at the age of twelve in May 1825, and Elizabeth in June of the same year, at the age of eleven. It is, however, with their three sisters that we have most concern,

[2] *Baptisms solemnised in the Parish of Bradford and Chapelry of Thornton in the County of York.*

When Baptized.	Child's Christian Name.	PARENTS' NAME.		Abode.	Quality, Trade or Profession.	By whom the Ceremony was Performed.
		Christian.	Surname.			
1816 29th June	Charlotte daughter of	The Rev. Patrick and Maria	Brontë	Thornton	Minister of Thornton	Wm. Morgan Minister of Christ Church Bradford.
1817 July 23	Patrick Branwell son of	Patrick and Maria	Brontë	Thornton	Minister	Jno. Fennell officiating Minister.
1818 20th August	Emily Jane daughter of	The Rev. Patrick and Maria	Brontë A.B.	Thornton Parsonage	Minister of Thornton	Wm. Morgan Minister of Christ Church Bradford.
1820 March 25th	Anne daughter of	The Rev. Patrick and Maria	Brontë	Minister of Haworth		Wm. Morgan Minister of Christ Church in Bradford.

CHARLOTTE BRONTË

although all the six children accompanied their parents to Haworth in 1820.

Haworth, we are told, has been over-described; and yet it may not be amiss to discover from the easily available directories what manner of place it was during the Brontë residence there. Pigot's Yorkshire Directory of 1828 gives the census during the first year of Mr. Brontë's incumbency thus: —

'HAWORTH, a populous manufacturing village, in the honour of Pontefract, Morley wapentake, and in the parish of Bradford, is four miles south of Keighley, containing, by the census of 1821, 4668 inhabitants.

'Gentry and Clergy: Brontë, Rev. Patrick, Haworth; Heaton, Robert, gent., Ponden Hall; Miles, Rev. Oddy, Haworth; Saunders, Rev. Moses, Haworth.'

From the same source twenty years later we obtain more explicit detail, which is not without interest to-day.

'HAWORTH is a chapelry, comprising the hamlets of Haworth, Stanbury, and Near and Far Oxenhope, in the parish of Bradford, and wapentake of Morley, West Riding — Haworth being ten miles from Bradford, about the same distance from Halifax, Colne, and Skipton, three and a half miles S. from Keighley, and eight from Hebden Bridge, at which latter place is a station on the Leeds and Manchester railway. Haworth is situated on the side of a hill, and consists of one irregularly built street — the habitations in that part called Oxenhope being yet more scattered, and Stanbury still farther distant; the entire chapelry occupying a wide space. The spinning of worsted, and the manufacture of stuffs, are branches which here prevail extensively.

'The Church or rather chapel (subject to Bradford), dedicated to St. Michael, was rebuilt in 1757: the living is a perpetual curacy, in the presentation of the vicar of Bradford and certain trustees; the present curate is the Rev. Patrick Brontë. The

other places of worship are two chapels for baptists, one each
for primitive and Wesleyan methodists, and another at Oxenhope for the latter denomination. There are two excellent free
schools — one at Stanbury, the other, called the Free Grammar
School, near Oxenhope ; besides which there are several neat
edifices erected for Sunday teaching. There are three annual
fairs : they are held on Easter-Monday, the second Monday
after St. Peter's day (old style), and the first Monday after
Old Michaelmas day. The chapelry of Haworth, and its dependent hamlets, contained by the returns for 1831, 5835 inhabitants ;
and by the census taken in June, 1841, the population amounted
to 6301.'

Haworth needs even to-day no further description, but
the house in which Mr. Brontë resided, from 1820 till his
death in 1861, has not been over-described, perhaps because
Mr. Brontë's successor has not been too well disposed to
receive the casual visitor to Haworth under his roof.

Many changes have been made since Mr. Brontë died,
but the house still retains its essentially interesting features.
In the time of the Brontës, it is true, the front outlook was
as desolate as to-day it is attractive. Then there was a little
piece of barren ground running down to the walls of the
churchyard, with here and there a currant-bush as the sole
adornment. Now we see an abundance of trees and a well-
kept lawn. Miss Ellen Nussey well remembers seeing Emily
and Anne, on a fine summer afternoon, sitting on stools in
this bit of garden plucking currants from the poor insignificant bushes. There was no premonition of the time, not so
far distant, when the rough doorway separating the churchyard from the garden, which was opened for their mother
when they were little children, should be opened again time
after time in rapid succession for their own biers to be
carried through. This gateway is now effectively bricked
up. In the days of the Brontës it was reserved for the
passage of the dead — a grim arrangement, which, strange

to say, finds no place in any one of the sisters' stories.
We enter the house, and the door on the right leads into
Mr. Brontë's study, always called the parlour; that on
the left into the dining-room, where the children spent a
great portion of their lives. From childhood to womanhood, indeed, the three girls regularly breakfasted with
their father in his study. In the dining-room — a square
and simple room of a kind common enough in the houses of
the poorer middle-classes — they ate their mid-day dinner,
their tea and supper. Mr. Brontë joined them at tea,
although he always dined alone in his study. The children's dinner-table has been described to me by a visitor
to the house. At one end sat Miss Branwell, at the other,
Charlotte, with Emily and Anne on either side. Branwell
was then absent. The living was of the simplest. A
single joint, followed invariably by one kind or another of
milk-pudding. Pastry was unknown in the Brontë household. Milk-puddings, or food composed of milk and rice,
would seem to have made the principal diet of Emily and
Anne Brontë, and to this they added a breakfast of Scotch
porridge, which they shared with their dogs. It is more
interesting, perhaps, to think of all the daydreams in that
room, of the mass of writing which was achieved there,
of the conversations and speculation as to the future.
Miss Nussey has given a pleasant picture of twilight when
Charlotte and she walked with arms encircling one another
round and round the table, and Emily and Anne followed
in similar fashion. There was no lack of cheerfulness
and of hope at that period. Behind Mr. Brontë's studio
was the kitchen; and there we may easily picture the
Brontë children telling stories to Tabby or Martha, or
to whatever servant reigned at the time, and learning,
as all of them did, to become thoroughly domesticated —
Emily most of all. Behind the dining-room was a peat-
room, which, when Charlotte was married in 1854, was

cleared out and converted into a little study for Mr. Nicholls. The staircase with its solid banister remains as it did half a century ago; and at its foot one is still shown the corner which tradition assigns as the scene of Emily's conflict with her dog Keeper. On the right, at the back, as you mount the staircase, was a small room allotted to Branwell as a studio. On the other side of this staircase, also at the back, was the servants' room. In the front of the house, immediately over the dining-room, was Miss Branwell's room, afterwards the spare bedroom until Charlotte Brontë married. In that room she died. On the left, over Mr. Brontë's study, was Mr. Brontë's bedroom. It was the room which, for many years, he shared with Branwell, and it was in that room that Branwell and his father died at an interval of twenty years. On the staircase, half-way up, was a grandfather's clock, which Mr. Brontë used to wind up every night on his way to bed. He always went to bed at nine o'clock, and Miss Nussey well remembers his stentorian tones as he called out as he left his study and passed the dining-room door — 'Don't be up late, children' — which they usually were. Between these two front rooms upstairs, and immediately over the passage, with a door facing the staircase, was a box room; but this was the children's nursery, where for many years the children slept, where the bulk of their little books were compiled, and where, it is more than probable, the 'Professor' and 'Jane Eyre' were composed.

Of the work of the Brontë children in these early years, a great deal might be written. Mrs. Gaskell gives a list of some eighteen booklets, but at least eighteen more from the pen of Charlotte are in existence. Branwell was equally prolific; and of him, also, there remains an immense mass of childish effort. That Emily and Anne were industrious in a like measure there is abundant reason to believe; but scarcely one of their juvenile efforts remains to us, nor even the unpublished fragments of later years, to which reference will be made a little later. Whether Emily and Anne on the eve of their death deliberately destroyed all their treasures, or whether they were destroyed by Charlotte in the days of her mourning, will never be known. Meanwhile one turns with interest to the efforts of Charlotte and Branwell. Charlotte's little stories commence in her thirteenth year, and go on until she is twenty-three. From thirteen to eighteen she would seem to have had one absorbing hero. It was the Duke of Wellington; and her hero-worship extended to the children of the Duke, who, indeed, would seem even more than their father to have absorbed her childish affections. Whether the stories are fairy tales or dramas of modern life, they all alike introduce the Marquis of Douro, who afterwards became the second Duke of Wellington, and Lord Charles Wellesley, whose son is now the third Duke of Wellington. The length of some of these fragments is indeed incredible. They fill but a few sheets of notepaper in that tiny handwriting; but when copied by zealous admirers, it is seen that more than one of them is twenty thousand words in length.

'The Foundling, by Captain Tree,' written in 1833, is a story of thirty-five thousand words, though the manuscript has only eighteen pages. 'The Green Dwarf,' written in the same year, is even longer, and indeed after her return from Roe Head in 1833, Charlotte must have devoted herself to continuous writing. 'The Adventures of Ernest Alembert' is a booklet of this date, and 'Arthuriana, or Odds and Ends: being a Miscellaneous Collection of Pieces in Prose and Verse, by Lord Charles Wellesley,' is yet another.

The son of the Iron Duke is made to talk, in these little books, in a way which would have gladdened the heart of a modern interviewer:

'Lord Charles,' said Mr. Rundle to me one afternoon lately, 'I have an engagement to drink tea with an old college chum this evening, so I shall give you sixty lines of the "Æneid" to get ready during my absence. If it is not ready by the time I come back you know the consequences.' 'Very well, Sir,' said I, bringing out the books with a prodigious bustle, and making a show as if I intended to learn a whole book instead of sixty lines of the "Æneid." This appearance of industry, however, lasted no longer than until the old gentleman's back was turned. No sooner had he fairly quitted the room than I flung aside the musty tomes, took my cap, and speeding through chamber, hall, and gallery, was soon outside the gates of Waterloo Palace.'

'The Secret,' another story, of which Mrs. Gaskell gave a facsimile of the first page, was also written in 1833, and indeed in this, her seventeenth year, Charlotte Brontë must have written as much as in any year of her life. When at Roe Head, 1832–3, she would seem to have worked at her studies, and particularly her drawing; but in the interval between Cowan Bridge and Roe Head she wrote a great deal. The earliest manuscripts in my possession bear date 1829 — that is to say, in Charlotte's thirteenth year. They are her 'Tales of the Islanders,' which extend to four little volumes in brown paper covers neatly inscribed 'First Volume,' 'Second Volume,' and so on. The Duke is of absorbing importance in these 'Tales.' 'One evening the Duke of Wellington was writing in his room in Downing Street. He was reposing at his ease in a simple easy chair, smoking a homely tobacco pipe, for he disdained all the modern frippery of cigars . . .' and so on in an abundance of childish imaginings. 'The Search after Happiness' and 'Characters of Great Men of the Present Time' were also written in 1829. Perhaps the only juvenile fragment which is worth anything is also the only one in which she escapes from the Wellington enthusiasm. It has an interest also in indicating that Charlotte in her girlhood heard something of her father's native land. It is called —

63

CHARLOTTE BRONTË

AN ADVENTURE IN IRELAND.

During my travels in the south of Ireland the following adventure happened to me. One evening in the month of August, after a long walk, I was ascending the mountain which overlooks the village of Cahin, when I suddenly came in sight of a fine old castle. It was built upon a rock, and behind it was a large wood and before it was a river. Over the river there was a bridge, which formed the approach to the castle. When I arrived at the bridge I stood still awhile to enjoy the prospect around me: far below was the wide sheet of still water in which the reflection of the pale moon was not disturbed by the smallest wave; in the valley was the cluster of cabins which is known by the appellation of Cahin, and beyond these were the mountains of Killala. Over all, the grey robe of twilight was now stealing with silent and scarcely perceptible advances. No sound except the hum of the distant village and the sweet song of the nightingale in the wood behind me broke upon the stillness of the scene. While I was contemplating this beautiful prospect, a gentleman, whom I had not before observed, accosted me with 'Good evening, sir; are you a stranger in these parts?' I replied that I was. He then asked me where I was going to stop for the night; I answered that I intended to sleep somewhere in the village. 'I am afraid you will find very bad accommodation there,' said the gentleman; 'but if you will take up your quarters with me at the castle, you are welcome.' I thanked him for his kind offer, and accepted it.

When we arrived at the castle I was shown into a large parlour, in which was an old lady sitting in an arm-chair by the fireside, knitting. On the rug lay a very pretty tortoise-shell cat. As soon as mentioned, the old lady rose; and when Mr. O'Callaghan (for that, I learned, was his name) told her who I was, she said in the most cordial tone that I was welcome, and asked me to sit down. In the course of conversation I learned that she was Mr. O'Callaghan's mother, and that his father had been dead about a year. We had sat about an hour, when supper was announced, and after supper Mr. O'Callaghan asked me if I should like to retire for the night. I answered in the affirmative, and a little boy was commissioned to show me to my apartment. It was a snug, clean, and comfortable little old-fashioned room at the top of the castle. As soon as we had entered, the boy, who appeared to be a shrewd, good-tempered little fellow, said with a shrug of the shoulder, 'If it was going to bed I was, it shouldn't be here that you'd catch me.' 'Why?' said I. 'Because,' replied the boy, 'they say that the ould masther's ghost has been seen sitting on that there chair.' 'And have you seen him?' 'No; but I've heard him washing his hands in that basin often and often.' 'What is your name, my little fellow?' 'Dennis Mulready, please your honour.' 'Well, good-night to you.' 'Good-night, masther; and may the saints keep you from all fairies and brownies,' said Dennis as he left the room.

As soon as I had laid down I began to think of what the boy had been telling me, and I confess I felt a strange kind of fear, and once or twice I even thought I could discern something white through the darkness which surrounded me. At length, by the help of reason, I succeeded in mastering these, what some would call idle fancies, and fell asleep. I had slept about an hour when a strange sound awoke me, and I saw looking through my curtains a skeleton wrapped in a white sheet. I was overcome with terror and tried to scream, but my tongue was paralysed and my whole frame shook with fear. In a deep hollow voice it said to me, 'Arise, that I may show thee this world's wonders,' and in an instant I found myself encompassed with clouds and darkness. But soon the roar of mighty waters fell upon my ear, and I saw some clouds of spray arising from high falls that rolled in awful majesty down tremendous precipices, and then foamed and thundered in the gulf beneath as if they had taken up their unquiet abode in some giant's cauldron. But soon the scene changed, and I found myself in the mines of Cracone. There were high pillars and stately arches, whose glittering splendour was never excelled by the brightest fairy palaces. There were not many lamps, only those of a few poor miners, whose rough visages formed a striking contrast to the dazzling figures and grandeur which surrounded them. But in the midst of all this magnificence I felt an indescribable sense of fear and terror, for the sea raged above us, and by the awful and tumultuous noises of roaring winds and dashing waves, it seemed as if the storm was violent. And now the mossy pillars groaned beneath the pressure of the ocean, and the glittering arches seemed about to be overwhelmed. When I heard the rushing waters and saw a mighty flood rolling towards me I gave a loud shriek of terror. The scene vanished, and I found myself in a wide desert full of barren rocks and high mountains. As I was approaching one of the rocks, in which there was a large cave, my foot stumbled and I fell. Just then I heard a deep growl, and saw by the unearthly light of his own fiery eyes a royal lion rousing himself from his kingly slumbers. His terrible eye was fixed upon me, and the desert rang and the rocks echoed with the tremendous roar of fierce delight which he uttered as he sprang towards me. 'Well, masther, it's been a windy night, though it's fine now,' said Dennis, as he drew the window-curtain and let the bright rays of the morning sun into the little old-fashioned room at the top of O'Callaghan Castle. C. BRONTË.

April the 28th, 1829.

Six numbers of 'The Young Men's Magazine' were written in 1829; a very juvenile poem, 'The Evening Walk,' by the Marquis of Douro, in 1830; and another, of greater literary value, 'The Violet,' in the same year. In 1831 we have an unfinished poem, 'The Trumpet Hath Sounded;' and in 1832 a very long poem called 'The Bridal.' Some of them, as for example a poem called 'Richard Cœur de Lion and Blondel,' are written in penny and twopenny notebooks of the kind used by laundresses. Occasionally her father has purchased a sixpenny book and has written within the cover —

'All that is written in this book must be in a good, plain, and legible hand. — P. B.'

While upon this topic, I may as well carry the record up to the date of publication of Currer Bell's poems. 'A Leaf from an unopened volume' was written in 1834, as were also 'The Death of Darius,' and 'Corner Dishes.' 'Saul: a Poem,' was written in 1835, and a number of other still unpublished verses. There is a story called 'Lord Douro,' bearing date 1837, and a manuscript book of verses of 1838, but that pretty well exhausts the manuscripts before me previous to the days of serious literary activity. During the years as private governess (1839–1841) and the Brussels experiences (1842–1844), Charlotte would seem to have put all literary effort on one side.

There is only one letter of Charlotte Brontë's childhood. It is indorsed by Mr. Brontë on the cover 'Charlotte's First Letter,' possibly for the guidance of Mrs. Gaskell, who may perhaps have thought it of insufficient importance. That can scarcely be the opinion of any one to-day. Charlotte, aged thirteen, is staying with the Fennells, her mother's friends of those early love-letters.

TO THE REV. P. BRONTË.

'Parsonage House, Crosstone,
'September 23, 1829.

'My dear Papa, — At Aunt's request I write these lines to in-form you that "if all be well" we shall be at home on Friday by dinner-time, when we hope to find you in good health. On account of the bad weather we have not been out much, but notwithstanding we have spent our time very pleasantly, be-tween reading, working, and learning our lessons, which Uncle Fennell has been so kind as to teach us every day. Branwell has taken two sketches from nature, and Emily, Anne, and myself have likewise each of us drawn a piece from some views of the lakes which Mr. Fennell brought with him from Westmoreland. The whole of these he intends keeping. Mr. Fennell is sorry he cannot accompany us to Haworth on Friday, for want of room,

but hopes to have the pleasure of seeing you soon. All unite in
sending their kind love with your affectionate daughter,

'CHARLOTTE BRONTË.'

The following list includes the whole of the early Brontë
Manuscripts known to me, or of which I can find any
record: —

UNPUBLISHED BRONTË LITERATURE.

BY CHARLOTTE BRONTË.

The Young Men's Magazines. In Six Numbers, ... 1829
[Only four out of these six numbers appear to have been preserved.]

The Search after Happiness: A Tale. By Charlotte
    Brontë, ... 1829
Two Romantic Tales; viz. The Twelve Adventures, and An
    Adventure in Ireland, ... 1829
Characters of Great Men of the Present Age, Dec. 17th, . 1829
Tales of the Islanders. By Charlotte Brontë : —
          Vol. i. dated June 31, 1829.
          Vol. ii. dated December 2, 1829.
          Vol. iii. dated May 8, 1830.
          Vol. iv. dated July 30, 1830.

[Accompanying these volumes is a one-page document detailing
'The Origin of the Islanders.' Dated March 12, 1829.]

The Evening Walk: A Poem. By the Marquis Douro, . 1830
A Translation into English Verse of the First Book of
    Voltaire's Henriade. By Charlotte Brontë, ... 1830
Albion and Marina: A Tale. By Lord Wellesley, . . . 1830
The Adventures of Ernest Alembert. A Fairy Tale. By
    Charlotte Brontë, ... 1830
The Violet: A Poem. With several smaller Pieces. By
    the Marquess of Douro. . . . Published by Seargeant
    Tree. Glasstown, 1830, ... 1830
The Bridal. By C. Brontë, ... 1832
Arthuriana; or, Odds and Ends: Being a Miscellaneous

Collection of Pieces in Prose and Verse. By Lord
Charles A. F. Wellesley, ... 1833

Something about Arthur. Written by Charles Albert Florian Wellesley, ... 1833

The Vision. By Charlotte Brontë, ... 1833

The Secret and Lily Hart : Two Tales. By Lord Charles
Wellesley, ... 1833

[The first page of this book is given in fac-simile in vol. i. of Mrs.
Gaskell's ' Life of Charlotte Brontë.']

Visits in Verdopolis. By the Honourable Charles Albert
Florian Wellesley. Two vols., ... 1833

The Green Dwarf : A Tale of the Perfect Tense. By Lord
Charles Albert Florian Wellesley. Charlotte Brontë, . 1833

The Foundling : A Tale of our own Times. By Captain
Tree, ... 1833

Richard Cœur de Lion and Blondel. By Charlotte Brontë.
8vo, pp. 20. Signed in full Charlotte Brontë, and
dated Haworth, near Bradford, Dec. 27th, 1833, . . 1833

My Angria and the Angrians. By Lord Charles Albert
Florian Wellesley, ... 1834

A Leaf from an Unopened Volume ; or, The Manuscript of
an Unfortunate Author. Edited by Lord Charles Albert Florian Wellesley, ... 1834

Corner Dishes : Being a small Collection of . . . Trifles in
Prose and Verse. By Lord Charles Albert Florian
Wellesley, ... 1834

The Spell : An Extravaganza. By Lord Charles Albert
Florian Wellesley. Signed Charlotte Brontë, June 21st,
1834. The contents include : 1. Preface, half page ;
2. The Spell, 26 pages ; 3. High Life in Verdopolis :
or The Difficulties of Annexing a Suitable Title to a
Work Practically Illustrated in Six Chapters. By
Lord C. A. F. Wellesley, March 20, 1834, 22 pages ;
4. The Scrap-Book : A Mingling of Many Things.
Compiled by Lord C. A. F. Wellesley. C. Brontë,
March 17th, 1835, 31 pages.

[This volume is in the British Museum.]

CHARLOTTE BRONTË

Death of Darius Cadomanus : A Poem. By Charlotte
    Brontë. Pp. 24. Signed in full, and dated, . . . 1835
Saul and Memory : Two Poems. By C. Brontë. Pp. 12, . 1835
Passing Events, ... 1836
' We Wove a Web in Childhood ' : A Poem (pp. vi.), signed
    C. Brontë, Haworth, Dec'br. 19th, 1835, ... 1835
The Wounded Stag, and other Poems. Signed C. Brontë.
    Jan'y. 19, 1836. Pp. 20, ... 1836
Lord Douro : A Story. Signed C. Brontë. July 21st,
    1837, ... 1837
Poems. By C. Brontë. Pp. 16, ... 1838
Lettre d'Invitation à un Ecclésiastique. Signed Charlotte
    Brontë. Le 21 Juillet, 1842. Large 8vo, pp. 4. A
    French exercise written at Brussels, ... 1842
John Henry. By Charlotte Brontë. Crown 8vo, pp. 36,
    written in pencil, ... circa 1852
Willie Ellin. By Charlotte Brontë. Crown 8vo, pp. 18,
                       May and June 1853

The following, included in Charlotte's ' Catalogue of my Books '
printed by Mrs. Gaskell, are not now forthcoming :

Leisure Hours : A Tale, and two Fragments, . . July 6th, 1829
The Adventures of Edward de Crak : A Tale, . Feb. 2nd, 1830
An Interesting Incident in the Lives of some of the most
    eminent Persons of the Age : A Tale, . June 10th, 1830
The Poetaster: A Drama. In two volumes, . July 12th, 1830
A Book of Rhymes, finished, ... December 17th, 1829
Miscellaneous Poems, finished, ... May 3rd, 1830

[These ' Miscellaneous Poems ' are probably poems written upon
separate sheets, and not forming a complete book — indeed, some
half dozen such separate poems are still extant. The last item
given in Charlotte's list of these ' Miscellaneous Poems ' is 'The
Evening Walk,' 1820; this is a separate book, and is included in
the list above.]

BY EMILY BRONTË.

A volume of Poems, 8vo, pp. 29 ; signed (at the top of
the first page) E. J. B. Transcribed February 1844.

Each poem is headed with the date of its composition. Of the poems included in this book four are still unprinted, the remainder were published in the 'Poems of 1846.' The whole are written in miscroscopic characters, ... 1844

A volume of Poems, square 8vo, pp. 24. Each poem is dated, and the first is signed 'E. J. Brontë, August 19th, 1837.' Written in an ordinary, and not a minute, handwriting. All unpublished, ... 1837–1839

A series of poems written in a minute hand upon both sides of fourteen or fifteen small slips of paper of various sizes. All unpublished, ... 1833–1839

Lettre and Réponse. An exercise in French. Large 8vo, pp. 4. Signed 'E. J. Brontë,' and dated '16 Juillet,' 1842

L'Amour Filial. An exercise in French. Small quarto, pp. 4. Signed in full 'Emily J. Brontë,' and dated '5 Aout,' 1842

BY ANNE BRONTË.

Verses by Lady Geralda, and other poems. A crown 8vo volume of 28 pages. Each poem is signed (or initialed) and dated, the dates extending from 1836 to 1837. The poems are all unpublished, . . . 1836–1837

The North Wind, and other poems. A crown 8vo volume of 26 pages. Each poem is signed (or initialed) and dated, some having in addition to her own name the nom-de-guerre 'Alexandrina Zenobia' or 'Olivia Vernon.' The dates extend from 1838 to 1840. The poems are all unpublished, ... 1838–1840

To Cowper, and other poems. 8vo, pp. 22. Of the nine poems contained in this volume three are signed 'Anne Brontë,' four are signed 'A. Brontë,' and two are initialed 'A. B.' All are dated. Part of these 'Poems' are unpublished, the remainder appeared in the 'Poems of 1846,' 1842–1845

A thin 8vo volume of poems (mostly dated 1845), pp. 14, each being signed 'A. Brontë,' or simply 'A. B.' —

CHARLOTTE BRONTË

some having in addition to, or instead of, her own
name the nom-de-guerre 'Zerona.' A few of these
poems are unprinted ; the remainder are a portion of
Anne's contribution to the ' Poems of 1846,' . .   circa 1845

Song : ' Should Life's first feelings be forgot ' (one octavo
leaf), ... 1845

[A fair copy (2 pp. 8vo) of a poem by Branwell Brontë, in the handwriting of Anne Brontë.]

The Power of Love, and other poems.   Post octavo,
pp. 26.   Each poem is signed (or initialed) and
dated, ... 1845–1846

Self Communion, a Poem.   8vo, pp. 19.   Signed 'A. B.'
and dated 'April 17th, 1848,' 1848

BY BRANWELL BRONTË.

The Battle of Washington.   By P. B. Brontë.   With full-
page coloured illustrations, ... 1827

[An exceedingly childish production, and the earliest of all the
Brontë manuscripts.]

History of the Rebellion in my Army, ... 1828

The Travels of Rolando Segur : Comprising his Adventures
throughout the Voyage, and in America, Europe, the
South Pole, etc.   By Patrick Branwell Brontë.   In
two volumes, ... 1829

A Collection of Poems.   By Young Soult the Rhymer.
Illustrated with Notes and Commentaries by Monsieur
Chateaubriand.   In two volumes, ... 1829

The Liar Detected.   By Captain Bud, ... 1830

Caractacus : A Dramatic Poem.   By Young Soult, . . . 1830

The Revenge : A Tragedy, in three Acts.   By Young Soult.
P. B. Brontë.   In two volumes.   Glasstown, . . . 1830

[Although the title page reads ' in two volumes,' the book is complete in one volume only.]

The History of the Young Men.   By John Bud, ... 1831

Letters from an Englishman.   By Captain John Flower.
In six volumes, ... 1830–1832

72

AND HER CIRCLE

The Monthly Intelligencer. No. 1., ... March 27, 1833

[The only number produced of a projected manuscript newspaper, by Branwell Brontë. The MS. consists of 4 pp. 4to, arranged in columns, precisely after the manner of an ordinary journal.]

Real Life in Verdopolis: A Tale. By Captain John
    Flower, M.P. In two volumes. P. B. Brontë, . . 1833

The Politics of Verdopolis: A Tale. By Captain John
    Flower. P. B. Brontë, ... 1833

The Pirate: A Tale. By Captain John Flower, ... 1833

[The most pretentious of Branwell's prose stories.]

Thermopylae: A Poem. By P. B. Brontë. 8vo, pp. 14 . 1834

And the Weary are at Rest: A Tale. By P. B. Brontë, . 1834

The Wool is Rising: An Augrian Adventure. By the Right
    Honourable John Baron Flower, ... 1834

Ode to the Polar Star, and other Poems. By P. B. Brontë.
    Quarto, pp. 24, ... 1834

The Life of Field Marshal the Right Honourable Alexander
    Percy, Earl of Northangerland. In two volumes. By
    John Bud. P. B. Brontë, ... 1835

The Rising of the Angrians: A Tale. By P. B. Brontë, . 1836

A Narrative of the First War. By P. B. Brontë, ... 1836

The Angrian Welcome: A Tale. By P. B. Brontë, . . . 1836

Percy: A Story. By P. B. Brontë, ... 1837

A packet containing four small groups of Poems, of about
    six or eight pages each, mostly without titles, but all
    either signed or initialed, and dated from 1836 to 1838

Love and Warfare: A Story. By P. B. Brontë, ... 1839

Lord Nelson, and other Poems. By P. B. Brontë. Written
    in pencil. Small 8vo, pp. 26, ... 1844

[This book contains a full-page pencil portrait of Branwell Brontë, drawn by himself, as well as four carefully finished heads. These give an excellent idea of the extent of Branwell's artistic skill.]

CHAPTER III.

SCHOOL AND GOVERNESS LIFE.

In seeking for fresh light upon the development of Charlotte Brontë, it is not necessary to discuss further her childhood's years at Cowan Bridge. She left the school at nine years of age, and what memories of it were carried into womanhood were, with more or less of picturesque colouring, embodied in 'Jane Eyre.'[1] From 1825 to 1831

[1] At the same time it is worth while quoting from a letter by 'A. H.' in August, 1855. A. H. was a teacher who was at Cowan Bridge during the time of the residence of the little Brontës there.

'In July, 1824, the Rev. Mr. Brontë arrived at Cowan Bridge with two of his daughters, Maria and Elizabeth, 12 and 10 years of age. The children were delicate; both had but recently recovered from the measles and whooping-cough — so recently, indeed, that doubts were entertained whether they could be admitted with safety to the other pupils. They were received, however, and went on so well that in September their father returned, bringing with him two more of his children — Charlotte, 9 (she was really but 8), and Emily, 6 years of age. During both these visits Mr. Brontë lodged at the school, sat at the same table with the children, saw the whole routine of the establishment, and, so far as I have ever known, was satisfied with everything that came under his observation.

' "*The two younger children enjoyed uniformly good health.*" Charlotte was a general favourite. To the best of my recollection she was never under disgrace, however slight; punishment she certainly did *not* experience while she was at Cowan Bridge.

'In size, Charlotte was remarkably diminutive; and if, as has been recently asserted, she never grew an inch after leaving the Clergy Daughters' School, she must have been a *literal dwarf*, and could not have obtained a situation as teacher in a school at Brussels, or anywhere else; the idea is absurd. In respect of the treatment of the pupils at Cowan Bridge, I will say that neither Mr. Brontë's daughters nor any other of the children were denied a sufficient quantity of food. Any statement to the contrary is entirely false. The daily dinner consisted of meat, vegetables, and pudding, in abundance; the children

74

CHARLOTTE BRONTË AND HER CIRCLE

Charlotte was at home with her sisters, reading and writing as we have seen, but learning nothing very systematically. In 1831–32 she was a boarder at Miss Wooler's school at Roe Head, some twenty miles from Haworth. Miss Wooler lived to a green old age, dying in the year 1885. She would seem to have been very proud of her famous pupil, and could not have been blind to her capacity in the earlier years. Charlotte was with her as governess at Roe Head, and later at Dewsbury Moor. It is quite clear that Miss Brontë was head of the school in all intellectual pursuits, and she made two firm friends — Ellen Nussey and Mary Taylor. A very fair measure of French and some skill in drawing appear to have been the most striking accomplish-

were permitted, and expected, to ask for whatever they desired, and were never limited.

'It has been remarked that the food of the school was such that none but starving children could eat it; and in support of this statement reference is made to a certain occasion when the medical attendant was consulted about it. In reply to this, let me say that during the spring of 1825 a low fever, although not an alarming one, prevailed in the school, and the managers, naturally anxious to ascertain whether any local cause occasioned the epidemic, took an opportunity to ask the physician's opinion of the food that happened to be then on the table. I recollect that he spoke rather scornfully of a baked rice pudding; but as the ingredients of this dish were chiefly rice, sugar, and milk, its effects could hardly have been so serious as have been affirmed. I thus furnish you with the simple fact from which those statements have been manufactured.

'I have not the least hesitation in saying that, upon the whole, the comforts were as many and the privations as few at Cowan Bridge as can well be found in so large an establishment. How far young or delicate children are able to contend with the necessary evils of a public school is, in my opinion, a very grave question, and does not enter into the present discussion.

'The younger children in all larger institutions are liable to be oppressed; but the exposure to this evil at Cowan Bridge was not more than in other schools, but, as I believe, far less. Then, again, thoughtless servants will occasionally spoil food, even in private families; and in public schools they are likely to be still less particular, unless they are well looked after.

'But in this respect the institution in question compares very favourably with other and more expensive schools, as from personal experience I have reason to know. — A. H., August, 1855.' — From 'A Vindication of the Clergy Daughters' School and the Rev. W. Cairns Wilson from the Remarks in "The Life of Charlotte Brontë,"' by the Rev. H. Shepheard, M. A. London: Seeley, Jackson, and Halliday, 1857.

ments which Charlotte carried back from Roe Head to Haworth. There are some twenty drawings of about this date, and a translation into English verse of the first book of Voltaire's 'Henriade.' With Ellen Nussey commenced a friendship which terminated only with the pencilled notes written from Charlotte Brontë's deathbed. The first suggestion of a regular correspondence is contained in the following letter.

TO MISS ELLEN NUSSEY.

'HAWORTH, July 21, 1832.

'MY DEAREST ELLEN, — Your kind and interesting letter gave me the sincerest pleasure. I have been expecting to hear from you almost every day since my arrival at home, and I at length began to despair of receiving the wished-for letter. You ask me to give you a description of the manner in which I have passed every day since I left school. This is soon done, as an account of one day is an account of all. In the mornings, from nine o'clock to half-past twelve, I instruct my sisters and draw, then we walk till dinner; after dinner I sew till tea-time, and after tea I either read, write, do a little fancy-work, or draw, as I please. Thus in one delightful, though somewhat monotonous course, my life is passed. I have only been out to tea twice since I came home. We are expecting company this afternoon, and on Tuesday next we shall have all the female teachers of the Sunday school to tea. I do hope, my dearest Ellen, that you will return to school again for your own sake, though for mine I would rather that you would remain at home, as we shall then have more frequent opportunities of correspondence with each other. Should your friends decide against your returning to school, I know you have too much good-sense and right feeling not to strive earnestly for your own improvement. Your natural abilities are excellent, and under the direction of a judicious and able friend (and I know you have many such), you might acquire a decided taste for elegant literature, and even poetry, which, indeed, is included under that general term. I was very much disappointed by your not sending the hair; you may be sure, my

dearest Ellen, that I would not grudge double postage to obtain
it, but I must offer the same excuse for not sending you any.
My aunt and sisters desire their love to you. Remember me
kindly to your mother and sisters, and accept all the fondest
expressions of genuine attachment, from your real friend

'CHARLOTTE BRONTË.

'P.S. — Remember the mutual promise we made of a regular
correspondence with each other. Excuse all faults in this wretched
scrawl. Give my love to the Miss Taylors when you see them.
Farewell, my *dear, dear, dear* Ellen.'

Reading, writing, and as thorough a domestic training as
the little parsonage could afford, made up the next few
years. Then came the determination to be a governess — a
not unnatural resolution when the size of the family and
the modest stipend of its head are considered. Far more
prosperous parents are content in our day that their
daughters should earn their living in this manner. In
1835 Charlotte went back to Roe Head as governess, and
she continued in that position when Miss Wooler removed
her school to Dewsbury Moor in 1836.

TO MISS ELLEN NUSSEY.

'DEWSBURY MOOR, August 24, 1837.

'MY DEAR ELLEN, — I have determined to write lest you
should begin to think I have forgotten you, and in revenge
resolve to forget me. As you will perceive by the date of this
letter, I am again engaged in the old business — teach, teach,
teach. Miss and Mrs. Wooler are coming here next Christmas.
Miss Wooler will then relinquish the school in favour of her
sister Eliza, but I am happy to say worthy Miss Wooler will
continue to reside in the house. I should be sorry indeed
to part with her. When will you come *home?* Make haste,
you have been at Bath long enough for all purposes. By this
time you have acquired polish enough, I am sure. If the varnish
is laid on much thicker, I am afraid the good wood underneath
will be quite concealed, and your old Yorkshire friends won't

stand that. Come, come, I am getting really tired of your absence. Saturday after Saturday comes round, and I can have no hope of hearing your knock at the door and then being told that " Miss E. N. is come." Oh dear ! in this monotonous life of mine that was a pleasant event. I wish it would recur again, but it will take two or three interviews before the stiffness, the estrangement of this long separation will quite wear away. I have nothing at all to tell you now but that Mary Taylor is better, and that she and Martha are gone to take a tour in Wales. Patty came on her pony about a fortnight since to inform me that this important event was in contemplation. She actually began to fret about your long absence, and to express the most eager wishes for your return. My own dear Ellen, good-bye. If we are all spared I hope soon to see you again. God bless you. C. BRONTË.'

Things were not always going on quite so smoothly, as the following letter indicates.

TO MISS ELLEN NUSSEY.

' DEWSBURY MOOR, January 4, 1838.

'Your letter, Ellen, was a welcome surprise, though it contained something like a reprimand. I had not, however, forgotten our agreement. You were right in your conjectures respecting the cause of my sudden departure. Anne continued wretchedly ill, neither the pain nor the difficulty of breathing left her, and how could I feel otherwise than very miserable. I looked on her case in a different light to what I could wish or expect any uninterested person to view it in. Miss Wooler thought me a fool, and by way of proving her opinion treated me with marked coldness. We came to a little éclaircissement one evening. I told her one or two rather plain truths, which set her a-crying ; and the next day, unknown to me, she wrote papa, telling him that I had reproached her bitterly, taken her severely to task, etc. Papa sent for us the day after he had received her letter. Meantime I had formed a firm resolution to quit Miss Wooler and her concerns for ever ; but just before I went away, she took me to her room, and giving way to her

feelings, which in general she restrains far too rigidly, gave me
to understand that in spite of her cold, repulsive manners, she
had a considerable regard for me, and would be very sorry to part
with me. If any body likes me, I cannot help liking them ; and
remembering that she had in general been very kind to me, I gave
in and said I would come back if she wished me. So we are settled again for the present, but I am not satisfied. I should have
respected her far more if she had turned me out of doors, instead
of crying for two days and two nights together. I was in a regular
passion ; my "*warm* temper" quite got the better of me, of which
I don't boast, for it was a weakness ; nor am I ashamed of it, for I
had reason to be angry.

'Anne is now much better, though she still requires a great deal
of care. However, I am relieved from my worst fears respecting
her. I approve highly of the plan you mention, except as it
regards committing a verse of the Psalms to memory. I do not
see the direct advantage to be derived from that. We have
entered on a new year. Will it be stained as darkly as the last
with all our sins, follies, secret vanities, and uncontrolled passions
and propensities? I trust not; but I feel in nothing better, neither
humbler nor purer. It will want three weeks next Monday to
the termination of the holidays. Come to see me, my dear Ellen,
as soon as you can ; however bitterly I sometimes feel towards
other people, the recollection of your mild, steady friendship con-
soles and softens me. I am glad you are not such a passionate
fool as myself. Give my best love to your mother and sisters.
Excuse the most hideous scrawl that ever was penned, and —
Believe me always tenderly yours,

'C. BRONTË.'

Dewsbury Moor, however, did not agree with Charlotte.
That was probably the core of the matter. She returned to
Haworth, but only to look around for another 'situation.'
This time she accepted the position of private governess in
the family of a Mr. Sidgwick, at Stonegappe, in the same
county. Her letters from his house require no comment.
A sentence from the first was quoted by Mrs. Gaskell.

CHARLOTTE BRONTË

TO MISS EMILY J. BRONTË.

'STONEGAPPE, June 8, 1839.

'DEAREST LAVINIA, — I am most exceedingly obliged to you for the trouble you have taken in seeking up my things and sending them all right. The box and its contents were most acceptable. I only wish I had asked you to send me some letter-paper. This is my last sheet but two. When you can send the other articles of raiment now manufacturing, I shall be right down glad of them.

'I have striven hard to be pleased with my new situation. The country, the house, and the grounds are, as I have said, divine. But, alack-a-day! there is such a thing as seeing all beautiful around you — pleasant woods, winding white paths, green lawns, and blue sunshiny sky — and not having a free moment or a free thought left to enjoy them in. The children are constantly with me, and more riotous, perverse, unmanageable cubs never grew. As for correcting them, I soon quickly found that was entirely out of the question : they are to do as they like. A complaint to Mrs. Sidgwick brings only black looks upon oneself, and unjust, partial excuses to screen the children. I have tried that plan once. It succeeded so notably that I shall try it no more. I said in my last letter that Mrs. Sidgwick did not know me. I now begin to find that she does not intend to know me, that she cares nothing in the world about me except to contrive how the greatest possible quantity of labour may be squeezed out of me, and to that end she overwhelms me with oceans of needlework, yards of cambric to hem, muslin night-caps to make, and, above all things, dolls to dress. I do not think she likes me at all, because I can't help being shy in such an entirely novel scene, surrounded as I have hitherto been by strange and constantly changing faces. I see now more clearly than I have ever done before that a private governess has no existence, is not considered as a living and rational being except as connected with the wearisome duties she has to fulfil. While she is teaching the children, working for them, amusing them, it is all right. If she steals a moment for herself she is a nuisance.

Nevertheless, Mrs. Sidgwick is universally considered an amiable woman. Her manners are fussily affable. She talks a great deal, but as it seems to me not much to the purpose. Perhaps I may like her better after a while. At present I have no call to her. Mr. Sidgwick is in my opinion a hundred times better — less profession, less bustling condescension, but a far kinder heart. It is very seldom that he speaks to me, but when he does I always feel happier and more settled for some minutes after. He never asks me to wipe the children's smutty noses or tie their shoes or fetch their pinafores or set them a chair. One of the pleasantest afternoons I have spent here — indeed, the only one at all pleasant — was when Mr. Sidgwick walked out with his children, and I had orders to follow a little behind. As he strolled on through his fields with his magnificent New-foundland dog at his side, he looked very like what a frank, wealthy, Conservative gentleman ought to be. He spoke freely and unaffectedly to the people he met, and though he indulged his children and allowed them to tease himself far too much, he would not suffer them grossly to insult others.

'I am getting quite to have a regard for the Carter family. At home I should not care for them, but here they are friends. Mr. Carter was at Mirfield yesterday and saw Anne. He says she was looking uncommonly well. Poor girl, *she* must indeed wish to be at home. As to Mrs. Collins' report that Mrs. Sidgwick intended to keep me permanently, I do not think that such was ever her design. Moreover, I would not stay without some alterations. For instance, this burden of sewing would have to be removed. It is too bad for anything. I never in my whole life had my time so fully taken up. Next week we are going to Swarcliffe, Mr. Greenwood's place near Harrogate, to stay three weeks or a month. After that time I hope Miss Hoby will return. Don't show this letter to papa or aunt, only to Branwell. They will think I am never satisfied wherever I am. I complain to you because it is a relief, and really I have had some unexpected mortifications to put up with. However, things may mend, but Mrs.

81

Sidgwick expects me to do things that I cannot do — to love her children and be entirely devoted to them. I am really very well. I am so sleepy that I can write no more. I must leave off. Love to all. — Good-bye.

'Direct your next dispatch — J. Greenwood, Esq., Swarcliffe, near Harrogate. C. Brontë.'

TO MISS ELLEN NUSSEY.

'SWARCLIFFE, June 15, 1839.

'My dearest Ellen, — I am writing a letter to you with pencil because I cannot just now procure ink without going into the drawing-room, where I do not wish to go. I only received your letter yesterday, for we are not now residing at Stonegappe but at Swarcliffe, a summer residence of Mr. Greenwood's, Mrs. Sidgwick's father; it is near Harrogate and Ripon. I should have written to you long since, and told you every detail of the utterly new scene into which I have lately been cast, had I not been daily expecting a letter from yourself, and wondering and lamenting that you did not write, for you will remember it was your turn. I must not bother you too much with my sorrows, of which, I fear, you have heard an exaggerated account. If you were near me, perhaps I might be tempted to tell you all, to grow egotistical, and pour out the long history of a private governess's trials and crosses in her first situation. As it is, I will only ask you to imagine the miseries of a reserved wretch like me thrown at once into the midst of a large family, proud as peacocks and wealthy as Jews, at a time when they were particularly gay, when the house was filled with company — all strangers : people whose faces I had never seen before. In this state I had a charge given of a set of horrid children, whom I was expected constantly to amuse, as well as instruct. I soon found that the constant demand on my stock of animal spirits reduced them to the lowest state of exhaustion; at times I felt — and, I suppose seemed — depressed. To my astonishment, I was taken to task on the subject by Mrs. Sidgwick, with a sternness of manner and a harshness of language scarcely credible. Like a fool, I cried most bitterly. I could not help it; my spirits quite failed me at first.

I thought I had done my best, strained every nerve to please her; and to be treated in that way, merely because I was shy and sometimes melancholy, was too bad. At first I was for giving all up and going home. But after a little reflection, I determined to summon what energy I had, and to weather the storm. I said to myself, "I had never yet quitted a place without gaining a friend; adversity is a good school; the poor are born to labour, and the dependent to endure." I resolved to be patient, to command my feelings, and to take what came; the ordeal, I reflected, would not last many weeks, and I trusted it would do me good. I recollected the fable of the willow and the oak; I bent quietly, and now I trust the storm is blowing over. Mrs. Sidgwick is generally considered an agreeable woman; so she is, I doubt not, in general society. Her health is sound, her animal spirits good, consequently she is cheerful in company. But oh! does this compensate for the absence of every fine feeling, of every gentle and delicate sentiment? She behaves somewhat more civilly to me now than she did at first, and the children are a little more manageable; but she does not know my character, and she does not wish to know it. I have never had five minutes conversation with her since I came, except when she was scolding me. I have no wish to be pitied, except by yourself. If I were talking to you I could tell you much more. Good-bye, dear, dear Ellen. Write to me again very soon, and tell me how you are.

'C. Brontë.'

TO MISS ELLEN NUSSEY.

'Haworth, July 26, 1839.

'Dear Ellen,— I left Swarcliffe a week since. I never was so glad to get out of a house in my life; but I'll trouble you with no complaints at present. Write to me directly; explain your plans more fully. Say when you go, and I shall be able in my answer to say decidedly whether I can accompany you or not. I must, I will, I'm set upon it — I'll be obstinate and bear down all opposition.— Good-bye, yours faithfully,

'C. Brontë.'

CHARLOTTE BRONTË

That experience with the Sidgwicks rankled for many a day, and we find Charlotte Brontë referring to it in her letters from Brussels. At the same time it is not necessary to assume any very serious inhumanity on the part of the Sidgwicks or their successors the Whites, to whom Charlotte was indebted for her second term as private governess. Hers was hardly a temperament adapted for that docile part, and one thinks of the author of 'Villette,' and the possessor of one of the most vigorous prose styles in our language, condemned to a perpetual manufacture of night-caps, with something like a shudder. And at the same time it may be urged that Charlotte Brontë did not suffer in vain, and that through her the calling of a nursery governess may have received some added measure of dignity and consideration on the part of sister-women.

A month or two later we find Charlotte dealing with the subject in a letter to Ellen Nussey.

TO MISS ELLEN NUSSEY.

'HAWORTH, January 24, 1840.

'MY DEAR ELLEN,— You could never live in an unruly, violent family of modern children, such for instance as those at Blake Hall. Anne is not to return. Mrs. Ingham is a placid, mild woman ; but as for the children, it was one struggle of life-wearing exertion to keep them in anything like decent order. I am miserable when I allow myself to dwell on the necessity of spending my life as a governess. The chief requisite for that station seems to me to be the power of taking things easily as they come, and of making oneself comfortable and at home wherever we may chance to be — qualities in which all our family are singularly deficient. I know I cannot live with a person like Mrs. Sidgwick, but I hope all women are not like her, and my motto is "try again." Mary Taylor, I am sorry to hear, is ill — have you seen her or heard anything of her lately? Sickness seems very general, and death too, at least in this neighbourhood. Ever yours,   C. B.'

AND HER CIRCLE

She 'tried again' but with just as little success. In March 1841 she entered the family of a Mr. White of Upperwood House, Rawdon.

TO MISS ELLEN NUSSEY.

'UPPERWOOD HOUSE, April 1, 1841.

'MY DEAR NELL, — It is twelve o'clock at night, but I must just write to you a word before I go to bed. If you think I am going to refuse your invitation, or if you sent it me with that idea, you're mistaken. As soon as I read your shabby little note, I gathered up my spirits directly, walked on the impulse of the moment into Mrs. White's presence, popped the question, and for two minutes received no answer. Will she refuse me when I work so hard for her? thought I. "Ye-e-es" was said in a reluctant cold tone. "Thank you, ma'am," said I, with extreme cordiality, and was marching from the room when she recalled me with : "You'd better go on Saturday afternoon then, when the children have holiday, and if you return in time for them to have all their lessons on Monday morning, I don't see that much will be lost." You *are* a genuine Turk, thought I, but again I assented. Saturday after next then is the day appointed — *not next Saturday mind.* I do not quite know whether the offer about the gig is not entirely out of your own head or if George has given his consent to it — whether that consent has not been wrung from him by the most persevering and irresistible teasing on the part of a certain young person of my acquaintance. I make no manner of doubt that if he does send the conveyance (as Miss Wooler used to denominate all wheeled vehicles) it will be to his own extreme detriment and inconvenience, but for once in my life, I'll not mind this, or bother my head about it. I'll come — God knows with a thankful and joyful heart — glad of a day's reprieve from labour. If you don't send the gig I'll walk. Now mind, I am not coming to Brookroyd with the idea of dissuading Mary Taylor from going to New Zealand. I've said everything I mean to say on that subject, and she has a perfect right to decide for herself. I am coming to taste

85

the pleasure of liberty, a bit of pleasant congenial talk, and a sight of two or three faces I like. God bless you. I want to see you again. Huzza for Saturday afternoon after next! Goodnight, my lass.   C. BRONTË.

'Have you lit your pipe with Mr. Weightman's valentine?'

TO MISS ELLEN NUSSEY.

'UPPERWOOD HOUSE, MAY 4, 1841.

'DEAR NELL,—I have been a long time without writing to you; but I think, knowing as you do how I am situated in the matter of time, you will not be angry with me. Your brother George will have told you that he did not go into the house when we arrived at Rawdon, for which omission of his Mrs. White was very near blowing me up. She went quite red in the face with vexation when she heard that the gentleman had just driven within the gates and then back again, for she is very touchy in the matter of opinion. Mr. White also seemed to regret the circumstance from more hospitable and kindly motives. I assure you, if you were to come and see me you would have quite a fuss made over you. During the last three weeks that hideous operation called "a thorough clean" has been going on in the house. It is now nearly completed, for which I thank my stars, as during its progress I have fulfilled the twofold character of nurse and governess, while the nurse has been transmuted into cook and housemaid. That nurse, by-the-bye, is the prettiest lass you ever saw, and when dressed has much more the air of a lady than her mistress. Well can I believe that Mrs. White has been an exciseman's daughter, and I am convinced also that Mr. White's extraction is very low. Yet Mrs. White talks in an amusing strain of pomposity about his and her family and connections, and affects to look down with wondrous hauteur on the whole race of tradesfolk, as she terms men of business. I was beginning to think Mrs. White a good sort of body in spite of all her bouncing and boasting, her bad grammar and worse orthography, but I have had experience of one little trait in her character which condemns her a long way with me. After treating a person in the most familiar terms of equality for a long time, if any little thing goes wrong she does not scruple to give way to anger in a very coarse, unladylike manner. I think passion is the true test of vulgarity or refinement.

'This place looks exquisitely beautiful just now. The grounds are certainly lovely, and all is as green as an emerald. I wish you would just come and look at it. Mrs. White would be as proud as Punch to show it you. Mr. White has been writing an urgent invitation to papa, entreating him to come and spend a week here. I don't at all wish papa to come, it would be like incurring an obligation. Somehow, I have managed to get a good deal more control over the children lately — this makes my life a good deal easier, also by dint of nursing the fat baby, it has got to know me and be fond of me. I suspect myself of growing rather fond of it. Exertion of any kind is always beneficial. Come and see me if you can in any way get, I *want* to see you. It seems Martha Taylor is fairly gone. Good-bye, my lassie. — Yours insufferably, C. BRONTE.'

TO REV. HENRY NUSSEY, EARNLEY RECTORY.

'UPPERWOOD HOUSE, RAWDON,
'May 9, 1841.

'DEAR SIR, — I am about to employ part of a Sunday evening in answering your last letter. You will perhaps think this hardly right, and yet I do not feel that I am doing wrong. Sunday evening is almost my only time of leisure. No one would blame me if I were to spend this spare hour in a pleasant chat with a friend — is it worse to spend it in a friendly letter?

'I have just seen my little noisy charges deposited snugly in their cribs, and I am sitting alone in the school-room with the quiet of a Sunday evening pervading the grounds and gardens outside my window. I owe you a letter — can I choose a better time than the present for paying my debt? Now, Mr. Nussey, you need not expect any gossip or news, I have none to tell you — even if I had I am not at present in the mood to communicate them. You will excuse an unconnected letter. If I had thought you critical or captious I would have declined the task of corresponding with you. When I reflect, indeed, it

seems strange that I should sit down to write without a feeling
of formality and restraint to an individual with whom I am
personally so little acquainted as I am with yourself; but the
fact is, I cannot be formal in a letter — if I write at all I must
write as I think. It seems Ellen has told you that I am become a
governess again. As you say, it is indeed a hard thing for flesh
and blood to leave home, especially a *good* home — not a wealthy
or splendid one. My home is humble and unattractive to strangers,
but to me it contains what I shall find nowhere else in the world
— the profound, the intense affection which brothers and sisters
feel for each other when their minds are cast in the same mould,
their ideas drawn from the same source — when they have clung to
each other from childhood, and when disputes have never sprung
up to divide them.

'We are all separated now, and winning our bread amongst
strangers as we can — my sister Anne is near York, my brother
in a situation near Halifax, I am here. Emily is the only one
left at home, where her usefulness and willingness make her
indispensable. Under these circumstances should we repine?
I think not — our mutual affection ought to comfort us under
all difficulties. If the God on whom we must all depend will but
vouchsafe us health and the power to continue in the strict
line of duty, so as never under any temptation to swerve from
it an inch, we shall have ample reason to be grateful and
contented.

'I do not pretend to say that I am always contented. A
governess must often submit to have the heartache. My employers, Mr. and Mrs. White, are kind worthy people in their
way, but the children are indulged. I have great difficulties
to contend with sometimes. Perseverance will perhaps conquer
them. And it has gratified me much to find that the parents
are well satisfied with their children's improvement in learning
since I came. But I am dwelling too much upon my own
concerns and feelings. It is true they are interesting to me,
but it is wholly impossible they should be so to you, and, therefore, I hope you will skip the last page, for I repent having
written it.

'A fortnight since I had a letter from Ellen urging me to go to Brookroyd for a single day. I felt such a longing to have a respite from labour, and to get once more amongst " old familiar faces," that I conquered diffidence and asked Mrs. White to let me go. She complied, and I went accordingly, and had a most delightful holiday. I saw your mother, your sisters Mercy, Ellen, and poor Sarah, and your brothers Richard and George — all were well. Ellen talked of endeavouring to get a situation somewhere. I did not encourage the idea much. I advised her rather to go to Earnley for a while. I think she wants a change, and I daresay you would be glad to have her as a companion for a few months. — I remain, yours respectfully,   C. BRONTË.'

The above letter was written to Miss Nussey's brother, whose attachment to Charlotte Brontë has already more than once been mentioned in the current biographies. The following letter to Miss Nussey is peculiarly interesting because of the reference to Ireland. It would have been strange if Charlotte Brontë had returned as a governess to her father's native land. Speculation thereon is sufficiently foolish, and yet one is tempted to ask if Ireland may not have gained some of that local literary colour — one of its greatest needs — which always makes Scotland dear to the readers of ' Waverley,' and Yorkshire classic ground to the admirers of ' Shirley.'

TO MISS ELLEN NUSSEY.

'UPPERWOOD HOUSE, June 10, 1841.

'DEAR NELL, — If I don't scrawl you a line of some sort I know you will begin to fancy that I neglect you, in spite of all I said last time we met. You can hardly fancy it possible, I dare say, that I cannot find a quarter of an hour to scribble a note in ; but when a note is written it is to be carried a mile to the post, and consumes nearly an hour, which is a large portion of the day. Mr. and Mrs. White have been gone a week. I heard from them this morning ; they are now at Hexham. No time is fixed for their return, but I hope it will not be delayed long, or I shall miss the chance of seeing Anne this vacation. She came home, I understand, last Wednesday, and is only to be allowed three weeks' holidays, because the family she is with are going to Scarborough. I should like to see her to judge for myself of the state of her health. I cannot trust any other person's report, no one seems minute enough in their observations. I should also very much have liked you to see her.

' I have got on very well with the servants and children so far, yet it is dreary, solitary work. You can tell as well as me the lonely feeling of being without a companion. I offered the Irish concern to Mary Taylor, but she is so circumstanced that she cannot accept it. Her brothers have a feeling of pride that revolts at the thought of their sister "going out." I hardly 'knew that it was such a degradation till lately.

' Your visit did me much good. I wish Mary Taylor would come, and yet I hardly know how to find time to be with her.— Good-bye. God bless you. C. BRONTË.

' I am very well, and I continue to get to bed before twelve o'clock P.M. I don't tell people that I am dissatisfied with my situation. I can drive on ; there is no use in complaining. I have lost my chance of going to Ireland.'

TO MISS ELLEN NUSSEY.

'HAWORTH, July 1, 1841.

' DEAR NELL, — I was not at home when I got your letter, but I am at home now, and it feels like paradise. I came last night. When I asked for a vacation, Mrs. White offered me a week or ten days, but I demanded three weeks, and stood to my tackle with a tenacity worthy of yourself, lassie. I gained the point, but I don't like such victories. I have gained another point. You are unanimously requested to come here next Tuesday and stay as long as you can. Aunt is in high good-humour. I need not write a long letter. — Good-bye, dear Nell. C. B.

' P. S. — I have lost the chance of seeing Anne. She is gone back to "The land of Egypt and the house of bondage." Also, little black Tom is dead. Every cup, however sweet, has its drop of bitterness in it. Probably you will be at a loss to ascertain the identity of black Tom, but don't fret about it, I 'll tell you when you come. Keeper is as well, big, and grim as ever. I 'm too happy to write. Come, come, lassie.'

It must have been during this holiday that the resolution concerning a school of their own assumed definite shape. Miss Wooler talked of giving up Dewsbury Moor — should Charlotte and Emily take it? Charlotte's recollections of her illness there settled the question in the negative, and Brussels was coming to the front.

TO MISS ELLEN NUSSEY.

'UPPERWOOD HOUSE, October 17, 1841.

'DEAR NELL, — It is a cruel thing of you to be always up-braiding me when I am a trifle remiss or so in writing a letter. I see I can't make you comprehend that I have not quite as much time on my hands as Miss Harris or Mrs. Mills. I never neglect you on purpose. I could not *do* it, you little teasing, faithless wretch.

'The humour I am in is worse than words can describe. I have had a hideous dinner of some abominable spiced-up inde-scribable mess, and it has exasperated me against the world at large. So you are coming home, are you? Then don't expect me to write a long letter. I am not going to Dewsbury Moor, as far as I can see at present. It was a decent friendly pro-posal on Miss Wooler's part, and cancels all or most of her little foibles, in my estimation ; but Dewsbury Moor is a poisoned place to me, besides, I burn to go somewhere else. I think, Nell, I see a chance of getting to Brussels. Mary Taylor advises me to this step. My own mind and feelings urge me. I can't write a word more.   C. B.'

TO MISS EMILY J. BRONTË.

'UPPERWOOD HOUSE, RAWDON,
'Nov. 7, 1841.

'DEAR E. J., — You are not to suppose that this note is written with a view of communicating any information on the subject we

91

CHARLOTTE BRONTË

both have considerably at heart : I have written letters but I have received no letters in reply yet. Belgium is a long way off, and people are everywhere hard to spur up to the proper speed. Mary Taylor says we can scarcely expect to get off before January. I have wished and intended to write to both Anne and Branwell, but really I have not had time.

'Mr. Jenkins I find was mistakenly termed the British Consul at Brussels ; he is in fact the English Episcopal clergyman.

'I think perhaps we shall find that the best plan will be for papa to write a letter to him by and bye, but not yet. I will give an intimation when this should be done, and also some idea of what had best be said. Grieve not over Dewsbury Moor. You were cut out there to all intents and purposes, so in fact was Anne, Miss Wooler would hear of neither for the first half year.

'Anne seems omitted in the present plan, but if all goes right I trust she will derive her full share of benefit from it in the end. I exhort all to hope. I believe in my heart this is acting for the best, my only fear is lest others should doubt and be dismayed. Before our half year in Brussels is completed, you and I will have to seek employment abroad. It is not my intention to retrace my steps home till twelve months, if all continues well and we and those at home retain good health.

'I shall probably take my leave of Upperwood about the 15th or 17th of December. When does Anne talk of returning ? How is she ? What does W. W.[1] say to these mattters ? How are papa and aunt, do they flag ? How will Anne get on with Martha ? Has W. W. been seen or heard of lately ? Love to all. Write quickly. — Good-bye.   C. BRONTË.

'I am well.'

TO MISS ELLEN NUSSEY.

'RAWDON, December 10, 1841.

'MY DEAR ELLEN, — I hear from Mary Taylor that you are come home, and also that you have been ill. If you are able to write comfortably, let me know the feelings that preceded your illness, and also its effects. I wish to see you. Mary Taylor

---

[1] The Rev. William Weightman.

92

reports that your looks are much as usual. I expect to get back to Haworth in the course of a fortnight or three weeks. I hope I shall then see you. I would rather you came to Haworth than I went to Brookroyd. My plans advance slowly and I am not yet certain where I shall go, or what I shall do when I leave Upperwood House. Brussels is still my promised land, but there is still the wilderness of time and space to cross before I reach it. I am not likely, I think, to go to the Château de Kockleberg. I have heard of a less expensive establishment. So far I had written when I received your letter. I was glad to get it. Why don't you mention your illness? I had intended to have got this note off two or three days past, but I am more straitened for time than ever just now. We have gone to bed at twelve or one o'clock during the last three nights. I must get this scrawl off to-day or you will think me negligent. The new governess, that is to be, has been to see my plans, etc. My dear Ellen, good-bye. — Believe me, in heart and soul, your sincere friend,   C. B.'

TO MISS ELLEN NUSSEY.

'DECEMBER 17, 1841.

'MY DEAR ELLEN, — I am yet uncertain when I shall leave Upperwood, but of one thing I am very certain, when I do leave I must go straight home. It is absolutely necessary that some definite arrangement should be commenced for our future plans before I go visiting anywhere. That I wish to see you I know, that I intend and *hope* to see you before long I also know, that you will at the first impulse accuse me of neglect, I fear, that upon consideration you will acquit me, I devoutly trust. Dear Ellen, come to Haworth if you can, if you cannot I will endeavour to come for a day at least to Brookroyd, but do not depend on this — come to Haworth. I thank you for Mr. Jenkins' address. You always think of other people's convenience, however ill and affected you are yourself. How very much I wish to see you, you do not know; but if I were to go to Brookroyd now, it would deeply disappoint those at home. I have some hopes of seeing Branwell at Xmas, and when

I shall be able to see him afterwards I cannot tell. He has never been at home for the last five months. — Good-night, dear Ellen,   C. B.'

TO MISS MERCY NUSSEY.

'RAWDON, December 17th.

'MY DEAR MISS MERCY, — Though I am very much engaged I must find time to thank you for the kind and polite contents of your note. I should act in the manner most consonant with my own feelings if I at once, and without qualification, accepted your invitation. I do not however consider it advisable to indulge myself so far at present. When I leave Upperwood I must go straight home. Whether I shall afterwards have time to pay a short visit to Brookroyd I do not yet know — circumstances must determine that. I would fain see Ellen at Haworth instead ; our visitations are not shared with any show of justice. It shocked me very much to hear of her illness — may it be the first and last time she ever experiences such an attack ! Ellen, I fear, has thought I neglected her, in not writing sufficiently long or frequent letters. It is a painful idea to me that she has had this feeling — it could not be more groundless. I know her value, and I would not lose her affection for any probable compensation I can imagine. Remember me to your mother. I trust she will soon regain her health. — Believe me, my dear Miss Mercy, yours sincerely,   C. BRONTË.'

TO MISS ELLEN NUSSEY.

'HAWORTH, January 10, 1842.

'MY DEAR ELLEN, — Will you write as soon as you get this and fix your own day for coming to Haworth. I got home on Christmas Eve. The parting scene between me and my late employers was such as to efface the memory of much that annoyed me while I was there, but indeed, during the whole of the last six months they only made too much of me. Anne has rendered herself so valuable in her difficult situation that they have entreated her to return to them, if it be but for a short time. I almost think she will go back, if we can get a good servant who will do all our work. We want one about forty or fifty years old, good-tempered, clean, and honest. You shall hear all about Brussels, etc., when you come. Mr. Weightman is still here, just the same as ever. I have a curiosity to see a meeting between you and him. He will be again desperately in love, I am convinced. *Come.* C. B.'[1]

[1] It is interesting to note that Charlotte sent one of her little pupils a gift-book during the holidays. The book is lost, but the fly-leaf of it, inscribed 'Sarah Louisa White, from her friend C. Brontë, July 20, 1841,' is in the possession of Mr. W. Lowe Fleeming, of Wolverhampton.

CHAPTER IV.

THE PENSIONNAT HÉGER, BRUSSELS.

HAD not the impulse come to Charlotte Brontë to add somewhat to her scholastic accomplishments by a sojourn in Brussels, our literature would have lost that powerful novel 'Villette,' and the singularly charming 'Professor.' The impulse came from the persuasion that without 'languages' the school project was an entirely hopeless one. Mary and Martha Taylor were at Brussels, staying with friends, and thence they had sent kindly presents to Charlotte, at this time raging under the yoke of governess at Upperwood House. Charlotte wrote the diplomatic letter to her aunt which ended so satisfactorily.[1] The good lady — Miss Bran-

[1] 'UPPERWOOD HOUSE, RAWDON, September 29, 1841.

'DEAR AUNT, — I have heard nothing of Miss Wooler yet since I wrote to her intimating that I would accept her offer. I cannot conjecture the reason of this long silence, unless some unforeseen impediment has occurred in concluding the bargain. Meantime, a plan has been suggested and approved by Mr. and Mrs. White, and others, which I wish now to impart to you. My friends recommend me, if I desire to secure permanent success, to delay commencing the school for six months longer, and by all means to contrive, by hook or by crook, to spend the intervening time in some school on the continent. They say schools in England are so numerous, competition so great, that without some such step towards attaining superiority we shall probably have a very hard struggle, and may fail in the end. They say, moreover, that the loan of £100, which you have been so kind as to offer us, will, perhaps, not be all required now, as Miss Wooler will lend us the furniture; and that, if the speculation is intended to be a good and successful one, half the sum, at least, ought to be laid out in the manner I have mentioned, thereby insuring a more speedy repayment both of interest and principal.

'I would not go to France or to Paris. I would go to Brussels, in Belgium. The cost of the journey there, at the dearest rate of travelling, would be £5 ;

well was then about sixty years of age — behaved hand-somely by her nieces, and it was agreed that Charlotte and Emily were to go to the Continent, Anne retaining her post of governess with Mrs. Robinson at Thorp Green. But Brussels schools did not seem at the first blush to be very satisfactory. Something better promised at Lille.

Here is a letter written at this period of hesitation and doubt. A portion of it only was printed by Mrs. Gaskell.

living is there little more than half as dear as it is in England, and the facili-ties for education are equal or superior to any other place in Europe. In half a year, I could acquire a thorough familiarity with French. I could improve greatly in Italian, and even get a dash of German, *i.e.*, providing my health continued as good as it is now. Martha Taylor is now staying in Brussels, at a first-rate establishment there. I should not think of going to the Château de Kockleberg, where she is resident, as the terms are much too high; but if I wrote to her, she, with the assistance of Mrs. Jenkins, the wife of the British Consul, would be able to secure me a cheap and decent residence and respect-able protection. I should have the opportunity of seeing her frequently, she would make me acquainted with the city; and, with the assistance of her cousins, I should probably in time be introduced to connections far more im-proving, polished, and cultivated, than any I have yet known.

'These are advantages which would turn to vast account, when we actually commenced a school — and, if Emily could share them with me, only for a sin-gle half-year, we could take a footing in the world afterwards which we can never do now. I say Emily instead of Anne; for Anne might take her turn at some future period, if our school answered. I feel certain, while I am writing, that you will see the propriety of what I say; you always like to use your money to the best advantage; you are not fond of making shabby purchases; when you do confer a favour, it is often done in style; and depend upon it £50, or £100, thus laid out, would be well employed. Of course, I know no other friend in the world to whom I could apply on this subject except yourself. I feel an absolute conviction that, if this advantage were allowed us, it would be the making of us for life. Papa will perhaps think it a wild and ambitious scheme; but who ever rose in the world without ambition? When he left Ireland to go to Cambridge University, he was as ambitious as I am now. I want us *all* to go on. I know we have talents, and I want them to be turned to account. I look to you, aunt, to help us. I think you will not refuse. I know, if you consent, it shall not be my fault if you ever repent your kindness. With love to all, and the hope that you are all well, — Believe me, dear aunt, your affectionate niece,

'MISS BRANWELL.   C. BRONTE.'

Mrs. Gaskell's 'Life.' Corrected and completed from original letter in the possession of Mr. A. B. Nicholls.

CHARLOTTE BRONTË

'JANUARY 20 1842.

TO MISS ELLEN NUSSEY.

'DEAR ELLEN, — I cannot quite enter into your friends' reasons for not permitting you to come to Haworth ; but as it is at present, and in all human probability will be for an indefinite time to come, impossible for me to get to Brookroyd, the balance of accounts is not so unequal as it might otherwise be. We expect to leave England in less than three weeks, but we are not yet certain of the day, as it will depend upon the convenience of a French lady now in London, Madame Marzials, under whose escort we are to sail. Our place of destination is changed. Papa received an unfavourable account from Mr. or rather Mrs. Jenkins, of the French schools in Brussels, and on further inquiry, an Institution in Lille, in the North of France, was recommended by Baptist Noel and other clergymen, and to that place it is decided that we are to go. The terms are fifty pounds for each pupil for board and French alone.

'I considered it kind in aunt to consent to an extra sum for a separate room. We shall find it a great privilege in many ways. I regret the change from Brussels to Lille on many accounts, chiefly that I shall not see Martha Taylor. Mary has been indefatigably kind in providing me with information. She has grudged no labour, and scarcely any expense, to that end. Mary's price is above rubies. I have, in fact, two friends — you and her — staunch and true, in whose faith and sincerity I have as strong a belief as I have in the Bible. I have bothered you both, you especially ; but you always get the tongs and heap coals of fire upon my head. I have had letters to write lately to Brussels, to Lille, and to London. I have lots of chemises, night-gowns, pocket-handkerchiefs, and pockets to make, besides clothes to repair. I have been, every week since I came home, expecting to see Branwell, and he has never been able to get over yet. We fully expect him, however, next Saturday. Under these circumstances how can I go visiting? You tantalise me to death with talking of conversations by the fireside. Depend upon it, we are not to have

98

any such for many a long month to come. I get an interesting impression of old age upon my face, and when you see me next I shall certainly wear caps and spectacles. — Yours affectionately,

'C. B.'

This Mr. Jenkins was chaplain to the British Embassy at Brussels, and not Consul as Charlotte at first supposed. The brother of his wife was a clergyman living in the neighbourhood of Haworth. Mr. Jenkins, whose English Episcopal chapel Charlotte attended during her stay in Brussels, finally recommended the Pensionnat Héger in the Rue d'Isabelle. Madame Héger wrote, accepting the two girls as pupils, and to Brussels their father escorted them in February 1842, staying one night at the house of Mr. Jenkins and then returning to Haworth.

The life of Charlotte Brontë at Brussels has been mirrored for us with absolute accuracy in 'Villette' and 'The Professor.' That, indeed, from the point of view of local colour, is made sufficiently plain to the casual visitor of to-day who calls in the Rue d'Isabelle. The house, it is true, is dismantled with a view to its incorporation into some city buildings in the background, but one may still eat pears from the 'old and huge fruit-trees' which flourished when Charlotte and Emily walked under them half a century ago; one may still wander through the school-rooms, the long dormitories, and into the 'vine-draped *berceau*'— little enough is changed within and without. Here is the dormitory with its twenty beds, the two end ones being occupied by Emily and Charlotte, they alone securing the privilege of age or English eccentricity to curtain off their beds from the gaze of the eighteen girls who shared the room with them. The crucifix, indeed, has been removed from the niche in the *Oratoire* where the children offered up prayer every morning; but with a copy of 'Villette' in hand it is possible to restore every feature of the place, not excluding the adjoining Athenée with its small window overlooking the garden of the Pen-

sionnat and the *allée défendu*. It was from this window that
Mr. Crimsworth of 'The Professor' looked down upon the
girls at play. It was here, indeed, at the Royal Athenée, that
M. Héger was Professor of Latin. Externally, then, the
Pensionnat Héger remains practically the same as it appeared
to Charlotte and Emily Brontë in February 1842, when they
made their first appearance in Brussels. The Rue Fossette
of 'Villette,' the Rue d'Isabelle of 'The Professor,' is the
veritable Rue d'Isabelle of Currer Bell's experience.

What, however, shall we say of the people who wandered
through these rooms and gardens — the hundred or more
children, the three or four governesses, the professor and his
wife? Here there has been much speculation and not a
little misreading of the actual facts. Charlotte and Emily
went to Brussels to learn. They did learn with energy. It was
their first experience of foreign travel, and it came too late
in life for them to enter into it with that breadth of mind
and tolerance of the customs of other lands, lacking which
the Englishman abroad is always an offence. Charlotte and
Emily hated the land and people. They had been brought
up ultra-Protestants. Their father was an Ulster man, and
his one venture into the polemics of his age was to attack
the proposals for Catholic emancipation. With this inherit-
ance of intolerance, how could Charlotte and Emily face
with kindliness the Romanism which they saw around
them? How heartily they disproved of it many a picture
in 'Villette' has made plain to us.

Charlotte had been in Brussels three months when she
made the friendship to which I am indebted for anything
that there may be to add to this episode in her life. Miss
Lætitia Wheelwright was one of five sisters, the daughters
of a doctor in Lower Phillimore Place, Kensington. Dr.
Wheelwright went to Brussels for his health and for his
children's education. The girls were day boarders at the
Pensionnat, but they lived in the house for a full month

or more at a time when their father and mother were on
a trip up the Rhine. Otherwise their abode was a flat in
the Hotel Clusyenaar in the Rue Royale, and there during her later stay in Brussels Charlotte frequently paid
them visits. In this earlier period Charlotte and Emily
were too busy with their books to think of 'calls' and
the like frivolities, and it must be confessed also that at
this stage Lætitia Wheelwright would have thought it
too high a price for a visit from Charlotte to receive as
a fellow-guest the apparently unamiable Emily. Miss
Wheelwright, who was herself fourteen years of age when
she entered the Pensionnat Héger, recalls the two sisters,
thin and sallow-looking, pacing up and down the garden,
friendless and alone. It was the sight of Lætitia standing
up in the class-room and glancing round with a semi-con-
temptuous air at all these Belgian girls which attracted
Charlotte Brontë to her. 'It was so very English,' Miss
Brontë laughingly remarked at a later period to her friend.
There was one other English girl at this time of sufficient
age to be companionable; but with Miss Maria Miller, whom
Charlotte Brontë has depicted under the guise of Ginevra
Fanshawe, she had less in common. In later years Miss
Miller became Mrs. Robertson, the wife of an author in one
form or another.

To Miss Wheelwright, and those of her sisters who are
still living, the descriptions of the Pensionnat Héger which
are given in 'Villette' and 'The Professor' are perfectly
accurate. M. Héger, with his heavy black moustache and
his black hair, entering the class-room of an evening to read
to his pupils was a sufficiently familiar object, and his keen
intelligence amounting almost to genuis had affected the
Wheelwright girls as forcibly as it had done the Brontës.
Mme. Héger, again, for ever peeping from behind doors and
through the plate-glass partitions which separate the passages from the school-rooms, was a constant source of

irritation to all the English pupils. This prying and spying is, it is possible, more of a fine art with the school-mistresses of the Continent than with those of our own land. In any case, Mme. Héger was an accomplished spy, and in the midst of the most innocent work or recreation the pupils would suddenly see a pair of eyes pierce the dusk and disappear. This, and a hundred similar trifles, went to build up an antipathy on both sides, which had, however, scarcely begun when Charlotte and Emily were suddenly called home by their aunt's death in October. A letter to Miss Nussey on her return sufficiently explains the situation.

TO MISS ELLEN NUSSEY.

'HAWORTH, November 10, 1842.

'MY DEAR ELLEN, —I was not yet returned to England when your letter arrived. We received the first news of aunt's illness, Wednesday, Nov. 2nd. We decided to come home directly. Next morning a second letter informed us of her death. We sailed from Antwerp on Sunday; we travelled day and night and got home on Tuesday morning — and of course the funeral and all was over. We shall see her no more. Papa is pretty well. We found Anne at home; she is pretty well also. You say you have had no letter from me for a long time. I wrote to you three weeks ago. When you answer this note, I will write to you more in detail. Aunt, Martha Taylor, and Mr. Weightman are now all gone; how dreary and void everything seems. Mr. Weightman's illness was exactly what Martha's was — he was ill the same length of time and died in the same manner. Aunt's disease was internal obstruction, she also was ill a fortnight.

'Good-bye, my dear Ellen. C. BRONTË.'

The aunt whose sudden death brought Charlotte and Fmily Brontë thus hastily from Brussels to Haworth must have been a very sensible woman in the main. She left her money to those of her nieces who most needed it. A perusal of her will is not without interest, and indeed it will be seen that it clears up one or two errors into which Mrs. Gaskell and subsequent biographers have rashly fallen through failing to expend the necessary half-guinea upon a copy. This is it : —

Extracted from the District Probate Registry at York attached to Her Majesty's High Court of Justice.

Depending on the Father, Son, and Holy Ghost for peace here, and glory and bliss forever hereafter, I leave this my last Will and Testament : Should I die at Haworth, I request that my remains may be deposited in the church in that place as near as convenient to the remains of my dear sister ; I moreover will that all my just debts and funeral expenses be paid out of my property, and that my funeral shall be conducted in a moderate and decent manner. My Indian workbox I leave to my niece, Charlotte Brontë ; my workbox with a china top I leave to my niece, Emily Jane Brontë, together with my ivory fan ; my Japan dressing-box I leave to my nephew, Patrick Branwell Brontë ; to my niece Anne Brontë, I leave my watch with all that belongs to it ; as also my eye-glass and its chain, my rings, silver-spoons, books, clothes, etc., etc., I leave to be divided between my above-named three nieces, Charlotte Brontë, Emily Jane Brontë, and Anne Brontë, according as their father shall think proper. And I will that all the money that shall remain, including twenty-five pounds sterling, being the part of the proceeds of the sale of my goods which belong to me in consequence of my having advanced to my sister Kingston the sum of twenty-five pounds in lieu of her share of the proceeds of my goods aforesaid, and deposited in the bank of Bolitho Sons and Co., Esqrs., of Chiandower, near Penzance, after the aforesaid sums and articles shall have been paid and deducted, shall be put into some safe bank or lent on good landed security, and there left to accumulate for the sole benefit of my four nieces, Charlotte Brontë, Emily Jane Brontë, Anne Brontë, and Elizabeth Jane Kingston ; and this sum or sums, and whatever other property I may have, shall be equally divided between them when the youngest of them then living shall have arrived at the age of twenty-one years. And should any one or more of these my four nieces die, her or their part or parts shall be equally divided amongst the survivors; and if but one is left, all shall go to that one : And should they all die before the age of twenty-one years, all their parts shall be given to my sister, Anne Kingston ; and should she die before that time specified, I will that all that was to have been hers shall be equally divided between all the surviving children of my dear brother and sisters. I appoint my brother-in-law, the Rev. P. Brontë, A.B., now Incumbent of Haworth, Yorkshire ; the Rev. John Fennell, now Incumbent of Cross Stone, near Halifax ; the Rev. Theodore Dury, Rector of Keighley, Yorkshire ; and Mr. George Taylor of Stanbury, in the chapelry of Haworth aforesaid, my executors. Written by me, ELIZABETH BRANWELL, and signed, sealed, and delivered on the 30th of April, in the year of our Lord one thousand eight hundred and thirty-three, ELIZABETH BRANWELL. Witnesses present, William Brown, John Tootill, William Brown, Junr.

> The twenty-eighth day of December, 1842, the Will of ELIZABETH BRANWELL, late of Haworth, in the parish of Bradford, in the county of York, spinster (having *bona notabilia* within the province of York), deceased, was proved in the prerogative court of York by the oaths of the Reverend Patrick Brontë, clerk, brother-in-law ; and George Taylor, two of the executors to whom administration was granted (the Reverend Theodore Dury, another of the executors, having renounced), they having been first sworn duly to administer.

Effects sworn under £1500.

Testatrix died 29th October 1842.

Now hear Mrs. Gaskell : —

'The small property, which she had accumulated by dint of personal frugality and self-denial, was bequeathed to her nieces. Branwell, her darling, was to have had his share, but his reckless expenditure had distressed the good old lady, and his name was omitted in her will.'

A perusal of the will in question indicates that it was made in 1833, before Branwell had paid his first visit to London, and when, as all his family supposed, he was on the high road to fame and fortune as an artist. The old lady doubtless thought that the boy would be able to take good care of himself. She had, indeed, other nieces down in Cornwall, but with the general sympathy of her friends and relatives in Penzance, Elizabeth Jane Kingston, who it was thought would want it most, was to have a share. Had the Kingston girl, her mother, and the Brontë girls all died before him, the boy Branwell, it will be seen, would have shared the property with his Branwell cousins in Penzance, of whom two are still alive. In any case, Branwell's name *was* mentioned, and he received 'my Japan dressing-box,' whatever that may have been worth.

Three or four letters, above and beyond these already published, were written by Charlotte to her friend in the interval between Miss Branwell's death and her return to Brussels; and she paid a visit to Miss Nussey at Brookroyd, and it was returned.

TO MISS ELLEN NUSSEY.

'HAWORTH, November 20, 1842.

'DEAR ELLEN, — I hope your brother is sufficiently recovered now to dispense with your constant attendance. Papa desires his compliments to you, and says he should be very glad if you could give us your company at Haworth a little while. Can you come on Friday next? I mention so early a day because Anne leaves us to return to York on Monday, and she wishes very much to see you before her departure. I think your brother is too good-natured to object to your coming. There is little enough pleasure in this world, and it would be truly unkind to deny to you and me that of meeting again after so long a separation. Do not fear to find us melancholy or depressed. We are all much as usual. You will see no difference from our former demeanour. Send an immediate answer.

' My love and best wishes to your sister and mother.

'C. BRONTË.'

TO MISS ELLEN NUSSEY.

'HAWORTH, November 25, 1842.

'MY DEAR ELLEN, — I hope that invitation of yours was given in real earnest, for I intend to accept it. I wish to see you, and

105

CHARLOTTE BRONTË

as in a few weeks I shall probably again leave England, I will not be too delicate and ceremonious and so let the present opportunity pass. Something says to me that it will not be too convenient to have a guest at Brookroyd while there is an invalid there—however, I listen to no such suggestions. Anne leaves Haworth on Tuesday at 6 o'clock in the morning, and we should reach Bradford at half-past eight. There are many reasons why I should have preferred your coming to Haworth, but as it appears there are always obstacles which prevent that, I'll break through ceremony, or pride, or whatever it is, and, like Mahomet, go to the mountain which won't or can't come to me. The coach stops at the Bowling Green Inn, in Bradford. Give my love to your sister and mother.   C. BRONTË.'

TO MISS ELLEN NUSSEY.

'HAWORTH, January 10, 1843.

'DEAR NELL, — It is a singular state of things to be obliged to write and have nothing worth reading to say. I am glad you got home safe. You are an excellent good girl for writing to me two letters, especially as they were such long ones. Branwell wants to know why you carefully exclude all mention of him when you particularly send your regards to every other member of the family. He desires to know whether and in what he has offended you, or whether it is considered improper for a young lady to mention the gentlemen of a house. We have been one walk on the moors since you left. We have been to Keighley, where we met a person of our acquaintance, who uttered an interjection of astonishment on meeting us, and when he could get his breath, informed us that he had heard I was dead and buried.   C. BRONTË.'

TO MISS ELLEN NUSSEY.

'HAWORTH, January 15, 1843.

'DEAR NELL, — I am much obliged to you for transferring the roll of muslin. Last Saturday I found the other gift, for which you deserve smothering. I will deliver Branwell your message.

106

You have left your Bible — how can I send it? I cannot tell precisely what day I leave home, but it will be the last week in this month. Are you going with me? I admire exceedingly the costume you have chosen to appear in at the Birstall rout. I think you say pink petticoat, black jacket, and a wreath of roses — beautiful! For a change I would advise a black coat, velvet stock and waistcoat, white pantaloons, and smart boots. Address Rue d'Isabelle. Write to me again, that's a good girl, very soon. Respectful remembrances to your mother and sister.

'C. Brontë.'

Then she is in Brussels again, as the following letter indicates.

TO MISS ELLEN NUSSEY.

'Brussels, January 30, 1843.

'Dear Ellen, — I left Leeds for London last Friday at nine o'clock; owing to delay we did not reach London till ten at night — two hours after time. I took a cab the moment I arrived at Euston Square, and went forthwith to London Bridge Wharf. The packet lay off that wharf, and I went on board the same night. Next morning we sailed. We had a prosperous and speedy voyage, and landed at Ostend at seven o'clock next morning. I took the train at twelve and reached Rue d'Isabelle at seven in the evening. Madame Héger received me with great kindness. I am still tired with the continued excitement of three days' travelling. I had no accident, but of course some anxiety. Miss Dixon called this afternoon.[1] Mary Taylor had told her I should be in Brussels the last week in January. I am going there on Sunday, D.V. Address — Miss Brontë, Chez Mme. Héger, 32 Rue d'Isabelle, Bruxelles. — Good-bye, dear.

'C. B.'

This second visit of Charlotte Brontë to Brussels has given rise to much speculation, some of it of not the

[1] Miss Mary Dixon, the sister of Mr. George Dixon, M.P., is still alive, but she has unfortunately not preserved her letters from Charlotte Brontë.

CHARLOTTE BRONTË

pleasantest kind. It is well to face the point bluntly, for it has been more than once implied that Charlotte Brontë was in love with M. Héger, as her prototype Lucy Snowe was in love with Paul Emanuel. The assumption, which is absolutely groundless, has had certain plausible points in its favour, not the least obvious, of course, being the inclination to read autobiography into every line of Charlotte Brontë's writings. Then there is a passage in a printed letter to Miss Nussey which has been quoted as if to bear out this suggestion : ' I returned to Brussels after aunt's death,' she writes, ' against my conscience, prompted by what then seemed an irresistible impulse. I was punished for my selfish folly by a total withdrawal for more than two years of happiness and peace of mind.'

It is perfectly excusable for a man of the world, unacquainted with qualifying facts, to assume that for these two years Charlotte Brontë's heart was consumed with an unquenchable love for her professor — held in restraint, no doubt, as the most censorious admit, but sufficiently marked to secure the jealousy and ill-will of Madame Héger. Madame Héger and her family, it must be admitted, have kept this impression afloat. Madame Héger refused to see Mrs. Gaskell when she called upon her in the Rue d'Isabelle ; and her daughters will tell you that their father broke off his correspondence with Miss Brontë because his favourite English pupil showed an undue extravagance of devotion. ' Her attachment after her return to Yorkshire,' to quote a recent essay on the subject, ' was expressed in her frequent letters in a tone that her Brussels friends considered it not only prudent but kind to check. She was warned by them that the exaltation these letters betrayed needed to be toned down and replaced by what was reasonable. She was further advised to write only once in six months, and then to limit the subject of her letters to her own health and that of her family, and to a plain account of her circumstances

108

and occupations.'[1] Now to all this I do not hesitate to give an emphatic contradiction, a contradiction based upon the only independent authority available. Miss Lætitia Wheelwright and her sisters saw much of Charlotte Brontë during this second sojourn in Brussels, and they have a quite different tale to tell. That misgiving of Charlotte, by the way, which weighed so heavily upon her mind afterwards, was due to the fact that she had left her father practically unprotected from the enticing company of a too festive curate. He gave himself up at this time to a very copious whisky drinking, from which Charlotte's homecoming speedily rescued him.[2]

Madame Héger did indeed hate Charlotte Brontë in her later years. This is not unnatural when we remember how that unfortunate woman has been gibbeted for all time in the characters of Mlle. Zoraïde Reuter and Madame Beck. But in justice to the creator of these scathing portraits, it may be mentioned that Charlotte Brontë took every precaution to prevent ' Villette ' from obtaining currency in the city which inspired it. She told Miss Wheelwright, with whom naturally, on her visits to London, she often discussed the Brussels life, that she had received a promise that there should be no translation, and that the book would never appear in the French language. One cannot therefore fix upon Charlotte Brontë any responsibility for the circumstance that immediately after her death the novel appeared in the only tongue understood by Madame Héger.

Miss Wheelwright informs me that Charlotte Brontë did certainly admire M. Héger, as did all his pupils, very heartily. Charlotte's first impression, indeed, was not flattering : ' He is professor of rhetoric, a man of power as to mind, but

---

[1] 'The Brontës at Brussels,' by Frederika Macdonald. — *The Woman at Home*, July 1894.

[2] This statement has received the separate endorsement of the Rev. A. B. Nicholls and of Miss Ellen Nussey.

very choleric and irritable in temperament ; a little black
being, with a face that varies in expression. Sometimes he
borrows the lineaments of an insane tom-cat, sometimes
those of a delirious hyena ; occasionally, but very seldom,
he discards these perilous attractions and assumes an air not
above 100 degrees removed from mild and gentleman-like.'
But he was particularly attentive to Charlotte ; and as he
was the first really intelligent man she had met, the first
man, that is to say, with intellectual interests — for we
know how much she despised the curates of her neighbourhood — she rejoiced at every opportunity of doing verbal
battle with him, for Charlotte inherited, it may be said, the
Irish love of debate.   Some time after Charlotte had returned
to England, and when in the height of her fame, she met
her Brussels school-fellow in London.   Miss Wheelwright
asked her whether she still corresponded with M. Héger.
Charlotte replied that she had discontinued to do so.   M.
Héger had mentioned in one letter that his wife did not like
the correspondence, and he asked her therefore to address
her letters to the Royal Athenée, where, as I have mentioned, he gave lessons to the boys.   ' I stopped writing at
once,' Charlotte told her friend.   ' I would not have dreamt
of writing to him when I found it was disagreeable to his
wife ; certainly I would not write unknown to her.'   ' She
said this,' Miss Wheelwright adds, ' with the sincerity of
manner which characterised her every utterance, and I
would sooner have doubted myself than her.'   Let, then,
this silly and offensive imputation be now and for ever dismissed from the minds of Charlotte Brontë's admirers, if
indeed it had ever lodged there.[1]

[1] M. and Mme. Héger celebrated their golden wedding in 1888, but Mme.
Héger died the next year.   M. Constantin Héger lived to be eighty-seven years
of age, dying at 72 Rue Nettoyer, Brussels, on the 6th of May 1896.   He was
born in Brussels in 1809, took part in the Belgian revolution of 1830, and fought
in the war of independence against the Dutch.   He was twice married, and it
was his second wife who was associated with Charlotte Brontë.   She started the

Charlotte had not visited the Wheelwrights in the Rue Royale during her first visit to Brussels. She had found the companionship of Emily all-sufficing, and Emily was not sufficiently popular with the Wheelwrights to have made her a welcome guest. They admitted her cleverness, but they considered her hard, unsympathetic, and abrupt in manner. We know that she was self-contained and homesick, pining for her native moors. This was not evident to a girl of ten, the youngest of the Wheelwright children, who was compelled to receive daily a music lesson from Emily in her play-hours. When, however, Charlotte came back to Brussels alone she was heartily welcomed into two or three English families, including those of Mr. Dixon, of the Rev. Mr. Jenkins, and of Dr. Wheelwright. With the Wheelwright children she sometimes spent the Sunday, and with them she occasionally visited the English Episcopal church which the Wheelwrights attended, and of which the clergyman was a Mr. Drury. When Dr. Wheelwright took his wife for a Rhine trip in May he left his four children — one little girl had died at Brussels, aged seven, in the preceding November — in the care of Madame Héger at the Pensionnat, and under the immediate supervision of Charlotte.

At this period there was plenty of cheerfulness in her life. She was learning German. She was giving English lessons to M. Héger and to his brother-in-law, M. Chappelle. She went to the Carnival, and described it as 'animating to see the immense crowds and the general gaiety.' 'When-

school in the Rue d'Isabelle, and M. Héger took charge of the upper French classes. In an obituary article written by M. Colin of 'L'Etoile Belge' in 'The Sketch' (June 5, 1896), which was revised by Dr. Héger, the only son of M. Héger, it is stated that Charlotte Brontë was piqued at being refused permission to return to the Pensionnat a third time, and that 'Villette' was her revenge. We know that this was not the case. The Pensionnat Héger was removed in 1894 to the Avenue Louise. The building in the Rue d'Isabelle will shortly be pulled down.

111

CHARLOTTE BRONTË

ever I turn back,' she writes, 'to compare what I am with what I was, my place here with my place at Mrs. Sidgwick's or Mrs. White's, I am thankful.'

In a letter to her brother, however, we find the darker side of the picture. It reveals many things apart from what is actually written down. In this, the only letter to Branwell that I have been able to discover, apart from one written in childhood, it appears that the brother and sister are upon very confidential terms. Up to this time, at any rate, Branwell's conduct had not excited any apprehension as to his future, and the absence of any substantial place in his aunt's will was clearly not due to misconduct. Branwell was now under the same roof as his sister Anne, having obtained an appointment as tutor to young Edmund Robinson at Thorp Green, near York, where Anne was governess. The letter is unsigned, concluding playfully with 'yourn,' and the initials follow a closing message to Anne on the same sheet of paper.

TO BRANWELL BRONTË.

'BRUSSELS, May 1, 1843.

'DEAR BRANWELL,—I hear you have written a letter to me. This letter, however, as usual, I have never received, which I am exceedingly sorry for, as I have wished very much to hear from you. Are you sure that you put the right address and that you paid the English postage, 1s. 6d.? Without that, letters are never forwarded. I heard from papa a day or two since. All appears to be going on reasonably well at home. I grieve only that Emily is so solitary; but, however, you and Anne will soon be returning for the holidays, which will cheer the house for a time. Are you in better health and spirits, and does Anne continue to be pretty well? I understand papa has been to see you. Did he seem cheerful and well? Mind when you write to me you answer these questions, as I wish to know. Also give me a detailed account as to how you get on with your pupil and the rest of the family. I have received a general assurance

112

that you do well and are in good odour, but I want to know particulars.

'As for me, I am very well and wag on as usual. I perceive, however, that I grow exceedingly misanthropic and sour. You will say that this is no news, and that you never knew me possessed of the contrary qualities — philanthropy and sugariness. *Das ist wahr* (which being translated means, that is true) ; but the fact is, the people here are no go whatsoever. Amongst 120 persons which compose the daily population of this house, I can discern only one or two who deserve anything like regard. This is not owing to foolish fastidiousness on my part, but to the absence of decent qualities on theirs. They have not intellect or politeness or good-nature or good-feeling. They are nothing. I don't hate them — hatred would be too warm a feeling. They have no sensations themselves and they excite none. But one wearies from day to day of caring nothing, fearing nothing, liking nothing, hating nothing, being nothing, doing nothing — yes, I teach and sometimes get red in the face with impatience at their stupidity. But don't think I ever scold or fly into a passion. If I spoke warmly, as warmly as I sometimes used to do at the Roe Head, they would think me mad. Nobody ever gets into a passion here. Such a thing is not known. The phlegm that thickens their blood is too gluey to boil. They are very false in their relations with each other, but they rarely quarrel, and friendship is a folly they are unacquainted with. The black Swan, M. Héger, is the only sole veritable exception to this rule (for Madame, always cool and always reasoning, is not quite an exception). But I rarely speak to Monsieur now, for not being a pupil I have little or nothing to do with him. From time to time he shows his kind-heartedness by loading me with books, so that I am still indebted to him for all the pleasure or amusement I have. Except for the total want of companionship I have nothing to complain of. I have not too much to do, sufficient liberty, and I am rarely interfered with. I lead an easeful, stagnant, silent life, for which, when I think of Mrs. Sidgwick, I ought to be very thankful. Be sure you write to me soon, and beg of Anne to inclose a small billet in the same letter; it will be a real charity to do me this kindness. Tell me everything you can think of.

'It is a curious metaphysical fact that always in the evening when I am in the great dormitory alone, having no other company than a number of beds with white curtains, I always recur as fanatically as ever to the old ideas, the old faces, and the old scenes in the world below.

'Give my love to Anne.— And believe me, yourn.

'DEAR ANNE,—Write to me.—Your affectionate Schwester,

'C. B.

'Mr. Héger has just been in and given me a little German Testament as a present. I was surprised, for since a good many days he has hardly spoken to me.'

A little later she writes to Emily in similar strain.

TO MISS EMILY J. BRONTË.

'BRUSSELS, May 29, 1843.

'DEAR E. J.,— The reason of the unconscionable demand for money is explained in my letter to papa. Would you believe it, Mdlle. Mühl demands as much for one pupil as for two, namely, 10 francs per month. This, with the five francs per month to the Blanchisseuse, makes havoc in £16 per annum. You will perceive I have begun again to take German lessons. Things wag on much as usual here. Only Mdlle. Blanche and Mdlle. Haussé are at present on a system of war without quarter. They hate each other like two cats. Mdlle. Blanche frightens Mdlle. Haussé by her white passions (for they quarrel venomously). Mdlle. Haussé complains that when Mdlle. Blanche is in fury, "*elle n'a pas de lèvres.*" I find also that Mdlle. Sophie dislikes Mdlle. Blanche extremely. She says she is heartless, insincere, and vindictive, which epithets, I assure you, are richly deserved. Also I find she is the regular spy of Mme. Héger, to whom she reports everything. Also she invents — which I should not have thought. I have now the entire charge of the English lessons. I have given two lessons to the first class. Hortense Jannoy was a picture on these occasions, her face was black as a "blue-piled thunder-loft," and her two ears were red as raw beef. To all questions asked her reply was, "*je ne sais pas.*" It is a pity but her friends could meet with a person qualified to cast out a devil. I am richly off for companionship in these parts. Of late days, M. and Mde. Héger rarely speak to me, and I really don't pretend to care a fig for any body else in the establishment. You are not to suppose by that expression that I am under the influence of *warm* affection for Mde. Héger. I am convinced she does not like me — why, I can't tell, nor do I think she herself has any definite reason for the aversion; but for one thing, she cannot comprehend why I do not make intimate friends of Mesdames Blanche, Sophie, and Haussé. M. Héger is wondrously influenced by Madame, and I should not wonder if he disapproves very much of my unamiable want of sociability. He has already given me a brief lecture on universal *bienveillance,* and perceiving that I don't improve in consequence, I fancy he has taken to considering me as a person to be let alone — left to the error of her ways; and consequently he has in a great measure withdrawn the light of his countenance, and I get on from day to day in a Robinson-Crusoe-like condition — very lonely. That does not signify. In other respects I have nothing substantial to complain of, nor is even this a cause for complaint. Except the loss of M. Héger's good-will (if I have lost it) I care for none of 'em. I hope you are well and hearty. Walk out often on the moors. Sorry am I to hear that Hannah is gone, and that she has left you burdened with the charge of the little girl, her sister. I hope Tabby will continue to stay with you — give my love to her. Regards to the fighting gentry, and to old asthma.— Your

'C. B.

'I have written to Branwell, though I never got a letter from him.'

In August she is still more dissatisfied, but 'I will continue to stay some months longer, till I have acquired German, and then I hope to see all your faces again.'

TO MISS ELLEN NUSSEY.

'BRUSSELS, August 6, 1843.

'DEAR ELLEN, — You never answered my last letter; but, however, forgiveness is a part of the Christian Creed, and so having an opportunity to send a letter to England, I forgive you and write to you again. Last Sunday afternoon, being at the Chapel Royal, in Brussels, I was surprised to hear a voice proceed from the pulpit which instantly brought all Birstall and Batley before my mind's eye. I could see nothing, but certainly thought that that unclerical little Welsh pony, Jenkins, was there. I buoyed up my mind with the expectation of receiving a letter from you, but as, however, I have got none, I suppose I must have been mistaken.

C. B.

'Mr. Jenkins has called. He brought no letter from you, but said you were at Harrogate, and that they could not find the letter you had *intended* to send. He informed me of the death of your sister. Poor Sarah, when I last bid her good-bye I little thought I should never see her more. Certainly, however, she is happy where she is gone — far happier than she was here. When the first days of mourning are past, you will see that you have reason rather to rejoice at her removal than to grieve for it. Your mother will have felt her death much — and you also. I fear from the circumstance of your being at Harrogate that you are yourself ill. Write to me soon.'

It was in September that the incident occurred which has found so dramatic a setting in 'Villette' — the confession to a priest of the Roman Catholic Church of a daughter of the most militant type of Protestantism; and not the least valuable of my newly-discovered Brontë treasures is the letter which Charlotte wrote to Emily giving an unembellished account of the incident.

TO MISS EMILY J. BRONTË.

'BRUXELLES, September 2, 1843.

'DEAR E. J., — Another opportunity of writing to you coming to pass, I shall improve it by scribbling a few lines. More than half the holidays are now past, and rather better than I expected. The weather has been exceedingly fine during the last fortnight, and yet not so Asiatically hot as it was last year at this time. Consequently I have tramped about a great deal and tried to get a clearer acquaintance with the streets of Bruxelles. This week, as no teacher is here except Mdlle. Blanche, who is returned from Paris, I am always alone except at meal-times, for Mdlle. Blanche's character is so false and so contemptible I can't force myself to associate with her. She perceives my utter dislike and never now speaks to me — a great relief.

'However, I should inevitably fall into the gulf of low spirits if I stayed always by myself here without a human being to speak to, so I go out and traverse the Boulevards and streets of Bruxelles sometimes for hours together. Yesterday I went on a pilgrimage to the cemetery, and far beyond it on to a hill where there was nothing but fields as far as the horizon. When I came back it was evening; but I had such a repugnance to return to the house, which contained nothing that I cared for, I still kept threading the streets in the neighbourhood of the Rue d'Isabelle and avoiding it. I found myself opposite to Ste. Gudule, and the bell, whose voice you know, began to toll for evening salut. I went in, quite alone (which procedure you will say is not much like me), wandered about the aisles where a few old women were saying their prayers, till vespers begun. I stayed till they were over. Still I could not leave the church or force myself to go home — to school I mean. An odd whim came into my head. In a solitary part of the Cathedral six or seven people still remained kneeling by the confessionals. In two confessionals I saw a priest. I felt as if I did not care what I did, provided it was not absolutely wrong, and that it served to vary my life and yield a moment's interest. I

117

CHARLOTTE BRONTË

took a fancy to change myself into a Catholic and go and make
a real confession to see what it was like. Knowing me as you
do, you will think this odd, but when people are by themselves they have singular fancies. A penitent was occupied in
confessing. They do not go into the sort of pew or cloister
which the priest occupies, but kneel down on the steps and
confess through a grating. Both the confessor and the penitent
whisper very low, you can hardly hear their voices. After I
had watched two or three penitents go and return I approached
at last and knelt down in a niche which was just vacated. I had
to kneel there ten minutes waiting, for on the other side was
another penitent invisible to me. At last that went away and
a little wooden door inside the grating opened, and I saw the
priest leaning his ear towards me. I was obliged to begin, and
yet I did not know a word of the formula with which they always
commence their confessions. It was a funny position. I felt
precisely as I did when alone on the Thames at midnight. I
commenced with saying I was a foreigner and had been brought
up a Protestant. The priest asked if I was a Protestant
then. I somehow could not tell a lie and said "yes." He
replied that in that case I could not *"jouir du bonheur de la
confesse;"* but I was determined to confess, and at last he said he
would allow me because it might be the first step towards returning to the true church. I actually did confess — a real confession. When I had done he told me his address, and said that
every morning I was to go to the rue du Parc — to his house —
and he would reason with me and try to convince me of the
error and enormity of being a Protestant! ! ! I promised faithfully to go. Of course, however, the adventure stops there, and I
hope I shall never see the priest again. I think you had better
not tell papa of this. He will not understand that it was
only a freak, and will perhaps think I am going to turn Catholic. Trusting that you and papa are well, and also Tabby and
the Holyes, and hoping you will write to me immediately, —
I am, yours,

'C. B.'

AND HER CIRCLE

The 'Holyes,' it is perhaps hardly necessary to add, is Charlotte's irreverent appellation for the curates — Mr. Smith and Mr. Grant.

TO MISS ELLEN NUSSEY.

'Brussels, October 13, 1843.

'Dear Ellen, — I was glad to receive your last letter ; but when I read it, its contents gave me some pain. It was melancholy indeed that so soon after the death of a sister you should be called from a distant county by the news of the severe illness of a brother, and, after your return home, your sister Ann should fall ill too. Mary Dixon informs me your brother is scarcely expected to recover — is this true? I hope not, for his sake and yours. His loss would indeed be a blow — a blow which I hope Providence may avert. Do not, my dear Ellen, fail to write to me soon of affairs at Brookroyd. I cannot fail to be anxious on the subject, your family being amongst the oldest and kindest friends I have. I trust this season of affliction will soon pass. It has been a long one.   C. B.'

TO MISS EMILY J. BRONTË.

'Brussels, December 19, 1843.

'Dear E. J., — I have taken my determination. I hope to be at home the day after New Year's Day. I have told Mme. Héger. But in order to come home I shall be obliged to draw on my cash for another £5. I have only £3 at present, and as there are several little things I should like to buy before I leave Brussels — which you know cannot be got as well in England — £3 would not suffice. Low spirits have afflicted me much lately, but I hope all will be well when I get home — above all, if I find papa and you and B. and A. well. I am not ill in body. It is only the mind which is a trifle shaken — for want of comfort.

'I shall try to cheer up now. — Good-bye.   C. B.'

119

CHAPTER V.

PATRICK BRANWELL BRONTË.

THE younger Patrick Brontë was always known by his mother's family name of Branwell. The name derived from the patron Saint of Ireland, with which the enthusiastic Celt, Romanist and Protestant alike, delights to disfigure his male child, was speedily banished from the Yorkshire Parsonage. Branwell was a year younger than Charlotte, and it is clear that she and her brother were 'chums,' in the same way as Emily and Anne were 'chums,' in the earlier years, before Charlotte made other friends. Even until two or three years from Branwell's death, we find Charlotte writing to him with genuine sisterly affection, and, indeed, the only two family letters addressed to Branwell which are extant are from her. One of them, written from Brussels, I have printed elsewhere. The other, written from Roe Head, when Charlotte, aged sixteen, was at school there, was partly published by Mrs. Gaskell, but may as well be given here, copied direct from the original.

TO BRANWELL BRONTË.

'ROE HEAD, May 17, 1832.

'DEAR BRANWELL, — As usual I address my weekly letter to you, because to you I find the most to say. I feel exceedingly anxious to know how and in what state you arrived at home after your long and (I should think) very fatiguing journey. I could perceive when you arrived at Roe Head that you were very much tired, though you refused to acknowledge it. After

PATRICK BRANWELL BRONTË.

From a Silhouette in the possession of Mr. A. B. Nicholls.

you were gone, many questions and subjects of conversation
recurred to me which I had intended to mention to you, but
quite forgot them in the agitation which I felt at the totally
unexpected pleasure of seeing you. Lately I had begun to
think that I had lost all the interest which I used formerly to
take in politics, but the extreme pleasure I felt at the news o
the Reform Bill's being thrown out by the House of Lords,
and of the expulsion or resignation of Earl Grey, etc., etc.,
convinced me that I have not as yet lost *all* my penchant for
politics. I am extremely glad that aunt has consented to take
in " Fraser's Magazine," for though I know from your description
of its general contents it will be rather uninteresting when compared with " Blackwood," still it will be better than remaining
the whole year without being able to obtain a sight of any
periodical publication whatever; and such would assuredly be
our case, as in the little wild, moorland village where we reside,
there would be no possibility of borrowing or obtaining a work
of that description from a circulating library. I hope with you
that the present delightful weather may contribute to the perfect restoration of our dear papa's health, and that it may give
aunt pleasant reminiscences of the salubrious climate of her native
place.

'With love to all, — Believe me, dear Branwell, to remain your
affectionate sister,   CHARLOTTE.'

'As to you I find the most to say' is significant. And to
Branwell, Charlotte refers again and again in most affectionate terms in many a later letter. It is to her enthusiasm,
indeed, that we largely owe the extravagant estimate of
Branwell's ability which has found so abundant expression
in books on the Brontës.

Branwell has himself been made the hero of at least three
biographies.[1] Mr. Francis Grundy has no importance for

[1] 'Pictures of the Past,' by Francis H. Grundy, C.E.: Griffiths & Farran,
1879; 'Emily Brontë,' by A. Mary F. Robinson: W. H. Allen, 1883; 'The
Brontë Family, with Special Reference to Patrick Branwell Brontë,' by
Francis A. Leyland: Hurst & Blackett, 2 vols. 1886.

our day other than that he prints certain letters from Branwell in his autobiography. Miss Mary F. Robinson, whatever distinction may pertain to her verse, should never have attempted a biography of Emily Brontë. Her book is mainly of significance because, appearing in a series of 'Eminent Women,' it served to emphasise the growing opinion that Emily, as well as Charlotte, had a place among the great writers of her day. Miss Robinson added nothing to our knowledge of Emily Brontë, and her book devoted inordinate space to the shortcomings of Branwell, concerning which she had no new information.

Mr. Leyland's book is professedly a biography of Branwell, and is, indeed, a valuable storehouse of facts. It might have had more success had it been written with greater brightness and verve. As it stands, it is a dull book, readable only by the Brontë enthusiast. Mr. Leyland has no literary perception, and in his eagerness to show that Branwell was a genius, prints numerous letters and poems which sufficiently demonstrate that he was not.

Charlotte never hesitated in the earlier years to praise her brother as the genius of the family. We all know how eagerly the girls in any home circle are ready to acknowledge and accept as signs of original power the most impudent witticisms of a fairly clever brother. The Brontë household was not exceptionally constituted in this respect. It is evident that the boy grew up with talent of a kind. He could certainly draw with more idea of perspective than his sisters, and one or two portraits by him are not wanting in merit. But there is no evidence of any special writing faculty, and the words 'genius' and 'brilliant' which have been freely applied to him are entirely misplaced. Branwell was thirty-one years of age when he died, and it was only during the last year or two of his life that opium and alcohol had made him intellectually hopeless. Yet, unless we accept the preposterous statement that he wrote 'Wuthering

Heights,' he would seem to have composed nothing which gives him the slightest claim to the most inconsiderable niche in the temple of literature.

Branwell appears to have worked side by side with his sisters in the early years, and innumerable volumes of the 'little writing' bearing his signature have come into my hands. Verdopolis, the imaginary city of his sisters' early stories, plays a considerable part in Branwell's. 'Real Life in Verdopolis' bears date 1833. 'The Battle of Washington' is evidently a still more childish effusion. 'Caractacus' is dated 1830, and the poems and tiny romances continue steadily on through the years until they finally stop short in 1837—when Branwell is twenty years old—with a story entitled 'Percy.' By the light of subsequent events it is interesting to note that a manuscript of 1830 bears the title of 'The Liar Unmasked.'

It would be unfair to take these crude productions of Branwell's Brontë's boyhood as implying that he had no possibilities in him of anything better, but judging from the fact that his letters, as a man of eight and twenty, are as undistinguished as his sister's are noteworthy at a like age, we might well dismiss Branwell Brontë once and for all, were not some epitome of his life indispensable in an account of the Brontë circle.

Branwell was born at Thornton in 1817. When the family removed to Haworth he studied at the Grammar School, although, doubtless, he owed most of his earlier tuition to his father. When school days were over it was decided that he should be an artist. To a certain William Robinson, of Leeds, he was indebted for his first lessons. Mrs. Gaskell describes a life-size drawing of Charlotte, Emily, and Anne which Branwell painted about this period. The huge canvas stood for many years at the top of the staircase at the parsonage.[1] In 1835 Branwell went up to

[1] After Mr. Brontë's death Mr. Nicholls removed it to Ireland. Being of

London with a view to becoming a pupil at the Royal Academy Art Schools. The reason for his almost immediate reappearance at Haworth has never been explained. Probably he wasted his money and his father refused supplies. He had certainly been sufficiently in earnest at the start, judging from this letter, of which I find a draft among his papers.

TO THE SECRETARY, ROYAL ACADEMY OF ARTS.

'SIR, — Having an earnest desire to enter as probationary student in the Royal Academy, but not being possessed of information as to the means of obtaining my desire, I presume to request from you, as Secretary to the Institution, an answer to the questions —

'Where am I to present my drawings?
'At what time?
        and especially,
'Can I do it in August or September?

Your obedient servant,   BRANWELL BRONTË.'

In 1836 we find him as 'brother' of the 'Lodge of the Three Graces' at Haworth. In the following year he is practising as an artist in Bradford, and painting a number of portraits of the townsfolk. At this same period he wrote to Wordsworth, sending verses, which he was at the time producing with due regularity. In January 1840 Branwell became tutor in the family of Mr. Postlethwaite at Broughton-in-Furness. It was from that place that he wrote the incoherent and silly letter which has been more than once printed, and which merely serves to show that then, as always, he had an ill-regulated mind. It was from

opinion that the only accurate portrait was that of Emily, he cut this out and destroyed the remainder. The portrait of Emily was given to Martha Brown, the servant, on one of her visits to Mr. Nicholls, and I have not been able to trace it. There are three or four so-called portraits of Emily in existence, but they are all repudiated by Mr. Nicholls as absolutely unlike her. The supposed portrait which appeared in the 'Woman at Home' for July 1894 is now known to have been merely an illustration from a 'Book of Beauty,' and entirely spurious.

Broughton-in-Furness also that he addresses Hartley Coleridge, and the letters are worth printing if only on account of the similar destiny of the two men.

TO HARTLEY COLERIDGE.

'Broughton-in-Furness,
'Lancashire, April 20, 1840.

'Sir, — It is with much reluctance that I venture to request, for the perusal of the following lines, a portion of the time of one upon whom I can have no claim, and should not dare to intrude, but I do not, personally, know a man on whom to rely for an answer to the questions I shall put, and I could not resist my longing to ask a man from whose judgment there would be little hope of appeal.

'Since my childhood I have been wont to devote the hours I could spare from other and very different employments to efforts at literary composition, always keeping the results to myself, nor have they in more than two or three instances been seen by any other. But I am about to enter active life, and prudence tells me not to waste the time which must make my independence; yet, sir, I like writing too well to fling aside the practice of it without an effort to ascertain whether I could turn it to account, not in *wholly* maintaining myself, but in *aiding* my maintenance, for I do not sigh after fame, and am not ignorant of the folly or the fate of those who, without ability, would depend for their lives upon their pens; but I seek to know, and venture, though with shame, to ask from one whose word I must respect: whether, by periodical or other writing, I could please myself with writing, and make it subservient to living.

'I would not, with this view, have troubled you with a composition in verse, but any piece I have in prose would too greatly trespass upon your patience, which, I fear, if you look over the verse, will be more than sufficiently tried.

'I feel the egotism of my language, but I have none, sir, in my heart, for I feel beyond all encouragement from myself, and I hope for none from you.

125

'Should you give any opinion upon what I send, it will, however condemnatory, be most gratefully received by, — Sir, your most humble servant, P. B. BRONTË.

'P.S. — The first piece is only the sequel of one striving to depict the fall from unguided passion into neglect, despair, and death. It ought to show an hour too near those of pleasure for repentance, and too near death for hope. The translations are two out of many made from Horace, and given to assist an answer to the question — would it be possible to obtain remuneration for translations for such as those from that or any other classic author?'

Branwell would appear to have gone over to Ambleside to see Hartley Coleridge, if we may judge by that next letter, written from Haworth upon his return.

TO HARTLEY COLERIDGE.

'HAWORTH, June 27, 1840.

'SIR, — You will, perhaps, have forgotten me, but it will be long before I forget my first conversation with a man of real intellect, in my first visit to the classic lakes of Westmoreland.

'During the delightful day which I had the honour of spending with you at Ambleside, I received permission to transmit to you, as soon as finished, the first book of a translation of Horace, in order that, after a glance over it, you might tell me whether it was worth further notice or better fit for the fire.

'I have — I fear most negligently, and amid other very different employments — striven to translate two books, the first of which I have presumed to send to you. And will you, sir, stretch your past kindness by telling me whether I should amend and pursue the work or let it rest in peace.

'Great corrections I feel it wants, but till I feel that the work might benefit me, I have no heart to make them; yet if your judgment prove in any way favourable, I will re-write the whole, without sparing labour to reach perfection.

'I dared not have attempted Horace but that I saw the utter worthlessness of all former translations, and thought that a better

126

one, by whomsoever executed, might meet with some little
encouragement. I long to clear up my doubts by the judgment
of one whose opinion I should revere, and — but I suppose I am
dreaming — one to whom I should be proud indeed to inscribe
anything of mine which any publisher would look at, unless, as
is likely enough, the work would disgrace the name as much as
the name would honour the work.

'Amount of remuneration I should not look to — as anything
would be everything — and whatever it might be, let me say that
my bones would have no rest unless by written agreement a
division should be made of the profits (little or much) between
myself and him through whom alone I could hope to obtain a
hearing with that formidable personage, a London bookseller.

'Excuse my unintelligibility, haste, and appearance of presumption, and — Believe me to be, sir, your most humble and grateful
servant,   P. B. BRONTË.

'If anything in this note should displease you, lay it, sir, to the
account of inexperience and *not* impudence.'

In October 1840, we find Branwell clerk-in-charge at the
Station of Sowerby Bridge on the Leeds and Manchester
Railway, and the following year at Luddenden Foot, where
Mr. Grundy, the railway engineer, became acquainted with
him, and commenced the correspondence contained in
'Pictures of the Past.'

I have in my possession a small memorandum book,
evidently used by Branwell when engaged as a railway clerk.
There are notes in it upon the then existing railways,
demonstrating that he was trying to prime himself with
the requisite facts and statistics for a career of that kind.
But side by side with these are verses upon 'Lord Nelson,'
'Robert Burns,' and kindred themes, with such estimable
sentiments as this : —

> 'Then England's love and England's tongue
> And England's heart shall reverence long
> The wisdom deep, the courage strong,
> Of English Johnson's name.'

127

CHARLOTTE BRONTË

Altogether a literary atmosphere had been kindled for the boy had he had the slightest strength of character to go with it. The railway company, however, were soon tired of his vagaries, and in the beginning of 1842 he returns to the Haworth parsonage. The following letter to his friend Mr. Grundy is of biographical interest.

TO FRANCIS H. GRUNDY.

'OCTOBER 25, 1842.

'MY DEAR SIR, — There is no misunderstanding. I have had a long attendance at the death-bed of the Rev. Mr. Weightman, one of my dearest friends, and now I am attending at the death-bed of my aunt, who has been for twenty years as my mother. I expect her to die in a few hours.

'As my sisters are far from home, I have had much on my mind, and these things must serve as an apology for what was never intended as neglect of your friendship to us.

'I had meant not only to have written to you, but to the Rev. James Martineau, gratefully and sincerely acknowledging the receipt of his most kindly and truthful criticism — at least in advice, though too generous far in praise; but one sad ceremony must, I fear, be gone through first. Give my most sincere respects to Mr. Stephenson, and excuse this scrawl — my eyes are too dim with sorrow to see well. — Believe me, your not very happy but obliged friend and servant,   P. B. BRONTË.'

A week later he writes to the same friend : —

'I am incoherent, I fear, but I have been waking two nights witnessing such agonising suffering as I would not wish my worst enemy to endure; and I have now lost the guide and director of all the happy days connected with my childhood. I have suffered much sorrow since I last saw you at Haworth.'

Charlotte and Emily, it will be remembered, were at this time on their way home from Brussels, and Anne had to seek relief from her governess bonds at Mrs. Robinson's.

128

Branwell would seem to have returned with Anne to Thorp Green, as tutor to Mr. Robinson's son. He commenced his duties in December, 1842.

It would not be rash to assume — although it is only an assumption — that Branwell took to opium soon after he entered upon his duties at Thorp Green. I have already said something of the trouble which befel Mrs. Gaskell in accepting the statements of Charlotte Brontë, and — after Charlotte's death — of her friends, to the effect that Branwell became the prey of a designing woman, who promised to marry him when her husband — a venerable clergyman — should be dead. The story has been told too often. Branwell was dismissed, and returned to the parsonage to rave about his wrongs. If Mr. Robinson should die, the widow had promised to marry him, he assured his friends. Mr. Robinson did die (May 26, 1846), and then Branwell insisted that by his will he had prohibited his wife from marrying, under penalties of forfeiting the estate. A copy of the document is in my possession : —

'The eleventh day of September 1846 the Will of the Reverend Edmund Robinson, late of Thorp Green, in the Parish of Little Ouseburn, in the County of York, Clerk, deceased, was proved in the Prerogative Court of York by the oaths of Lydia Robinson, Widow, his Relict ; the Venerable Charles Thorp and Henry Newton, the Executors, to whom administration was granted.'

Needless to say, the will, a lengthy document, put no restraint whatever upon the actions of Mrs. Robinson. Upon the publication of Mrs. Gaskell's Life she was eager to clear her character in the law-courts, but was dissuaded therefrom by friends, who pointed out that a withdrawal of the obnoxious paragraphs in succeeding editions of the Memoir, and the publication of a letter in the 'Times,' would sufficiently meet the case.

CHARLOTTE BRONTË

Here is a letter from the advertisement pages of the 'Times.'

'8 BEDFORD ROW,
'LONDON, May 26, 1857.

'DEAR SIR, — As solicitor for and on behalf of the Rev. W. Gaskell and of Mrs. Gaskell, his wife, the latter of whom is authoress of the "Life of Charlotte Brontë," I am instructed to retract every statement contained in that work which imputes to a widowed lady, referred to, but not named therein, any breach of her conjugal, of her maternal, or of her social duties, and more especially of the statement contained in chapter 13 of the first volume, and in chapter 2 of the second volume, which imputes to the lady in question a guilty intercourse with the late Branwell Brontë. All those statements were made upon information which at the time Mrs. Gaskell believed to be well founded, but which, upon investigation, with the additional evidence furnished to me by you, I have ascertained not to be trustworthy. I am therefore authorised not only to retract the statements in question, but to express the deep regret of Mrs. Gaskell that she should have been led to make them. — I am, dear sirs, yours truly,

'WILLIAM SHAEN.

'Messrs. Newton & Robinson, Solicitors, York.'

A certain 'Note' in the 'Athenæum' a few days later is not without interest now.

'We are sorry to be called upon to return to Mrs. Gaskell's "Life of Charlotte Brontë," but we must do so, since the book has gone forth with our recommendation. Praise, it is needless to point out, implied trust in the biographer as an accurate collector of facts. This, we regret to state, Mrs. Gaskell proves not to have been. To the gossip which for weeks past has been seething and circulating in the London *coteries*, we gave small heed; but the "Times" advertises a legal apology, made on behalf of Mrs. Gaskell, withdrawing the statements put forth in her book respecting the cause of Mr. Branwell Brontë's wreck and ruin. These Mrs. Gaskell's lawyer is now fain to confess his client advanced on insufficient testimony. The telling of an episodical and gratuitous tale so dismal as concerns the dead, so damaging to the living, could only be excused by the story of sin being severely, strictly true ; and every one will have cause to regret that due caution was not used to test representations not, it seems, to be justified. It is in the interest of Letters that biographers should be deterred from rushing into print with mere impressions in place of proofs, however eager and sincere those impressions may be. They *may be* slanders, and as such they may sting cruelly. Meanwhile the "Life of Charlotte Brontë" must undergo modification ere it can be further circulated.'

Meanwhile let us return to Branwell Brontë's life as it is contained in his sister's correspondence.

TO MISS ELLEN NUSSEY.
'JANUARY 3, 1846.

' DEAR ELLEN, — I must write to you to-day whether I have anything to say or not, or else you will begin to think that I have forgotten you ; whereas, never a day passes, seldom an hour, that I do not think of you, *and the scene of trial* in which you live, move, and have your being. Mary Taylor's letter was deeply interesting and strongly characteristic. I have no news whatever to communicate. No changes take place here. Branwell offers no prospect of hope ; he professes to be too ill to think of seeking for employment ; he makes comfort scant at home. I hold to my intention of going to Brookroyd as soon as I can — that is, provided you will have me.

' Give my best love to your mother and sisters. — Yours, dear Nell, always faithful,   C. BRONTË.'

TO MISS ELLEN NUSSEY.
'JANUARY 13, 1845.

' MY DEAR ELLEN, — I have often said and thought that you have had many and heavy trials to bear in your still short life. You have always borne them with great firmness and calm so far — I hope fervently you will still be enabled to do so. Yet there is something in your letter that makes me fear the present is

CHARLOTTE BRONTE

the greatest trial of all, and the most severely felt by you. I hope it will soon pass over and leave no shadow behind it. I do earnestly desire to be with you, to talk to you, to give you what comfort I can. Branwell and Anne leave us on Saturday. Branwell has been quieter and less irritable on the whole this time than he was in summer. Anne is as usual — always good, mild, and patient. I think she too is a little stronger than she was. — Goodbye, dear Ellen.   C. Brontë.'

TO MISS ELLEN NUSSEY.

'December 31, 1845.

'Dear Ellen, — I don't know whether most to thank you for the very pretty slippers you have sent me or to scold you for occasioning yourself, in the slightest degree, trouble or expense on my account. I will have them made up and bring them with me, if all be well, when I come to Brookroyd.

'Never doubt that I shall come to Brookroyd as soon as I can, Nell. I daresay my wish to see you is equal to your wish to see me.

'I had a note on Saturday from Ellen Taylor, informing me that letters have been received from Mary in New Zealand, and that she was well and in good spirits. I suppose you have not yet seen them, as you do not mention them ; but you will probably have them in your possession before you get this note.

'You say well in speaking of Branwell that no sufferings are so awful as those brought on by dissipation. Alas ! I see the truth of this observation daily proved.

'Your friends must have a weary and burdensome life of it in waiting upon *their* unhappy brother. It seems grievous, indeed, that those who have not sinned should suffer so largely.

'Write to me a little oftener, Ellen — I am very glad to get your notes. Remember me kindly to your mother and sisters. — Yours faithfully,   C. Brontë.'

TO MISS WOOLER.

'January 30, 1846.

'My dear Miss Wooler, — I have not yet paid my usual visit to Brookroyd, but I frequently hear from Ellen, and she

132

did not fail to tell me that you were gone into Worcestershire.
She was unable, however, to give me your address; had I known
it I should have written to you long since.

'I thought you would wonder how we were getting on when
you heard of the Railway Panic, and you may be sure I am very
glad to be able to answer your kind inquiries by an assurance
that our small capital is as yet undiminished. The "York and
Midland" is, as you say, a very good line, yet I confess to you
I should wish, for my part, to be wise in time. I cannot think
that even the very best lines will continue for many years at
their present premiums, and I have been most anxious for us
to sell our shares ere it be too late, and to secure the proceeds
in some safer, if, for the present, less profitable investment. I
cannot, however, persuade my sisters to regard the affair precisely from my point of view, and I feel as if I would rather
run the risk of loss than hurt Emily's feelings by acting in direct
opposition to her opinion. She managed in a most handsome
and able manner for me when I was at Brussels, and prevented
by distance from looking after my own interests; therefore, I will
let her manage still, and take the consequences. Disinterested
and energetic she certainly is, and if she be not quite so tracta-
ble or open to conviction as I could wish, I must remember
perfection is not the lot of humanity. And as long as we can
regard those we love, and to whom we are closely allied, with
profound and very unshaken esteem, it is a small thing that they
should vex us occasionally by, what appear to us, unreasonable
and headstrong notions. You, my dear Miss Wooler, know full
as well as I do the value of sisters' affection to each other;
there is nothing like it in this world, I believe, when they
are nearly equal in age, and similar in education, tastes, and
sentiments.

'You ask about Branwell. He never thinks of seeking
employment, and I begin to fear he has rendered himself
incapable of filling any respectable station in life; besides,
if money were at his disposal he would use it only to his
own injury; the faculty of self-government is, I fear, almost
destroyed in him. You ask me if I do not think men are

strange beings. I do, indeed — I have often thought so ; and I think too that the mode of bringing them up is strange, they are not half sufficiently guarded from temptations. Girls are protected as if they were something very frail and silly indeed, while boys are turned loose on the world as if they, of all beings in existence, were the wisest and the least liable to be led astray.

'I am glad you like Bromsgrove. I always feel a peculiar satisfaction when I hear of your enjoying yourself, because it proves to me that there is really such a thing as retributive justice even in this life ; now you are free, and that while you have still, I hope, many years of vigour and health in which you can enjoy freedom. Besides, I have another and very egotistical motive for being pleased : it seems that even "a lone woman" can be happy, as well as cherished wives and proud mothers. I am glad of that — I speculate much on the existence of unmarried and never-to-be married woman now-a-days, and I have already got to the point of considering that there is no more respectable character on this earth than an unmarried woman who makes her own way through life quietly, perseveringly, without support of husband or mother, and who, having attained the age of forty-five or upwards, retains in her possession a well-regulated mind, a disposition to enjoy simple pleasures, fortitude to support inevitable pains, sympathy with the sufferings of others, and willingness to relieve want as far as her means extend. I wish to send this letter off by to-day's post, I must therefore conclude in haste. — Believe me, my dear Miss Wooler, yours, most affectionately,   C. BRONTË.'

TO MISS ELLEN NUSSEY.

'NOVEMBER 4, 1845.

'DEAR ELLEN, — You do not reproach me in your last, but I fear you must have thought me unkind in being so long without answering you. The fact is, I had hoped to be able to ask you to come to Haworth. Branwell seemed to have a prospect of getting employment, and I waited to know the result of his efforts in order to say, "Dear Ellen, come and see us"; but the place (a secretaryship to a Railroad Committee) is given to another person. Branwell still remains at home, and while he is here you shall not come. I am more confirmed in that resolution the more I know of him. I wish I could say one word to you in his favour, but I cannot, therefore I will hold my tongue.

'Emily and Anne wish me to tell you that they think it very unlikely for little Flossy to be expected to rear so numerous a family; they think you are quite right in protesting against all the pups being preserved, for, if kept, they will pull their poor little mother to pieces. — Yours faithfully,

'C. B.'

TO MISS ELLEN NUSSEY.

'APRIL 14, 1846.

'DEAR ELLEN, — I assure you I was very glad indeed to get your last note; for when three or four days elapsed after my second despatch to you and I got no answer, I scarcely doubted something was wrong. It relieved me much to find my apprehensions unfounded. I return you Miss Ringrose's notes with thanks. I always like to read them, they appear to me so true an index of an amiable mind, and one not too conscious of its own worth; beware of awakening in her this consciousness by undue praise. It is the privilege of simple-hearted, sensible, but not brilliant people, that they can *be* and *do* good without comparing their own thoughts and actions too closely with those of other people, and thence drawing strong food for self-appreciation. Talented people almost always know full well the excellence that is in them. I wish I could say anything favourable, but how can we be more comfortable so long as Branwell stays at home, and degenerates instead of improving? It has been lately intimated to him, that he would be received again on the railroad where he was formerly stationed if he would behave more steadily, but he refuses to make an effort; he will not work; and at home he is a drain on every resource — an impediment to all happiness. But there is no use in complaining.

'My love to all. Write again soon. C. B.'

135

CHARLOTTE BRONTË

TO MISS ELLEN NUSSEY.

'JUNE 17, 1846.

'DEAR ELLEN,— I was glad to perceive, by the tone of your last letter, that you are beginning to be a little more settled. We, I am sorry to say, have been somewhat more harassed than usual lately. The death of Mr. Robinson, which took place about three weeks or a month ago, served Branwell for a pretext to throw all about him into hubbub and confusion with his emotions, etc., etc. Shortly after came news from all hands that Mr. Robinson had altered his will before he died, and effectually prevented all chance of a marriage between his widow and Branwell, by stipulating that she should not have a shilling if she ever ventured to re-open any communication with him. Of course he then became intolerable. To papa he allows rest neither day nor night, and he is continually screwing money out of him, sometimes threatening that he will kill himself if it is withheld from him. He says Mrs. Robinson is now insane; that her mind is a complete wreck owing to remorse for her conduct towards Mr. Robinson (whose end it appears was hastened by distress of mind) and grief for having lost him. I do not know how much to believe of what he says, but I fear she is very ill. Branwell declares that he neither can nor will do anything for himself. Good situations have been offered him more than once, for which, by a fortnight's work, he might have qualified himself, but he will do nothing, except drink and make us all wretched. I had a note from Ellen Taylor a week ago, in which she remarks that letters were received from New Zealand a month since, and that all was well. I should like to hear from you again soon. I hope one day to see Brookroyd again, though I think it will not be yet — these are not times of amusement. Love to all.
C. B.'

TO MISS ELLEN NUSSEY.

'HAWORTH, March 1, 1847.

'DEAR ELLEN,—Branwell has been conducting himself very badly lately. I expect from the extravagance of his behaviour, and from mysterious hints he drops (for he never will speak out plainly), that we shall be hearing news of fresh debts contracted by him soon. The Misses Robinson, who had entirely ceased their correspondence with Anne for half a year after their father's death, have lately recommenced it. For a fortnight they sent her a letter almost every day, crammed with warm protestations of endless esteem and gratitude. They speak with great affection too of their mother, and never make any allusion intimating acquaintance with her errors. We take special care that Branwell does not know of their writing to Anne. My health is better: I lay the blame of its feebleness on the cold weather more than on an uneasy mind, for, after all, I have many things to be thankful for. Write again soon.

'C. BRONTË.'

TO MISS ELLEN NUSSEY.

'MAY 12, 1847.

'DEAR ELLEN, — We shall all be glad to see you on the Thursday or Friday of next week, whichever day will suit you best. About what time will you be likely to get here, and how will you come? By coach to Keighley, or by a gig all the way to Haworth? There must be no impediments now? I cannot do with them, I want very much to see you. I hope you will be decently comfortable while you stay.

'Branwell is quieter now, and for a good reason: he has got to the end of a considerable sum of money, and consequently is obliged to restrict himself in some degree. You must expect to find him weaker in mind, and a complete rake in appearance. I have no apprehension of his being at all uncivil to you; on the contrary, he will be as smooth as oil. I pray for fine weather that we may be able to get out while you stay. Good-bye for the present. Prepare for much dulness and monotony. Give my love to all at Brookroyd.   C. BRONTË.'

TO MISS ELLEN NUSSEY.

'JULY 28, 1848.

'DEAR ELLEN, — Branwell is the same in conduct as ever. His constitution seems much shattered. Papa, and sometimes all of us, have sad nights with him : he sleeps most of the day, and consequently will lie awake at night. But has not every house its trial ?

'Write to me very soon, dear Nell, and — Believe me, yours sincerely,
C. BRONTË.'

Branwell Brontë died on Sunday, September the 24th, 1848,[1] and the two following letters from Charlotte to her friend Mr. Williams are peculiarly interesting.

TO W. S. WILLIAMS.

'OCTOBER 2, 1848.

'MY DEAR SIR, — "We have hurried our dead out of our sight." A lull begins to succeed the gloomy tumult of last week. It is not permitted us to grieve for him who is gone as others grieve for those they lose. The removal of our only brother must necessarily be regarded by us rather in the light of a mercy than a chastisement. Branwell was his father's and his sisters' pride and hope in boyhood, but since manhood the case has been otherwise. It has been our lot to see him take a wrong bent ; to hope, expect, wait his return to the right path ; to know the sickness of hope deferred, the dismay of prayer baffled ; to experience despair at last — and now to behold the sudden early obscure close of what might have been a noble career.

'I do not weep from a sense of bereavement — there is no prop withdrawn, no consolation torn away, no dear companion lost — but for the wreck of talent, the ruin of promise, the untimely dreary extinction of what might have been a burning and a shining light. My brother was a year my junior. I had aspirations and ambitions for him once, long ago — they have perished mournfully. Nothing remains of him but a memory

[1] There are two portraits of Branwell in existence, both of them in the possession of Mr. Nicholls. One of them is a medallion by his friend Leyland, the other the silhouette which accompanies this chapter. They both suggest, mainly on account of the clothing, a man of more mature years than Branwell actually attained to.

of errors and sufferings. There is such a bitterness of pity for his life and death, such a yearning for the emptiness of his whole existence as I cannot describe. I trust time will allay these feelings.

'My poor father naturally thought more of his *only* son than of his daughters, and, much and long as he had suffered on his account, he cried out for his loss like David for that of Absalom — my son! my son! — and refused at first to be comforted. And then when I ought to have been able to collect my strength and be at hand to support him, I fell ill with an illness whose approaches I had felt for some time previously, and of which the crisis was hastened by the awe and trouble of the death-scene — the first I had ever witnessed. The past has seemed to me a strange week. Thank God, for my father's sake, I am better now, though still feeble. I wish indeed I had more general physical strength — the want of it is sadly in my way. I cannot do what I would do for want of sustained animal spirits and efficient bodily vigour.

'My unhappy brother never knew what his sisters had done in literature — he was not aware that they had ever published a line. We could not tell him of our efforts for fear of causing him too deep a pang of remorse for his own time mis-spent, and talents misapplied. Now he will *never* know. I cannot dwell longer on the subject at present — it is too painful.

'I thank you for your kind sympathy, and pray earnestly that your sons may all do well, and that you may be spared the sufferings my father has gone through. — Yours sincerely,

'C. Brontë.'

TO W. S. WILLIAMS.

'Haworth, October 6, 1848.

'My dear Sir, — I thank you for your last truly friendly letter, and for the number of "Blackwood" which accompanied it. Both arrived at a time when a relapse of illness had depressed me much. Both did me good, especially the letter. I have only one fault to find with your expressions of friendship: they make me ashamed, because they seem to imply that you think better of me than I merit. I believe you are prone to think too highly of your fellow-creatures in general — to see too exclusively the good points of those for whom you have a regard. Disappointment must be the inevitable result of this habit. Believe all men, and women too, to be dust and ashes — a spark of the divinity now and then kindling in the dull heap — that is all. When I looked on the noble face and forehead of my dead brother (nature had favoured him with a fairer outside, as well as a finer constitution, than his sisters) and asked myself what had made him go ever wrong, tend ever downwards, when he had so many gifts to induce to, and aid in, an upward course, I seemed to receive an oppressive revelation of the feebleness of humanity — of the inadequacy of even genius to lead to true greatness if unaided by religion and principle. In the value, or even the reality, of these two things he would never believe till within a few days of his end; and then all at once he seemed to open his heart to a conviction of their existence and worth. The remembrance of this strange change now comforts my poor father greatly. I myself, with painful, mournful joy, heard him praying softly in his dying moments; and to the last prayer which my father offered up at his bedside he added, "Amen." How unusual that word appeared from his lips, of course you, who did not know him, cannot conceive. Akin to this alteration was that in his feelings towards his relations — all the bitterness seemed gone.

'When the struggle was over, and a marble calm began to succeed the last dread agony, I felt, as I had never felt before, that there was peace and forgiveness for him in Heaven. All his errors — to speak plainly, all his vices — seemed nothing to me in that moment: every wrong he had done, every pain he had caused, vanished; his sufferings only were remembered; the wrench to the natural affections only was left. If man can thus experience total oblivion of his fellow's imperfections, how much more can the Eternal Being, who made man, forgive His creature?

'Had his sins been scarlet in their dye, I believe now they are white as wool. He is at rest, and that comforts us all.

Long before he quitted this world, life had no happiness for him.

' " Blackwood's " mention of " Jane Eyre " gratified me much, and will gratify me more, I daresay, when the ferment of other feelings than that of literary ambition shall have a little subsided in my mind.

'The doctor has told me I must not expect too rapid a restoration to health; but to-day I certainly feel better. I am thankful to say my father has hitherto stood the storm well; and so have my *dear* sisters, to whose untiring care and kindness I am chiefly indebted for my present state of convalescence. — Believe me, my dear sir, yours faithfully,

' C. Brontë.'

The last letter in order of date that I have concerning Branwell is addressed to Ellen Nussey's sister: —

TO MISS MERCY NUSSEY.

'Haworth, October 25, 1848.

' My dear Miss Nussey, — Accept my sincere thanks for your kind letter. The event to which you allude came upon us with startling suddenness, and was a severe shock to us all. My poor brother has long had a shaken constitution, and during the summer his appetite had been diminished, and he had seemed weaker, but neither we, nor himself, nor any medical man who was consulted on the case, thought it one of immediate danger. He was out of doors two days before death, and was only confined to bed one single day.

'I thank you for your kind sympathy. Many, under the circumstances, would think our loss rather a relief than otherwise; in truth, we must acknowledge, in all humility and gratitude, that God has greatly tempered judgment with mercy. But yet, as you doubtless know from experience, the last earthly separation cannot take place between near relatives without the keenest pangs on the part of the survivors. Every wrong and sin is forgotten then, pity and grief share the heart and the memory between them. Yet we are not without comfort in our

CHARLOTTE BRONTË

affliction. A most propitious change marked the few last days of poor Branwell's life : his demeanour, his language, his sentiments were all singularly altered and softened. This change could not be owing to the fear of death, for till within half-an-hour of his decease he seemed unconscious of danger. In God's hands we leave him : He sees not as man sees.

'Papa, I am thankful to say, has borne the event pretty well. His distress was great at first — to lose an only son is no ordinary trial, but his physical strength has not hitherto failed him, and he has now in a great measure recovered his mental composure ; my dear sisters are pretty well also. Unfortunately, illness attacked me at the crisis when strength was most needed. I bore up for a day or two, hoping to be better, but got worse. Fever, sickness, total loss of appetite, and internal pain were the symptoms. The doctor pronounced it to be bilious fever, but I think it must have been in a mitigated form ; it yielded to medicine and care in a few days. I was only confined to my bed a week, and am, I trust, nearly well now. I felt it a grievous thing to be incapacitated from action and effort at a time when action and effort were most called for. The past month seems an overclouded period in my life.

'Give my best love to Mrs. Nussey and your sister, and — Believe me, my dear Miss Nussey, yours sincerely,   C. BRONTË.'

My unhappy brother never knew what his sisters had done in literature — he was not aware that they had ever published a line.

Who that reads these words addressed to Mr. Williams can for a moment imagine that Charlotte is speaking other than the truth ? And yet we have Mr. Grundy writing:

'Patrick Brontë declared to me that he wrote a great portion of " Wuthering Heights " himself.'

And Mr. George Searle Phillips,[1] with more vivid imagination, describes Branwell holding forth to his friends in the

[1] In the 'Mirror,' 1872. Mr. Phillips, under the pseudonym of ' January Searle,' wrote a readable biography of Wordsworth.

parlour of the 'Black Bull' at Haworth, upon the genius of his sisters, and upon the respective merits of 'Jane Eyre' and other works.   Mr. Leyland is even so foolish as to compare Branwell's poetry with Emily's, to the advantage of the former — which makes further comment impossible. 'My unhappy brother never knew what his sisters had done in literature '— these words of Charlotte's may be taken as final for all who had any doubts concerning the authorship of 'Wuthering Heights.'

CHAPTER VI.

EMILY JANE BRONTË.

EMILY BRONTË is the sphinx of our modern literature. She came into being in the family of an obscure clergyman, and she went out of it at twenty-nine years of age without leaving behind her one single significant record which was any key to her character or to her mode of thought, save only the one famous novel, 'Wuthering Heights,' and a few poems — some three or four of which will live in our poetic anthologies for ever. And she made no single friend other than her sister Anne. With Anne she must have corresponded during the two or three periods of her life when she was separated from that much loved sister; and we may be sure that the correspondence was of a singularly affectionate character. Charlotte, who never came very near to her in thought or sympathy, although she loved her younger sister so deeply, addressed her in one letter as 'mine own bonnie love'; and it is certain that her own letters to her two sisters, and particularly to Anne, must have been peculiarly tender and in no way lacking in abundant self-revelation. When Emily and Anne had both gone to the grave, Charlotte, it is probable, carefully destroyed every scrap of their correspondence, and, indeed, of their literary effects; and thus it is that, apart from her books and literary fragments, we know Emily only by two formal letters to her sister's friend. Beyond these there is not one scrap of information as to Emily's outlook upon life. In infancy she went with Charlotte to

Cowan Bridge, and was described by the governess as 'a pretty little thing.' In girlhood she went to Miss Wooler's school at Roe Head; but there, unlike Charlotte, she made no friends. She and Anne were inseparable when at home, but of what they said to one another there is no record. The sisters must have differed in many ways. Anne, gentle and persuasive, grew up like Charlotte, devoted to the Christianity of her father and mother, and entirely in harmony with all the conditions of a parsonage. It is impossible to think that the author of 'The Old Stoic' and 'Last Lines' was equally attached to the creeds of the churches; but what Emily thought on religious subjects the world will never know. Mrs. Gaskell put to Miss Nussey this very question: 'What was Emily's religion?' But Emily was the last person in the world to have spoken to the most friendly of visitors about so sacred a theme. For a short time, as we know, Emily was in a school at Law Hill near Halifax — a Miss Patchet's.[1] She was, for a still longer period, at the Héger Pensionnat at Brussels. Mrs. Gaskell's business was to write the life of Charlotte Brontë and not of her sister Emily; and as a result there is little enough of Emily in Mrs. Gaskell's book — no record of the Halifax and Brussels life as seen through Emily's eyes. Time, however, has brought its revenge. The cult which started with Mr. Sydney Dobell, and found poetic expression in Mr. Matthew Arnold's fine lines on her,

'Whose soul
Knew no fellow for might,
Passion, vehemence, grief,
Daring, since Byron died,'[2]

[1] Charlotte writes from Dewsbury Moor (October 2, 1836): — 'My sister Emily is gone into a situation as teacher in a large school of near forty pupils, near Halifax. I have had one letter from her since her departure — it gives an appalling account of her duties. Hard labour from six in the morning until near eleven at night, with only one half-hour of exercise between. This is slavery. I fear she will never stand it.' — *Mrs. Gaskell's Life.*

[2] 'Haworth Churchyard, April 1855,' by Matthew Arnold. Macmillan & Co.

culminated in an enthusiastic eulogy by Mr. Swinburne, who placed her in the very forefront of English women of genius.

We have said that Emily Brontë is a sphinx whose riddle no amount of research will enable us to read; and this chapter, it may be admitted, adds but little to the longed-for knowledge of an interesting personality. One scrap of Emily's handwriting, of a personal character, has indeed come to me — overlooked, I doubt not, by Charlotte when she burnt her sister's effects. I have before me a little tin box about two inches long, which one day last year Mr. Nicholls turned out from the bottom of a desk. It is of a kind in which one might keep pins or beads, certainly of no value whatever apart from its associations. Within were four little pieces of paper neatly folded to the size of a sixpence. These papers were covered with handwriting, two of them by Emily, and two by Anne Brontë. They revealed a pleasant if eccentric arrangement on the part of the sisters, which appears to have been settled upon even after they had passed their twentieth year. They had agreed to write a kind of reminiscence every four years, to be opened by Emily on her birthday. The papers, however, tell their own story, and I give first the two which were written in 1841. Emily writes at Haworth, and Anne from her situation as governess to Mr. Robinson's children at Thorp Green. At this time, at any rate, Emily was fairly happy and in excellent health; and although it is five years from the publication of the volume of poems, she is full of literary projects, as is also her sister Anne. The 'Gondaland Chronicles,' to which reference is made, must remain a mystery for us. They were doubtless destroyed, with abundant other memorials of Emily, by the heart-broken sister who survived her. We have plentiful material in the way of childish effort by Charlotte and by Branwell, but there is not one scrap in the early handwriting of Emily and Anne. This chapter would have been more interesting if

146

only one possessed 'Solala Vernon's Life' by Anne Brontë, or the 'Gondaland Chronicles' by Emily!

'A PAPER to be opened
when Anne is
25 years old,
or my next birthday after
if
all be well.
EMILY JANE BRONTË. July 30, 1841.

'It is Friday evening, near 9 o'clock — wild rainy weather. I am seated in the dining-room, having just concluded tidying our desk boxes, writing this document. Papa is in the parlour — aunt upstairs in her room. She has been reading "Blackwood's Magazine" to papa. Victoria and Adelaide are ensconced in the peat-house. Keeper is in the kitchen — Hero in his cage. We are all stout and hearty, as I hope is the case with Charlotte, Branwell, and Anne, of whom the first is at John White, Esq., Upperwood House, Rawdon ; the second is at Luddenden Foot ; and the third is, I believe, at Scarborough, enditing perhaps a paper corresponding to this.

'A scheme is at present in agitation for setting us up in a school of our own ; as yet nothing is determined, but I hope and trust it may go on and prosper and answer our highest expectations. This day four years I wonder whether we shall still be dragging on in our present condition or established to our hearts' content. Time will show.

'I guess that at the time appointed for the opening of this paper we, *i. e.* Charlotte, Anne, and I, shall be all merrily seated in our own sitting-room in some pleasant and flourishing seminary, having just gathered in for the midsummer ladyday. Our debts will be paid off, and we shall have cash in hand to a considerable amount. Papa, aunt, and Branwell will either have been or be coming to visit us. It will be a fine warm summer evening, very different from this bleak look-out, and Anne and I will perchance

147

slip out into the garden for a few minutes to peruse our papers. I hope either this or something better will be the case.

'The Gondaliand are at present in a threatening state, but there is no open rupture as yet. All the princes and princesses of the Royalty are at the Palace of Instruction. I have a good many books on hand, but I am sorry to say that as usual I make small progress with any. However, I have just made a new regularity paper! and I must *verb sap* to do great things. And now I close, sending from far an exhortation of courage, boys! courage, to exiled and harassed Anne, wishing she was here.'

Anne, as I have said, writes from Thorp Green.

'July the 30th, A.D. 1841.

'This is Emily's birthday. She has now completed her 23rd year, and is, I believe at home. Charlotte is a governess in the family of Mr. White. Branwell is a clerk in the railroad station at Luddenden Foot, and I am a governess in the family of Mr. Robinson. I dislike the situation and wish to change it for another. I am now at Scarborough. My pupils are gone to bed and I am hastening to finish this before I follow them.

'We are thinking of setting up a school of our own, but nothing definite is settled about it yet, and we do not know whether we shall be able to or not. I hope we shall. And I wonder what will be our condition and how or where we shall all be on this day four years hence; at which time, if all be well, I shall be 25 years and 6 months old, Emily will be 27 years old, Branwell 28 years and 1 month, and Charlotte 29 years and a quarter. We are now all separate and not likely to meet again for many a weary week, but we are none of us ill that I know of and all are doing something for our own livelihood except Emily, who, however, is as busy as any of us, and in reality earns her food and raiment as much as we do.

'How little know we what we are
How less what we may be!

148

FACSIMILE OF PAGE OF EMILY BRONTE'S DIARY.

'Four years ago I was at school. Since then I have been a governess at Blake Hall, left it, come to Thorp Green, and seen the sea and York Minster. Emily has been a teacher at Miss Patchet's school, and left it. Charlotte has left Miss Wooler's, been a governess at Mrs. Sidgwick's, left her, and gone to Mrs. White's. Branwell has given up painting, been a tutor in Cumberland, left it, and become a clerk on the railroad. Tabby has left us, Martha Brown has come in her place. We have got Keeper, got a sweet little cat and lost it, and also got a hawk. Got a wild goose which has flown away, and three tame ones, one of which has been killed. All these diversities, with many others, are things we did not expect or foresee in the July of 1837. What will the next four years bring forth? Providence only knows. But we ourselves have sustained very little alteration since that time. I have the same faults that I had then, only I have more wisdom and experience, and a little more self-possession than I then enjoyed. How will it be when we open this paper and the one 'Emily has written? I wonder whether the " Gondaliand " will still be flourishing, and what will be their condition. I am now engaged in writing the fourth volume of "Solala Vernon's Life."

'For some time I have looked upon 25 as a sort of era in my existence. It may prove a true presentiment, or it may be only a superstitious fancy ; the latter seems most likely, but time will show.

'Anne Brontë.'

Let us next take up the other two little scraps of paper. They are dated July the 30th, 1845, or Emily's twenty-seventh birthday. Many things have happened, as she says. She has been to Brussels, and she has settled definitely at home again. They are still keenly interested in literature, and we still hear of the Gondals. There is wonderfully little difference in the tone or spirit of the journals. The concluding ' best wishes for this whole house till July the 30th, 1848, and as much longer as may be,' contain no

CHARLOTTE BRONTË

premonition of coming disaster. Yet July 1848 was to find Branwell Brontë on the verge of the grave, and Emily on her deathbed. She died on the 14th of December of that year.

'HAWORTH, Thursday, July 30, 1845.

'My birthday — showery, breezy, cool. I am twenty-seven years old to-day. This morning Anne and I opened the papers we wrote four years since, on my twenty-third birthday. This paper we intend, if all be well, to open on my thirtieth — three years hence, in 1848. Since the 1841 paper the following events have taken place. Our school scheme has been abandoned, and instead Charlotte and I went to Brussels on the 8th of February 1842.

'Branwell left his place at Luddenden Foot. C. and I returned from Brussels, November 8th 1842, in consequence of aunt's death.

'Branwell went to Thorp Green as a tutor, where Anne still continued, January 1843.

'Charlotte returned to Brussels the same month, and, after staying a year, came back again on New Year's Day 1844.

'Anne left her situation at Thorp Green of her own accord, June 1845.

'Anne and I went our first long journey by ourselves together, leaving home on the 30th of June, Monday, sleeping at York, returning to Keighley Tuesday evening, sleeping there and walking home on Wednesday morning. Though the weather was broken we enjoyed ourselves very much, except during a few hours at Bradford. And during our excursion we were, Ronald Macalgin, Henry Angora, Juliet Angusteena, Rosabella Esmaldan, Ella and Julian Egremont, Catharine Navarre, and Cordelia Fitzaphnold, escaping from the palaces of instruction to join the Royalists who are hard driven at present by the victorious Republicans. The Gondals still flourish bright as ever. I am at present writing a work on the First War. Anne has been writing some articles on this, and a book by Henry Sophona. We intend

150

sticking firm by the rascals as long as they delight us, which I am glad to say they do at present. I should have mentioned that last summer the school scheme was revived in full vigour. We had prospectuses printed, despatched letters to all acquaintances imparting our plans, and did our little all; but it was found no go. Now I don't desire a school at all, and none of us have any great longing for it. We have cash enough for our present wants, with a prospect of accumulation. We are all in decent health, only that papa has a complaint in his eyes, and with the exception of B., who, I hope, will be better and do better hereafter. I am quite contented for myself: not as idle as formerly, altogether as hearty, and having learnt to make the most of the present and long for the future with the fidgetiness that I cannot do all I wish; seldom or ever troubled with nothing to do, and merely desiring that everybody could be as comfortable as myself and as undesponding, and then we should have a very tolerable world of it.

'By mistake I find we have opened the paper on the 31st instead of the 30th. Yesterday was much such a day as this, but the morning was divine.

'Tabby, who was gone in our last paper, is come back, and has lived with us two years and a half, and is in good health. Martha, who also departed, is here too. We have got Flossy; got and lost Tiger; lost the hawk Hero, which, with the geese, was given away, and is doubtless dead, for when I came back from Brussels I inquired on all hands and could hear nothing of him. Tiger died early last year. Keeper and Flossy are well, also the canary acquired four years since. We are now all at home, and likely to be there some time. Branwell went to Liverpool on Tuesday to stay a week. Tabby has just been teasing me to turn as formerly to "Pilloputate." Anne and I should have picked the black currants if it had been fine and sunshiny. I must hurry off now to my turning and ironing. I have plenty of work on hand, and writing, and am altogether full of business. With best wishes for the whole house till 1848, July 30th, and as much longer as may be, —I conclude.   EMILY BRONTË.'

151

Finally, I give Anne's last fragment, concerning which silence is essential. Interpretation of most of the references would be mere guess-work.

'Thursday, July the 31st, 1845. Yesterday was Emily's birthday, and the time when we should have opened our 1845 paper, but by mistake we opened it to-day instead. How many things have happened since it was written — some pleasant, some far otherwise. Yet I was then at Thorp Green, and now I am only just escaped from it. I was wishing to leave it then, and if I had known that I had four years longer to stay how wretched I should have been; but during my stay I have had some very unpleasant and undreamt-of experience of human nature. Others have seen more changes. Charlotte has left Mr. White's and been twice to Brussels, where she stayed each time nearly a year. Emily has been there too, and stayed nearly a year. Branwell has left Luddenden Foot, and been a tutor at Thorp Green, and had much tribulation and ill health. He was very ill on Thursday, but he went with John Brown to Liverpool, where he now is, I suppose; and we hope he will be better and do better in future. This is a dismal, cloudy, wet evening. We have had so far a very cold wet summer. Charlotte has lately been to Hathersage, in Derbyshire, on a visit of three weeks to Ellen Nussey. She is now sitting sewing in the dining-room. Emily is ironing upstairs. I am sitting in the dining-room in the rocking-chair before the fire with my feet on the fender. Papa is in the parlour. Tabby and Martha are, I think, in the kitchen. Keeper and Flossy are, I do not know where. Little Dick is hopping in his cage. When the last paper was written we were thinking of setting up a school. The scheme has been dropt, and long after taken up again and dropt again because we could not get pupils. Charlotte is thinking about getting another situation. She wishes to go to Paris. Will she go? She has let Flossy in, by-the-bye, and he is now lying on the sofa. Emily is engaged in writing the Emperor Julius's life. She has read some of it, and I want very much to hear the rest. She is writing some poetry, too. I wonder what it is about? I have begun the third volume of " Passages in the Life of an Individual." I

See I can't tell if ever I can till
writing a word on the first wine Anne but
by every Stephen... on all order but
she could be long or way ought to which
I am glad to my stay do it present. I should
have mentioned last Summer she still
school... resided in full vigour... and you
... retains painful disposition times... in all opinions
... our plan but did... little she but
it... find... of... I go... now I... desire... a short
if we have can carry the one present want
... pursuit of accumulation — we am still
direct health — only one pipe... in... ...is
... eye and... the last exception of B who
... will be better and... better... health
I am quite certain... from myself — ... while
... formally straitened... trusty and having lived
... make the most of one present and by
... to... extravagant on our trusted
count as all I... slidden our own trials
with waiting to disease and mostly delaying
but certainly... is... comfortable way
... and so indifferent — a tone... we shall
and a very filiastic world of it —

By notice I find we have opened the year
on the 30th (September of... 30th yesterday)
... much such a day as this but the more
by it is divine —

Totally who was June is our last piece
is come to be and I... lived with us — two
... and... I built and it is good health — thank
we're all slipped... I hope to... we have got
Flossy got and lost Tiger — lost the Hawk Nero
which got and lost two... hang away and

wish I had finished it. This afternoon I began to set about making my grey figured silk frock that was dyed at Keighley. What sort of a hand shall I make of it? E. and I have a great deal of work to do. When shall we sensibly diminish it? I want to get a habit of early rising. Shall I succeed? We have not yet finished our "Gondal Chronicles" that we began three years and a half ago. When will they be done? The Gondals are at present in a sad state. The Republicans are uppermost, but the Royalists are not quite overcome. The young sovereigns, with their brothers and sisters, are still at the Palace of Instruction. The Unique Society, above half a year ago, were wrecked on a desert island as they were returning from Gaul. They are still there, but we have not played at them much yet. The Gondals in general are not in first-rate playing condition. Will they improve? I wonder how we shall all be and where and how situated on the thirtieth of July 1848, when, if we are all alive, Emily will be just 30. I shall be in my 29th year, and Charlotte in her 33rd, and Branwell in his 32nd; and what changes shall we have seen and known; and shall we be much changed ourselves? I hope not, for the worst at least. I for my part cannot well be *flatter* or older in mind than I am now. Hoping for the best, I conclude.

'ANNE BRONTË.'

Exactly fifty years were to elapse before these pieces of writing saw the light. The interest which must always centre in Emily Brontë amply justifies my publishing a fragment in fac-simile; and it has the greater moment on account of the rough drawing which Emily has made of herself and of her dog Keeper. Emily's taste for drawing is a pathetic element in her always pathetic life. I have seen a number of her sketches. There is one in the possession of Mr. Nicholls of Keeper and Flossy, the former the bull-dog which followed her to the grave, the latter a little King Charlie which one of the Miss Robinsons gave to Anne. The sketch, however, like most of Emily's drawings, is technically full of errors. She was not a born artist, and possibly she had not the best opportunities of becoming one by hard work. Another drawing before me is of the hawk mentioned in the above fragment; and yet another is of the dog Growler, a predecessor of Keeper, which is not, however, mentioned in the correspondence. Upon Emily Brontë, the poet, I do not propose to write here. She left behind her, and Charlotte preserved, a manuscript volume containing the whole of the poems in the two collections of her verse, and there are other poems not yet published. Here, for example, are some verses in which the Gondals make a slight reappearance.

'MAY 21, 1838.

GLENEDEN'S DREAM.

' Tell me, whether is it winter?
Say how long my sleep has been.
Have the woods I left so lovely
Lost their robes of tender green?

'Is the morning slow in coming?
Is the night time loth to go?
Tell me, are the dreary mountains
Drearier still with drifted snow?

' " Captive, since thou sawest the forest,
All its leaves have died away,
And another March has woven
Garlands for another May.

' " Ice has barred the Arctic waters;
Soft Southern winds have set it free;
And once more to deep green valley
Golden flowers might welcome thee."

' Watcher in this lonely prison,
Shut from joy and kindly air,
Heaven descending in a vision
Taught my soul to do and bear.

154

AND HER CIRCLE

'It was night, a night of winter,
I lay on the dungeon floor,
And all other sounds were silent —
All, except the river's roar.

'Over Death and Desolation,
Fireless hearths, and lifeless homes;
Over orphans' heartsick sorrows,
Patriot fathers' bloody tombs;

'Over friends, that my arms never
Might embrace in love again;
Memory ponderous until madness
Struck its poniard in my brain.

'Deepest slumbers followed raving,
Yet, methought, I brooded still;
Still I saw my country bleeding,
Dying for a Tyrant's will.

'Not because my bliss was blasted,
Burned within the avenging flame;
Not because my scattered kindred
Died in woe or lived in shame.

'God doth know I would have given
Every bosom dear to me,
Could that sacrifice have purchased
Tortured Gondal's liberty!

'But that at Ambition's bidding
All her cherished hopes should wane,
That her noblest sons should muster,
Strive and fight and fall in vain.

'Hut and castle, hall and cottage,
  Roofless, crumbling to the ground,
  Mighty Heaven, a glad Avenger
  Thy eternal Justice found.

'Yes, the arm that once would shudder
  Even to grieve a wounded deer,
  I beheld it, unrelenting,
  Clothe in blood its sovereign's prayer.

'Glorious Dream! I saw the city
  Blazing in Imperial shine,
  And among adoring thousands
  Stood a man of form divine.

'None need point the princely victim —
  Now he smiles with royal pride!
  Now his glance is bright as lightning,
  Now the knife is in his side!

'Ah! I saw how death could darken,
  Darken that triumphant eye!
  His red heart's blood drenched my dagger;
  My ear drank his dying sigh!

'Shadows come! what means this midnight?
  O my God, I know it all!
  Know the fever dream is over,
  Unavenged the Avengers fall!'

There are, indeed, a few fragments, all written in that
tiny handwriting which the girls affected, and bearing
various dates from 1833 to 1840. A new edition of Emily's
poems, will, by virtue of these verses, have a singular interest
for her admirers. With all her gifts as a poet, however,
it is by 'Wuthering Heights' that Emily Brontë is best

known to the world; and the weirdness and force of that book suggest an inquiry concerning the influences which produced it. Dr. Wright, in his entertaining book, 'The Brontës in Ireland,' recounts the story of Patrick Brontë's origin, and insists that it was in listening to her father's anecdotes of his own Irish experiences that Emily obtained the weird material of 'Wuthering Heights.' It is not, of course, enough to point out that Dr. Wright's story of the Irish Brontës is full of contradictions. A number of tales picked up at random from an illiterate peasantry might very well abound in inconsistencies, and yet contain some measure of truth. But nothing in Dr. Wright's narrative is confirmed, save only the fact that Patrick Brontë continued throughout his life in some slight measure of correspondence with his brothers and sisters — a fact rendered sufficiently evident by a perusal of his will. Dr. Wright tells of many visits to Ireland in order to trace the Brontë traditions to their source ; and yet he had not — in his first edition — marked the elementary fact that the registry of births in County Down records the existence of innumerable Bruntys and not a single Brontë. Dr. Wright probably made his inquiries with the stories of Emily and Charlotte well in mind. He sought for similar traditions, and the quick-witted Irish peasantry gave him all that he wanted. They served up and embellished the current traditions of the neighbourhood for his benefit, as the peasantry do everywhere for folklore enthusiasts. Charlotte Brontë's uncle Hugh, we are told, read the 'Quarterly Review' article upon 'Jane Eyre,' and, armed with a shillelagh, came to England, in order to wreak vengeance upon the writer of the bitter attack. He landed at Liverpool, walked from Liverpool to Haworth, saw his nieces, who 'gathered round him,' and listened to his account of his mission. He then went to London and made abundant inquiries — but why pursue this ludicrous story further ? In the first place, the

'Quarterly Review' article was published in December 1848
— after Emily was dead, and while Anne was dying. Very
soon after the review appeared Charlotte was informed of its
authorship, and references to Miss Rigby and the 'Quarterly'
are found more than once in her correspondence with Mr.
Williams.[1]

This is a lengthy digression from the story of Emily's life,
but it is of moment to discover whether there is any evidence of influences other than those which her Yorkshire
home afforded. I have discussed the matter with Miss
Ellen Nussey, and with Mr. Nicholls. Miss Nussey never,
in all her visits to Haworth, heard a single reference to the
Irish legends related by Dr. Wright, and firmly believes
them to be mythical. Mr. Nicholls, during the six years
that he lived alone at the parsonage with his father-in-law,
never heard one single word from Mr. Brontë — who was by
no means disposed to reticence — about these stories, and is
also of opinion that they are purely legendary.

It has been suggested that Emily would have been guilty
almost of a crime to have based the more sordid part of her
narrative upon her brother's transgressions. This is sheer
nonsense. She wrote 'Wuthering Heights' because she was
impelled thereto, and the book, with all its morbid force
and fire, will remain, for all time, as a monument of the
most striking genius that nineteenth century womanhood
has given us. It was partly her life in Yorkshire — the local
colour was mainly derived from her brief experience as a
governess at Halifax — but it was partly, also, the German
fiction which she had devoured during the Brussels period,
that inspired 'Wuthering Heights.'

Here, however, are glimpses of Emily Brontë on a more
human side.

[1] See chap. xiii., page 346.

TO MISS ELLEN NUSSEY.

'MARCH 25, 1844.

'DEAR NELL, — I got home safely, and was not too much tired on arriving at Haworth. I feel rather better to-day than I have been, and in time I hope to regain more strength. I found Emily and Papa well, and a letter from Branwell intimating that he and Anne are pretty well too. Emily is much obliged to you for the flower seeds. She wishes to know if the Sicilian pea and crimson corn-flower are hardy flowers, or if they are delicate, and should be sown in warm and sheltered situations? Tell me also if you went to Mrs. John Swain's on Friday, and if you enjoyed yourself; talk to me, in short, as you would do if we were together. Good-morning, dear Nell; I will say no more to you at present. C. BRONTË.'

TO MISS ELLEN NUSSEY.

'APRIL 5, 1844.

'DEAR NELL, — We were all very glad to get your letter this morning. *We*, I say, as both Papa and Emily were anxious to hear of the safe arrival of yourself and the little *varmint*.[1] As you conjecture, Emily and I set-to to shirt-making the very day after you left, and we have stuck to it pretty closely ever since. We miss your society at least as much as you miss ours, depend upon it; would that you were within calling distance. Be sure you write to me. I shall expect another letter on Thursday — don't disappoint me. Best regards to your mother and sisters. — Yours, somewhat irritated, C. BRONTË.'

Earlier than this Emily had herself addressed a letter to Miss Nussey, and, indeed, the two letters from Emily Brontë to Ellen Nussey which I print here are, I imagine, the only letters of Emily's in existence. Mr. Nicholls informs me that he has never seen a letter in Emily's handwriting. The

---

[1] A dog, referred to elsewhere as Flossie, junior.

CHARLOTTE BRONTË

following letter is written during Charlotte's second stay in Brussels, and at a time when Ellen Nussey contemplated joining her there — a project never carried out.

TO MISS ELLEN NUSSEY.

'MAY 12, 1843.

'DEAR MISS NUSSEY, — I should be wanting in common civility if I did not thank you for your kindness in letting me know of an opportunity to send postage free.

'I have written as you directed, though if next Tuesday means to-morrow I fear it will be too late. Charlotte has never mentioned a word about coming home. If you would go over for half-a-year, perhaps you might be able to bring her back with you — otherwise, she might vegetate there till the age of Methuselah for mere lack of courage to face the voyage.

'All here are in good health; so was Anne according to her last account. The holidays will be here in a week or two, and then, if she be willing, I will get her to write you a proper letter, a feat that I have never performed. — With love and good wishes,
'EMILY J. BRONTË.'

The next letter is written at the time that Charlotte is staying with her friend at Mr. Henry Nussey's house at Hathersage in Derbyshire.

TO MISS ELLEN NUSSEY.

'HAWORTH, February 9, 1846.

'DEAR MISS NUSSEY, — I fancy this note will be too late to decide one way or other with respect to Charlotte's stay. Yours only came this morning (Wednesday), and unless mine travels faster you will not receive it till Friday. Papa, of course, misses Charlotte, and will be glad to have her back. Anne and I ditto; but as she goes from home so seldom, you may keep her a day or two longer, if your eloquence is equal to the task of persuading

her — that is, if she still be with you when you get this permission. Love from Anne. — Yours truly,

'EMILY J. BRONTË.'

'Wuthering Heights' and 'Agnes Grey,' by 'Ellis and
Acton Bell,' were published together in three volumes in
1847. The former novel occupied two volumes, and the
latter one. By a strange freak of publishing, the book was
issued as 'Wuthering Heights,' vol. I. and II., and 'Agnes
Grey,' vol. III., in deference, it must be supposed, to the
passion for the three volume novel. Charlotte refers to the
publication in the next letter, which contained as inclosure
the second preface to 'Jane Eyre' — the preface actually
published.[1] An earlier preface, entitled 'A Word to the
"Quarterly,"' was cancelled.

TO W. S. WILLIAMS.

'DECEMBER 21, 1847.

'DEAR SIR, — I am, for my own part, dissatisfied with the
preface I sent — I fear it savours of flippancy. If you see no
objection I should prefer substituting the inclosed. It is rather
more lengthy, but it expresses something I have long wished to
express.

'Mr. Smith is kind indeed to think of sending me "The Jar of
Honey." When I receive the book I will write to him. I cannot
thank you sufficiently for your letters, and I can give you but
a faint idea of the pleasure they afford me; they seem to
introduce such light and life to the torpid retirement where
we live like dormice. But, understand this distinctly, you
must never write to me except when you have both leisure
and inclination. I know your time is too fully occupied and too
valuable to be often at the service of any one individual.

'You are not far wrong in your judgment respecting "Wuthering
Heights" and "Agnes Grey." Ellis has a strong, original mind,

[1] It was sent to Mr. Williams on six half-sheets of note-paper and was
preserved by him.

CHARLOTTE BRONTË

full of strange though sombre power. When he writes poetry that power speaks in language at once condensed, elaborated, and refined, but in prose it breaks forth in scenes which shock more than they attract. Ellis will improve, however, because he knows his defects. "Agnes Grey" is the mirror of the mind of the writer. The orthography and punctuation of the books are mortifying to a degree : almost all the errors that were corrected in the proof-sheets appear intact in what should have been the fair copies. If Mr. Newby always does business in this way, few authors would like to have him for their publisher a second time. — Believe me, dear sir, yours respectfully,   C. BELL.'

When 'Jane Eyre' was performed at a London Theatre — and it has been more than once adapted for the stage, and performed many hundreds of times in England and America — Charlotte Brontë wrote to her friend Mr. Williams as follows : —

TO W. S. WILLIAMS.

'FEBRUARY 5, 1848.

'DEAR SIR, — A representation of "Jane Eyre" at a minor theatre would no doubt be a rather afflicting spectacle to the author of that work. I suppose all would be wofully exaggerated and painfully vulgarised by the actors and actresses on such a stage. What, I cannot help asking myself, would they make of Mr. Rochester? And the picture my fancy conjures up by way of reply is a somewhat humiliating one. What would they make of Jane Eyre? I see something very pert and very affected as an answer to that query.

'Still, were it in my power, I should certainly make a point of being myself a witness of the exhibition. Could I go quietly and alone, I undoubtedly should go ; I should endeavour to endure both rant and whine, strut and grimace, for the sake of the useful observations to be collected in such a scene.

'As to whether I wish *you* to go, that is another question. I am afraid I have hardly fortitude enough really to wish it. One

162

AND HER CIRCLE

can endure being disgusted with one's own work, but that a friend should share the repugnance is unpleasant. Still, I know it would interest me to hear both your account of the exhibition and any ideas which the effect of the various parts on the spectators might suggest to you. In short, I should like to know what you would think, and to hear what you would say on the subject. But you must not go merely to satisfy my curiosity ; you must do as you think proper. Whatever you decide on will content me : if you do *not* go, you will be spared a vulgarising impression of the book ; if you *do* go, I shall perhaps gain a little information — either alternative has its advantage.[1]

'I am glad to hear that the second edition is selling, for the sake of Messrs. Smith & Elder. I rather feared it would remain on hand, and occasion loss. "Wuthering Heights" it appears is selling too, and consequently Mr. Newby is getting into marvellously good tune with his authors. — I remain, my dear sir, yours faithfully,   CURRER BELL.'

I print the above letter here because of its sequel, which has something to say of Ellis — of Emily Brontë.

[1] Although 'Jane Eyre' has been dramatised by several hands, the play has never been as popular as one might suppose from a story of such thrilling incident. I can find no trace of the particular version which is referred to in this letter, but in the next year the novel was dramatised by John Brougham, the actor and dramatist, and produced in New York on March 26, 1849. Brougham is rather an interesting figure. An Irishman by birth, he had a chequered experience of every phase of theatrical life both in London and New York. It was he who adapted 'The Queen's Motto' and 'Lady Audley's Secret,' and he collaborated with Dion Boucicault in 'London Assurance.' In 1849 he seems to have been managing Niblo's Garden in New York, and in the following year the Lyceum Theatre in Broadway. Miss Wemyss took the title rôle in 'Jane Eyre,' J. Gilbert was Rochester, and Mrs. J. Gilbert was Lady Ingram ; and though the play proved but only moderately successful, it was revived in 1856 at Laura Keene's Varieties at New York, with Laura Keene as Jane Eyre. This version has been published by Samuel French, and is also in Dick's 'Penny Plays.' Divided into five Acts and twelve Scenes, Brougham starts the story at Lowood Academy. The second Act introduces us to Rochester's house, and the curtain descends in the fourth as Jane announces that the house is in flames. At the end of the fifth, Brougham reproduced *verbatim* much of the conversation of the dialogue between Rochester

163

CHARLOTTE BRONTË

TO W. S. WILLIAMS.

'FEBRUARY 15, 1848.

'DEAR SIR, — Your letter, as you may fancy, has given me something to think about. It has presented to my mind a curious picture, for the description you give is so vivid, I seem to realise it all. I wanted information and I have got it. You have raised the veil from a corner of your great world — your London — and have shown me a glimpse of what I might call loathsome, but which I prefer calling *strange*. Such, then, is a sample of what amuses the metropolitan populace! Such is a view of one of their haunts!

'Did I not say that I would have gone to this theatre and witnessed this exhibition if it had been in my power? What absurdities people utter when they speak of they know not what!

'You must try now to forget entirely what you saw.

'As to my next book, I suppose it will grow to maturity in

and Jane. Perhaps the best-known dramatisation of the novel was that by the late W. G. Wills, who divided the story into four Acts. His play was produced on Saturday, December 23, 1882, at the Globe Theatre, by Mrs. Bernard-Beere, with the following cast : —

JANE EYRE,	. . . . .	Mrs. Bernard-Beere.
LADY INGRAM,	. . . . .	Miss Carlotta Leclercq.
BLANCHE INGRAM,	. . . .	Miss Kate Bishop.
MARY INGRAM,	. . . . .	Miss Maggie Hunt.
MISS BEECHEY,	. . . . .	Miss Nellie Jordan.
MRS. FAIRFAX,	. . . . .	Miss Alexes Leighton.
GRACE POOL,	. . . . .	Miss Masson.
BERTHA,	. . . . .	Miss D'Almaine.
ADELE,	. . . . . .	Mdlle. Clemence Colle.
MR. ROCHESTER,	. . . .	Mr. Charles Kelly.
LORD DESMOND,	. . . .	Mr. A. M. Denison.
REV. MR. PRICE,	. . . .	Mr. H. E. Russel.
NAT LEE,	. . . . .	Mr. H. H. Cameron.
JAMES,	. . . . . .	Mr. C. Stevens.

Mr. Wills confined the story to Thornfield Hall. One critic described the drama at the time as 'not so much a play as a long conversation.' A few years ago James Willing made a melodrama of 'Jane Eyre' under the title of 'Poor Relations.' This piece was performed at the Standard, Surrey, and Park Theatres. A version of the story, dramatised by Charlotte Birch-Pfeiffer, called 'Die Waise von Lowood,' has been rather popular in Germany.

time, as grass grows or corn ripens; but I cannot force it. It makes slow progress thus far: it is not every day, nor even every week that I can write what is worth reading; but I shall (if not hindered by other matters) be industrious when the humour comes, and in due time I hope to see such a result as I shall not be ashamed to offer you, my publishers, and the public.

'Have you not two classes of writers — the author and the bookmaker? And is not the latter more prolific than the former? Is he not, indeed, wonderfully fertile; but does the public, or the publisher even, make much account of his productions? Do not both tire of him in time?

'Is it not because authors aim at a style of living better suited to merchants, professed gain-seekers, that they are often compelled to degenerate to mere bookmakers, and to find the great stimulus of their pen in the necessity of earning money? If they were not ashamed to be frugal, might they not be more independent?

'I should much — very much — like to take that quiet view of the "great world" you allude to, but I have as yet won no right to give myself such a treat :. it must be for some future day — when, I don't know. Ellis, I imagine, would soon turn aside from the spectacle in disgust. I do not think he admits it as his creed that "the proper study of mankind is man" — at least not the artificial man of cities. In some points I consider Ellis somewhat of a theorist: now and then he broaches ideas which strike my sense as much more daring and original than practical; his reason may be in advance of mine, but certainly it often travels a different road. I should say Ellis will not be seen in his full strength till he is seen as an essayist.

'I return to you the note inclosed under your cover, it is from the editor of the "Berwick Warder"; he wants a copy of "Jane Eyre" to review.

'With renewed thanks for your continued goodness to me, — I remain, my dear sir, yours faithfully,   CURRER BELL.'

A short time afterwards the illness came to Emily from which she died the next year. Branwell died in September

1848, and a month later Charlotte writes with a heart full of misgivings.

TO MISS ELLEN NUSSEY.

'OCTOBER 29, 1848.

' DEAR ELLEN, — I am sorry you should have been uneasy at my not writing to you ere this, but you must remember it is scarcely a week since I received your last, and my life is not so varied that in the interim much should have occurred worthy of mention. You insist that I should write about myself; this puts me in straits, for I really have nothing interesting to say about myself. I think I have now nearly got over the effects of my late illness, and am almost restored to my normal condition of health. I sometimes wish that it was a little higher, but we ought to be content with such blessings as we have, and not pine after those that are out of our reach. I feel much more uneasy about my sisters than myself just now. Emily's cold and cough are very obstinate. I fear she has pain in the chest, and I sometimes catch a shortness in her breathing, when she has moved at all quickly. She looks very, very thin and pale. Her reserved nature occasions me great uneasiness of mind. It is useless to question her — you get no answers. It is still more useless to recommend remedies — they are never adopted. Nor can I shut my eyes to the fact of Anne's great delicacy of constitution. The late sad event has, I feel, made me more apprehensive than common. I cannot help feeling much depressed sometimes. I try to leave all in God's hands; to trust in His goodness; but faith and resignation are difficult to practise under some circumstances. The weather has been most unfavourable for invalids of late : sudden changes of temperature, and cold penetrating winds have been frequent here. Should the atmosphere become settled, perhaps a favourable effect might be produced on the general health, and those harassing coughs and colds be removed. Papa has not quite escaped, but he has, so far, stood it out better than any of us. You must not mention my going to Brookroyd this winter. I could not, and would not, leave home on any account. I am truly sorry to hear of Miss Heald's serious illness, it seems to me she has been for some years out of health now. These things make one *feel* as well as *know*, that this world is not our abiding-place. We should not knit human ties too close, or clasp human affections too fondly. They must leave us, or we must leave them, one day. Good-bye for the present. God restore health and strength to you and to all who need it. — Yours faithfully,   C. Brontë.'

TO W. S. WILLIAMS.

'November 2, 1848.

' My dear Sir, — I have received, since I last wrote to you, two papers, the "Standard of Freedom" and the "Morning Herald," both containing notices of the Poems ; which notices, I hope, will at least serve a useful purpose to Mr. Smith in attracting public attention to the volume. As critiques, I should have thought more of them had they more fully recognised Ellis Bell's merits ; but the lovers of abstract poetry are few in number.

' Your last letter was very welcome, it was written with so kind an intention : you made it so interesting in order to divert my mind. I should have thanked you for it before now, only that I kept waiting for a cheerful day and mood in which to address you, and I grieve to say the shadow which has fallen on our quiet home still lingers round it. I am better, but others are ill now. Papa is not well, my sister Emily has something like a slow inflammation of the lungs, and even our old servant, who has lived with us nearly a quarter of a century, is suffering under serious indisposition.

' I would fain hope that Emily is a little better this evening, but it is difficult to ascertain this. She is a real stoic in illness : she neither seeks nor will accept sympathy. To put any questions, to offer any aid, is to annoy ; she will not yield a step before pain or sickness till forced ; not one of her ordinary avocations will she voluntarily renounce. You must look on and see her do what she is unfit to do, and not dare to say a word — a painful necessity for those to whom her health and existence are as precious as the life in their veins. When she is ill there seems to be no sunshine in the world for me. The tie of sister is near and dear indeed,

and I think a certain harshness in her powerful and peculiar
character only makes me cling to her more. But this is all
family egotism (so to speak) — excuse it, and, above all, never
allude to it, or to the name Emily, when you write to me. I do
not always show your letters, but I never withhold them when
they are inquired after.

'I am sorry I cannot claim for the name Brontë the honour of
being connected with the notice in the "Bradford Observer." That
paper is in the hands of dissenters, and I should think the best
articles are usually written by one or two intelligent dissenting
ministers in the town. Alexander Harris[1] is fortunate in your
encouragement, as Currer Bell once was. He has not forgotten
the first letter he received from you, declining indeed his MS. of
"The Professor," but in terms so different from those in which the
rejections of the other publishers had been expressed — with so
much more sense and kind feeling, it took away the sting of disappointment and kindled new hope in his mind.

'Currer Bell might expostulate with you again about thinking
too well of him, but he refrains; he prefers acknowledging that
the expression of a fellow creature's regard — even if more than
he deserves — does him good: it gives him a sense of content.
Whatever portion of the tribute is unmerited on his part, would,
he is aware, if exposed to the test of daily acquaintance, disperse
like a broken bubble, but he has confidence that a portion, however
minute, of solid friendship would remain behind, and that portion
he reckons amongst his treasures.

'I am glad, by-the-bye, to hear that "Madeline" is come out
at last, and was happy to see a favourable notice of that work
and of "The Three Paths" in the "Morning Herald." I wish
Miss Kavanagh all success.[2]

[1] Alexander Harris wrote 'A Converted Atheist's Testimony to the Truth
of Christianity,' and other now forgotten works.
[2] Julia Kavanagh (1824–1877). Her father, M. P. Kavanagh, wrote 'The
Wanderings of Lucan and Dinah,' a poetical romance, and other works. Miss
Kavanagh was born at Thurles and died at Nice. Her first book, 'The
Three Paths,' a tale for children, was published in 1847. 'Madeline,' a story
founded on the life of a peasant girl of Auvergne, in 1848. 'Women in France
during the Eighteenth Century' appeared in 1850, 'Nathalie' the same year.

'Trusting that Mrs. Williams's health continues strong, and that your own and that of all your children is satisfactory, for without health there is little comfort, — I am, my dear sir, yours sincerely, C. BRONTË.'

The next letter gives perhaps the most interesting glimpse of Emily that has been afforded us.

TO W. S. WILLIAMS.

'NOVEMBER 22, 1848.

'MY DEAR SIR, — I put your most friendly letter into Emily's hands as soon as I had myself perused it, taking care, however, not to say a word in favour of homœopathy — that would not have answered. It is best usually to leave her to form her own judgment, and *especially* not to advocate the side you wish her to favour; if you do, she is sure to lean in the opposite direction, and ten to one will argue herself into non-compliance. Hitherto she has refused medicine, rejected medical advice; no reasoning, no entreaty, has availed to induce her to see a physician. After reading your letter she said, "Mr. Williams's intention was kind and good, but he was under a delusion : Homœopathy was only another form of quackery." Yet she may reconsider this opinion and come to a different conclusion; her second thoughts are often the best.

'The "North American Review" is worth reading; there is no mincing the matter there. What a bad set the Bells must be! What appalling books they write! To-day, as Emily appeared a little easier, I thought the "Review" would amuse her, so I read it aloud to her and Anne. As I sat between them at our quiet but now somewhat melancholy fireside, I studied the two ferocious authors. Ellis, the "man of uncommon talents, but dogged, brutal, and morose," sat leaning back in his easy chair drawing his impeded breath as he best could, and looking, alas! piteously pale and wasted; it is not his wont to laugh, but he smiled half-amused and half in scorn as he listened. Acton

In the succeeding years she wrote innumerable stories and biographical sketches.

CHARLOTTE BRONTË

was sewing, no emotion ever stirs him to loquacity, so he only smiled too, dropping at the same time a single word of calm amazement to hear his character so darkly pourtrayed. I wonder what the reviewer would have thought of his own sagacity could he have beheld the pair as I did. Vainly, too, might he have looked round for the masculine partner in the firm of " Bell & Co." How I laugh in my sleeve when I read the solemn assertions that " Jane Eyre " was written in partnership, and that it " bears the marks of more than one mind and one sex."

'The wise critics would certainly sink a degree in their own estimation if they knew that yours or Mr. Smith's was the first masculine hand that touched the ms. of " Jane Eyre," and that till you or he read it no masculine eye had scanned a line of its contents, no masculine ear heard a phrase from its pages. However, the view they take of the matter rather pleases me than otherwise. If they like, I am not unwilling they should think a dozen ladies and gentlemen aided at the compilation of the book. Strange patchwork it must seem to them — this chapter being penned by Mr., and that by Miss or Mrs. Bell; that character or scene being delineated by the husband, that other by the wife! The gentleman, of course, doing the rough work, the lady getting up the finer parts. I admire the idea vastly.

' I have read " Madeline." It is a fine pearl in simple setting. Julia Kavanagh has my esteem; I would rather know her than many far more brilliant personages. Somehow my heart leans more to her than to Eliza Lynn, for instance. Not that I have read either " Amymone " or " Azeth," but I have seen extracts from them which I found it literally impossible to digest. They presented to my imagination Lytton Bulwer in petticoats — an overwhelming vision. By-the-bye, the American critic talks admirable sense about Bulwer — candour obliges me to confess that.

' I must abruptly bid you good-bye for the present. — Yours sincerely,   CURRER BELL.'

TO W. S. WILLIAMS.

'DECEMBER 7, 1848.

'MY DEAR SIR, — I duly received Dr. Curie's work on Homœopathy, and ought to apologise for having forgotten to thank you for it. I will return it when I have given it a more attentive perusal than I have yet had leisure to do. My sister has read it, but as yet she remains unshaken in her former opinion : she will not admit there can be efficacy in such a system. Were I in her place, it appears to me that I should be glad to give it a trial, confident that it can scarcely do harm and might do good.

'I can give no favourable report of Emily's state. My father is very despondent about her. Anne and I cherish hope as well as we can, but her appearance and her symptoms tend to crush that feeling. Yet I argue that the present emaciation, cough, weakness, shortness of breath are the results of inflammation, now, I trust, subsided, and that with time these ailments will gradually leave her. But my father shakes his head and speaks of others of our family once similarly afflicted, for whom he likewise persisted in hoping against hope, and who are now removed where hope and fear fluctuate no more. There were, however, differences between their case and hers — important differences I think. I must cling to the expectation of her recovery, I cannot renounce it.

'Much would I give to have the opinion of a skilful professional man. It is easy, my dear sir, to say there is nothing in medicine, and that physicians are useless, but we naturally wish to procure aid for those we love when we see them suffer, most painful is it to sit still, look on, and do nothing. Would that my sister added to her many great qualities the humble one of tractability ! I have again and again incurred her displeasure by urging the necessity of seeking advice, and I fear I must yet incur it again and again. Let me leave the subject ; I have no right thus to make you a sharer in our sorrow.

'I am indeed surprised that Mr. Newby should say that he is to publish another work by Ellis and Acton Bell. Acton has had quite enough of him. I think I *have* before intimated that that

171

author never more intends to have Mr. Newby for a publisher. Not only does he seem to forget that engagements made should be fulfilled, but by a system of petty and contemptible manœuvring he throws an air of charlatanry over the works of which he has the management. This does not suit the " Bells " : they have their own rude north-country ideas of what is delicate, honourable, and gentlemanlike.

' Newby's conduct in no sort corresponds with these notions ; they have found him — I will not say what they have found him. Two words that would exactly suit him are at my pen point, but I shall not take the trouble to employ them.

' Ellis Bell is at present in no condition to trouble himself with thoughts either of writing or publishing. Should it please Heaven to restore his health and strength, he reserves to himself the right of deciding whether or not Mr. Newby has forfeited every claim to his second work.

' I have not yet read the second number of " Pendennis." The first I thought rich in indication of ease, resource, promise ; but it is not Thackeray's way to develop his full power all at once. " Vanity Fair " began very quietly — it was quiet all through, but the stream as it rolled gathered a resistless volume and force. Such, I doubt not, will be the case with " Pendennis."

' You must forget what I said about Eliza Lynn. She may be the best of human beings, and I am but a narrow-minded fool to express prejudice against a person I have never seen.

' Believe me, my dear sir, in haste, yours sincerely,

'C. BRONTË.'

The next four letters speak for themselves.

TO W. S. WILLIAMS.

'DECEMBER 9, 1848.

' MY DEAR SIR, — Your letter seems to relieve me from a difficulty and to open my way. I know it would be useless to consult Drs. Elliotson or Forbes : my sister would not see the most skilful physician in England if he were brought to her just now, nor would she follow his prescription. With regard to Homœopathy, she has at least admitted that it cannot do much

harm, perhaps if I get the medicines she may consent to try them ;
at any rate, the experiment shall be made.

'Not knowing Dr. Epps's address, I send the inclosed statement
of her case through your hands.[1]

'I deeply feel both your kindness and Mr. Smith's in thus
interesting yourselves in what touches me so nearly. — Believe
me, yours sincerely,   C. BRONTË.'

TO MISS ELLEN NUSSEY.

'DECEMBER 15, 1848.

'MY DEAR ELLEN, — I mentioned your coming here to Emily
as a mere suggestion, with the faint hope that the prospect might
cheer her, as she really esteems you perhaps more than any other

---

[1] It runs thus : —

'DECEMBER 9, 1848.

'The patient, respecting whose case Dr. Epps is consulted, and for whom
his opinion and advice are requested, is a female in her 29th year. A peculiar
reserve of character renders it difficult to draw from her all the symptoms of
her malady, but as far as they can be ascertained they are as follows : —

'Her appetite failed ; she evinced a continual thirst, with a craving for
acids, and required a constant change of beverage. In appearance she grew
rapidly emaciated ; her pulse — the only time she allowed it to be felt — was
found to be 115 per minute. The patient usually appeared worse in the forenoon, she was then frequently exhausted and drowsy ; toward evening she
often seemed better.

'Expectoration accompanies the cough. The shortness of breath is aggravated by the slightest exertion. The patient's sleep is supposed to be
tolerably good at intervals, but disturbed by paroxysms of coughing. Her
resolution to contend against illness being very fixed, she has never consented
to lie in bed for a single day — she sits up from 7 in the morning till 10 at
night. All medical aid she has rejected, insisting that Nature should be left
to take her own course. She has taken no medicine, but occasionally a mild
aperient and Locock's cough wafers, of which she has used about 3 per diem,
and considers their effect rather beneficial. Her diet, which she regulates
herself, is very simple and light.

'The patient has hitherto enjoyed pretty good health, though she has never
looked strong, and the family constitution is not supposed to be robust. Her
temperament is highly nervous. She has been accustomed to a sedentary and
studious life.

'If Dr. Epps can, from what has here been stated, give an opinion on the case
and prescribe a course of treatment, he will greatly oblige the patient's friends.

'Address — Miss Brontë, Parsonage, Haworth, Bradford, Yorks.'

173

person out of this house. I found, however, it would not do ; any, the slightest excitement or putting out of the way is not to be thought of, and indeed I do not think the journey in this unsettled weather, with the walk from Keighley and walk back, at all advisable for yourself. Yet I should have liked to see you, and so would Anne. Emily continues much the same ; yesterday I thought her a little better, but to-day she is not so well. I hope still, for I *must* hope — she is dear to me as life. If I let the faintness of despair reach my heart I shall become worthless. The attack was, I believe, in the first place, inflammation of the lungs ; it ought to have been met promptly in time. She is too intractable. I *do* wish I knew her state and feelings more clearly. The fever is not so high as it was, but the pain in the side, the cough, the emaciation are there still.

'Remember me kindly to all at Brookroyd, and believe me, yours faithfully, C. BRONTË.'

TO MISS ELLEN NUSSEY.

'DECEMBER 21, 1848.

'MY DEAR ELLEN, — Emily suffers no more from pain or weakness now. She will never suffer more in this world. She is gone, after a hard, short conflict. She died on *Tuesday*, the very day I wrote to you. I thought it very possible she might be with us still for weeks, and a few hours afterwards she was in eternity. Yes, there is no Emily in time or on earth now. Yesterday we put her poor, wasted, mortal frame quietly under the church pavement. We are very calm at present. Why should we be otherwise ? The anguish of seeing her suffer is over ; the spectacle of the pains of death is gone by ; the funeral day is past. We feel she is at peace. No need now to tremble for the hard frost and the keen wind. Emily does not feel them. She died in a time of promise. We saw her taken from life in its prime. But it is God's will, and the place where she is gone is better than she has left.'

TO W. S. WILLIAMS.

'DECEMBER 25, 1848.

'MY DEAR SIR, — I will write to you more at length when my heart can find a little rest — now I can only thank you very briefly for your letter, which seemed to me eloquent in its sincerity.

'Emily is nowhere here now, her wasted mortal remains are taken out of the house. We have laid her cherished head under the church aisle beside my mother's, my two sisters' — dead long ago — and my poor, hapless brother's. But a small remnant of the race is left — so my poor father thinks.

'Well, the loss is ours, not hers, and some sad comfort I take, as I hear the wind blow and feel the cutting keenness of the frost, in knowing that the elements bring her no more suffering; their severity cannot reach her grave; her fever is quieted, her restlessness soothed, her deep, hollow cough is hushed for ever; we do not hear it in the night nor listen for it in the morning; we have not the conflict of the strangely strong spirit and the fragile frame before us — relentless conflict — once seen, never to be forgotten. A dreary calm reigns round us, in the midst of which we seek resignation.

'My father and my sister Anne are far from well. As for me, God has hitherto most graciously sustained me; so far I have felt adequate to bear my own burden and even to offer a little help to others. I am not ill; I can get through daily duties, and do something towards keeping hope and energy alive in our mourning household. My father says to me almost hourly, "Charlotte, you must bear up, I shall sink if you fail me"; these words, you can conceive, are a stimulus to nature. The sight, too, of my sister Anne's very still but deep sorrow wakens in me such fear for her that I dare not falter. Somebody *must* cheer the rest.

'So I will not now ask why Emily was torn from us in the fulness of our attachment, rooted up in the prime of her own days, in the promise of her powers; why her existence now lies like a field of green corn trodden down, like a tree in full bearing struck at the root. I will only say, sweet is rest after labour and calm after tempest, and repeat again and again that Emily knows that now. — Yours sincerely,

'C. BRONTË.'

CHARLOTTE BRONTË

And then there are these last pathetic references to the beloved sister.

TO W. S. WILLIAMS.

'MY DEAR SIR, — Untoward circumstances come to me, I think, less painfully than pleasant ones would just now. The lash of the "Quarterly," however severely applied, cannot sting — as its praise probably would not elate me. Currer Bell feels a sorrowful independence of reviews and reviewers ; their approbation might indeed fall like an additional weight on his heart, but their censure has no bitterness for him.

'My sister Anne sends the accompanying answer to the letter received through you the other day ; will you be kind enough to post it. She is not well yet, nor is papa, both are suffering under severe influenza colds. My letters had better be brief at present — they cannot be cheerful. I am, however, still sustained. While looking with dismay on the desolation sickness and death have wrought in our home, I can combine with awe of God's judgments a sense of gratitude for his mercies. Yet life has become very void, and hope has proved a strange traitor ; when I shall again be able to put confidence in her suggestions, I know not : she kept whispering that Emily would not, *could* not die, and where is she now ?   Out of my reach, out of my world — torn from me. — Yours sincerely,   C. BRONTË.'

'MARCH 3, 1849.

'MY DEAR SIR, — Hitherto, I have always forgotten to acknowledge the receipt of the parcel from Cornhill. It came at a time when I could not open it nor think of it ; its contents are still a mystery. I will not taste, till I can enjoy them. I looked at it the other day. It reminded me too sharply of the time when the first parcel arrived last October : Emily was then beginning to be ill — the opening of the parcel and examination of the books cheered her ; their perusal occupied her for many a weary day. The very evening before her last morning dawned I read to her one of Emerson's essays. I read on, till I found

176

she was not listening — I thought to recommence next day. Next day, the first glance at her face told me what would happen before night-fall.   C. BRONTË.'

'NOVEMBER 19, 1849.

'MY DEAR SIR,— I am very sorry to hear that Mr. Taylor's illness has proved so much more serious than was anticipated, but I do hope he is now better. That he should be quite well cannot be as yet expected, for I believe rheumatic fever is a complaint slow to leave the system it has invaded.

'Now that I have almost formed the resolution of coming to London, the thought begins to present itself to me under a pleasant aspect. At first it was sad; it recalled the last time I went and with whom, and to whom I came home, and in what dear companionship I again and again narrated all that had been seen, heard, and uttered in that visit. Emily would never go into any sort of society herself, and whenever I went I could on my return communicate to her a pleasure that suited her, by giving the distinct faithful impression of each scene I had witnessed. When pressed to go, she would sometimes say, " What is the use? Charlotte will bring it all home to me." And indeed I delighted to please her thus. My occupation is gone now.

'I shall come to be lectured. I perceive you are ready with animadversion; you are not at all well satisfied on some points, so I will open my ears to hear, nor will I close my heart against conviction; but I forewarn you, I have my own doctrines, not acquired, but innate, some that I fear cannot be rooted up without tearing away all the soil from which they spring, and leaving only unproductive rock for new seed.

'I have read the " Caxtons," I have looked at " Fanny Hervey." I think I will not write what I think of either — should I see you I will speak it.

'Take a hundred, take a thousand of such works and weigh them in the balance against a page of Thackeray. I hope Mr. Thackeray is recovered.

'The " Sun," the " Morning Herald," and the " Critic " came

177

this morning. None of them express disappointment from "Shirley,"
or on the whole compare her disadvantageously with "Jane." It
strikes me that those worthies — the "Athenæum," "Spectator,"
"Economist," made haste to be first with their notices that they might
give the tone; if so, their manœuvre has not yet quite succeeded.

'The "Critic," our old friend, is a friend still. Why does the
pulse of pain beat in every pleasure? Ellis and Acton Bell are
referred to, and where are they? I will not repine. Faith
whispers they are not in those graves to which imagination turns
— the feeling, thinking, the inspired natures are beyond earth,
in a region more glorious. I believe them blessed. I think, I
will think, my loss has been *their* gain. Does it weary you that
I refer to them? If so, forgive me.— Yours sincerely,

'C. BRONTË.

'Before closing this I glanced over the letter inclosed under
your cover. Did you read it? It is from a lady, not quite an
old maid, but nearly one, she says; no signature or date; a queer,
but good-natured production, it made me half cry, half laugh. I
am sure "Shirley" has been exciting enough for her, and too
exciting. I cannot well reply to the letter since it bears no address,
and I am glad — I should not know what to say. She is not sure
whether I am a gentleman or not, but I fancy she thinks so. Have
you any idea who she is? If I were a gentleman and like my
heroes, she suspects she should fall in love with me. She had
better not. It would be a pity to cause such a waste of sensibility.
You and Mr. Smith would not let me announce myself as a single
gentleman of mature age in my preface, but if you had permitted it, a great many elderly spinsters would have been
pleased.'

The last words that I have to say concerning Emily are
contained in a letter to me from Miss Ellen Nussey.

'So very little is known of Emily Brontë,' she writes, 'that
every little detail awakens an interest. Her extreme reserve
seemed impenetrable, yet she was intensely loveable; she invited

confidence in her moral power. Few people have the gift of looking and smiling as she could look and smile. One of her rare expressive looks was something to remember through life, there was such a depth of soul and feeling, and yet a shyness of revealing herself — a strength of self-containment seen in no other. She was in the strictest sense a law unto herself, and a heroine in keeping to her law. She and gentle Anne were to be seen twined together as united statues of power and humility. They were to be seen with their arms lacing each other in their younger days whenever their occupations permitted their union. On the top of a moor or in a deep glen Emily was a child in spirit for glee and enjoyment; or when thrown entirely on her own resources to do a kindness, she could be vivacious in conversation and enjoy giving pleasure. A spell of mischief also lurked in her on occasions when out on the moors. She enjoyed leading Charlotte where she would not dare to go of her own free-will. · Charlotte had a mortal dread of unknown animals, and it was Emily's pleasure to lead her into close vicinity, and then to tell her of how and of what she had done, laughing at her horror with great amusement. If Emily wanted a book she might have left in the sitting-room she would dart in again without looking at any one, especially if any guest were present. Among the curates, Mr. Weightman was her only exception for any conventional courtesy. The ability with which she took up music was amazing; the style, the touch, and the expression was that of a professor absorbed heart and soul in his theme. The two dogs, Keeper and Flossy, were always in quiet waiting by the side of Emily and Anne during their breakfast of Scotch oatmeal and milk, and always had a share handed down to them at the close of the meal. Poor old Keeper, Emily's faithful friend and worshipper, seemed to understand her like a human being. One evening, when the four friends were sitting closely round the fire in the sitting-room, Keeper forced himself in between Charlotte and Emily and mounted himself on Emily's lap; finding the space too limited for his comfort he pressed himself forward on to the guest's knees, making himself quite comfortable. Emily's heart was won by the unresisting endurance of the visitor, little guessing that she herself, being in close contact, was the inspiring cause of submission to Keeper's preference. Sometimes Emily would delight in showing off Keeper — make him frantic in action, and roar with the voice of a lion. It was a terrifying exhibition within the walls of an ordinary sitting-room. Keeper was a solemn mourner at Emily's funeral and never recovered his cheerfulness.'

CHAPTER VII.

ANNE BRONTË.

IT can scarcely be doubted that Anne Brontë's two novels, 'Agnes Grey' and 'The Tenant of Wildfell Hall,' would have long since fallen into oblivion but for the inevitable association with the romances of her two greater sisters. While this may be taken for granted, it is impossible not to feel, even at the distance of half a century, a sense of Anne's personal charm. Gentleness is a word always associated with her by those who knew her. When Mr. Nicholls saw what professed to be a portrait of Anne in a magazine article, he wrote: 'What an awful caricature of the dear, gentle Anne Brontë!' Mr. Nicholls has a portrait of Anne in his possession, drawn by Charlotte, which he pronounces to be an admirable likeness, and this does convey the impression of a sweet and gentle nature.

Anne, as we have seen, was taken in long clothes from Thornton to Haworth. Her godmother was a Miss Outhwaite, a fact I learn from an inscription in Anne's 'Book of Common Prayer.' 'Miss Outhwaite to her goddaughter, Anne Brontë, July 13th, 1827.' Miss Outhwaite was not forgetful of her goddaughter, for by her will she left Anne £200.

There is a sampler worked by Anne, bearing date January 23rd, 1830, and there is a later book than the Prayer Book, with Anne's name in it, and, as might be expected, it is a good-conduct prize. 'Prize for good conduct presented to Miss A. Brontë with Miss Wooler's kind love,

CHARLOTTE BRONTE

Roe Head, Dec. 14th, 1836,' is the inscription in a copy of Watts 'On the Improvement of the Mind.'

Apart from the correspondence we know little more than this — that Anne was the least assertive of the three sisters, and that she was more distinctly a general favourite. We have Charlotte's own word for it that even the curates ventured upon 'sheep's eyes' at Anne. We know all too little of her two experiences as governess, first at Blake Hall with Mrs. Ingham, and later at Thorp Green with Mrs. Robinson. The painful episode of Branwell's madness came to disturb her sojourn at the latter place, but long afterwards her old pupils, the Misses Robinson, called to see her at Haworth; and one of them, who became a Mrs. Clapham of Keighley, always retained the most kindly memories of her gentle governess.

With the exception of these two uncomfortable episodes as governess, Anne would seem to have had no experience of the larger world. Even before Anne's death, Charlotte had visited Brussels, London, and Hathersage (in Derbyshire). Anne never, I think, set foot out of her native county, although she was the only one of her family to die away from home. Of her correspondence I have only the two following letters: —

TO MISS ELLEN NUSSEY.

'HAWORTH, October 4, 1847.

MY DEAR MISS NUSSEY, — Many thanks to you for your unexpected and welcome epistle. Charlotte is well, and meditates writing to you. Happily for all parties the east wind no longer prevails. During its continuance she complained of its influence as usual. I too suffered from it in some degree, as I always do, more or less; but this time, it brought me no reinforcement of colds and coughs, which is what I dread the most. Emily considers it a very uninteresting wind, but it does not affect her nervous system. Charlotte

ANNE BRONTË.

From a Drawing by Charlotte in the possession of Mr. Nicholls.

agrees with me in thinking the ———— [1] a very provoking affair. You are quite mistaken about her parasol; she affirms she brought it back, and I can bear witness to the fact, having seen it yesterday in her possession. As for my book, I have no wish to see it again till I see you along with it, and then it will be welcome enough for the sake of the bearer. We are all here much as you left us. I have no news to tell you, except that Mr. Nicholls begged a holiday and went to Ireland three or four weeks ago, and is not expected back till Saturday; but that, I dare say, is no news at all. We were all and severally pleased and gratified for your kind and judiciously selected presents, from papa down to Tabby, or down to myself, perhaps I ought rather to say. The crab-cheese is excellent, and likely to be very useful, but I don't intend to need it. It is not choice but necessity has induced me to choose such a tiny sheet of paper for my letter, having none more suitable at hand; but perhaps it will contain as much as you need wish to read, and I to write, for I find I have nothing more to say, except that your little Tabby must be a charming little creature. That is all, for as Charlotte is writing, or about to write to you herself, I need not send any messages from her. Therefore accept my best love. I must not omit the Major's [2] compliments. And — Believe me to be your affectionate friend,

'ANNE BRONTË.'

TO MISS ELLEN NUSSEY.

'HAWORTH, January 4, 1848.

'MY DEAR MISS NUSSEY, — I am not going to give you a "nice *long* letter" — on the contrary, I mean to content myself with a shabby little note, to be ingulfed in a letter of Charlotte's, which will, of course, be infinitely more acceptable to you than any production of mine, though I do not question your friendly regard for me, or the indulgent welcome you would accord to a missive of mine, even without a more agreeable companion to

---

[1] The original of this letter is lost, so that it is not possible to fill in the hiatus.

[2] Emily — who was called the Major, because on one occasion she guarded Miss Nussey from the attentions of Mr. Weightman during an evening walk.

back it; but you must know there is a lamentable deficiency in my organ of language, which makes me almost as bad a hand at writing as talking, unless I have something particular to say. I have now, however, to thank you and your friend for your kind letter and her pretty watch-guards, which I am sure we shall all of us value the more for being the work of her own hands. You do not tell us how *you* bear the present unfavourable weather. We are all cut up by this cruel east wind. Most of us, *i. e.* Charlotte, Emily, and I have had the influenza, or a bad cold instead, twice over within the space of a few weeks. Papa has had it once. Tabby has escaped it altogether. I have no news to tell you, for we have been nowhere, seen no one, and done nothing (to speak of) since you were here — and yet we contrive to be busy from morning till night. Flossy is fatter than ever, but still active enough to relish a sheep-hunt. I hope you and your circle have been more fortunate in the matter of colds than we have.

' With kind regards to all, — I remain, dear Miss Nussey, yours ever affectionately,   ANNE BRONTË.'

' Agnes Grey,' as we have noted, was published by Newby, in one volume, in 1847. ' The Tenant of Wildfell Hall' was issued by the same publisher, in three volumes, in 1848. It is not generally known that ' The Tenant of Wildfell Hall' went into a second edition the same year; and I should have pronounced it incredible, were not a copy of the later issue in my possession, and Anne Brontë had actually written a preface to this edition. The fact is entirely ignored in the correspondence. The preface in question makes it quite clear, if any evidence of that were necessary, that Anne had her brother in mind in writing the book. ' I could not be understood to suppose,' she says, ' that the proceedings of the unhappy scapegrace, with his few profligate companions I have here introduced, are a specimen of the common practices of society: the case is an extreme one, as I trusted none would fail to perceive; but I

knew that such characters do exist, and if I have warned
one rash youth from following in their steps, or prevented
one thoughtless girl from falling into the very natural error
of my heroine, the book has not been written in vain.'
' One word more and I have done,' she continues. ' Respecting the author's identity, I would have it to be distinctly understood that Acton Bell is neither Currer nor
Ellis Bell, and, therefore, let not his faults be attributed to
them. As to whether the name is real or fictitious, it cannot
greatly signify to those who know him only by his works.'

TO W. S. WILLIAMS.

' JANUARY 18, 1849.

' MY DEAR SIR, — In sitting down to write to you I feel as if I
were doing a wrong and a selfish thing. I believe I ought to dis-
continue my correspondence with you till times change, and the
tide of calamity which of late days has set so strongly in against us
takes a turn. But the fact is, sometimes I feel it absolutely necessary to unburden my mind. To papa I must only speak cheer-
ingly, to Anne only encouragingly — to you I may give some hint
of the dreary truth.

' Anne and I sit alone and in seclusion as you fancy us, but we
do not study. Anne cannot study now, she can scarcely read ; she
occupies Emily's chair ; she does not get well. A week ago we
sent for a medical man of skill and experience from Leeds to see
her. He examined her with the stethoscope. His report I forbear
to dwell on for the present — even skilful physicians have often
been mistaken in their conjectures.

' My first impulse was to hasten her away to a warmer climate,
but this was forbidden : she must not travel ; she is not to stir
from the house this winter ; the temperature of her room is to be
kept constantly equal.

' Had leave been given to try change of air and scene, I should
hardly have known how to act. I could not possibly leave papa ;
and when I mentioned his accompanying us, the bare thought distressed him too much to be dwelt upon. Papa is now upwards of

185

seventy years of age; his habits for nearly thirty years have been those of absolute retirement; any change in them is most repugnant to him, and probably could not, at this time especially when the hand of God is so heavy upon his old age, be ventured upon without danger.

' When we lost Emily I thought we had drained the very dregs of our cup of trial, but now when I hear Anne cough as Emily coughed, I tremble lest there should be exquisite bitterness yet to taste. However, I must not look forwards nor must I look backwards. Too often I feel like one crossing an abyss on a narrow plank — a glance round might quite unnerve.

' So circumstanced, my dear sir, what claim have I on your friendship, what right to the comfort of your letters? My literary character is effaced for the time, and it is by that only you know me. Care of papa and Anne is necessarily my chief present object in life, to the exclusion of all that could give me interest with my publishers or their connections. Should Anne get better, I think I could rally and become Currer Bell once more, but if otherwise, I look no farther : sufficient for the day is the evil thereof.

' Anne is very patient in her illness, as patient as Emily was unflinching. I recall one sister and look at the other with a sort of reverence as well as affection — under the test of suffering neither has faltered.

' All the days of this winter have gone by darkly and heavily like a funeral train. Since September, sickness has not quitted the house. It is strange it did not use to be so, but I suspect now all this has been coming on for years. Unused, any of us, to the possession of robust health, we have not noticed the gradual approaches of decay; we did not know its symptoms : the little cough, the small appetite, the tendency to take cold at every variation of atmosphere have been regarded as things of course. I see them in another light now.

' If you answer this, write to me as you would to a person in an average state of tranquillity and happiness. I want to keep myself as firm and calm as I can. While papa and Anne want me, I hope, I pray, never to fail them. Were I to see you I should endeavour to converse on ordinary topics, and I should wish to write on the same — besides, it will be less harassing to yourself to address me as usual.

'May God long preserve to you the domestic treasures you value; and when bereavement at last comes, may He give you strength to bear it. — Yours sincerely,   C. BRONTË.'

TO W. S. WILLIAMS.

'FEBRUARY 1, 1849.

'MY DEAR SIR, — Anne seems so tranquil this morning, so free from pain and fever, and looks and speaks so like herself in health, that I too feel relieved, and I take advantage of the respite to write to you, hoping that my letter may reflect something of the comparative peace I feel.

'Whether my hopes are quite fallacious or not, I do not know; but sometimes I fancy that the remedies prescribed by Mr. Teale, and approved — as I was glad to learn — by Dr. Forbes, are working a good result. Consumption, I am aware, is a flattering malady, but certainly Anne's illness has of late assumed a less alarming character than it had in the beginning: the hectic is allayed; the cough gives a more frequent reprieve. Could I but believe she would live two years — a year longer, I should be thankful: I dreaded the terrors of the swift messenger which snatched Emily from us, as it seemed, in a few days.

'The parcel came yesterday. You and Mr. Smith do nothing by halves. Neither of you care for being thanked, so I will keep my gratitude in my own mind. The choice of books is perfect. Papa is at this moment reading Macaulay's "History," which he had wished to see. Anne is engaged with one of Frederika Bremer's tales.

'I wish I could send a parcel in return; I had hoped to have had one by this time ready to despatch. When I saw you and Mr. Smith in London, I little thought of all that was to come between July and Spring: how my thoughts were to be caught away from imagination, enlisted and absorbed in realities the most cruel.

'I will tell you what I want to do; it is to show you the first
187

volume of my MS., which I have copied. In reading "Mary Barton" (a clever though painful tale) I was a little dismayed to find myself in some measure anticipated both in subject and incident. I should like to have your opinion on this point, and to know whether the resemblance appears as considerable to a stranger as it does to myself. I should wish also to have the benefit of such general strictures and advice as you choose to give. Shall I therefore send the MS. when I return the first batch of books?

'But remember, if I show it to you it is on two conditions: the first, that you give me a faithful opinion — I do not promise to be swayed by it, but I should like to have it; the second, that you show it and speak of it to *none* but Mr. Smith. I have always a great horror of premature announcements — they may do harm and can never do good. Mr. Smith must be so kind as not to mention it yet in his quarterly circulars. All human affairs are so uncertain, and my position especially is at present so peculiar, that I cannot count on the time, and would rather that no allusion should be made to a work of which great part is yet to create.

'There are two volumes in the first parcel which, having seen, I cannot bring myself to part with, and must beg Mr. Smith's permission to retain: Mr. Thackeray's "Journey from Cornhill," etc. and "The Testimony to the Truth." That last is indeed a book after my own heart. I *do* like the mind it discloses — it is of a fine and high order. Alexander Harris may be a clown by birth, but he is a nobleman by nature. When I could read no other book, I read his and derived comfort from it. No matter whether or not I can agree in all his views, it is the principles, the feelings, the heart of the man I admire.

'Write soon and tell me whether you think it advisable that I should send the MS. — Your sincerely, C. BRONTË.'

TO W. S. WILLIAMS.

'HAWORTH, February 4, 1849.

'MY DEAR SIR, — I send the parcel up without delay, according to your request. The manuscript has all its errors upon it, not having been read through since copying. I have kept "Madeline," along with the two other books I mentioned; I shall consider it the gift of Miss Kavanagh, and shall value it both for its literary excellence and for the modest merit of the giver. We already possess Tennyson's "Poems" and "Our Street." Emerson's "Essays" I read with much interest, and often with admiration, but they are of mixed gold and clay — deep and invigorating truth, dreary and depressing fallacy seem to me combined therein. In George Borrow's works I found a wild fascination, a vivid graphic power of description, a fresh originality, an athletic simplicity (so to speak), which give them a stamp of their own. After reading his "Bible in Spain" I felt as if I had actually travelled at his side, and seen the "wild Sil" rush from its mountain cradle; wandered in the hilly wilderness of the Sierras; encountered and conversed with Manehegan, Castillian, Andalusian, Arragonese, and, above all, with the savage Gitanos.

'Your mention of Mr. Taylor suggests to me that possibly you and Mr. Smith might wish him to share the little secret of the MS. — that exclusion might seem invidious, that it might make your mutual evening chat less pleasant. If so, admit him to the confidence by all means. He is attached to the firm, and will no doubt keep its secrets. I shall be glad of another censor, and if a severe one, so much the better, provided he is also just. I court the keenest criticism. Far rather would I never publish more, than publish anything inferior to my first effort. Be honest, therefore, all three of you. If you think this book promises less favourably than "Jane Eyre," say so, it is but trying again, i. e., if life and health be spared.

'Anne continues a little better — the mild weather suits her. At times I hear the renewal of hope's whisper, but I dare not listen too fondly; she deceived me cruelly before. A sudden change to cold would be the test. I dread such change, but must not anticipate. Spring lies before us, and then summer — surely we may hope a little!

'Anne expresses a wish to see the notices of the poems. You had better, therefore, send them. We shall expect to find painful allusions to one now above blame and beyond praise; but these must be borne. For ourselves, we are almost indifferent to censure. I read the "Quarterly" without a pang, except that I thought there were some sentences disgraceful to the critic. He seems anxious to let it be understood that he is a person well acquainted with the habits of the upper classes. Be this as it may, I am afraid he is no gentleman ; and moreover, that no training could make him such.[1] Many a poor man, born and bred to labour, would disdain that reviewer's cast of feeling. — Yours sincerely,   C. BRONTË.'

TO W. S. WILLIAMS.

'MARCH 2, 1849.

' MY DEAR SIR, — My sister still continues better : she has less languor and weakness ; her spirits are improved. This change gives cause, I think, both for gratitude and hope.

'I am glad that you and Mr. Smith like the commencement of my present work. I wish it were *more than a commencement ;* for how it will be reunited after the long break, or how it can gather force of flow when the current has been checked or rather drawn off so long, I know not.

' I sincerely thank you both for the candid expression of your objections. What you say with reference to the first chapter shall be duly weighed. At present I feel reluctant to withdraw it, because, as I formerly said of the Lowood part of " Jane Eyre," *it is true.* The curates and their ongoings are merely photographed from the life. I should like you to explain to me more fully the ground of your objections. Is it because you think this chapter will render the work liable to severe handling by the press ? Is it because knowing as you now do the identity of " Currer Bell," this scene strikes you as unfeminine ? Is it because it is intrinsically defective and inferior ? I am afraid the two first reasons would not weigh with me — the last would.

' Anne and I thought it very kind in you to preserve all the notices of the Poems so carefully for us. Some of them, as you said, were well worth reading. We were glad to find that our old

---

[1] In his next letter Mr. Williams informed her that Miss Rigby was the writer of the ' Quarterly ' article.

friend the "Critic" has again a kind word for us. I was struck with one curious fact, viz., that four of the notices are facsimiles of each other. How does this happen? I suppose they copy.'

TO MISS ELLEN NUSSEY.

'MARCH 8, 1849.

'DEAR ELLEN, — Anne's state has apparently varied very little during the last fortnight or three weeks. I wish I could say she gains either flesh, strength, or appetite; but there is no progress on these points, nor I hope, as far as regards the two last at least, any falling off; she is piteously thin. Her cough, and the pain in her side, continue the same.

'I write these few lines that you may not think my continued silence strange; anything like frequent correspondence I cannot keep up, and you must excuse me. I trust you and all at Brookroyd are happy and well. Give my love to your mother and all the rest, and — Believe me, yours sincerely,

'C. BRONTË.'

TO W. S. WILLIAMS.

'MARCH 11, 1849.

'MY DEAR SIR, — My sister has been something worse since I wrote last. We have had nearly a week of frost, and the change has tried her, as I feared it would do, though not so severely as former experience had led me to apprehend. I am thankful to say she is now again a little better. Her state of mind is usually placid, and her chief sufferings consist in the harassing cough and a sense of languor.

'I ought to have acknowledged the safe arrival of the parcel before now, but I put it off from day to day, fearing I should write a sorrowful letter. A similar apprehension induces me to abridge this note.

'Believe me, whether in happiness or the contrary, yours sincerely, C. BRONTË.'

TO MISS LÆTITIA WHEELWRIGHT.

'HAWORTH, March 15, 1849.

'DEAR LÆTITIA, — I have not quite forgotten you through the winter, but I have remembered you only like some pleasant waking idea struggling through a dreadful dream. You say my last letter was dated September 14th. You ask how I have passed the time since. What has happened to me? Why have I been silent?

'It is soon told.

'On the 24th of September my only brother, after being long in weak health, and latterly consumptive — though we were far from apprehending immediate danger — died, quite suddenly as it seemed to us. He had been out two days before. The shock was great. Ere he could be interred I fell ill. A low nervous fever left me very weak. As I was slowly recovering, my sister Emily, whom you knew, was seized with inflammation of the lungs; suppuration took place; two agonising months of hopes and fears followed, and on the 19th of December *she died.*

'She was scarcely cold in her grave when Anne, my youngest and last sister, who has been delicate all her life, exhibited symptoms that struck us with acute alarm. We sent for the first advice that could be procured. She was examined with the stethoscope, and the dreadful fact was announced that her lungs too were affected, and that tubercular consumption had already made considerable progress. A system of treatment was prescribed, which has since been ratified by the opinion of Dr. Forbes, whom your papa will, I dare say, know. I hope it has somewhat delayed disease. She is now a patient invalid, and I am her nurse. God has hitherto supported me in some sort through all these bitter calamities, and my father, I am thankful to say, has been wonderfully sustained; but there have been hours, days, weeks of inexpressible anguish to undergo, and the cloud of impending distress still lowers dark and sullen above us. I cannot write much. I can only pray Providence to preserve you and yours from such affliction as He has seen good to accumulate on me and mine.

'With best regards to your dear mamma and all your circle, — Believe me, yours faithfully,   C. BRONTË.'

TO MISS WOOLER.

'HAWORTH, March 24, 1849.

'MY DEAR MISS WOOLER, — I have delayed answering your letter in the faint hope that I might be able to reply favourably to your inquiries after my sister's health. This, however, is not permitted me to do. Her decline is gradual and fluctuating, but its nature is not doubtful. The symptoms of cough, pain in the side and chest, wasting of flesh, strength, and appetite, after the sad experience we have had, cannot but be regarded by us as equivocal.

'In spirit she is resigned ; at heart she is, I believe, a true Christian. She looks beyond this life, and regards her home and rest as elsewhere than on earth. May God support her and all of us through the trial of lingering sickness, and aid her in the last hour when the struggle which separates soul from body must be gone through !

'We saw Emily torn from the midst of us when our hearts clung to her with intense attachment, and when, loving each other as we did — well, it seemed as if (might we but have been spared to each other) we could have found complete happiness in our mutual society and affection. She was scarcely buried when Anne's health failed, and we were warned that consumption had found another victim in her, and that it would be vain to reckon on her life.

'These things would be too much if Reason, unsupported by Religion, were condemned to bear them alone. I have cause to be most thankful for the strength which has hitherto been vouchsafed both to my father and myself. God, I think, is specially merciful to old age ; and for my own part, trials which in perspective would have seemed to me quite intolerable, when they actually came, I endured without prostration. Yet, I must confess, that in the time which has elapsed since Emily's death, there have been moments of solitary, deep, inert affliction, far harder to bear than those which immediately followed our loss. The crisis of bereavement has an acute pang which goads to exertion, the desolate after-feeling sometimes paralyses.

CHARLOTTE BRONTË

'I have learned that we are not to find solace in our own strength : we must seek it in God's omnipotence. Fortitude is good, but fortitude itself must be shaken under us to teach us how weak we are.

'With best wishes to yourself and all dear to you, and sincere thanks for the interest you so kindly continue to take in me and my sister, — Believe me, my dear Miss Wooler, yours faithfully,

'C. BRONTË.'

TO W. S. WILLIAMS.

'APRIL 16, 1849.

'MY DEAR SIR, — Your kind advice on the subject of Homœopathy deserves and has our best thanks. We find ourselves, however, urged from more than one quarter to try different systems and medicines, and I fear we have already given offence by not listening to all. The fact is, were we in every instance compliant, my dear sister would be harassed by continual changes. Cod-liver oil and carbonate of iron were first strongly recommended. Anne took them as long as she could, but at last she was obliged to give them up : the oil yielded her no nutriment, it did not arrest the progress of emaciation, and as it kept her always sick, she was prevented from taking food of any sort. Hydropathy was then strongly advised. She is now trying Gobold's Vegetable Balsam ; she thinks it does her some good ; and as it is the first medicine which has had that effect, she would wish to persevere with it for a time. She is also looking hopefully forward to deriving benefit from change of air. We have obtained Mr. Teale's permission to go to the seaside in the course of six or eight weeks. At first I felt torn between two duties — that of staying with papa and going with Anne ; but as it is papa's own most kindly expressed wish that I should adopt the latter plan, and as, besides, he is now, thank God ! in tolerable health, I hope to be spared the pain of resigning the care of my sister to other hands, however friendly. We wish to keep together as long as we can. I hope, too, to derive from the change some renewal of physical strength and mental composure (in neither of which points am I what I ought or wish to be) to make me a better and more cheery nurse.

'I fear I must have seemed to you hard in my observations about "The Emigrant Family." The fact was, I compared Alexander Harris with himself only. It is not equal to the "Testimony to the Truth," but, tried by the standard of other and very popular books too, it is very clever and original. Both subject and the manner of treating it are unhackneyed : he gives new views of new scenes and furnishes interesting information on interesting topics. Considering the increasing necessity for and tendency to emigration, I should think it has a fair chance of securing the success it merits.

'I took up Leigh Hunt's book "The Town" with the impression that it would be interesting only to Londoners, and I was surprised, ere I had read many pages, to find myself enchained by his pleasant, graceful, easy style, varied knowledge, just views, and kindly spirit. There is something peculiarly anti-melancholic in Leigh Hunt's writings, and yet they are never boisterous. They resemble sunshine, being at once bright and tranquil.

'I like Carlyle better and better. His style I do not like, nor do I always concur in his opinions, nor quite fall in with his hero worship; but there is a manly love of truth, an honest recognition and fearless vindication of intrinsic greatness, of intellectual and moral worth, considered apart from birth, rank, or wealth, which commands my sincere admiration. Carlyle would never do for a contributor to the "Quarterly." I have not read his "French Revolution."

'I congratulate you on the approaching publication of Mr. Ruskin's new work. If the "Seven Lamps of Architecture" resemble their predecessor, "Modern Painters," they will be no lamps at all, but a new constellation — seven bright stars, for whose rising the reading world ought to be anxiously agaze.

'Do not ask me to mention what books I should like to read. Half the pleasure of receiving a parcel from Cornhill consists in having its contents chosen for us. We like to discover, too, by the leaves cut here and there, that the ground has been travelled before us. I may however say, with reference to works of fiction, that I should much like to see one of Godwin's

works, never having hitherto had that pleasure — "Caleb
Williams" or "Fleetwood," or which you thought best worth
reading.

'But it is yet much too soon to talk of sending more books;
our present stock is scarcely half exhausted. You will perhaps
think I am a slow reader, but remember, Currer Bell is a country
housewife, and has sundry little matters connected with the
needle and kitchen to attend to which take up half his day,
especially now when, alas! there is but one pair of hands where
once there were three. I did not mean to touch that chord, its
sound is too sad.

'I try to write now and then. The effort was a hard one at
first. It renewed the terrible loss of last December strangely.
Worse than useless did it seem to attempt to write what there
no longer lived an "Ellis Bell" to read; the whole book with
every hope founded on it, faded to vanity and vexation of
spirit.

'One inducement to persevere and do my best I still have,
however, and I am thankful for it: I should like to please my
kind friends at Cornhill. To that end I wish my powers would
come back; and if it would please Providence to restore my
remaining sister, I think they would.

'Do not forget to tell me how you are when you write again.
I trust your indisposition is quite gone by this time. — Believe
me, yours sincerely, C. BRONTË.'

TO MISS ELLEN NUSSEY.

'MAY 1, 1849.

'DEAR ELLEN, — I returned Mary Taylor's letter to Hunsworth
as soon as I had read it. Thank God she was safe up to that
time, but I do not think the earthquake was then over. I shall
long to hear tidings of her again.

'Anne was worse during the warm weather we had about a
week ago. She grew weaker, and both the pain in her side
and her cough were worse; strange to say, since it is colder,
she has appeared rather to revive than sink. I still hope that
if she gets over May she may last a long time.

'We have engaged lodgings at Scarboro'. We stipulated for a good-sized sitting-room and an airy double-bedded lodging room, with a sea view, and if not deceived, have obtained these desiderata at No. 2 Cliff. Anne says it is one of the best situations in the place. It would not have done to have taken lodgings either in the town or on the bleak steep coast, where Miss Wooler's house is situated. If Anne is to get any good she must have every advantage. Miss Outhwaite [her godmother] left her in her will a legacy of £200, and she cannot employ her money better than in obtaining what may prolong existence, if it does not restore health. We hope to leave home on the 23rd, and I think it will be advisable to rest at York, and stay all night there. I hope this arrangement will suit you. We reckon on your society, dear Ellen, as a real privilege and pleasure. We shall take little luggage, and shall have to buy bonnets and dresses and several other things either at York or Scarboro'; which place do you think would be best? Oh, if it would please God to strengthen and revive Anne, how happy we might be together! His will, however, must be done, and if she is not to recover, it remains to pray for strength and patience.   C. B.'

TO W. S. WILLIAMS.

'MAY 8, 1849.

'MY DEAR SIR,— I hasten to acknowledge the two kind letters for which I am indebted to you. That fine spring weather of which you speak did not bring such happiness to us in its sunshine as I trust it did to you and thousands besides — the change proved trying to my sister. For a week or ten days I did not know what to think, she became so weak, and suffered so much from increased pain in the side, and aggravated cough. The last few days have been much colder, yet, strange to say, during their continuance she has appeared rather to revive than sink. She not unfrequently shows the very same symptoms which were apparent in Emily only a few days before she died — fever in the evenings, sleepless nights, and a sort of lethargy in the morning hours; this creates acute anxiety — then comes an improvement, which reassures. In about three weeks, should the weather be genial and her strength continue at all equal to the journey, we hope to go to Scarboro'. It is not without misgiving that I contemplate a departure from home under such circumstances; but since she herself earnestly wishes the experiment to be tried, I think it ought not to. be neglected. We are in God's hands, and must trust the results to Him. An old school-fellow of mine, a tried and faithful friend, has volunteered to accompany us. I shall have the satisfaction of leaving papa to the attentions of two servants equally tried and faithful. One of them is indeed now old and infirm, and unfit to stir much from her chair by the kitchen fireside; but the other is young and active, and even she has lived with us seven years. I have reason, therefore, you see, to be thankful amidst sorrow, especially as papa still possesses every faculty unimpaired, and though not robust, has good general health — a sort of chronic cough is his sole complaint.

' I hope Mr. Smith will not risk a cheap edition of " Jane Eyre " yet, he had better wait awhile — the public will be sick of the name of that one book. I can make no promise as to when another will be ready — neither my time nor my efforts are my own. That absorption in my employment to which I gave myself up without fear of doing wrong when I wrote " Jane Eyre," would now be alike impossible and blamable; but I do what I can, and have made some little progress. We must all be patient.

' Meantime, I should say, let the public forget at their ease, and let us not be nervous about it. And as to the critics, if the Bells possess real merit, I do not fear impartial justice being rendered them one day. I have a very short mental as well as physical sight in some matters, and am far less uneasy at the idea of public impatience, misconstruction, censure, etc., than I am at the thought of the anxiety of those two or three friends in Cornhill to whom I owe much kindness, and whose expectations I would earnestly wish not to disappoint. If they can make up their minds to wait tranquilly, and put some confidence in my good-will, if not my power, to get on as well as may be, I shall not repine ; but I verily believe that the " nobler sex " find it more difficult to wait, to plod, to work out their destiny inch by inch, than their sisters do. They are always for walking so fast and taking such long steps, one cannot keep up with them. One should never tell a gentleman that one has commenced a task till it is nearly achieved. Currer Bell, even if he had no let or hindrance, and if his path were quite smooth, could never march with the tread of a Scott, a Bulwer, a Thackeray, or a Dickens. I want you and Mr. Smith clearly to understand this. I have always wished to guard you against exaggerated anticipations — calculate low when you calculate on me. An honest man — and woman too — would always rather rise above expectation than fall below it.

'Have I lectured enough ? and am I understood ?

'Give my sympathising respects to Mrs. Williams. I hope her little daughter is by this time restored to perfect health. It pleased me to see with what satisfaction you speak of your son. I was glad, too, to hear of the progress and welfare of Miss Kavanagh. The notices of Mr. Harris's works are encouraging and just — may they contribute to his success !

'Should Mr. Thackeray again ask after Currer Bell, say the secret is and will be well kept because it is not worth disclosure. This fact his own sagacity will have already led him to divine. In the hope that it may not be long ere I hear from you again, — Believe me, yours sincerely,   C. BRONTË.'

TO MISS WOOLER.

'HAWORTH, May 16, 1849.

'MY DEAR MISS WOOLER, — I will lose no time in thanking you for your letter and kind offer of assistance. We have, however, already engaged lodgings. I am not myself acquainted with Scarboro', but Anne knows it well, having been there three or four times. She had a particular preference for the situation of some lodgings (No. 2 Cliff). We wrote about them, and finding them disengaged, took them. Your information is, notwithstanding, valuable, should we find this place in any way ineligible. It is a satisfaction to be provided with directions for future use.

'Next Wednesday is the day fixed for our departure. Ellen Nussey accompanies us (by Anne's expressed wish). I could not refuse her society, but I dared not urge her to go, for I have little hope that the excursion will be one of pleasure or benefit to those engaged in it. Anne is extremely weak. She herself has a fixed impression that the sea air will give her a chance of regaining strength; that chance, therefore, we must have. Having resolved to try the experiment, misgivings are useless; and yet, when I look at her, misgivings will rise. She is more emaciated than Emily was at the very last; her breath scarcely serves her to mount the stairs, however slowly. She sleeps very little at night, and often passes most of the forenoon in a semi-lethargic state. Still, she is up all day, and even goes out a little when it is fine. Fresh air usually acts as a stimulus, but its reviving power diminishes.

'With best wishes for your own health and welfare, — Believe me, my dear Miss Wooler, yours sincerely, C. BRONTË.'

TO W. S. WILLIAMS.

'NO. 2 CLIFF, SCARBORO', May 27, 1849.

'MY DEAR SIR, — The date above will inform you why I have not answered your last letter more promptly. I have been busy with preparations for departure and with the journey. I am thankful to say we reached our destination safely, having rested one night at York. We found assistance wherever we needed it; there was always an arm ready to do for my sister what I was not quite strong enough to do: lift her in and out of the carriages, carry her across the line, etc.

'It made her happy to see both York and its Minster, and Scarboro' and its bay once more. There is yet no revival of bodily strength —I fear indeed the slow ebb continues. People who see her tell me I must not expect her to last long — but it is something to cheer her mind.

'Our lodgings are pleasant. As Anne sits at the window she can look down on the sea, which this morning is calm as glass. She says if she could breathe more freely she would be comfortable at this moment — but she cannot breathe freely.

' My friend Ellen is with us. I find her presence a solace. She is a calm, steady girl — not brilliant, but good and true. She suits and has always suited me well. I like her, with her phlegm, repose, sense, and sincerity, better than I should like the most talented without these qualifications.

' If ever I see you again I should have pleasure in talking over with you the topics you allude to in your last — or rather, in hearing *you* talk them over. We see these things through a glass darkly — or at least I see them thus. So far from objecting to speculation on, or discussion of, the subject, I should wish to hear what others have to say. By *others*, I mean only the serious and reflective — levity in such matters shocks as much as hypocrisy.

' Write to me. In this strange place your letters will come like the visits of a friend. Fearing to lose the post, I will add no more at present. — Believe me, yours sincerely,

'C. Brontë.'

TO W. S. WILLIAMS.

'May 30, 1849.

' My dear Sir, — My poor sister is taken quietly home at last. She died on Monday. With almost her last breath she said she was happy, and thanked God that death was come, and come so gently. I did not think it would be so soon.

' You will not expect me to add more at present. — Yours faithfully,   C. Brontë.'

TO W. S. WILLIAMS.

'June 25, 1849.

' My dear Sir, — I am now again at home, where I returned last Thursday. I call it *home* still — much as London would be called London if an earthquake should shake its streets to ruins. But let me not be ungrateful : Haworth parsonage is still a home for me, and not quite a ruined or desolate home either. Papa is there, and two most affectionate and faithful

servants, and two old dogs, in their way as faithful and affectionate, Emily's large house-dog, which lay at the side of her
dying bed, and followed her funeral to the vault, lying in the
pew couched at our feet while the burial service was being
read, and Anne's little spaniel. The ecstasy of these poor
animals when I came in was something singular. At former
returns from brief absences they always welcomed me warmly
— but not in that strange, heart-touching way. I am certain
they thought that, as I was returned, my sisters were not far
behind. But here my sisters will come no more. Keeper may
visit Emily's little bed-room — as he still does day by day — and
Flossy may look wistfully round for Anne, they will never see
them again — nor shall I — at least the human part of me. I
must not write so sadly, but how can I help thinking and
feeling sadly? In the daytime effort and occupation aid me,
but when evening darkens, something in my heart revolts
against the burden of solitude — the sense of loss and want grows
almost too much for me. I am not good or amiable in such
moments, I am rebellious, and it is only the thought of my
dear father in the next room, or of the kind servants in the
kitchen, or some caress from the poor dogs, which restores me
to softer sentiments and more rational views. As to the night
— could I do without bed, I would never seek it. Waking, I
think, sleeping, I dream of them; and I cannot recall them as
they were in health, still they appear to me in sickness and
suffering. Still, my nights were worse after the first shock of
Branwell's death — they were terrible then; and the impressions experienced on waking were at that time such as we do
not put into language. Worse seemed at hand than was yet
endured — in truth, worse awaited us.

'All this bitterness must be tasted. Perhaps the palate will
grow used to the draught in time, and find its flavour less
acrid. This pain must be undergone; its poignancy, I trust,
will be blunted one day. Ellen would have come back with
me but I would not let her. I knew it would be better to face
the desolation at once — later or sooner the sharp pang must be
experienced.

'Labour must be the cure, not sympathy. Labour is the only radical cure for rooted sorrow. The society of a calm, serenely cheerful companion — such as Ellen — soothes pain like a soft opiate, but I find it does not probe or heal the wound; sharper, more severe means, are necessary to make a remedy. Total change might do much; where that cannot be obtained, work is the best substitute.

'I by no means ask Miss Kavanagh to write to me. Why should she trouble herself to do it? What claim have I on her? She does not know me — she cannot care for me except vaguely and on hearsay. I have got used to your friendly sympathy, and it comforts me. I have tried and trust the fidelity of one or two other friends, and I lean upon it. The natural affection of my father and the attachment and solicitude of our two servants are precious and consolatory to me, but I do not look round for general pity; conventional condolence I do not want, either from man or woman.

'The letter you inclosed in your last bore the signature H. S. Mayers — the address, Sheepscombe, Stroud, Gloucestershire; can you give me any information respecting the writer? It is my intention to acknowledge it one day. I am truly glad to hear that your little invalid is restored to health, and that the rest of your family continue well. Mrs. Williams should spare herself for her husband's and children's sake. Her life and health are too valuable to those round her to be lavished — she should be careful of them. — Believe me, yours sincerely,

'C. Brontë.'

It is not necessary to tell over again the story of Anne's death. Miss Ellen Nussey, who was an eye witness, has related it once for all in Mrs. Gaskell's Memoir. The tomb at Scarborough bears the following inscription : —

HERE LIE THE REMAINS OF
ANNE BRONTË
DAUGHTER OF THE REV. P. BRONTË
INCUMBENT OF HAWORTH, YORKSHIRE
She Died, Aged 28, May 28th, 1849

CHAPTER VIII.

ELLEN NUSSEY.

IF to be known by one's friends is the index to character that it is frequently assumed to be, Charlotte Brontë comes well out of that ordeal. She was discriminating in friendship and leal to the heart's core. With what gratitude she thought of the publisher who gave her the 'first chance' we know by recognising that the manly Dr. John of 'Villette' was Mr. George Smith of Smith & Elder. Mr. W. S. Williams, again, would seem to have been a singularly gifted and amiable man. To her three girl friends, Ellen Nussey, Mary Taylor, and Lætitia Wheelwright, she was loyal to her dying day, and pencilled letters to the two of them who were in England were written in her last illness. Of all her friends, Ellen Nussey must always have the foremost place in our esteem. Like Mary Taylor, she made Charlotte's acquaintance when, at fifteen years of age, she first went to Roe Head School. Mrs. Gaskell has sufficiently described the beginnings of that friendship which death was not to break. Ellen Nussey and Charlotte Brontë corresponded with a regularity which one imagines would be impossible had they both been born half a century later. The two girls loved one another profoundly. They wrote at times almost daily. They quarrelled occasionally over trifles, as friends will, but Charlotte was always full of contrition when a few hours had passed. Towards the end of her life she wrote to Mr. Williams a letter concerning Miss Nussey which may well be printed here.

MISS ELLEN NUSSEY AS A SCHOOL-GIRL.
From a Photograph.

MISS ELLEN NUSSEY TO-DAY.
From a Photograph.

CHARLOTTE BRONTË AND HER CIRCLE

TO W. S. WILLIAMS.

'JANUARY 3, 1850.

'MY DEAR SIR, — I have to acknowledge the receipt of the "Morning Chronicle" with a good review, and of the "Church of England Quarterly" and the "Westminster" with bad ones. I have also to thank you for your letter, which would have been answered sooner had I been alone; but just now I am enjoying the treat of my friend Ellen's society, and she makes me indolent and negligent — I am too busy talking to her all day to do anything else. You allude to the subject of female friendships, and express wonder at the infrequency of sincere attachments amongst women. As to married women, I can well understand that they should be absorbed in their husbands and children — but single women often like each other much, and derive great solace from their mutual regard. Friendship, however, is a plant which cannot be forced. True friendship is no gourd, springing in a night and withering in a day. When I first saw Ellen I did not care for her; we were school-fellows. In course of time we learnt each other's faults and good points. We were contrasts — still, we suited. Affection was first a germ, then a sapling, then a strong tree — now, no new friend, however lofty or profound in intellect — not even Miss Martineau herself — could be to me what Ellen is; yet she is no more than a conscientious, observant, calm, well-bred Yorkshire girl. She is without romance. If she attempts to read poetry, or poetic prose, aloud, I am irritated and deprive her of the book — if she talks of it, I stop my ears; but she is good; she is true; she is faith-ful, and I love her.

'Since I came home, Miss Martineau has written me a long and truly kindly letter. She invites me to visit her at Ambleside. I like the idea. Whether I can realise it or not, it is pleasant to have in prospect.

'You ask me to write to Mrs. Williams. I would rather she wrote to me first; and let her send any kind of letter she likes, without studying mood or manner — Yours sincerely,

'C. BRONTË.'

205

CHARLOTTE BRONTË

Good, True, Faithful — friendship has no sweeter words than these; and it was this loyalty in Miss Nussey which has marked her out in our day as a fine type of sweet womanliness, and will secure to her a lasting name as the friend of Charlotte Brontë.

Miss Ellen Nussey was one of a large family of children, all of whom she survives. Her home during the years of her first friendship with Charlotte Brontë was at the Rydings, at that time the property of an uncle, Reuben Walker, a distinguished court physician. The family in that generation and in this has given many of its members to high public service in various professions. Two Nusseys, indeed, and two Walkers, were court physicians in their day. When Earl Fitzwilliam was canvassing for the county in 1809, he was a guest at the Rydings for two weeks, and on his election was chaired by the tenantry. Reuben Walker, this uncle of Miss Nussey's, was the only Justice of the Peace for the district which included Leeds, Bradford, Huddersfield, and Halifax, during the Luddite riots — a significant reminder of the growth of population since that day. Ellen Nussey's home was at the Rydings, then tenanted by her brother John, until 1837, and she then removed to Brookroyd, where she lived until long after Charlotte Brontë died.

The first letter to Ellen Nussey is dated May 31, 1831, Charlotte having become her school-fellow in the previous January. It would seem to have been a mere play exercise across the school-room, as the girls were then together at Roe Head.

'DEAR MISS NUSSEY,—I take advantage of the earliest opportunity to thank you for the letter you favoured me with last week, and to apologise for having so long neglected to write to you ; indeed, I believe this will be the first letter or note I have ever addressed to you. I am extremely obliged to Mary for her kind invitation, and I assure you that I should very much have liked to hear the Lectures on Galvanism, as they would doubtless have been amusing and instructive. But we are often compelled to bend our inclination to our duty (as Miss Wooler observed the other day), and since there are so many holidays this half-year, it would have appeared almost unreasonable to ask for an extra holiday; besides, we should perhaps have got behindhand with our lessons, so that every-thing considered, it is perhaps as well that circumstances have deprived us of this pleasure. — Believe me to remain, your affectionate friend, C. Brontë.'

But by the Christmas holidays, 'Dear Miss Nussey' has become 'Dear Ellen,' and the friendship has already well commenced.

TO MISS ELLEN NUSSEY.
'Haworth, January 13, 1832.

' Dear Ellen, — The receipt of your letter gave me an agree-able surprise, for notwithstanding your faithful promises, you must excuse me if I say that I had little confidence in their fulfilment, knowing that when school girls once get home they willingly abandon every recollection which tends to remind them of school, and indeed they find such an infinite variety of circumstances to engage their attention and employ their leisure hours, that they are easily persuaded that they have no *time* to fulfil promises made at school. It gave me great pleasure, however, to find that you and Miss Taylor are exceptions to the general rule. The cholera still seems slowly advancing, but let us yet hope, knowing that all things are under the guidance of a merciful Providence. England has hitherto been highly favoured, for the disease has neither raged with the astounding violence, nor extended itself with the frightful rapidity which marked its progress in many of the continental countries. — From your affectionate friend, Charlotte Brontë.'

TO MISS ELLEN NUSSEY.
'Haworth, January 1, 1833.

' Dear Ellen, — I believe we agreed to correspond once a

207

month. That space of time has now elapsed since I received
your last interesting letter, and I now therefore hasten to reply.
Accept my congratulations on the arrival of the New Year,
every succeeding day of which will, I trust, find you *wiser*
and *better* in the true sense of those much-used words. The
first day of January always presents to my mind a train of
very solemn and important reflections, and a question more
easily asked than answered frequently occurs, viz. — How have
I improved the past year, and with what good intentions do I
view the dawn of its successor? These, my dearest Ellen, are
weighty considerations which (young as we are) neither you
nor I can too deeply or too seriously ponder. I am sorry your
too great diffidence, arising, I think, from the want of sufficient
confidence in your own capabilities, prevented you from writing
to me in French, as I think the attempt would have materially
contributed to your improvement in that language. You very
kindly caution me against being tempted by the fondness of my
sisters to consider myself of too much importance, and then in a
parenthesis you beg me not to be offended. O Ellen, do you
think I could be offended by any good advice you may give me?
No, I thank you heartily, and love you, if possible, better for it.
I am glad you like " Kenilworth." It is certainly a splendid production, more resembling a romance than a novel, and, in my
opinion, one of the most interesting works that ever emanated
from the great Sir Walter's pen. I was exceedingly amused
at the characteristic and naive manner in which you expressed
your detestation of Varney's character — so much so, indeed, that
I could not forbear laughing aloud when I perused that part of
your letter. He is certainly the personification of consummate
villainy ; and in the delineation of his dark and profoundly artful
mind, Scott exhibits a wonderful knowledge of human nature as
well as surprising skill in embodying his perceptions so as to
enable others to become participators in that knowledge. Excuse
the want of *news* in this very barren epistle, for I really have
none to communicate. Emily and Anne beg to be kindly
remembered to you. Give my best love to your mother and
sisters, and as it is very late permit me to conclude with the

AND HER CIRCLE

assurance of my unchanged, unchanging, and unchangeable affection for you. — Adieu, my sweetest Ellen, I am ever yours,

'CHARLOTTE.'

Here is a pleasant testimony to Miss Nussey's attractions from Emily and Anne.

TO MISS ELLEN NUSSEY.

'HAWORTH, September 11, 1833.

'DEAR ELLEN, — I have hitherto delayed answering your last letter because from what you said I imagined you might be from home. Since you were here Emily has been very ill. Her ailment was erysipelas in the arm, accompanied by severe bilious attacks, and great general debility. Her arm was obliged to be cut in order to relieve it. It is now, I am happy to say, nearly healed — her health is, in fact, almost perfectly re-established. The sickness still continues to recur at intervals. Were I to tell you of the impression you have made on every one here you would accuse me of flattery. Papa and aunt are continually adducing you as an example for me to shape my actions and behaviour by. Emily and Anne say "they never saw any one they liked so well as Miss Nussey," and Tabby talks a great deal more nonsense about you than I choose to report. You must read this letter, dear Ellen, without thinking of the writing, for I have indited it almost all in the twilight. It is now so dark that, notwithstanding the singular property of "seeing in the night-time" which the young ladies at Roe Head used to attribute to me, I can scribble no longer. All the family unite with me in wishes for your welfare. Remember me respectfully to your mother and sisters, and supply all those expressions of warm and genuine regard which the increasing darkness will not permit me to insert. CHARLOTTE BRONTË.'

TO MISS ELLEN NUSSEY.

'HAWORTH, February 11, 1834.

'DEAR ELLEN, — My letters are scarcely worth the postage, and therefore I have, till now, delayed answering your last

209

communication; but upwards of two months having elapsed since I received it, I have at length determined to take up my pen in reply lest your anger should be roused by my apparent negligence. It grieved me extremely to hear of your precarious state of health. I trust sincerely that your medical adviser is mistaken in supposing you have any tendency to a pulmonary affection. Dear Ellen, that would indeed be a calamity. I have seen enough of consumption to dread it as one of the most insidious and fatal diseases incident to humanity. But I repeat it, I *hope*, nay *pray*, that your alarm is groundless. If you remember, I used frequently to tell you at school that you were constitutionally nervous — guard against the gloomy impressions which such a state of mind naturally produces. Take constant and regular exercise, and all, I doubt not, will yet be well. What a remarkable winter we have had! Rain and wind continually, but an almost total absence of frost and snow. Has *general* ill health been the consequence of wet weather at Birstall or not? With us an unusual number of deaths have lately taken place. According to custom I have no news to communicate, indeed I do not write either to retail gossip or to impart solid information ; my motives for maintaining our mutual correspondence are, in the first place, to get intelligence from you, and in the second that we may remind each other of our separate existences ; without some such medium of reciprocal converse, according to the nature of things, *you*, who are surrounded by society and friends, would soon forget that such an insignificant being as myself ever lived. *I*, however, in the solitude of our wild little hill village, think of my only unrelated friend, my dear ci-devant school companion daily — nay, almost hourly. Now, Ellen, don't you think I have very cleverly contrived to make up a letter out of nothing? Good-bye, dearest. That God may bless you is the earnest prayer of your ever faithful friend,   CHARLOTTE BRONTË.'

TO MISS ELLEN NUSSEY.

'HAWORTH, November 10, 1834.

'DEAR ELLEN, — I have been a long while, a very long while without writing to you. A letter I received from Mary Taylor this morning reminded me of my neglect, and made me instantly sit down to atone for it, if possible. She tells me your aunt, of Brookroyd, is dead, and that Sarah is very ill; for this I am truly sorry, but I hope her case is not yet without hope. You should however remember that death, should it happen, will undoubtedly be great gain to her. In your last, dear Ellen, you ask my opinion respecting the amusement of dancing, and whether I thought it objectionable when indulged in for an hour or two in parties of boys and girls. I should hesitate to express a difference of opinion from Mr. Atkinson, but really the matter seems to me to stand thus : It is allowed on all hands that the sin of dancing consists not in the mere action of shaking the shanks (as the Scotch say), but in the consequences that usually attend it — namely, frivolity and waste of time ; when it is used only, as in the case you state, for the exercise and amusement of an hour among young people (who surely may without any breach of God's commandments be allowed a little light-heartedness), these consequences cannot follow. Ergo (according to my manner of arguing), the amusement is at such times perfectly innocent. Having nothing more to say, I will conclude with the expression of my sincere and earnest attachment for, Ellen, your own dear self. CHARLOTTE BRONTË '

TO MISS ELLEN NUSSEY.

'HAWORTH, January 12, 1835.

'DEAREST ELLEN,—I thought it better not to answer your kind letter too soon, lest I should (in the present fully occupied state of your time) appear intrusive. I am happy to inform you papa has given me permission to accept the invitation it conveyed, and ere long I hope once more to have the pleasure of seeing *almost* the *only* and certainly the *dearest* friend I possess (out of our own family). I leave it to you to fix the time, only requesting you not to appoint too early a day ; let it be a fortnight or three weeks at least from the date of the present letter. I am greatly obliged to you for your kind offer of meeting me at Bradford, but papa thinks that such a plan would involve uncertainty, and be productive of trouble to you. He recommends that I should go direct in a gig from Haworth at the time you shall determine, or, if that day should prove unfavourable, the first subsequent fine one. Such an arrangement would leave us both free, and if it meets with your approbation would perhaps be the best we could finally resolve upon. Excuse the brevity of this epistle, dear Ellen, for I am in a great hurry, and we shall, I trust, soon see each other face to face, which will be better than a hundred letters. Give my respectful love to your mother and sisters, accept the kind remembrances of all our family, and — Believe me in particular to be, your firm and faithful friend, CHARLOTTE BRONTË.

'P. S. — You ask me to stay a month when I come, but as I do not wish to tire you with my company, and as, besides, papa and aunt both think a fortnight amply sufficient, I shall not exceed that period. Farewell, *dearest, dearest.*'

TO MISS ELLEN NUSSEY.

'ROE HEAD, September 10, 1835.

'MY DEAR ELLEN,— You are far too kind and frequent in your invitations. You puzzle me : I hardly know how to refuse, and it is still more embarrassing to accept. At any rate, I cannot come this week for we are in the very thickest *mêlée* of the repetitions ; I was hearing the terrible fifth section when your note arrived. But Miss Wooler says I must go to Gomersall next Friday as she promised for me on Whitsunday ; and on Sunday morning I will join you at church, if it be convenient, and stay at Rydings till Monday morning. There's a free and easy proposal ! Miss Wooler has driven me to it — she says her character is implicated ! I am very sorry to hear that your mother has been ill. I do hope she is better now, and that all the rest of the family are well. Will you be so kind as to deliver the accompanying note to Miss Taylor when you see her at church on Sunday. Dear Ellen, excuse the most horrid scrawl ever penned by mortal hands. Remember me to your mother and sisters, and — Believe me, E. Nussey's friend, CHARLOTTE.'

TO MISS ELLEN NUSSEY.

'FEBRUARY 20, 1837.

'I read your letter with dismay, Ellen — what shall I do without you? Why are we so to be denied each other's society? It is an inscrutable fatality. I long to be with you because it seems as if two or three days or weeks spent in your company would beyond measure strengthen me in the enjoyment of those feelings which I have so lately begun to cherish. You first pointed out to me that way in which I am so feebly endeavouring to travel, and now I cannot keep you by my side, I must proceed sorrowfully alone.

'Why are we to be divided? Surely, Ellen, it must be because we are in danger of loving each other too well — of losing sight of the *Creator* in idolatry of the *creature*. At first I could not say, "Thy will be done." I felt rebellious; but I know it was wrong to feel so. Being left a moment alone this morning I prayed fervently to be enabled to resign myself to *every* decree of God's will — though it should be dealt forth with a far severer hand than the present disappointment. Since then, I have felt calmer and humbler — and consequently happier. Last Sunday I took up my Bible in a gloomy frame of mind; I began to read; a feeling stole over me such as I have not known for many long years — a sweet placid sensation like those that I remember used to visit me when I was a little child, and on Sunday evenings in summer stood by the open window reading the life of a certain French nobleman who attained a purer and higher degree of sanctity than has been known since the days of the early Martyrs. I thought of my own Ellen — I wished she had been near me that I might have told her how happy I was, how bright and glorious the pages of God's holy word seemed to me. But the "foretaste" passed away, and earth and sin returned. I must see you before you go, Ellen; if you cannot come to Roe Head I will contrive to walk over to Brookroyd, provided you will let me know the time of your departure. Should you not be at home at Easter I dare not promise to accept your mother's and sisters' invitation.

213

I should be miserable at Brookroyd without you, yet I would contrive to visit them for a few hours if I could not for a few days. I love them for your sake. I have written this note at a venture. When it will reach you I know not, but I was determined not to let slip an opportunity for want of being prepared to embrace it. Farewell, may God bestow on you all His blessings. My darling — Farewell. Perhaps you may return before midsummer — do you think you possibly can? I wish your brother John knew how unhappy I am; he would almost pity me. C. Brontë.'

TO MISS ELLEN NUSSEY.
'June 8, 1837.

' My dearest Ellen, — The inclosed, as you will perceive, was written before I received your last. I had intended to send it by this, but what you said altered my intention. I scarce dare build a hope on the foundation your letter lays — we have been disappointed so often, and I fear I shall not be able to prevail on them to part with you; but I will try my utmost, and at any rate there is a chance of our meeting soon; with that thought I will comfort myself. You do not know how selfishly *glad I* am that you still continue to dislike London and the Londoners — it seems to afford a sort of proof that your affections are not changed. Shall we really stand once again together on the moors of Haworth? I *dare* not flatter myself with too sanguine an expectation. I see many doubts and difficulties. But with Miss Wooler's leave, which I have asked and in part obtained, I will go to-morrow and try to remove them. — Believe me, my own Ellen, yours always truly, C. Brontë.'

TO MISS ELLEN NUSSEY.
'January 12, 1839.

' My *dear kind* Ellen, — I can hardly help laughing when I reckon up the number of urgent invitations I have received from you during the last three months. Had I accepted all or even half of them, the Birstallians would certainly have concluded that I had come to make Brookroyd my permanent residence. When you set your mind upon it, you have a peculiar way of edging one in with a circle of dilemmas, so that they hardly know how to refuse you ; however, I shall take a running leap and clear them all. Frankly, my dear Ellen, I *cannot come.* Reflect for yourself a moment. Do you see nothing absurd in the idea of a person coming again into a neighbourhood within a month after they have taken a solemn and formal leave of all their acquaintance ? However, I thank both you and your mother for the invitation, which was most kindly expressed. You give no answer to my proposal that you should come to Haworth with the Taylors. I still think it would be your best plan. I wish you and the Taylors were safely here ; there is no pleasure to be had without toiling for it. You must invite me no more, my dear Ellen, until next Midsummer at the nearest. All here desire to be remembered to you, aunt particularly. Angry though you are, I will venture to sign myself as usual (no, not as usual, but as suits circumstances).—Yours, under a cloud,

' C. BRONTË.'

TO MISS ELLEN NUSSEY.

' MAY 5, 1838.

'MY DEAREST ELLEN,— Yesterday I heard that you were ill. Mr. and Miss Heald were at Dewsbury Moor, and it was from them I obtained the information. This morning I set off to Brookroyd to learn further particulars, from whence I am but just returned. Your mother is in great distress about you, she can hardly mention your name without tears ; and both she and Mercy wish very much to see you at home again. Poor girl, you have been a fortnight confined to your bed ; and while I was blaming you in my own mind for not writing, you were suffering in sickness without one kind *female* friend to watch over you. I should have heard all this before and have hastened to express my sympathy with you in this crisis had I been able to visit Brookroyd in the Easter holidays, but an unexpected summons back to Dewsbury Moor, in consequence of the illness and death of Mr. Wooler, prevented it. Since that time I have been a fortnight and two days quite alone, Miss Wooler being detained in the interim at Rouse Mill. You will now see, Ellen, that it was not neglect or failure of affection which has occasioned my silence, though I fear you will long ago have attributed it to those causes. If you are well enough, do write to me just two lines — just to assure me of your convalescence; not a word, however, if it would harm you — not a syllable. They value you at home. Sickness and absence call forth expressions of attachment which might have remained long enough unspoken if their object had been present and well. I wish your *friends* (I include myself in that word) may soon cease to have cause for so painful an excitement of their regard. As yet I have but an imperfect idea of the nature of your illness — of its extent — or of the degree in which it may now have subsided. When you can let me know all, no particular, however minute, will be uninteresting to me. How have your spirits been? I trust not much overclouded, for that is the most melancholy result of illness. You are not, I understand, going to Bath at present; they seem to have arranged matters strangely. When I parted from you near White-lee Bar, I had a more sorrowful feeling than ever I experienced before in our temporary separations. It is foolish to dwell too much on the idea of presentiments, but I certainly had a feeling that the time of our reunion had never been so indefinite or so distant as then. I doubt not, my dear Ellen, that amidst your many trials, amidst the sufferings that you have of late felt in yourself, and seen in several of your relations, you have still been able to look up and find support in trial, consolation in affliction, and repose in tumult, where human interference can make no change. I think you know in the right spirit how to withdraw yourself from the vexation, the care, the meanness of life, and to derive comfort from purer sources than this world can afford. You know how to do it silently, unknown to others, and can avail yourself of that hallowed communion the Bible gives us with God. I am charged to transmit your mother's and sister's love. Receive mine in the same parcel, I think it will scarcely be the smallest share. Farewell, my dear Ellen.   C. Brontë.'

TO MISS ELLEN NUSSEY.

'May 15, 1840.

' My dear Ellen, — I read your last letter with a great deal of interest. Perhaps it is not always well to tell people when we approve of their actions, and yet it is very pleasant to do so ; and as if you had done wrongly, I hope I should have had honesty enough to tell you so, so now as you have done rightly, I shall gratify myself by telling you what I think.

'If I made you my father confessor I could reveal weaknesses which you do not dream of. I do not mean to intimate that I attach a *high value* to empty compliments, but a word of panegyric has often made me feel a sense of confused pleasure which it required my strongest effort to conceal — and on the other hand, a hasty expression which I could construe into neglect or disapprobation, has tortured me till I have lost half a night's rest from its rankling pangs.　　　　　　　　　　　　C. Brontë.

'P. S. — Don't talk any more of sending for me — when I come I will *send* myself. All send their love to you. I have no prospect of a situation any more than of going to the moon. Write to me again as soon as you can.'

Here is the only glimpse that we find of her Penzance relatives in these later years. They would seem to have visited Haworth when Charlotte was twenty-four years of age. The impression they left was not a kindly one.

TO MISS ELLEN NUSSEY.

'August 14, 1840.

' My dear Ellen, — As you only sent me a note, I shall only send you one, and that not out of revenge, but because like you I have but little to say. The freshest news in our house is that we had, a fortnight ago, a visit from some of our South of England relations, John Branwell and his wife and daughter. They have been staying above a month with Uncle Fennell at Crosstone. They reckon to be very grand folks indeed, and talk largely — I

217

thought assumingly. I cannot say I much admired them. To my eyes there seemed to be an attempt to play the great Mogul down in Yorkshire. Mr. Branwell was much less assuming than the womenites; he seemed a frank, sagacious kind of man, very tall and vigorous, with a keen active look. The moment he saw me he exclaimed that I was the very image of my aunt Charlotte. Mrs. Branwell sets up for being a woman of great talent, tact, and accomplishment. I thought there was much more noise than work. My cousin Eliza is a young lady intended by nature to be a bouncing, good-looking girl — art has trained her to be a languishing, affected piece of goods. I would have been friendly with her, but I could get no talk except about the Low Church, Evangelical clergy, the Millennium, Baptist Noel, botany, and her own conversion. A mistaken education has utterly spoiled the lass. Her face tells that she is naturally good-natured, though perhaps indolent. Her affectations were so utterly out of keeping with her round rosy face and tall bouncing figure, I could hardly refrain from laughing as I watched her. Write a long letter next time and I 'll write you ditto. Goodbye.'

We have already read the letters which were written to Miss Nussey during the governess period, and from Brussels. On her final return from Brussels, Charlotte implores a letter.

TO MISS ELLEN NUSSEY.

'HAWORTH, February 10, 1844.

'DEAR ELLEN, — I cannot tell what occupies your thoughts and time. Are you ill? Is some one of your family ill? Are you married? Are you dead? If it be so, you may as well write a word and let me know — for my part, I am again in old England. I shall tell you nothing further till you write to me.

'C. BRONTË.

'Write to me directly, that is a good girl; I feel really anxious, and have felt so for a long time to hear from you.'

She visits Miss Nussey soon afterwards at Brookroyd, and a little later writes as follows: —

TO MISS ELLEN NUSSEY.

'APRIL 7, 1844.

'DEAR NELL, — I have received your note. It communicated a piece of good news which I certainly did not expect to hear. I want, however, further enlightenment on the subject. Can you tell me what has caused the change in Mary's plans, and brought her so suddenly back to England? Is it on account of Mary Dixon? Is it the wish of her brother, or is it her own determination? I hope, whatever the reason be, it is nothing which can give her uneasiness or do her harm. Do you know how long she is likely to stay in England? or when she arrives at Hunsworth?

'You ask how I am. I really have felt much better the last week — I think my visit to Brookroyd did me good. What delightful weather we have had lately! I wish we had had such while I was with you. Emily and I walk out a good deal on the moors, to the great damage of our shoes, but I hope to the benefit of our health.

'Good-bye, dear Ellen. Send me another of your little notes soon. Kindest regards to all,   C. B.'

TO MISS ELLEN NUSSEY.

'JUNE 9, 1844.

'MY DEAR ELLEN, — Anne and Branwell are now at home, and they and Emily add their request to mine, that you will join us at the beginning of next week. Write and let us know what day you will come, and how — if by coach, we will meet you at Keighley. Do not let your visit be later than the beginning of next week, or you will see little of Anne and Branwell as their holidays are very short. They will soon have to join the family at Scarborough. Remember me kindly to your mother and sisters. I hope they are all well.   C. B.'

CHARLOTTE BRONTË

TO MISS ELLEN NUSSEY.

'NOVEMBER 14, 1844.

'DEAR ELLEN, — Your letter came very apropos, as, indeed, your letters always do; but this morning I had something of a headache, and was consequently rather out of spirits, and the epistle (scarcely legible though it be — excuse a rub) cheered me. In order to evince my gratitude, as well as to please my own inclination, I sit down to answer it immediately. I am glad, in the first place, to hear that your brother is going to be married, and still more so to learn that his wife-elect has a handsome fortune — not that I advocate marrying for money in general, but I think in many cases (and this is one) money is a very desirable contingent of matrimony.

'I wonder when Mary Taylor is expected in England. I trust you will be at home while she is at Hunsworth, and that you, she, and I may meet again somewhere under the canopy of heaven. I cannot, dear Ellen, make any promise about myself and Anne going to Brookroyd at Christmas; her vacations are so short she would grudge spending any part of them from home.

'The catastrophe, which you related so calmly, about your book-muslin dress, lace bertha, etc., convulsed me with cold shudderings of horror. You have reason to curse the day when so fatal a present was offered you as that infamous little "varmint." The perfect serenity with which you endured the disaster proves most fully to me that you would make the best wife, mother, and mistress in the world. You and Anne are a pair for marvellous philosophical powers of endurance; no spoilt dinners, scorched linen, dirtied carpets, torn sofa-covers, squealing brats, cross husbands, would ever discompose either of you. You ought never to marry a good-tempered man, it would be mingling honey with sugar, like sticking white roses upon a black-thorn cudgel. With this very picturesque metaphor I close my letter. Good-bye, and write very soon.

'C. BRONTË.'

Much has been said concerning Charlotte Brontë's visit to Hathersage in Derbyshire, and it is interesting because of the fact that Miss Brontë obtained the name of 'Eyre' from a family in that neighbourhood, and Morton in 'Jane Eyre' may obviously be identified with Hathersage.[1] Miss Ellen Nussey's brother Henry became Vicar of Hathersage, and he married shortly afterwards. While he was on his honeymoon his sister went to Hathersage to keep house for him, and she invited her friend Charlotte Brontë to stay with her. The visit lasted three weeks. This was the only occasion that Charlotte visited Hathersage. Here are two or three short notes referring to that visit.

TO MISS ELLEN NUSSEY.

'JUNE 10, 1845.

'DEAR ELLEN, — It is very vexatious for you to have had to go to Sheffield in vain. I am glad to hear that there is an omnibus on Thursday, and I have told Emily and Anne I will try to come on that day. The opening of the railroad is now postponed till July 7th. I should not like to put you off again, and for that and some other reasons they have decided to give up the idea of going to Scarboro', and instead, to make a little excursion next Monday and Tuesday, to Ilkley or elsewhere. I hope no other obstacle will arise to prevent my going to Hathersage. I do long to be with you, and I feel nervously afraid of being prevented, or put off in some way. Branwell only stayed a week with us, but he is to come home again when the family go to Scarboro'. I will write to Brookroyd directly. Yesterday I had a little note from Henry inviting me to go to see you. This is one of your contrivances, for which you deserve smothering. You have written to Henry to tell him to write to me. Do you think I stood on ceremony about the matter?

[1] In Hathersage Church is the altar tomb of Robert Eyre who fought at Agincourt and died on the 21st of May 1459, also of his wife Joan Eyre who died on the 9th of May 1464. This Joan Eyre was heiress of the house of Padley, and brought the Padley estates into the Eyre family. There is a Sanctus bell of the fifteenth century with a Latin inscription, 'Pray for the souls of Robert Eyre and Joan his wife.' — Rev. Thomas Keyworth on 'Morton Village and "Jane Eyre"' — a paper read before the Brontë Society at Keighley, 1895.

'The French papers have ceased to come. Good-bye for the present. C. B.'

TO MRS. NUSSEY.

'JULY 23, 1845.

'MY DEAR MRS. NUSSEY, — I lose no time after my return home in writing to you and offering you my sincere thanks for the kindness with which you have repeatedly invited me to go and stay a few days at Brookroyd. It would have given me great pleasure to have gone, had it been only for a day, just to have seen you and Miss Mercy (Miss Nussey I suppose is not at home) and to have been introduced to Mrs. Henry, but I have stayed so long with Ellen at Hathersage that I could not possibly now go to Brookroyd. I was expected at home; and after all *home* should always have the first claim on our attention. When I reached home (at ten o'clock on Saturday night) I found papa, I am thankful to say, pretty well, but he thought I had been a long time away.

'I left Ellen well, and she had generally good health while I stayed with her, but she is very anxious about matters of business, and apprehensive lest things should not be comfortable against the arrival of Mr. and Mrs. Henry — she is so desirous that the day of their arrival at Hathersage should be a happy one to both.

'I hope, my dear Mrs. Nussey, you are well; and I should be very happy to receive a little note either from you or from Miss Mercy to assure me of this. — Believe me, yours affectionately and sincerely, C. BRONTË.'

TO MISS ELLEN NUSSEY.

'JULY 24, 1845.

'DEAR ELLEN, — A series of toothaches, prolonged and severe, bothering me both day and night, have kept me very stupid of late, and prevented me from writing to you. More than once I have sat down and opened my desk, but have not been able to get up to par. To-day, after a night of fierce pain, I am better — much better, and I take advantage of the interval of ease to discharge my debt. I wish I had £50 to spare at present, and that you, Emily, Anne, and I were all at liberty to leave home without our absence being detrimental to any body. How pleasant to set off *en masse* to the seaside, and stay there a few weeks, taking in a stock of health and strength. — We could all do with recreation. Adversity agrees with you, Ellen. Your good qualities are never so obvious as when under the pressure of affliction. Continued prosperity might develop too much a certain germ of ambition latent in your character. I saw this little germ putting out green shoots when I was staying with you at Hathersage. It was not then obtrusive, and perhaps might never become so. Your good sense, firm principle, and kind feeling might keep it down. Holding down my head does not suit my toothache. Give my love to your mother and sisters. Write again as soon as may be. — Yours faithfully,   C. B.'

TO MISS ELLEN NUSSEY.

'AUGUST 18, 1845.

' DEAR ELLEN, — I am writing to you, not because I have any-thing to tell you, but because I want you to write to me. I am glad to see that you were pleased with your new sister. When I was at Hathersage you were talking of writing to Mary Taylor. I have lately written to her a brief, shabby epistle of which I am ashamed, but I found when I began to write I had really very little to say. I sent the letter to Hunsworth, and I suppose it will go sometime. You must write to me soon, a long letter. Remember me respectfully to Mr. and Mrs. Henry Nussey. Give my love to Miss R. — Yours,   C. B.'

TO MISS ELLEN NUSSEY.

'DECEMBER 14, 1845.

' DEAR ELLEN, — I was glad to get your last note, though it was so short and crusty. Three weeks had elapsed without my having heard a word from you, and I began to fear some new misfortune had occurred. I was relieved to find such was not the case. Anne is obliged by the kind regret you express at

CHARLOTTE BRONTË

not being able to ask her to Brookroyd. She wishes you could come to Haworth. Do you scold me out of habit, or are you really angry? In either case it is all nonsense. You know as well as I do that to go to Brookroyd is always a pleasure to me, and that to one who has so little change, and so few friends as I have, it must be a *great pleasure,* but I am not at all times in the mood or circumstances to take my pleasure. I wish so much to see you, that I shall certainly sometime after New Year's Day, if all be well, be going over to Birstall. *Now* I could *not* go if I *would.* If you think I stand upon ceremony in this matter, you miscalculate sadly. I have known you, and your mother and sisters, too long to be ceremonious with any of you. Invite me no more now, till I invite myself — be too proud to trouble yourself; and if, when at last I mention coming (for I shall give you warning), it does not happen to suit you, tell me so, with quiet hauteur. I should like a long letter next time. No more lover's quarrels.

'Good-bye. Best love to your mother and sisters. C. B.'

TO MISS ELLEN NUSSEY.

'JANUARY 28, 1847.

'DEAR ELLEN, — Long may you look young and handsome enough to dress in white, dear, and long may you have a right to feel the consciousness that you look agreeable. I know you have too much judgment to let an overdose of vanity spoil the blessing and turn it into a misfortune. After all though, age will come on, and it is well you have something better than a nice face for friends to turn to when that is changed. I hope this excessively cold weather has not harmed you or yours much. It has nipped me severely, taken away my appetite for a while and given me toothache; in short, put me in the ailing condition, in which I have more than once had the honour of making myself such a nuisance both at Brookroyd and Hunsworth. The consequence is that at this present speaking I look almost old enough to be your mother — grey, sunk, and withered. To-day, however, it is milder, and I hope soon to feel better; indeed I am not *ill* now, and my toothache is now subsided, but I

224

experience a loss of strength and a deficiency of spirit which
would make me a sorry companion to you or any one else. I
would not be on a visit now for a large sum of money.

'Write soon. Give my best love to your mother and sisters. —
Good-bye, dear Nell,   C. BRONTË.'

TO MISS ELLEN NUSSEY.

'APRIL 21, 1847.

'DEAR NELL, — I am very much obliged to you for your gift,
which you must not undervalue, for I like the articles; they
look extremely pretty and light. They are for wrist frills, are
they not? Will you condescend to accept a yard of lace made
up into nothing? I thought I would not offer to spoil it by
stitching it into any shape. Your creative fingers will turn it
to better account than my destructive ones. I hope, such as it
is, they will not peck it out of the envelope at the Bradford
Post-office, where they generally take the liberty of opening
letters when they feel soft as if they contained articles. I had
forgotten all about your birthday and mine, till your letter
arrived to remind me of it. I wish you many happy returns of
yours. Of course your visit to Haworth must be regulated by
Miss Ringrose's movements. I was rather amused at your fearing
I should be jealous. I never thought of it. She and I could
not be rivals in your affections. You allot her, I know, a
different set of feelings to what you allot me. She is amiable
and estimable, I am not amiable, but still we shall stick to the
last I don't doubt. In short, I should as soon think of being
jealous of Emily and Anne in these days as of you. If Miss
Ringrose does not come to Brookroyd about Whitsuntide, I should
like you to come. I shall feel a good deal disappointed if the
visit is put off — I would rather Miss Ringrose fixed her time in
summer, and then I would come to see you (D.V.) in the autumn.
I don't think it will be at all a good plan to go back with you.
We see each other so seldom, that I would far rather divide the
visits. Remember me to all. — Yours faithfully,

'C. BRONTË.'

CHARLOTTE BRONTË

TO MISS ELLEN NUSSEY.

'MAY 25, 1847.

'DEAR NELL, — I have a small present for Mercy. You must fetch it, for I repeat you shall *come to Haworth before I go to Brookroyd*.

'I do not say this from pique or anger — I am not angry now — but because my leaving home at present would from solid reasons be difficult to manage. If all be well I will visit you in the autumn, at present I *cannot* come. Be assured that if I could come I should, after your last letter, put scruples and pride away and "go over into Macedonia" at once. I never could manage to help you yet. You have always found me something like a new servant, who requires to be told where everything is, and shown how everything is to be done.

'My sincere love to your mother and Mercy. — Yours,

'C. BRONTË.'

TO MISS ELLEN NUSSEY.

'MAY 29, 1847.

'DEAR ELLEN, — Your letter and its contents were most welcome. You must direct your luggage to Mr. Brontë's, and we will tell the carrier to inquire for it. The railroad has been opened some time, but it only comes as far as Keighley. If you arrive about 4 o'clock in the afternoon, Emily, Anne, and I will all meet you at the station. We can take tea jovially together at the Devonshire Arms, and walk home in the cool of the evening. This arrangement will be much better than fagging through four miles in the heat of noon. Write by return of post if you can, and say if this plan suits you. — Yours,

'C. BRONTË.'

TO MISS ELLEN NUSSEY.

'NOVEMBER 10, 1847.

'DEAR ELLEN, — The old pang of fearing you should fancy I forget you drives me to write to you, though heaven knows I have precious little to say, and if it were not that I wish to hear from you, and hate to appear disregardful when I am not so, I might let another week or perhaps two slip away without writing. There is much in Ruth's letter that I thought very melancholy. Poor girls! theirs, I fear, must be a very unhappy home. Yours and mine, with all disadvantages, all absences of luxury and wealth and style, are, I doubt not, happier. I wish to goodness you were rich that you might give her a temporary asylum, and a relief from uneasiness, suffering, and gloom. What you say about the effects of ether on your sister rather startled me. I had always consoled myself with the idea of having some teeth extracted some day under its soothing influence, but now I should think twice before I consented to inhale it; one would not like to make a fool of one's self.— I am, yours faithfully, C. BRONTË.'

TO MISS ELLEN NUSSEY.
'MARCH 11, 1848.

'DEAR ELLEN,— There is a great deal of good-sense in your last letter. Be thankful that God gave you sense, for what are beauty, wealth, or even health without it? I had a note from Miss Ringrose the other day. I do not think I shall write again, for the reasons I before mentioned to you; but the note moved me much, it was almost all about her dear Ellen, a kind of gentle enthusiasm of affection, enough to make one smile and weep — her feelings are half truth, half illusion. No human being could be altogether what she supposes you to be, yet your kindness must have been very great. If one were only rich, how delightful it would be to travel and spend the winter in climates where there are no winters. Give my love to your mother and sisters.— Believe me, faithfully yours, C. BRONTË.'

TO MISS ELLEN NUSSEY.
'APRIL 22, 1848.

'DEAR ELLEN,— I have just received your little parcel, and beg to thank you in all our names for its contents, and also for your letter, of the arrival of which I was, to speak truth, getting rather impatient.
'The housewife's travelling companion is a most commodious

thing — just the sort of article which suits one to a T, and which yet I should never have the courage or industry to sit down and make for myself. I shall keep it for occasions of going from home, it will save me a world of trouble. It must have required some thought to arrange the various compartments and their contents so aptly. I had quite forgotten till your letter reminded me that it was the anniversary of your birthday and mine. I am now thirty-two. Youth is gone — gone — and will never come back ; can't help it. I wish you many returns of your birthday and increase of happiness with increase of years. It seems to me that sorrow must come sometime to every body, and those who scarcely taste it in their youth often have a more brimming and bitter cup to drain in after-life ; whereas, those who exhaust the dregs early, who drink the lees before the wine, may reasonably expect a purer and more palatable draught to succeed. So, at least, one fain would hope. It touched me at first a little painfully to hear of your purposed governessing, but on second thoughts I discovered this to be quite a foolish feeling. You are doing right even though you should not gain much. The effort will do you good ; no one ever does regret a step towards self-help ; it is so much gained in independence.

'Give my love to your mother and sisters.— Yours faithfully,

'C. Brontë.'

TO MISS ELLEN NUSSEY.

'May 24, 1848.

'Dear Ellen,— I shall begin by telling you that you have no right to be angry at the length of time I have suffered to slip by, since receiving your last, without answering it, because you have often kept me waiting much longer; and having made this gracious speech, thereby obviating reproaches, I will add that I think it a great shame when you receive a long and thoroughly interesting letter, full of the sort of details you fully relish, to read the same with selfish pleasure and not even have the manners to thank your correspondent, and express how much you enjoyed the narrative. I *did* enjoy the narrative in your last very keenly ; the exquisitely characteristic traits concerning the Bakers were worth gold; just like not only them but all their class — respectable, well-meaning people enough, but with all that petty assumption of dignity, that small jealousy of senseless formalities, which to such people seems to form a second religion. Your position amongst them was detestable. I admire the philosophy with which you bore it. Their taking offence because you stayed all night at their aunt's is rich. It is right not to think much of casual attentions; it is quite justifiable also to derive from them temporary gratification, insomuch as they prove that their object has the power of pleasing. Let them be as ephemera — to last an hour, and not be regretted when gone.

'Write to me again soon and — Believe me, yours faithfully,

'C. Brontë.'

TO MISS ELLEN NUSSEY.

'August 3, 1849.

'Dear Ellen, — I have received the furs safely. I like the sables very much, and shall keep them; and "to save them" shall keep the squirrel, as you prudently suggested. I hope it is not too much like the steel poker to save the brass one. I return Mary's letter. It is another page from the volume of life, and at the bottom is written "Finis" — mournful word. Macaulay's "History" was only *lent* to myself — all the books I have from London I accept only as a loan, except in peculiar cases, where it is the author's wish I should possess his work.

'Do you think in a few weeks it will be possible for you to come to see me? I am only waiting to get my labour off my hands to permit myself the pleasure of asking you. At our house you can read as much as you please.

'I have been much better, very free from oppression or irritation of the chest, during the last fortnight or ten days. Love to all. — Good-bye, dear Nell.   C. B.'

TO MISS ELLEN NUSSEY.

'August 23, 1849.

'Dear Ellen, — Papa has not been well at all lately — he has had another attack of bronchitis. I felt very uneasy about him for

229

some days, more wretched indeed than I care to tell you. After what has happened, one trembles at any appearance of sickness, and when anything ails papa I feel too keenly that he is the *last* the *only* near and dear relation I have in the world. Yesterday and to-day he has seemed much better, for which I am truly thankful.

'For myself, I should be pretty well but for a continually recurring feeling of slight cold, slight soreness in the throat and chest, of which, do what I will, I cannot quite get rid. Has your cough entirely left you? I wish the atmosphere would return to a salubrious condition, for I really think it is not healthy. English cholera has been very prevalent here.

' I *do* wish to see you.'

TO MISS ELLEN NUSSEY.

'August 16, 1850.

'Dear Nell, — I am going on Monday (d.v.) a journey, whereof the prospect cheers me not at all, to Windermere, in Westmoreland, to spend a few days with Sir J. K. S., who has taken a house there for the autumn and winter. I consented to go with reluctance, chiefly to please papa, whom a refusal on my part would have much annoyed; but I dislike to leave him. I trust he is not worse, but his complaint is still weakness. It is not right to anticipate evil, and to be always looking forward in an apprehensive spirit; but I think grief is a two-edged sword — it cuts both ways: the memory of one loss is the anticipation of another. Take moderate exercise and be careful, dear Nell, and — Believe me, yours sincerely,   C. Brontë.'

TO MISS ELLEN NUSSEY.

'May 10, 1851.

'Dear Nell, — Poor little Flossy! I have not yet screwed up nerve to tell papa about her fate, it seems to me so piteous. However, she had a happy life with a kind mistress, whatever her death has been. Little hapless plague! She had more goodness and patience shown her than she deserved, I fear.

'C. Brontë.'

AND HER CIRCLE

TO MISS ELLEN NUSSEY.

'HAWORTH, July 26, 1852.

'DEAR ELLEN, — I should not have written to you to-day by choice. Lately I have again been harassed with headache — the heavy electric atmosphere oppresses me much, yet I am less miserable just now than I was a little while ago. A severe shock came upon me about papa. He was suddenly attacked with acute inflammation of the eye. Mr. Ruddock was sent for; and after he had examined him, he called me into another room, and said papa's pulse was bounding at 150 per minute, that there was a strong pressure of blood upon the brain, that, in short, the symptoms were decidedly apoplectic.

'Active measures were immediately taken. By the next day the pulse was reduced to ninety. Thank God he is now better, though not well. The eye is a good deal inflamed. He does not know his state. To tell him he had been in danger of apoplexy would almost be to kill him at once — it would increase the rush to the brain and perhaps bring about rupture. He is kept very quiet.

'Dear Nell, you will excuse a short note. Write again soon. Tell me all concerning yourself that can relieve you. — Yours faithfully,   C. B.'

TO MISS ELLEN NUSSEY.

'AUGUST 3, 1852.

'DEAR ELLEN, — I write a line to say that papa is now considered out of danger. His progress to health is not without relapse, but I think he gains ground, if slowly, surely. Mr. Ruddock says the seizure was quite of an apoplectic character; there was a partial paralysis for two days, but the mind remained clear, in spite of a high degree of nervous irritation. One eye still remains inflamed, and papa is weak, but all muscular affection is gone, and the pulse is accurate. One cannot be too thankful that papa's sight is yet spared — it was the fear of losing that which chiefly distressed him.

'With best wishes for yourself, dear Ellen, — I am, yours faithfully,   C. BRONTË.

'My headaches are better. I have needed no help, but I thank you sincerely for your kind offers.'

TO MISS ELLEN NUSSEY.

'HAWORTH, August 12, 1852.

'DEAR ELLEN, — Papa has varied occasionally since I wrote to you last. Monday was a very bad day, his spirits sunk painfully. Tuesday and yesterday, however, were much better, and to-day he seems wonderfully well. The prostration of spirits which accompanies anything like a relapse is almost the most difficult point to manage. Dear Nell, you are tenderly kind in offering your society ; but rest very tranquil where you are ; be fully assured that it is not now, nor under present circumstances, that I feel the lack either of society or occupation ; my time is pretty well filled up, and my thoughts appropriated.

'Mr. Ruddock now seems quite satisfied there is no present danger whatever ; he says papa has an excellent constitution and may live many years yet. The true balance is not yet restored to the circulation, but I believe that impetuous and dangerous termination to the head is quite obviated. I cannot permit myself to comment much on the chief contents of your last ; advice is not necessary. As far as I can judge, you seem hitherto enabled to take these trials in a good and wise spirit. I can only pray that such combined strength and resignation may be continued to you. Submission, courage, exertion, when practicable — these seem to be the weapons with which we must fight life's long battle. — Yours faithfully,   C. BRONTË.'

To Miss Nussey we owe many other letters than those here printed — indeed, they must need play an important part in Charlotte Brontë's biography. They do not deal with the intellectual interests which are so marked in the letters to W. S. Williams, and which, doubtless, characterised the letters to Miss Mary Taylor. 'I ought to have written this letter to Mary,' Charlotte says, when on one occasion

she dropped into literature to her friend; but the friendship
was as precious as most intellectual friendships, because it
was based upon a common esteem and an unselfish devotion. Ellen Nussey, as we have seen, accompanied Anne
Brontë to Scarborough, and was at her death-bed. She
attended Charlotte's wedding, and lived to mourn over her
tomb. For forty years she has been the untiring advocate
and staunch champion, hating to hear a word in her great
friend's dispraise, loving to note the glorious recognition,
of which there has been so rich and so full a harvest. That
she still lives to receive our reverent gratitude for preserving
so many interesting traits of the Brontës, is matter for full
and cordial congratulation, wherever the names of the authors
of 'Jane Eyre' and 'Wuthering Heights' are held in just
and wise esteem.

CHAPTER IX.

MARY TAYLOR.

MARY TAYLOR, the 'M——' of Mrs. Gaskell's biography, and the 'Rose Yorke' of 'Shirley' will always have a peculiar interest to those who care for the Brontës. She shrank from publicity, and her name has been less mentioned than that of any other member of the circle. And yet hers was a personality singularly strenuous and strong. She wrote two books 'with a purpose,' and, as we shall see, vigorously embodied her teaching in her life. It will be remembered that Charlotte Brontë, Ellen Nussey, and Mary Taylor first met at Roe Head School, when Charlotte and Mary were fifteen and her friend about fourteen years of age. Here are Miss Nussey's impressions : —

'She was pretty and very childish-looking, dressed in a red-coloured frock with short sleeves and low neck, as then worn by young girls. Miss Wooler in later years used to say that when Mary went to her as a pupil she thought her too pretty to live. She was not talkative at school, but industrious, and always ready with lessons. She was always at the top in class lessons, with Charlotte Brontë and the writer ; seldom a change was made, and then only with the three — one move. Charlotte and she were great friends for a time, but there was no withdrawing from me on either side, and Charlotte never quite knew how an estrangement arose with Mary, but it lasted a long time. Then a time came that both Charlotte and Mary were so proficient in schoolroom attainments there was no more for them to learn, and Miss Wooler set them Blair's "Belles

Lettres " to commit to memory. We all laughed at their studies. Charlotte persevered, but Mary took her own line, flatly refused, and accepted the penalty of disobedience, going supperless to bed for about a month before she left school. When it was moonlight, we always found her engaged in drawing on .the chest of drawers, which stood in the bay window, quite happy and cheerful. Her rebellion was never outspoken. She was always quiet in demeanour. Her sister Martha, on the contrary, spoke out vigorously, daring Miss Wooler so much, face to face, that she sometimes received a box on the ear, which hardly any saint could have withheld. Then Martha would expatiate on the danger of boxing ears, quoting a reverend brother of Miss Wooler's. Among her school companions, Martha was called " Miss Boisterous," but was always a favourite, so piquant and fascinating were her ways. She was not in the least pretty, but something much better, full of change and variety, rudely outspoken, lively, and original, producing laughter with her own good-humour and affection. She was her father's pet child. He delighted in hearing her sing, telling her to go to the piano, with his affectionate " Patty lass."

'Mary never had the impromptu vivacity of her sister, but was lively in games that engaged her mind. Her music was very correct, but entirely cultivated by practice and perseverance. Anything underhand was detestable to both Mary and Martha; they had no mean pride towards others, but accepted the incidents of life with imperturbable good-sense and insight. They were not dressed as well as other pupils, for economy at that time was the rule of their household. The girls had to stitch all over their new gloves before wearing them, by order of their mother, to make them wear longer. Their dark blue cloth coats were worn when *too short,* and black beaver bonnets quite plainly trimmed, with the ease and contentment of a fashionable costume. Mr. Taylor was a banker as well as a monopolist of army cloth manufacture in the district. He lost money, and gave up banking. He set his mind on paying all creditors, and effected this during his lifetime as far as possible, willing that his sons were to do the remainder, which two of his sons carried out, as was understood, during their lifetime — Mark and Martin of "Shirley." '

Let us now read Charlotte's description in 'Shirley,' and I think we have a tolerably fair estimate of the sisters.

'The two next are girls, Rose and Jessie; they are both now at their father's knee; they seldom go near their mother, except when obliged to do so. Rose, the elder, is twelve years old; she is like her father — the most like him of the whole group — but it is a granite head copied in ivory; all is softened in colour and line. Yorke himself has a harsh face; his daughter's is not harsh, neither is it quite pretty; it is simple — childlike in feature; the round cheeks bloom; as to the grey eyes, they are otherwise than childlike — a serious soul lights them — a young soul yet, but it will mature, if the body lives; and neither father nor mother has a spirit to compare with it. Partaking of the essence of each, it will one day be better than either — stronger, much purer, more aspiring. Rose is a still, and sometimes a stubborn girl now; her mother wants to make of her such a woman as she is herself — a woman of dark and dreary duties; and Rose has a mind full-set, thick-sown with the germs of ideas her mother never knew. It is agony to her often to have these ideas trampled on and repressed. She has never rebelled yet; but if hard driven, she will rebel one day, and then it will be once for all. Rose loves her father; her father does not rule her with a rod of iron; he is good to her. He sometimes fears she will not live, so bright are the sparks of intelligence which, at moments, flash from her glance and gleam in her language. This idea makes him often sadly tender to her.

'He has no idea that little Jessie will die young, she is so gay and chattering, arch — original even now; passionate when provoked, but most affectionate if caressed; by turns gentle and rattling; exacting yet generous; fearless — of her mother, for instance, whose irrationally hard and strict rule she has often defied — yet reliant on any who will help her. Jessie, with her little piquant face, engaging prattle, and winning ways, is made to be a pet ; and her father's pet she accordingly is.'

Mary Taylor was called 'Pag' by her friends, and the first important reference to her that I find is contained in a letter written by Charlotte to Ellen Nussey, when she was seventeen years of age.

TO MISS ELLEN NUSSEY.

'HAWORTH, June 20, 1833.

' DEAR ELLEN, — I know you will be very angry because I have not written sooner ; my reason, or rather my motive for this apparent neglect was, that I had determined not to write until I could ask you to pay us your long-promised visit. Aunt thought it would be better to defer it until about the middle of summer, as the winter and even the spring seasons are remarkably cold and bleak among our mountains. Papa now desires me to present his respects to your mother, and say that he should feel greatly obliged if she would allow us the pleasure of your company for a few weeks at Haworth. I will leave it to you to fix whatever day may be most convenient, but let it be an early one. I received a letter from Pag Taylor yesterday ; she was in high dudgeon at my inattention in not promptly answering her last epistle. I however sat down immediately and wrote a very humble reply, candidly confessing my faults and soliciting forgiveness ; I hope it has proved successful. Have you suffered much from that troublesome though not (I am happy to hear) generally fatal disease, the influenza? We have so far steered clear of it, but I know not how long we may continue to escape. Your last letter revealed a state of mind which seemed to promise much. As I read it I could not help wishing that my own feelings more resembled yours ; but unhappily all the good thoughts that enter *my mind* evaporate almost before I have had time to ascertain their existence ; every right resolution which I form is so transient, so fragile, and so easily broken, that I sometimes fear I shall never be what I ought. Earnestly hoping that this may not be your case, that

237

you may continue steadfast till the end, — I remain, dearest Ellen, your ever faithful friend, CHARLOTTE BRONTË.'

The next letter refers to Mr. Taylor's death. Mr. Taylor, it is scarcely necessary to add, is the Mr. Yorke of Briarmains, who figures so largely in ' Shirley.' I have visited the substantial red-brick house near the high-road at Gomersall, but descriptions of the Brontë country do not come within the scope of this volume.

TO MISS ELLEN NUSSEY.

'JANUARY 3, 1841.

' MY DEAR ELLEN, — I received the news in your last with no surprise, and with the feeling that this removal must be a relief to Mr. Taylor himself and even to his family. The bitterness of death was past a year ago, when it was first discovered that his illness must terminate fatally ; all between has been lingering suspense. This is at an end now, and the present certainty, however sad, is better than the former doubt. What will be the consequence of his death is another question ; for my own part, I look forward to a dissolution and dispersion of the family, perhaps not immediately, but in the course of a year or two. It is true, causes may arise to keep them together awhile longer, but they are restless, active spirits, and will not be restrained always. Mary alone has more energy and power in her nature than any ten men you can pick out in the united parishes of Birstall and Haworth. It is vain to limit a character like hers within ordinary boundaries — she will overstep them. I am morally certain Mary will establish her own landmarks, so will the rest of them. C. BRONTË.'

Soon after her father's death Mary Taylor turned her eyes towards New Zealand, where she had friends, but two years were to go by before anything came of the idea.

TO MISS EMILY J. BRONTË.

' UPPERWOOD HOUSE, April 2, 1841.

' DEAR E. J., — I received your last letter with delight as usual. I must write a line to thank you for it and the

238

inclosure, which however is too bad — you ought not to have
sent me those packets. I had a letter from Anne yesterday ;
she says she is well. I hope she speaks absolute truth. I
had written to her and Branwell a few days before. I have
not heard from Branwell yet. It is to be hoped that his removal to another station will turn out for the best. As you say,
it *looks* like getting on at any rate.

'I have got up my courage so far as to ask Mrs. White to
grant me a day's holiday to go to Birstall to see Ellen Nussey,
who has offered to send a gig for me. My request was granted,
but so coldly and slowly. However, I stuck to my point in a
very exemplary and remarkable manner. I hope to go next
Saturday. Matters are progressing very strangely at Gomersall.
Mary Taylor and Waring have come to a singular determination,
but I almost think under the peculiar circumstances a defensible
one, though it sounds outrageously odd at first. They are
going to emigrate — to quit the country altogether. Their
destination unless they change is Port Nicholson, in the
northern island of New Zealand !!! Mary has made up her
mind she cannot and will not be a governess, a teacher, a
milliner, a bonnet-maker nor housemaid. She sees no means
of obtaining employment she would like in England, so she is
leaving it. I counselled her to go to France likewise and stay
there a year before she decided on this strange unlikely-
sounding plan of going to New Zealand, but she is quite
resolved. I cannot sufficiently comprehend what her views
and those of her brothers' may be on the subject, or what is
the extent of their information regarding Port Nicholson, to
say whether this is rational enterprise or absolute madness.
With love to papa, aunt, Tabby, etc. — Good-bye.   C. B.

'P.S. — I am very well ; I hope you are. Write again soon.'

Soon after this **Mary** went on a long visit to Brussels,
which, as we have seen, was the direct cause of Charlotte
and Emily establishing themselves at the Pensionnat Héger.
In Brussels Martha Taylor found a grave. Here is one of
her letters.

CHARLOTTE BRONTË

TO MISS ELLEN NUSSEY.

'BRUSSELS, September 9, 1841.

'MY DEAR ELLEN, — I received your letter from Mary, and you say I am to write though I have nothing to say. My sister will tell you all about me, for she has more time to write than I have.

'Whilst Mary and John have been with me, we have been to Liege and Spa, where we stayed eight days. I found my little knowledge of French very useful in our travels. I am going to begin working again very hard, now that John and Mary are going away. I intend beginning German directly. I would write some more but this pen of Mary's won't write; you must scold her for it, and tell her to write you a long account of my proceedings. You must write to me sometimes. George Dixon is coming here the last week in September, and you must send a letter for me to Mary to be forwarded by him. Good-bye. May you be happy.   MARTHA TAYLOR.'

It was while Charlotte was making her second stay in Brussels that she heard of Mary's determination to go with her brother Waring to New Zealand, with a view to earning her own living in any reasonable manner that might offer.

TO MISS ELLEN NUSSEY.

'BRUSSELS, April 1, 1843.

'DEAR ELLEN, — That last letter of yours merits a good dose of panegyric — it was both long and interesting; send me quickly such another, longer still if possible. You will have heard of Mary Taylor's resolute and intrepid proceedings. Her public letters will have put you in possession of all details — nothing is left for me to say except perhaps to express my opinion upon it. I have turned the matter over on all sides and really I cannot consider it otherwise than as very rational. Mind, I did not jump to this opinion at once, but was several days before I formed it conclusively.   C. B.'

TO MISS ELLEN NUSSEY.

'SUNDAY EVENING, June 1, 1845.

'DEAR ELLEN, — You probably know that another letter has been received from Mary Taylor. It is, however, possible that your absence from home will have prevented your seeing it, so I will give you a sketch of its contents. It was written at about 4° N. of the Equator. The first part of the letter contained an account of their landing at Santiago. Her health at that time was very good, and her spirits seemed excellent. They had had contrary winds at first setting out, but their voyage was then prosperous. In the latter portion of the letter she complains of the excessive heat, and says she lives chiefly on oranges; but still she was well, and freer from headache and other ailments than any other person on board. The receipt of this letter will have relieved all her friends from a weight of anxiety. I am uneasy about what you say respecting the French newspapers — do you mean to intimate that you have received none? I have despatched them regularly. Emily and I keep them usually three days, sometimes only two, and then send them forward to you. I see by the cards you sent, and also by the newspaper, that Henry is at last married. How did you like your office of bridesmaid? and how do you like your new sister and her family? You must write to me as soon as you can, and give me an *observant* account of everything.   C. BRONTË.'

TO MISS ELLEN NUSSEY.

'MANCHESTER, September 13, 1846.

'DEAR ELLEN, — Papa thinks his own progress rather slow, but the doctor affirms he is getting on very well. He complains of extreme weakness and soreness in the eye, but I suppose that is to be expected for some time to come. He is still kept in the dark, but now sits up the greater part of the day, and is allowed a little fire in the room, from the light of which he is carefully screened.

'By this time you will have got Mary's letters; most interesting they are, and she is in her element because she is where she has a toilsome task to perform, an important improvement to effect, a weak vessel to strengthen. You ask if I had any enjoyment here; in truth, I can't say I have, and I long to get home, though, unhappily, home is not now a place of complete rest. It is sad to think how it is disquieted by a constant phantom, or rather two — sin and suffering; they seem to obscure the cheerfulness of day, and to disturb the comfort of evening.

'Give my love to all at Brookroyd, and believe me, yours faithfully,   C. B.'

TO MISS ELLEN NUSSEY.

'June 5, 1847.

'Dear Ellen, — I return you Mary Taylor's letter; it made me somewhat sad to read it, for I fear she is not quite content with her existence in New Zealand. She finds it too barren. I believe she is more homesick than she will confess. Her gloomy ideas respecting you and me prove a state of mind far from gay. I have also received a letter; its tone is similar to your own, and its contents too.

'What brilliant weather we have had. Oh! I do indeed regret you could not come to Haworth at the time fixed, these warm sunny days would have suited us exactly; but it is not to be helped. Give my best love to your mother and Mercy. — Yours faithfully,   C. Brontë.'

TO MISS ELLEN NUSSEY.

'Haworth, June 26, 1848.

'Dear Ellen, — I should have answered your last long ago if I had known your address, but you omitted to give it me, and I have been waiting in the hope that you would perhaps write again and repair the omission. Finding myself deceived in this expectation however, I have at last hit on the plan of sending the letter to Brookroyd to be directed; be sure to give me your address when you reply to this.

'I was glad to hear that you were well received at London, and that you got safe to the end of your journey. Your *naïveté* in gravely inquiring my opinion of the "last new novel" amuses me. We do not subscribe to a circulating library at Haworth, and consequently "new novels" rarely indeed come in our way, and consequently, again, we are not qualified to give opinions thereon.

'About three weeks ago, I received a brief note from Hunsworth to the effect that Mr. Joe Taylor and his cousin Henry would make some inquiries respecting Mme. Héger's school on account of Ellen Taylor, and that if I had no objection, they would ride over to Haworth in a day or two. I said they might come if they would. They came, accompanied by Miss Mossman, of Bradford, whom I had never seen, only heard of occasionally. It was a pouring wet and windy day; we had quite ceased to expect them. Miss Mossman was quite wet, and we had to make her change her things, and dress her out in ours as well as we could. I do not know if you are acquainted with her; I thought her unaffected and rather agreeable looking, though she has very red hair. Henry Taylor does indeed resemble John most strongly. Joe looked thin; he was in good spirits, and I think in tolerable good-humour. I would have given much for you to have been there. I had not been very well for some days before, and had some difficulty in keeping up the talk, but I managed on the whole better than I expected. I was glad Miss Mossman came, for she helped. Nothing new was communicated respecting Mary. Nothing of importance in any way was said the whole time; it was all rattle, rattle, of which I should have great difficulty now in recalling the substance. They left almost immediately after tea. I have not heard a word respecting them since, but I suppose they got home all right. The visit strikes me as an odd whim. I consider it quite a caprice, prompted probably by curiosity.

'Joe Taylor mentioned that he had called at Brookroyd, and that Anne had told him you were ill, and going into the South for change of air.

'I hope you will soon write to me again and tell me particularly how your health is, and how you get on. Give my regards to

CHARLOTTE BRONTË

Mary Gorham, for really I have a sort of regard for her by hearsay, and — Believe me, dear Nell, yours faithfully,

'C. Brontë.'

The Ellen Taylor mentioned in the above letter did not go to Brussels. She joined her cousin Mary in New Zealand instead.

TO MISS CHARLOTTE BRONTË.

'Wellington, April 10, 1849.

'Dear Charlotte, — I 've been delighted to receive a very interesting letter from you with an account of your visit to London, etc. I believe I have tacked this acknowledgment to the tail of my last letter to you, but since then it has dawned on my comprehension that you are becoming a very important personage in this little world, and therefore, d' ye see? I must write again to you. I wish you would give me some account of Newby, and what the man said when confronted with the real Ellis Bell. By the way, having got your secret, will he keep it? And how do you contrive to get your letters under the address of Mr. Bell? The whole scheme must be particularly interesting to hear about, if I could only talk to you for half a day. When do you intend to tell the good people about you?

'I am now hard at work expecting Ellen Taylor. She may possibly be here in two months. I once thought of writing you some of the dozens of schemes I have for Ellen Taylor, but as the choice depends on her I may as well wait and tell you the one she chooses. The two most reasonable are keeping a school and keeping a shop. The last is evidently the most healthy, but the most difficult of accomplishment. I have written an account of the earthquakes for "Chambers," and intend (now don't remind me of this a year hence, because *la femme propose*) to write some more. What else I shall do I don't know. I find the writing faculty does not in the least depend on the leisure I have, but much more on the *active* work I have to do. I write at my novel a little and think of my other book. What this will turn out, God only knows. It is not, and never can be forgotten. It is my child, my baby, and *I assure you* such a

244

wonder as never was. I intend him when full grown to revolu-
tionise society and *faire époque* in history.

'In the meantime I'm doing a collar in crochet work.

'Pag.'

TO MISS CHARLOTTE BRONTË.

'Wellington, New Zealand.
'July 24, 1849.

'Dear Charlotte, — About a month since I received and read
"Jane Eyre." It seemed to me incredible that you had actually
written a book. Such events did not happen while I was in England. I begin to believe in your existence much as I do in Mr.
Rochester's. In a believing mood I don't doubt either of them.
After I had read it I went on to the top of Mount Victoria and
looked for a ship to carry a letter to you. There was a little thing
with one mast, and also H. M. S. "Fly," and nothing else. If a
cattle vessel came from Sydney she would probably return in a few
days, and would take a mail, but we have had east wind for a
month and nothing can come in.

'*Aug.* 1. — The "Harlequin" has just come from Otago, and is
to sail for Singapore *when the wind changes*, and by that route
(which I hope to take myself sometime) I send you this.
Much good may it do you. Your novel surprised me by
being so perfect as a work of art. I expected something more
changeable and unfinished. You have polished to some purpose.
If I were to do so I should get tired, and weary every one
else in about two pages. No sign of this weariness in your
book — you must have had abundance, having kept it all to
yourself!

'You are very different from me in having no doctrine to
preach. It is impossible to squeeze a moral out of your
production. Has the world gone so well with you that you
have no protest to make against its absurdities? Did you
never sneer or declaim in your first sketches? I will scold
you well when I see you. I do not believe in Mr. Rivers.
There are no *good* men of the Brocklehurst species. A
missionary either goes into his office for a piece of bread, or

245

he goes from enthusiasm, and that is both too good and too bad a quality for St. John. It's a bit of your absurd charity to believe in such a man. You have done wisely in choosing to imagine a high class of readers. You never stop to explain or defend anything, and never seem bothered with the idea. If Mrs. Fairfax or any other well-intentioned fool gets hold of this what will she think? And yet, you know, the world is made up of such, and worse. Once more, how have you written through three volumes without declaring war to the knife against a few dozen absurd doctrines, each of which is supported by "a large and respectable class of readers"? Emily seems to have had such a class in her eye when she wrote that strange thing "Wuthering Heights." Anne, too, stops repeatedly to preach commonplace truths. She has had a still lower class in her mind's eye. Emily seems to have followed the bookseller's advice. As to the price you got, it was certainly Jewish. But what could the people do? If they had asked you to fix it, do you know yourself how many ciphers your sum would have had? And how should they know better? And if they did, that's the knowledge they get their living by. If I were in your place, the idea of being bound in the sale of two more would prevent me from ever writing again. Yet you are probably now busy with another. It is curious for me to see among the old letters one from Anne sending a *copy of a whole article* on the currency question written by Fonblanque! I exceedingly regret having burnt your letters in a fit of caution, and I've forgotten all the names. Was the reader Albert Smith? What do they all think of you?

'I mention the book to no one and hear no opinions. I lend it a good deal because it's a novel, and *it's as good as another!* They say "it makes them cry." They are not literary enough to give an opinion. If ever I hear one I'll embalm it for you. As to my own affair, I have written 100 pages, and lately 50 more. It's no use writing faster. I get so disgusted, I can do nothing.

'If I could command sufficient money for a twelvemonth, I would go home by way of India and write my travels, which would prepare the way for my novel. With the benefit of your experience I should perhaps make a better bargain than you. I am most afraid of my health. Not that I should die, but perhaps sink into a state of betweenity, neither well nor ill, in which I should observe nothing, and be very miserable besides. My life here is not disagreeable. I have a great resource in the piano, and a little enployment in teaching.

'It 's a pity you don't live in this world, that I might entertain you about the price of meat. Do you know, I bought six heifers the other day for £23, and now it is turned so cold I expect to hear one-half of them are dead. One man bought twenty sheep for £8, and they are all dead but one. Another bought 150 and has 40 left.

'I have now told you everything I can think of except that the cat 's on the table and that I 'm going to borrow a new book to read — no less than an account of all the systems of philosophy of modern Europe. I have lately met with a wonder, a man who thinks Jane Eyre would have done better to marry Mr. Rivers ! He gives no reason — such people never do.

'MARY TAYLOR.'

TO MISS CHARLOTTE BRONTË.

'WELLINGTON, NEW ZEALAND.

'DEAR CHARLOTTE,— I have set up shop ! I am delighted with it as a whole — that is, it is as pleasant or as little disagreeable as you can expect an employment to be that you earn your living by. The best of it is that your labour has some return, and you are not forced to work on hopelessly without result. Du reste, it is very odd. I keep looking at myself with one eye while I 'm using the other, and I sometimes find myself in very queer positions. Yesterday I went along the shore past the wharfs and several warehouses on a street where I had never been before during all the five years I have been in Wellington. I opened the door of a long place filled with packages, with passages up the middle, and a row of high windows on one side. At the far end of the room a man was writing at a desk beneath a window. I walked all the length of the room very slowly, for

what I had come for had completely gone out of my head.
Fortunately the man never heard me until I had recollected it.
Then he got up, and I asked him for some stone-blue, saltpetre,
tea, pickles, salt, etc. He was very civil. I bought some things
and asked for a note of them. He went to his desk again; I
looked at some newspapers lying near. On the top was a
circular from Smith & Elder containing notices of the most
important new works. The first and longest was given to "Shirley," a book I had seen mentioned in the "Manchester Examiner"
as written by Currer Bell. I blushed all over. The man got up,
folding the note. I pulled it out of his hand and set off to the
door, looking odder than ever, for a partner had come in and
was watching. The clerk said something about sending them,
and I said something too — I hope it was not very silly — and
took my departure.

'I have seen some extracts from "Shirley" in which you talk of
women working. And this first duty, this great necessity, you
seem to think that some women may indulge in, if they give up
marriage, and don't make themselves too disagreeable to the
other sex. You are a coward and a traitor. A woman who
works is by that alone better than one who does not; and a
woman who does not happen to be rich and who *still* earns no
money and does not wish to do so, is guilty of a great fault,
almost a crime — a dereliction of duty which leads rapidly and
almost certainly to all manner of degradation. It is very wrong
of you to *plead* for toleration for workers on the ground of their
being in peculiar circumstances, and few in number or singular
in disposition. Work or degradation is the lot of all except the
very small number born to wealth.

'Ellen is with me, or I with her. I cannot tell how our shop
will turn out, but I am as sanguine as ever. Meantime we
certainly amuse ourselves better than if we had nothing to
do. We *like* it, and that's the truth. By the "Cornelia" we
are going to send our sketches and fern leaves. You must look
at them, and it will need all your eyes to understand them, for
they are a mass of confusion. They are all within two miles of
Wellington, and some of them rather like — Ellen's sketch of

me especially. During the last six months I have seen more
"society" than in all the last four years. Ellen is half the
reason of my being invited, and my improved circumstances
besides. There is no one worth mentioning particularly. The
women are all ignorant and narrow, and the men selfish. They
are of a decent, honest kind, and some intelligent and able.
A Mr. Woodward is the only *literary* man we know, and
he seems to have fair sense. This was the clerk I bought
the stone-blue of. We have just got a mechanic's institute, and weekly lectures delivered there. It is amusing to
see people trying to find out whether or not it is fashionable
and proper to patronise it. Somehow it seems it is. I think I
have told you all this before, which shows I have got to the end
of my news. Your next letter to me ought to bring me good
news, more cheerful than the last. You will somehow get
drawn out of your hole and find interests among your fellow-
creatures. Do you know that living among people with whom
you have not the slightest interest in common is just like
living alone, or worse. Ellen Nussey is the only one you
can talk to, that I know of at least. Give my love to her
and to Miss Wooler, if you have the opportunity. I am writing
this on just such a night as you will likely read it — rain and
storm, coming winter, and a glowing fire. Ours is on the
ground, wood, no fender or irons; no matter, we are very
comfortable.   Pag.'

TO MISS CHARLOTTE BRONTË.

'Wellington, N. Z., April 3, 1850.

'Dear Charlotte, — About a week since I received your last
melancholy letter with the account of Anne's death and your
utter indifference to everything, even to the success of your
last book. Though you do not say this, it is pretty plain to be
seen from the style of your letter. It seems to me hard indeed
that you who would succeed, better than any one, in making
friends and keeping them, should be condemned to solitude
from your poverty. To no one would money bring more happiness, for no one would use it better than you would. For me,

with my headlong self-indulgent habits, I am perhaps better without it, but I am convinced it would give you great and noble pleasures. Look out then for success in writing; you ought to care as much for that as you do for going to heaven. Though the advantages of being employed appear to you now the best part of the business, you will soon, please God, have other enjoyments from your success. Railway shares will rise, your books will sell, and you will acquire influence and power; and then most certainly you will find something to use it in which will interest you and make you exert yourself.

'I have got into a heap of social trickery since Ellen came, never having troubled my head before about the comparative numbers of young ladies and young gentlemen. To Ellen it is quite new to be of such importance by the mere fact of her femininity. She thought she was coming wofully down in the world when she came out, and finds herself better received than ever she was in her life before. And the class are not *in education* inferior, though they are in money. They are decent well-to-do people: six grocers, one draper, two parsons, two clerks, two lawyers, and three or four nondescripts. All these but one have families to "take tea with," and there are a lot more single men to flirt with. For the last three months we have been out every Sunday sketching. We seldom succeed in making the slightest resemblance to the thing we sit down to, but it is wonderfully interesting. Next year we hope to send a lot home. With all this my novel stands still; it might have done so if I had had nothing to do, for it is not want of time but want of freedom of mind that makes me unable to direct my attention to it. Meantime it grows in my head, for I never give up the idea. I have written about a volume I suppose. Read this letter to Ellen Nussey. MARY TAYLOR.'

TO MISS CHARLOTTE BRONTË.

'WELLINGTON, August 13, 1850.

'DEAR CHARLOTTE, — After writing about six months we have just got "Shirley." It was landed from the "Constantinople" on Monday afternoon, just in the thick of our preparations for a

AND HER CIRCLE

"small party" for the next day. We stopped spreading red
blankets over everything (New Zealand way of arranging the
room) and opened the box and read all the letters. Soyer's
"Housewife" and "Shirley" were there all right, but Miss Martineau's book was not. In its place was a silly child's tale called
"Edward Orland." On Tuesday we stayed up dancing till three
or four o'clock, what for I can't imagine. However, it was a
piece of business done. On Wednesday I began "Shirley" and
continued in a curious confusion of mind till now, principally at
the handsome foreigner who was nursed in our house when I
was a little girl. By the way, you 've put him in the servant's
bedroom. You make us all talk much as I think we should
have done if we 'd ventured to speak at all. What a little
lump of perfection you 've made me! There is a strange feeling
in reading it of hearing us all talking. I have not seen the
matted hall and painted parlour windows so plain these five
years. But my father is not like. He hates well enough and
perhaps loves too, but he is not honest enough. It was from
my father I learnt not to marry for money nor to tolerate any
one who did, and he never would advise any one to do so, or fail
to speak with contempt of those who did. "Shirley" is much
more interesting than "Jane Eyre," who never interests you at
all until she has something to suffer. All through this last novel
there is so much more life and stir that it leaves you far more
to remember than the other. Did you go to London about this
too? What for? I see by a letter of yours to Mr. Dixon that
you have been. I wanted to contradict some of your opinions,
now I can't. As to when I 'm coming home, you may well ask.
I have wished for fifteen years to begin to earn my own living;
last April I began to try — it is too soon to say yet with what
success. I am wofully ignorant, terribly wanting in tact, and
obstinately lazy, and almost too old to mend. Luckily there
is no other dance for me, so I must work. Ellen takes to it
kindly, it gratifies a deep ardent *wish* of hers as of mine, and
she is habitually industrious. For *her*, ten years younger, our
shop will be a blessing. She may possibly secure an independence, and skill to keep it and use it, before the prime of life

251

is past. As to my writings, you may as well ask the Fates about that too. I can give you no information. I write a page now and then. I never forget or get strange to what I have written. When I read it over it looks very interesting.

'MARY TAYLOR.'

The Ellen Taylor referred to so frequently was, as I have said, a cousin of Mary's. Her early death in New Zealand gives the single letter I have of hers a more pathetic interest.

TO MISS CHARLOTTE BRONTË.

'WELLINGTON, N. Z.

'MY DEAR MISS BRONTË, — I shall tell you everything I can think of, since you said in one of your letters to Pag that you wished me to write to you. I have been here a year. 'It seems a much shorter time, and yet I have thought more and done more than I ever did in my life before. When we arrived, Henry and I were in such a hurry to leave the ship that we didn't wait to be fetched, but got into the first boat that came alongside. When we landed we inquired where Waring lived, but hadn't walked far before we met him. I had never seen him before, but he guessed we were the cousins he expected, so caught us and took us along with him. Mary soon joined us, and we went home together. At first I thought Mary was not the least altered, but when I had seen her for about a week I thought she looked rather older. The first night Mary and I sat up till 2 A.M. talking. Mary and I settled we would do something together, and we talked for a fortnight before we decided whether we would have a school or shop; it ended in favour of the shop. Waring thought we had better be quiet, and I believe he still thinks we are doing it for amusement; but he never refuses to help us. He is teaching us book-keeping, and he buys things for us now and then. Mary gets as fierce as a dragon and goes to all the wholesale stores and looks at things, gets patterns, samples, etc., and asks prices, and then comes home, and we talk it over; and then she goes again and buys what we want. She says the people are

252

always civil to her. Our keeping shop astonishes everybody here, I believe they think we do it for fun. Some think we shall make nothing of it, or that we shall get tired; and all laugh at us. Before I left home I used to be afraid of being laughed at, but now it has very little effect upon me.

'Mary and I are settled together now : I can't do without Mary and she couldn't get on by herself. I built the house we live in, and we made the plan ourselves, so it suits us. We take it in turns to serve in the shop, and keep the accounts, and do the housework — I mean, Mary takes the shop for a week and I the kitchen, and then we change. I think we shall do very well if no more severe earthquakes come, and if we can prevent fire. When a wooden house takes fire it doesn't stop; and we have got an oil cask about as high as I am, that would help it. If some sparks go out at the chimney-top the shingles are in danger. ·The last earthquake but one about a fortnight ago threw down two medicine bottles that were standing on the table and made other things jingle, but did no damage. If we have nothing worse than that I don't care, but I don't want the chimney to come down — it would cost £10 to build it up again. Mary is making me stop because it is nearly 9 P.M. and we are going to Waring's to supper. Good-bye. — Yours truly,

'ELLEN TAYLOR.'

TO MISS ELLEN NUSSEY.

'HAWORTH, July 4, 1849.

'I get on as well as I can. Home is not the home it used to be — that you may well conceive; but so far, I get on.

'I cannot boast of vast benefits derived from change of air yet; but unfortunately I brought back the seeds of a cold with me from that dismal Easton, and I have not got rid of it yet. Still I think I look better than I did before I went. How are you? You have never told me.

'Mr. Williams has written to me twice since my return, chiefly on the subject of his third daughter, who wishes to be a governess, and has some chances of a presentation to Queen's College, an establishment connected with the Governess Institution ; this will secure her four years of instruction. He says Mr. George Smith is kindly using his influence to obtain votes, but there are so many candidates he is not sanguine of success.

'I had a long letter from Mary Taylor — interesting but sad, because it contained many allusions to those who are in this world no more. She mentioned you, and seemed impressed with an idea of the lamentable nature of your unoccupied life. She spoke of her own health as being excellent.

'Give my love to your mother and sisters, and, — Believe me, yours,   C. B.'

TO MISS ELLEN NUSSEY.

'HAWORTH, May 18.

'DEAR ELLEN, — I inclose Mary Taylor's letter announcing Ellen's death, and two last letters — sorrowful documents, all of them. I received them this morning from Hunsworth without any note or directions where to send them, but I think, if I mistake not, Amelia in a previous note told me to transmit them to you. — Yours faithfully,   C. B.'

TO MISS CHARLOTTE BRONTË.

'WELLINGTON, N. Z.

'DEAR CHARLOTTE, — I began a letter to you one bitter cold evening last week, but it turned out such a sad one that I have left it and begun again. I am sitting all alone in my own house, or rather what is to be mine when I've paid for it. I bought it of Henry when Ellen died — shop and all, and carry on by myself. I have made up my mind not to get any assistance. I have not too much work, and the annoyance of having an unsuitable companion was too great to put up with without necessity. I find now that it was Ellen that made me so busy, and without her to nurse I have plenty of time. I have begun to keep the house very tidy; it makes it less desolate. I take great interest in my trade — as much as I could do in anything that was not *all* pleasure. But the best part of my life is the excitement of arrivals from England. Reading all the news, written and printed, is like living another life quite separate from this one. The old letters are strange — very, when

I begin to read them, but quite familiar notwithstanding. So are all the books and newspapers, though I never see a human being to whom it would ever occur to me to mention anything I read in them. I see your *nom de guerre* in them sometimes. I saw a criticism on the preface to the second edition of "Wuthering Heights." I saw it among the notables who attended Thackeray's lectures. I have seen it somehow connected with Sir J. K. Shuttleworth. Did he want to marry you, or only to lionise you? *or was it somebody else?*

'Your life in London is a "new country" to me, which I cannot even picture to myself. You seem to like it — at least some things in it, and yet your late letters to Mrs. J. Taylor talk of low spirits and illness. "What's the matter with you now," as my mother used to say, as if it were the twentieth time in a fortnight. It is really melancholy that now, in the prime of life, in the flush of your hard-earned prosperity, you can't be well. Did not Miss Martineau improve you? If she did, why not try her and her plan again? But I suppose if you had hope and energy to try, you would be well. Well, it's nearly dark and you will surely be well when you read this, so what's the use of writing? I should like well to have some details of your life, but how can I hope for it? I have often tried to give you a picture of mine, but I have not the skill. I get a heap of details, mostly paltry in themselves, and not enough to give you an idea of the whole. Oh, for one hour's talk! You are getting too far off and beginning to look strange to me. Do you look as you used to do, I wonder? What do you and Ellen Nussey talk about when you meet? There! it's dark.

'*Sunday night.* — I have let the vessel go that was to take this. As there were others going soon I did not much care. I am in the height of cogitation whether to send for some worsted stockings, etc. They will come next year at this time, and who can tell what I shall want then, or shall be doing. Yet hitherto we have sent such orders, and have guessed or known pretty well what we should want. I have just been looking over a list of four pages long in Ellen's handwriting. These things ought to come by the next vessel, or part of them at least.

CHARLOTTE BRONTË

When tired of that I began to read some pages of "my book," intending to write some more, but went on reading for pleasure. I often do this, and find it very interesting indeed. It does not get on fast, though I have written about one volume and a half. It's full of music, poverty, disputing, politics, and original views of life. I can't for the life of me bring the lover into it, nor tell what he's to do when he comes. Of the men generally I can never tell what they'll do next. The women I understand pretty well, and rare *tracasserie* there is among them — they are perfectly *feminine* in that respect at least.

'I am just now in a state of famine. No books and no news from England for this two months. I am thinking of visiting a circulating library from sheer dulness. If I had more time I should get melancholy. No one can prize activity more than I do. I never am long without it than a gloom comes over me. The cloud seems to be always there behind me, and never quite out of sight but when I keep on at a good rate. Fortunately, the more I work the better I like it. I shall take to scrubbing the floor before it's dirty and polishing pans on the outside in my old age. It is the only thing that gives me an appetite for dinner.   PAG.

'Give my love to Ellen Nussey.'

TO MISS ELLEN NUSSEY.

'WELLINGTON, N. Z., Jan. 8, 1857.

'DEAR ELLEN, — A few days ago I got a letter from you, dated 2nd May 1856, along with some patterns and fashion-book. They seem to have been lost somehow, as the box ought to have come by the "Hastings," and only now makes its appearance by the "Philip Lang." It has come very *apropos* for a new year's gift, and the patterns were not opened twenty-four hours before a silk cape was cut out by one of them. I think I made a very impertinent request when I asked you to give yourself so much trouble. The poor woman for whom I wanted them is now a first-rate dressmaker, her drunken husband, who was her main misfortune, having taken himself off and not been heard of lately.

'I am glad to hear that Mrs. Gaskell is progressing with the "Life."

'I wish I had kept Charlotte's letters now, though I never felt it safe to do so until latterly that I have had a home of my own. They would have been much better evidence than my imperfect recollection, and infinitely more interesting. A settled opinion is very likely to look absurd unless you give the grounds for it, and even if I could remember them it might look as if there might be other facts which I have neglected which ought to have altered it. Your news of the "neighbours" is very interesting, especially of Miss Wooler and my old school-fellows. I wish I knew how to give you some account of my ways here and the effect of my position on me. First of all, it agrees with me. I am in better health than at any time since I left school. My life now is not overburdened with work, and what I do has interest and attraction in it. I think it is that part that I shall think most agreeable when I look back on my death-bed — a number of small pleasures scattered over my way, that, when seen from a distance, will seem to cover it thick. They don't cover it by any means, but I never had so many.

'I look after my shopwoman, make out bills, decide who shall have "trust" and who not. Then I go a-buying, not near such an anxious piece of business now that I understand my trade, and have, moreover, a good "credit." I read a good deal, sometimes on the sofa, a vice I am much given to in hot weather. Then I have some friends — not many, and no geniuses, which fact pray keep strictly to yourself, for how the doings and sayings of Wellington people in England always come out again to New Zealand! They are not very interesting any way. This is my fault in part, for I can't take interest in their concerns. A book is worth any of them, and a good book worth them all put together.

'*Our* east winds are much the pleasantest and healthiest we have. The soft moist north-west brings headache and depression — it even blights the trees. — Yours affectionately,

'MARY TAYLOR.'

CHARLOTTE BRONTË

TO MISS ELLEN NUSSEY.

'WELLINGTON, June 4, 1858.

'DEAR ELLEN, — I have lately heard that you are leaving Brookroyd. I shall not even see Brookroyd again, and one of the people who lived there; and *one* whom I used to see there I shall never see more. Keep yourself well, dear Ellen, and gather round you as much happiness and interest as you can, and let me find you cheery and thriving when I come. When that will be I don't yet know; but one thing is sure, I have given over ordering goods from England, so that I must sometime give over for want of anything to sell. The last things ordered I expect to arrive about the beginning of the year 1859. In the course of that year, therefore, I shall be left without anything to do or motive for staying. Possibly this time twelve months I may be leaving Wellington.

'We are here in the height of a political crisis. The election for the highest office in the province (Superintendent) comes off in about a fortnight. There is altogether a small storm going on in our teacup, quite brisk enough to stir everything in it. My principal interest therein is the sale of election ribbons, though I am afraid, owing to the bad weather, there will be little display. Besides the elections, there is nothing interesting. We all go on pretty well. I have got a pony about four feet high, that carries me about ten miles from Wellington, which is much more than walking distance, to which I have been confined for the last ten years. I have given over most of the work to Miss Smith, who will finally take the business, and if we had fine weather I think I should enjoy myself. My main want here is for books enough to fill up my idle time. It seems to me that when I get home I will spend half my income on books, and sell them when I have read them to make it go further. I know this is absurd, but people with an unsatisfied appetite think they can eat enormously.

'Remember me kindly to Miss Wooler, and tell me all about her in your next. — Yours affectionately,

'MARY TAYLOR.'

AND HER CIRCLE

Miss Taylor wrote one or two useful letters to Mrs. Gaskell, while the latter was preparing her Memoir of Charlotte Brontë, and her favourable estimate of the book we have already seen. About 1859 or 1860 she returned to England and lived out the remainder of her days in complete seclusion in a Yorkshire home that she built for herself. The novel to which she refers in a letter to her friend never seems to have 'got itself written,' or at least published, for it was not until 1890 that Miss Mary Taylor produced a work of fiction —'Miss Miles.'[1] This novel strives to inculcate the advantages as well as the duty of women learning to make themselves independent of men. It is well, though not brilliantly written, and might, had the author possessed any of the latter-day gifts of self-advertisement, have attracted the public, if only by the mere fact that its author was a friend of Currer Bell's. But Miss Taylor, it is clear, hated advertisement, and severely refused to be lionised by Brontë worshippers. Twenty years earlier than ' Miss Miles,' I may add, she had preached the same gospel in less attractive guise. A series of papers in the ' Victorian Magazine ' were reprinted under the title of 'The First Duty of Women.'[2] ' To inculcate the duty of earning money,' she declares, ' is the principal point in these articles.' ' It is to the feminine half of the world that the commonplace duty of providing for themselves is recommended,' and she enforces her doctrine with considerable point, and by means of arguments much more accepted in our day than in hers. Miss Taylor died in March 1893, at High Royd, in Yorkshire, at the age of seventy-six. She will always occupy an honourable place in the Brontë story.

[1] 'Miss Miles, or A Tale of Yorkshire Life Sixty Years Ago,' by Mary Taylor. Rivington & Co., 1890.
[2] 'The First Duty of Women.' A Series of Articles reprinted from the 'Victorian Magazine,' 1865 to 1870, by Mary Taylor. 1870.

CHAPTER X.

MARGARET WOOLER.

THE kindly, placid woman who will ever be remembered as Charlotte Brontë's schoolmistress, had, it may be safely said, no history. She was a good-hearted woman, who did her work and went to her rest with no possible claim to a place in biography, save only that she assisted in the education of two great women. For that reason her brief story is worth setting forth here.

'I am afraid we cannot give you very much information about our aunt, Miss Wooler,' writes one of her kindred. 'She was the eldest of a large family, born June 10th, 1792. She was extremely intelligent and highly educated, and throughout her long life, which lasted till within a week of completing her ninety-third year, she took the greatest interest in religious, political, and every charitable work, being a life governor to many institutions. Part of her early life was spent in the Isle of Wight with relations, where she was very intimate with the Sewell family, one of whom was the author of "Amy Herbert." By her own family, she was ever looked up to with the greatest respect, being always called "Sister" by her brothers and sisters all her life. After she retired from her school at Roe Head, and afterwards Dewsbury Moor, she used sometimes to make her home for months together with my father and mother at Heckmondwike Vicarage; then she would go away for a few months to the sea-side, either alone or with one of her sisters. The last ten or twelve years of her life were spent at Gomersall, along with two of her sisters and a niece. The three sisters all died within a year, the youngest going first and the eldest last. They are buried in Birstall Churchyard, close to my parents and sister.

'Miss Brontë was her pupil when at Roe Head; the late Miss Taylor and Miss E. Nussey were also her pupils at the same time. Afterwards Miss Brontë stayed on as governess. My father prepared Miss Brontë for confirmation when he was curate-in-charge at Mirfield Parish Church. When Miss Brontë was married, Miss Wooler was one of the guests. Mr. Brontë not feeling well enough to go to Church that morning, my aunt gave her away, as she had no other relative there to do it.

'Miss Wooler kept up a warm friendship with her former pupil, up to the time of her death.

'My aunt was a most loyal subject, and devotedly attached to the Church. She made a point of reading the Bible steadily through every year, and a chapter out of her Italian Testament each day, for she used to say "she never liked to lose anything she had learnt." It was always a pleasure, too, if she met with any one who could converse with her in French.

'I fear these few items will not be of much use, but it is difficult to record anything of one who led such a quiet and retiring, but useful life.'

'My recollections of Miss Wooler,' writes Miss Nussey, 'are, that she was short and stout, but graceful in her movements, very fluent in conversation and with a very sweet voice. She had Charlotte and myself to stay with her sometimes after we left school. We had delightful sitting-up times with her when the pupils had gone to bed. She would treat us so confidentially, relating her six years' residence in the Isle of Wight with an uncle and aunt — Dr. More and his wife. Dr. More was on the military staff, and the society of the island had claims upon him. Mrs. More was a fine woman and very benevolent. Personally, Miss Wooler was like a lady abbess. She wore white, well-fitting dresses embroidered. Her long hair plaited, formed a coronet, and long large ringlets fell from her head to shoulders. She was not pretty or handsome, but her quiet dignity made her presence imposing. She was nobly scrupulous and conscientious — a woman of the greatest self-denial. Her income was small. She lived on half of it, and gave the remainder to charitable objects.'

It is clear that Charlotte was very fond of her school-mistress, although they had one serious difference during the brief period of her stay at Dewsbury Moor with Anne. Anne was homesick and ill, and Miss Wooler, with her own robust constitution, found it difficult to understand Anne's illness. Charlotte, in arms for her sister, spoke out with vehemence, and both the sisters went home soon afterwards.[1] Here are a bundle of letters addressed to Miss Wooler.

TO MISS WOOLER.

'HAWORTH, August 28, 1848.

' MY DEAR MISS WOOLER, — Since you wish to hear from me while you are from home, I will write without further delay. It often happens that when we linger at first in answering a friend's letter, obstacles occur to retard us to an inexcusably late period.

' In my last I forgot to answer a question you asked me, and was sorry afterwards for the omission ; I will begin, therefore, by replying to it, though I fear what I can give will now come a little late. You said Mrs. Chapman had some thoughts of sending her daughter to school, and wished to know whether the Clergy Daughters' School at Casterton was an eligible place.

' My personal knowledge of that institution is very much out of date, being derived from the experience of twenty years ago ; the establishment was at that time in its infancy, and a sad rickety infancy it was. Typhus fever decimated the school periodically, and consumption and scrofula in every variety of form which bad air and water, and bad, insufficient diet, can generate, preyed on the ill-fated pupils. It would not *then* have been a fit place for any of Mrs. Chapham's children. But, I understand, it is very much altered for the better since those

[1] See letter to Ellen Nussey, page 78.

days. The school is removed from Cowan Bridge (a situation as unhealthy as it was picturesque — low, damp, beautiful with wood and water) to Casterton; the accommodation, the diet, the discipline, the system of tuition, all are, I believe, entirely altered and greatly improved. I was told that such pupils as behaved well and remained at school till their educations were finished were provided with situations as governesses if they wished to adopt that vocation, and that much care was exercised in the selection; it was added they were also furnished with an excellent wardrobe on quitting Casterton.

'If I have the opportunity of reading "The Life of Dr. Arnold," I shall not fail to profit thereby; your recommendation makes me desirous to see it. Do you remember once speaking with approbation of a book called "Mrs. Leicester's School," which you said you had met with, and you wondered by whom it was written? I was reading the other day a lately published collection of the "Letters of Charles Lamb," edited by Sargeant Talford, where I found it mentioned that "Mrs. Leicester's School" was the first production of Lamb and his sister. These letters are themselves singularly interesting; they have hitherto been suppressed in all previous collections of Lamb's works and relics, on account of the frequent allusions they contain to the unhappy malady of Miss Lamb, and a frightful incident which darkened her earlier years. She was, it appears, a woman of the sweetest disposition, and, in her normal state, of the highest and dearest intellect, but afflicted with periodical insanity which came on once a year, or oftener. To her parents she was a most tender and dutiful daughter, nursing them in their old age, when one was physically and the other mentally infirm, with unremitting care, and at the same time toiling to add something by needlework to the slender resources of the family. A succession of laborious days and sleepless nights brought on a frenzy fit, in which she had the miserable misfortune to kill her own mother. She was afterwards placed in a madhouse, where she would have been detained for life, had not her brother Charles promised to devote himself to her and take her under his care — and for her sake renounce a project of marriage he then entertained. An instance of abnegation of self scarcely, I think, to be paralleled in the annals of the "coarser sex." They passed their subsequent lives together — models of fraternal affection, and would have been very happy but for the dread visitation to which Mary Lamb continued liable all her life. I thought it both a sad and edifying history. Your account of your little niece's naive delight in beholding the morning sea for the first time amused and pleased me ; it proves she has some sensations — a refreshing circumstance in a day and generation when the natural phenomenon of children wholly destitute of all pretension to the same is by no means an unusual occurrence.

'I have written a long letter as you requested me, but I fear you will not find it very amusing. With love to your little companion, — Believe me, my dear Miss Wooler, yours affectionately and respectfully, C. BRONTË.'

' Papa, I am most thankful to say, continues in very good health, considering his age. My sisters likewise are pretty well.'

TO MISS WOOLER.

'HAWORTH, March 31, 1848.

'MY DEAR MISS WOOLER, — I had been wishing to hear from you for some time before I received your last. There has been so much sickness during the last winter, and the influenza especially has been so severe and so generally prevalent, that the sight of suffering around us has frequently suggested fears for absent friends. Ellen Nussey told me, indeed, that neither you nor Miss C. Wooler had escaped the influenza, but, since your letter contains no allusion to your own health or hers, I trust you are completely recovered. I am most thankful to say that papa has hitherto been exempted from any attack. My sister and myself have each had a visit from it, but Anne is the only one with whom it stayed long or did much mischief ; in her case it was attended with distressing cough and fever ; but she is now better, though it has left her chest weak.

' I remember well wishing my lot had been cast in the troubled times of the late war, and seeing in its exciting inci-

dents a kind of stimulating charm which it made my pulse beat
fast only to think of — I remember even, I think, being a little
impatient that you would not fully sympathise with my feelings
on this subject, that you heard my aspirations and speculations
very tranquilly, and by no means seemed to think the flaming
sword could be any pleasant addition to the joys of paradise.
I have now outlived youth; and, though I dare not say that
I have outlived all its illusions, that the romance is quite gone
from life, the veil fallen from truth, and that I see both in
naked reality, yet, certainly, many things are not to me what
they were ten years ago; and amongst the rest, "the pomp
and circumstance of war" have quite lost in my eyes their
factitious glitter. I have still no doubt that the shock of
moral earthquakes wakens a vivid sense of life both in nations
and individuals; that the fear of dangers on a broad national
scale diverts men's minds momentarily from brooding over
small private perils, and, for the time gives them something
like largeness of views; but as little doubt have I that con-
vulsive revolutions put back the world in all that is good, check
civilisation, bring the dregs of society to its surface — in short,
it appears to me that insurrections and battles are the acute
diseases of nations, and that their tendency is to exhaust by
their violence the vital energies of the countries where they
occur. That England may be spared the spasms, cramps, and
frenzy-fits now contorting the Continent and threatening Ireland, I earnestly pray!

'With the French and Irish I have no sympathy. With the
Germans and Italians I think the case is different — as different as
the love of freedom is from the lust of license.'

TO MISS WOOLER.

'HAWORTH, September 27, 1850.

'MY DEAR MISS WOOLER, — When I tell you that I have
already been to the Lakes this season, and that it is scarcely
more than a month since I returned, you will understand
that it is no longer within my power to accept your kind
invitation.

CHARLOTTE BRONTË

'I wish I could have gone to you. I wish your invitation had come first; to speak the truth, it would have suited me better than the one by which I profited. It would have been pleasant, soothing, in many ways beneficial, to have spent two weeks with you in your cottage-lodgings. But these reflections are vain. I have already had my excursion, and there is an end of it. Sir J. K. Shuttleworth is residing near Windermere, at a house called "The Briary," and it was there I was staying for a little while in August. He very kindly showed me the scenery — *as it can be seen from a carriage* — and I discerned that the "Lake Country" is a glorious region, of which I had only seen the similitude in dream — waking or sleeping. But, my dear Miss Wooler, I only half enjoyed it, because I was only half at my ease. Decidedly I find it does not agree with me to prosecute the search of the picturesque in a carriage; a waggon, a spring-cart, even a post-chaise might do, but the carriage upsets everything. I longed to slip out unseen, and to run away by myself in amongst the hills and dales. Erratic and vagrant instincts tormented me, and these I was obliged to control, or rather, suppress, for fear of growing in any degree enthusiastic, and thus drawing attention to the "lioness," the authoress, the artist. Sir J. K. Shuttleworth is a man of ability and intellect, but not a man in whose presence one willingly unbends.

'You say you suspect I have found a large circle of acquaintance by this time. No, I cannot say that I have. I doubt whether I possess either the wish or the power to do so. A few friends I should like to know well; if such knowledge brought proportionate regard I could not help concentrating my feelings. Dissipation, I think, appears synonymous with dilution. However, I have as yet scarcely been tried. During the month I spent in London in the spring, I kept very quiet, having the fear of "lionising" before my eyes. I only went out once to dinner, and was once present at an evening party; and the only visits I have paid have been to Sir J. K. Shuttleworth and my publishers. From this system I should not like to depart. As far as I can see, indiscriminate visiting tends only to a waste of time and a vulgarising of character. Besides, it would be wrong to leave papa often; he is now in his 75th year, the infirmities of age begin to creep upon him. During the summer he has been much harassed by chronic bronchitis, but, I am thankful to say, he is now somewhat better. I think my own health has derived benefit from change and exercise.

'You ask after Ellen Nussey. When I saw Ellen, about two months ago, she looked remarkably well. I sometimes hear small fragments of gossip which amuse me. Somebody professes to have authority for saying that "When Miss Brontë was in London she neglected to attend divine service on the Sabbath, and in the week spent her time in going about to balls, theatres, and operas." On the other hand, the London quidnuncs make my seclusion a matter of wonder, and devise twenty romantic fictions to account for it. Formerly I used to listen to report with interest and a certain credulity; I am now grown deaf and sceptical. Experience has taught me how absolutely devoid of foundations her stories may be.

'With the sincere hope that your own health is better, and kind remembrances to all old friends whenever you see them or write to them (and whether or not their feeling to me has ceased to be friendly, which I fear is the case in some instances),— I am, my dear Miss Wooler, always yours, affectionately and respect-fully, C. BRONTË.'

TO MISS WOOLER.

'HAWORTH, July 14, 1851.

'MY DEAR MISS WOOLER,— My first feeling on receiving your note was one of disappointment; but a little consideration sufficed to show me that "all was for the best." In truth, it was a great piece of extravagance on my part to ask you and Ellen together; it is much better to divide such good things. To have your visit in *prospect* will console me when hers is in *retrospect*. Not that I mean to yield to the weakness of clinging dependently to the society of friends, however dear, but still as an occasional treat I must value and even seek such society as a necessary of life. Let me know, then, whenever it suits your convenience to come to Haworth, and, unless some change I cannot now foresee occurs, a ready and warm welcome will await you. Should there be any cause rendering it desirable to defer the visit, I will tell you frankly.

'The pleasures of society I cannot offer you, nor those of fine scenery, but I place very much at your command the moors, some books, a series of "curling-hair times," and an old pupil into the bargain. Ellen may have told you that I have spent a month in London this summer. When you come you shall ask what questions you like on that point, and I will answer to the best of my stammering ability. Do not press me much on the subject of the "Crystal Palace." I went there five times, and certainly saw some interesting things, and the *coup d'œil* is striking and bewildering enough, but I never was able to get up any raptures on the subject, and each renewed visit was made under coercion rather than my own free-will. It is an excessively bustling place ; and, after all, its wonders appeal too exclusively to the eye and rarely touch the heart or head. I make an exception to the last assertion in favour of those who possess a large range of scientific knowledge. Once I went with Sir David Brewster, and perceived that he looked on objects with other eyes than mine.

'Ellen I find is writing, and will therefore deliver her own messages of regard. If papa were in the room he would, I know, desire his respects ; and you must take both respects and a good bundle of something more cordial from yours very faithfully,   C. BRONTË.'

TO MISS WOOLER.

'HAWORTH, September 22, 1851.

'MY DEAR MISS WOOLER,— Our visitor (a relative from Cornwall) having left us, the coast is now clear, so that whenever you feel inclined to come, papa and I will be truly glad to see you. I *do* wish the splendid weather we have had and are having may accompany you here. I fear I have somewhat grudged the fine days, fearing a change before you come.—

Believe me, with papa's regards, yours respectfully and affectionately,   C. Brontë.

'Come soon; if you can, on Wednesday.'

TO MISS ELLEN NUSSEY.

'October 3, 1851.

'Dear Nell, — Do not think I have forgotten you because I have not written since your last.   Every day I have had you more or less in my thoughts, and wondered how your mother was getting on; let me have a line of information as soon as possible.   I have been busy, first with a somewhat unexpected visitor, a cousin from Cornwall, who has been spending a few days with us, and now with Miss Wooler, who came on Monday. The former personage we can discuss any time when we meet. Miss Wooler is and has been very pleasant.   She is like good wine : I think time improves her; and really whatever she may be in person, in mind she is younger than when at Roe Head. Papa and she get on extremely well.   I have just heard papa walk into the dining-room and pay her a round compliment on her good-sense.   I think so far she has been pretty comfortable and likes Haworth, but as she only brought a small hand-basket of luggage with her she cannot stay long.

'How are *you?*   Write directly.   With my love to your mother, etc., good-bye, dear Nell. — Yours faithfully,

'C. Brontë.'

TO MISS WOOLER.

'February 6, 1852.

'Ellen Nussey, it seems, told you I spent a fortnight in London last December; they wished me very much to stay a month, alleging that I should in that time be able to secure a complete circle of acquaintance, but I found a fortnight of such excitement quite enough.   The whole day was usually spent in sight-seeing, and often the evening was spent in society; it was more than I could bear for a length of time.   On one occasion I met a party of my critics — seven of them ; some of them had been very bitter foes in print, but they were prodigiously civil face to face.   These gentlemen seemed infinitely

269

grander, more pompous, dashing, showy, than the few authors I saw. Mr. Thackeray, for instance, is a man of quiet, simple demeanour; he is however looked upon with some awe and even distrust. His conversation is very peculiar, too perverse to be pleasant. It was proposed to me to see Charles Dickens, Lady Morgan, Mesdames Trollope, Gore, and some others, but I was aware these introductions would bring a degree of notoriety I was not disposed to encounter; I declined, therefore, with thanks.

'Nothing charmed me more during my stay in town than the pictures I saw. One or two private collections of Turner's best water-colour drawings were indeed a treat; his later oil-paintings are strange things — things that baffle description.

'I twice saw Macready act — once in "Macbeth" and once in "Othello." I astonished a dinner-party by honestly saying I did not like him. It is the fashion to rave about his splendid acting. Anything more false and artificial, less genuinely impressive than his whole style I could scarcely have imagined. The fact is, the stage-system altogether is hollow nonsense. They act farces well enough: the actors comprehend their parts and do them justice. They comprehend nothing about tragedy or Shakespeare, and it is a failure. I said so; and by so saying produced a blank silence — a mute consternation. I was, indeed, obliged to dissent on many occasions, and to offend by dissenting. It seems now very much the custom to admire a certain wordy, intricate, obscure style of poetry, such as Elizabeth Barrett Browning writes. Some pieces were referred to about which Currer Bell was expected to be very rapturous, and failing in this, he disappointed.

'London people strike a provincial as being very much taken up with little matters about which no one out of particular town-circles cares much; they talk, too, of persons — literary men and women — whose names are scarcely heard in the country, and in whom you cannot get up an interest. I think I should scarcely like to live in London, and were I obliged to live there, I should certainly go little into company, especially I should eschew the literary coteries.

'You told me, my dear Miss Wooler, to write a long letter. I have obeyed you. — Believe me now, yours affectionately and respectfully,   C. Brontë.'

TO MISS WOOLER.

'Haworth, March 12, 1852.

'My dear Miss Wooler, — Your kind note holds out a strong temptation, but one that *must be resisted*. From home I must not go unless health or some cause equally imperative render a change necessary. For nearly four months now (*i. e.* since I became ill) I have not put pen to paper. My work has been lying untouched, and my faculties have been rusting for want of exercise. Further relaxation is out of the question, and I *will not permit myself to think of it*. My publisher groans over my long delays; I am sometimes provoked to check the expression of his impatience with short and crusty answers.

'Yet the pleasure I now deny myself I would fain regard as only deferred. I heard something about your proposing to visit Scarboro' in the course of the summer, and could I by the close of July or August bring my task to a certain point, how glad should I be to join you there for awhile!

'Ellen will probably go to the south about May to make a stay of two or three months; she has formed a plan for my accompanying her and taking lodgings on the Sussex Coast; but the scheme seems to me impracticable for many reasons, and, moreover, my medical man doubts the advisability of my going southward in summer, he says it might prove very enervating, whereas Scarboro' or Burlington would brace and strengthen. However, I dare not lay plans at this distance of time. For me so much must depend, first on papa's health (which throughout the winter has been, I am thankful to say, really excellent), and second, on the progress of work, a matter not wholly contingent on wish or will, but lying in a great measure beyond the reach of effort and out of the pale of calculation.

'I will not write more at present as I wish to save this post. All in the house would join in kind remembrances to you if they knew I was writing. Tabby and Martha both frequently inquire

CHARLOTTE BRONTË

after Miss Wooler, and desire their respects when an opportunity
offers of presenting the same. — Believe me, yours always affectionately and respectfully,   C. Brontë.'

TO MISS WOOLER.

'Haworth, September 2, 1852.

'My dear Miss Wooler, — I have delayed answering your very
kind letter till I could speak decidedly respecting papa's health.
For some weeks after the attack there were frequent variations,
and once a threatening of a relapse, but I trust his convalescence
may now be regarded as confirmed. The acute inflammation of
the eye, which distressed papa so much as threatening loss of
sight, but which I suppose was merely symptomatic of the rush
of blood to the brain, is now quite subsided ; the partial paralysis
has also disappeared ; the appetite is better ; weakness with occasional slight giddiness seem now the only lingering traces of
disease.   I am assured that with papa's excellent constitution,
there is every prospect of his still being spared to me for many
years.

'For two things I have reason to be most thankful, viz., that the
mental faculties have remained quite untouched, and also that my
own health and strength have been found sufficient for the occasion.   Solitary as I certainly was at Filey, I yet derived great
benefit from the change.

'It would be pleasant at the sea-side this fine warm weather, and
I should dearly like to be there with you ; to such a treat, however, I do not now look forward at all.   You will fully understand
the impossibility of my enjoying peace of mind during absence
from papa under present circumstances ; his strength must be
very much more fully restored before I can think of leaving
home.

'My dear Miss Wooler, in case you should go to Scarboro' this
season, may I request you to pay one visit to the churchyard and
see if the inscription on the stone has been altered as I directed.
We have heard nothing since on the subject, and I fear the alteration may have been neglected.

'Ellen has made a long stay in the south, but I believe she

272

will soon return now, and I am looking forward to the pleasure of having her company in the autumn.

'With kind regards to all old friends, and sincere love to yourself, — I am, my dear Miss Wooler, yours affectionately and respectfully.   C. BRONTË.'

TO MISS WOOLER.

'HAWORTH, September 21, 1852.

'MY DEAR MISS WOOLER, — I was truly sorry to hear that when Ellen called at the Parsonage you were suffering from influenza. I know that an attack of this debilitating complaint is no trifle in your case, as its effects linger with you long. It has been very prevalent in this neighbourhood. I did not escape, but the sickness and fever only lasted a few days and the cough was not severe. Papa, I am thankful to say, continues pretty well; Ellen thinks him little, if at all altered.

'And now for your kind present. The book will be precious to me — chiefly, perhaps, for the sake of the giver, but also for its own sake, for it is a good book; and I wish I may be enabled to read it with some approach to the spirit you would desire. Its perusal came recommended in such a manner as to obviate danger of neglect; its place shall always be on my dressing-table.

'As to the other part of the present, it arrived under these circumstances:

'For a month past an urgent necessity to buy and make some things for winter-wear had been importuning my conscience; the *buying* might be soon effected, but the *making* was a more serious consideration. At this juncture Ellen arrives with a good-sized parcel, which, when opened, discloses the things I required, perfectly made and of capital useful fabric; adorned too — which seemly decoration it is but too probable I might myself have foregone as an augmentation of trouble not to be lightly incurred. I felt strong doubts as to my right to profit by this sort of fairy gift, so unlooked for and so curiously opportune; on reading the note accompanying the garments, I am told that to accept will be to confer a favour (!)

273

The doctrine is too palatable to be rejected; I even waive all nice scrutiny of its soundness — in short, I submit with as good a grace as may be.

'Ellen has only been my companion one little week. I would not have her any longer, for I am disgusted with myself and my delays, and consider it was a weak yielding to temptation in me to send for her at all; but, in truth, my spirits were getting low — prostrate sometimes, and she has done me inexpressible good. I wonder when I shall see you at Haworth again. Both my father and the servants have again and again insinuated a distinct wish that you should be requested to come in the course of the summer and autumn, but I always turned a deaf ear: "Not yet," was my thought, "I want first to be free — work first, then pleasure."

'I venture to send by Ellen a book which may amuse an hour: a Scotch tale by a minister's wife. It seems to me well told, and may serve to remind you of characters and manners you have seen in Scotland. When you have time to write a line, I shall feel anxious to hear how you are. With kind regards to all old friends, and truest affection to yourself, in which Ellen joins me, — I am, my dear Miss Wooler, yours gratefully and respectfully, C. BRONTË.'

TO MISS WOOLER.

'HAWORTH, October 8, 1852.

'MY DEAR MISS WOOLER, — I wished much to write to you immediately on my return home, but I found several little matters demanding attention, and have been kept busy till now.

'I reached home about five o'clock in the afternoon, and the anxiety which is inseparable from a return after absence was pleasantly relieved by finding papa well and cheerful. He inquired after you with interest. I gave him your kind regards, and he specially charged me whenever I wrote to present his in return, and to say also that he hoped to see you at Haworth at the earliest date which shall be convenient to you.

'The week I spent at Hornsea was a happy and pleasant

week. Thank you, my dear Miss Wooler, for the true kindness which gave it its chief charm. I shall think of you often, especially when I walk out, and during the long evenings. I believe the weather has at length taken a turn: to-day is beautifully fine. I wish I were at Hornsea and just now preparing to go out with you to walk on the sands or along the lake.

'I would not have you to fatigue yourself with writing to me when you are not inclined, but yet I should be glad to hear from you some day ere long. When you *do* write, tell me how you liked "The Experience of Life," and whether you have read "Esmond," and what you think of it. — Believe me always yours, with true affection and respect,   C. BRONTË.'

TO MISS WOOLER.

'BROOKROYD, December 7, 1852.

'MY DEAR MISS WOOLER, — Since you were so kind as to take some interest in my small tribulation of Saturday, I write a line to tell you that on Sunday morning a letter came which put me out of pain and obviated the necessity of an impromptu journey to London.

'The *money transaction*, of course, remains the same, and perhaps is not quite equitable; but when an author finds that his work is cordially approved, he can pardon the rest — indeed, my chief regret now lies in the conviction that papa will be disappointed: he expected me to earn £500, nor did I myself anticipate that a lower sum would be offered; however, £250 is not to be despised.[1]

'Your sudden departure from Brookroyd left a legacy of consternation to the bereaved breakfast-table. Ellen was not easily to be soothed, though I diligently represented to her that you had quitted Haworth with the same inexorable haste. I am commissioned to tell you, first, that she has decided not to go to Yarmouth till after Christmas, her mother's health having within the last few days betrayed some symptoms not unlike those which preceded her

---

[1] Miss Brontë was paid £1500 in all for her three novels, and Mr. Nicholls received an additional £250 for the copyright of 'The Professor.'

275

former illness; and though it is to be hoped that those may pass without any untoward result, yet they naturally increase Ellen's reluctance to leave home for the present.

'Secondly, I am to say, that when the present you left came to be examined, the costliness and beauty of it inspired some concern. Ellen thinks you are too kind, as I also think every morning, for I am now benefiting by your kind gift.

'With sincere regards to all at the Parsonage, — I am, my dear Miss Wooler, yours respectfully and affectionately,

'C. Brontë.

'P. S. — I shall direct that "Esmond" (Mr. Thackeray's work) shall be sent on to you as soon as the Hunsworth party have read it. It has already reached a second edition.'

TO MISS WOOLER.

'Haworth, January 20, 1853.

'My dear Miss Wooler, — Your last kind note would not have remained so long unanswered if I had been in better health. While Ellen was with me, I seemed to revive wonderfully, but began to grow worse again the day she left; and this falling off proved symptomatic of a relapse. My doctor called the next day; he said the headache from which I was suffering arose from inertness in the liver.

'Thank God I now feel better; and very grateful am I for the improvement — grateful no less for my dear father's sake than for my own.

'Most fully can I sympathise with you in the anxiety you express about your friend. The thought of his leaving England and going out alone to a strange country, with all his natural sensitiveness and retiring diffidence, is indeed painful; still, my dear Miss Wooler, should he actually go to America, I can but then suggest to you the same source of comfort and support you have suggested to me, and of which indeed I know you never lose sight — namely, reliance on Providence. "God tempers the wind to the shorn lamb," and He will doubtless care for a good, though afflicted man, amidst whatever difficulties he may be thrown. When you write again, I should be glad to know whether your anxiety on this subject is released. I was truly glad to learn through Ellen that Ilkley still continued to agree with your health. Earnestly trusting that the New Year may prove to you a happy and tranquil time, — I am, my dear Miss Wooler, sincerely and affectionately yours,

'C. BRONTË.'

TO MISS WOOLER.

'JANUARY 27, 1853.

'MY DEAR MISS WOOLER, — I received your letter here in London where I have been staying about three weeks, and shall probably remain a few days longer. "Villette" is to be published to-morrow. Its appearance has been purposely delayed hitherto, to avoid discourteous clashing with Mrs. Gaskell's new work. Your name was one of the first on the list of presentees, and directed to the Parsonage, where I shall also send this letter, as you mention that you are to leave Halifax at the close of this week. I will bear in mind what you say about Mrs. Morgan ; and should I ever have an opportunity of serving her, will not omit to do so. I only wish my chance of being useful were greater. Schools seem to be considered almost obsolete in London. Ladies' colleges, with professors for every branch of instruction, are superseding the old-fashioned seminary. How the system will work I can't tell. I think the college classes might be very useful for finishing the education of ladies intended to go out as governesses, but what progress little girls will make in them seems to me another question.

'My dear Miss Wooler, I read attentively all you say about Miss Martineau ; the sincerity and constancy of your solicitude touches me very much. I should grieve to neglect or oppose your advice, and yet I do not feel that it would be right to give Miss Martineau up entirely. There is in her nature much that is very noble. Hundreds have forsaken her, more, I fear, in the apprehension that their fair names may suffer if seen in connection with hers, than from any pure convictions, such as you suggest, of harm consequent on her fatal tenets. With these fair-weather friends I cannot bear to rank. And for her

277

sin, is it not one of those which God and not man must judge?

'To speak the truth, my dear Miss Wooler, I believe if you were in my place, and knew Miss Martineau as I do — if you had shared with me the proofs of her rough but genuine kindliness, and had seen how she secretly suffers from abandonment, you would be the last to give her up; you would separate the sinner from the sin, and feel as if the right lay rather in quietly adhering to her in her strait, while that adherence is unfashionable and unpopular, than in turning on her your back when the world sets the example. I believe she is one of those whom opposition and desertion make obstinate in error, while patience and tolerance touch her deeply and keenly, and incline her to ask of her own heart whether the course she has been pursuing may not possibly be a faulty course. However, I have time to think of this subject, and I shall think of it seriously.

'As to what I have seen in London during my present visit, I hope one day to tell you all about it by our fireside at home. When you write again will you name a time when it would suit you to come and see me; everybody in the house would be glad of your presence; your last visit is pleasantly remembered by all.

'With kindest regards, — I am always, affectionately and respectfully yours, C. BRONTË.'

A note to Miss Nussey written after Charlotte's death indicates a fairly shrewd view on the part of Miss Wooler as regards the popularity of her friend.

TO MISS ELLEN NUSSEY.

'MY DEAR MISS ELLEN, — The third edition of Charlotte's Life has at length ventured out. Our curate tells me he is assured it is quite inferior to the former ones. So you see Mrs. Gaskell displayed worldly wisdom in going out of her way to furnish gossip for the discerning public. Did I mention to you that Mrs. Gibson knows two or three young ladies in Hull who finished their education at Mme. Héger's pension. Mrs. G. said they read "Villette" with keen interest — of course they would. I had a nice walk with a Suffolk lady, who was evidently delighted to meet with one who had personally known our dear C. B., and would not soon have wearied of a conversation in which she was the topic. — Love to yourself and sisters, from — Your affectionate, M. WOOLER.'

CHAPTER XI.

THE CURATES AT HAWORTH.

SOMETHING has already been said concerning the growth of the population of Haworth during the period of Mr. Brontë's Incumbency. It was 4668 in 1821, and 6301 in 1841. This makes it natural that Mr. Brontë should have applied to his Bishop for assistance in his pastoral duty, and such aid was permanently granted him in 1838, when Mr. William Weightman became his first curate. [1] Mr. Weightman would appear to have been a favourite. He many times put in an appearance at the parsonage, although I do not recognise him in any one of Charlotte's novels, and he certainly has no place among the three famous curates of 'Shirley.' He would seem to have been the only man, other than her father and brother, whom Emily was known to tolerate. We know that the girls considered him effeminate, and they called him 'Celia Amelia,' under which name he frequently appears in Charlotte's letters to Ellen Nussey. That he was good-natured seems to be indisputable. There is one story of his walking to Bradford to post valentines to the incumbent's daughters, when he found they had never received any. There is another story of a trip to Keighley to hear him lecture. He was a bit of a poet, it seems, and Ellen Nussey was the heroine of some of his verses when she

---

[1] A Mr. Hodgson is spoken of earlier, but he would seem to have been only a temporary help.

visited at Haworth. Here is a letter which throws some light upon Charlotte's estimate of the young man — he was twenty-three years of age at this time.

TO MISS ELLEN NUSSEY.

'MARCH 17, 1840.

' MY DEAR MRS. ELEANOR, — I wish to scold you with a forty-horse power for having told Mary Taylor that I had requested you not to tell her everything, which piece of information has thrown her into tremendous ill-humour, besides setting the teeth of her curiosity on edge. Tell her forthwith every individual occurrence, including valentines, " Fair E—, Fair E—," etc.; "Away fond love," etc.; "Soul divine," and all; likewise the painting of Miss Celia Amelia Weightman's portrait, and that *young lady's* frequent and agreeable visits. By-the-bye, I inquired into the opinion of that intelligent and interesting young person respecting you. It was a favourable one. "She" thought you a fine-looking girl, and a very good girl into the bargain. Have you received the newspaper which has been despatched, containing a notice of "her" lecture at Keighley. Mr. Morgan came and stayed three days. By Miss Weightman's aid, we got on pretty well. It was amazing to see with what patience and good-temper the innocent creature endured that fat Welshman's prosing, though she confessed afterwards that she was almost done up by his long stories. We feel very dull without you. I wish those three weeks were to come over again. Aunt has been at times precious cross since you went — however, she is rather better now. I had a bad cold on Sunday and stayed at home most of the day. Anne's cold is better, but I don't consider her strong yet. What did your sister Anne say about my omitting to send a drawing for the Jew basket. I hope she was too much occupied with the thoughts of going to Earnley to think of it. I am obliged to cut short my letter. Everybody in the house unites in sending their love to you. Miss Celia Amelia Weightman also desires to be remembered. Write soon again and — Believe me, yours unalterably,   CHARIVARI.'

CHARLOTTE BRONTË

He would seem to have been a much teased curate. Now it is Miss Ellen Nussey, now a Miss Agnes Walton, who is supposed to be the object of his devotion.

TO MISS ELLEN NUSSEY.

'APRIL 9, 1840.

'MY DEAR MRS. MENELAUS, — I think I am exceedingly good to write to you so soon, indeed I am quite afraid you will begin to consider me intrusive with my frequent letters. I ought by right to let an interval of a quarter of a year elapse between each communication, and I will, in time, never fear me. I shall improve in procrastination as I get older.

'My hand is trembling like that of an old man, so I don't expect you will be able to read my writing; never mind, put the letter by and I'll read it to you the next time I see you.

'I have been painting a portrait of Agnes Walton for our friend Miss Celia Amelia. You would laugh to see how his eyes sparkle with delight when he looks at it, like a pretty child pleased with a new plaything. Good-bye to you. Let me have no more of your humbug about Cupid, etc. You know as well as I do it is all groundless trash.   C. BRONTË.'

TO MISS ELLEN NUSSEY.

'AUGUST 20, 1840.

'DEAR MRS. ELLEN, — I was very well pleased with your capital long letter. A better farce than the whole affair of that letter-opening (ducks and Mr. Weightman included) was never imagined.[1] By-the-bye, speaking of Mr. W., I told you he was gone to pass his examination at Ripon six weeks ago. He is not come back yet, and what has become of him we don't know. Branwell has received one letter since he went, speaking rapturously of Agnes Walton, describing certain balls at which he had figured, and announcing that he had been twice over head and ears desperately in love. It is my devout belief that his reverence left Haworth with the fixed intention of never returning. If he does return, it will be because he

---

[1] Referring to a present of birds which the curate had sent to Miss Nussey.

282

has not been able to get a "living." Haworth is not the place
for him. He requires novelty, a change of faces, difficulties to
be overcome. He pleases so easily that he soon gets weary of
pleasing at all. He ought not to have been a parson; certainly
he ought not. Our *august* relations, as you choose to call them,
are gone back to London. They never stayed with us, they
only spent one day at our house. Have you seen anything of
the Miss Woolers lately? I wish they, or somebody else, would
get me a situation. I have answered advertisements without
number, but my applications have met with no success.

'CALIBAN.'

One wonders if a single letter by Charlotte Brontë apply-
ing for a 'situation' has been preserved! I have not seen
one.

TO MISS ELLEN NUSSEY

' SEPTEMBER 29, 1840.

'I know Mrs. Ellen is burning with eagerness to hear something about William Weightman. I think I'll plague her by not
telling her a word. To speak heaven's truth, I have precious little
to say, inasmuch as I seldom see him, except on a Sunday, when
he looks as handsome, cheery, and good-tempered as usual. I
have indeed had the advantage of one long conversation since
his return from Westmoreland, when he poured out his whole
warm fickle soul in fondness and admiration of Agnes Walton.
Whether he is in love with her or not I can't say; I can only
observe that it sounds very like it. He sent us a prodigious
quantity of game while he was away — a brace of wild ducks,
a brace of black grouse, a brace of partridges, ditto of snipes,
ditto of curlews, and a large salmon. If you were to ask Mr.
Weightman's opinion of my character just now, he would say that
at first he thought me a cheerful chatty kind of body, but that
on farther acquaintance he found me of a capricious changeful
temper, never to be reckoned on. He does not know that I
have regulated my manner by his — that I was cheerful and
chatty so long as he was respectful, and that when he grew
almost contemptuously familiar I found it necessary to adopt a

degree of reserve which was not natural, and therefore was very painful to me. I find this reserve very convenient, and consequently I intend to keep it up.'

TO MISS ELLEN NUSSEY.

'NOVEMBER 12, 1840.

'MY DEAR NELL,— You will excuse this scrawled sheet of paper, inasmuch as I happen to be out of that article, this being the only available sheet I can find in my desk. I have effaced one of the delectable portraitures, but have spared the others — lead pencil sketches of horse's head, and man's head — being moved to that act of clemency by the recollection that they are not the work of my hand, but of the sacred fingers of his reverence William Weightman. You will discern that the eye is a little too elevated in the horse's head, otherwise I can assure you it is no such bad attempt. It shows taste and something of an artist's eye. The fellow had no copy for it. He sketched it, and one or two other little things, when he happened to be here one evening, but you should have seen the vanity with which he afterwards regarded his productions. One of them represented the flying figure of Fame inscribing his own name on the clouds.

'Mrs. Brook and I have interchanged letters. She expressed herself pleased with the style of my application — with its candour, etc. (I took care to tell her that if she wanted a showy, elegant, fashionable personage, I was not the man for her), but she wants music and singing. I can't give her music and singing, so of course the negotiation is null and void. Being once up, however, I don't mean to sit down till I have got what I want; but there is no sense in talking about unfinished projects, so we'll drop the subject. Consider this last sentence a hint from me to be applied practically. It seems Miss Wooler's school is in a consumptive state of health. I have been endeavouring to obtain a reinforcement of pupils for her, but I cannot succeed, because Mrs. Heap is opening a new school in Bradford. C. BRONTË.'

284

TO MISS ELLEN NUSSEY.

'JANUARY 10, 1841.

'MY DEAR ELLEN, — I promised to write to you, and therefore I must keep my promise, though I have neither much to say nor much time to say it in.

'Mary Taylor's visit has been a very pleasant one to us, and I believe to herself also. She and Mr. Weightman have had several games at chess, which generally terminated in a species of mock hostility. Mr. Weightman is better in health; but don't set your heart on him, I'm afraid he is very fickle — not to you in particular, but to half a dozen other ladies. He has just cut his *inamorata* at Swansea, and sent her back all her letters. His present object of devotion is Caroline Dury, to whom he has just despatched a most passionate copy of verses. Poor lad, his sanguine temperament bothers him grievously.

'That Swansea affair seems to me somewhat heartless as far as I can understand it, though I have not heard a very clear explanation. He sighs as much as ever. I have not mentioned your name to him yet, nor do I mean to do so until I have a fair opportunity of gathering his real mind. Perhaps I may never mention it at all, but on the contrary carefully avoid all allusion to you. It will just depend upon the further opinion I may form of his character. I am not pleased to find that he was carrying on a regular correspondence with this lady at Swansea all the time he was paying such pointed attention to you; and now the abrupt way in which he has cut her off, and the evident wandering instability of his mind is no favourable symptom at all. I shall not have many opportunities of observing him for a month to come. As for the next fortnight, he will be sedulously engaged in preparing for his ordination, and the fortnight after he will spend at Appleby and Crackenthorp with Mr. and Miss Walton. Don't think about him; I am not afraid you will break your heart, but don't think about him.

'Give my love to Mercy and your mother, and, — Believe me, yours sincerely,　　　　　　　　　　　　　　　　　CA'IRA.'

CHARLOTTE BRONTË

TO MISS ELLEN NUSSEY.

' RAWDON, March 3, 1841.

' MY DEAR ELLEN, — I dare say you have received a valentine this year from our bonny-faced friend the curate of Haworth. I got a precious specimen a few days before I left home, but I knew better how to treat it than I did those we received a year ago. I am up to the dodges and artifices of his lordship's character. He knows I know him, and you cannot conceive how quiet and respectful he has long been. Mind I am not writing against him — I never *will* do that. I like him very much. I honour and admire his generous, open disposition, and sweet temper — but for all the tricks, wiles, and insincerities of love, the gentleman has not his match for twenty miles round. He would fain persuade every woman under thirty whom he sees that he is desperately in love with her. I have a great deal more to say, but I have not a moment's time to write it in. My dear Ellen, *do* write to me soon, don't forget. — Good-bye.'

TO MISS ELLEN NUSSEY.

' MARCH 21, 1841.

' MY DEAREST ELLEN, — I do not know how to wear your pretty little handcuffs. When you come you shall explain the mystery. I send you the precious valentine. Make much of it. Remember the writer's blue eyes, auburn hair, and rosy cheeks. You may consider the concern addressed to yourself, for I have no doubt he intended it to suit anybody.

' Fare-thee-well. C. B.'

Then there are these slighter inferences, that concerning Anne being particularly interesting.

'Write long letters to me, and tell me everything you can think of, and about everybody. "His young reverence," as you tenderly call him, is looking delicate and pale; poor thing, don't you pity him? I do from my heart! When he is well, and fat, and jovial, I never think of him, but when anything ails him I am always sorry. He sits opposite to Anne at church,

sighing softly, and looking out of the corners of his eyes to win
her attention, and Anne is so quiet, her look so downcast, they are
a picture.'

'JULY 19, 1841.

' Our revered friend, W. W., is quite as bonny, pleasant, light-
hearted, good-tempered, generous, careless, fickle, and unclerical
as ever. He keeps up his correspondence with Agnes Walton.
During the last spring he went to Appleby, and stayed upwards of
a month.'

During the governess and Brussels episodes in Charlotte's
life we lose sight of Mr. Weightman, and the next record
is of his death, which took place in September 1842, while
Charlotte and Emily were in Brussels. Mr. Brontë preached
the funeral sermon,[1] stating by way of introduction that for
the twenty years and more that he had been in Haworth
he had never before read his sermon. 'This is owing to a
conviction in my mind,' he says, 'that in general, for the
ordinary run of hearers, extempore preaching, though accompanied with some peculiar disadvantages, is more likely
to be of a colloquial nature, and better adapted, on the
whole, to the majority.' His departure from the practice
on this occasion, he explains, is due to the request that his
sermon should be printed.

Mr. Weightman, he told his hearers, was a native of
Westmoreland, educated at the University of Durham.
'While he was there,' continued Mr. Brontë, 'I applied
to the justly venerated Apostolical Bishop of this diocese,
requesting his Lordship to send me a curate adequate to
the wants and wishes of the parishioners. This application was not in vain. Our Diocesan, in the scriptural

[1] A Funeral Sermon for the late Rev. William Weightman, M.A., preached
in the Church at Haworth on Sunday the 2nd of October 1842 by the Rev.
Patrick Brontë, A.B., Incumbent. The profits, if any, to go in aid of the
Sunday School. Halifax — Printed by J. U. Walker, George Street, 1842.
Price sixpence.

character of the Overlooker and Head of his clergy, made an admirable choice, which more than answered my expectations, and probably yours. The Church Pastoral Aid Society, in their pious liberality, lent their pecuniary aid, without which all efforts must have failed.' 'He had classical attainments of the first order, and, above all, his religious principles were sound and orthodox,' concludes Mr. Brontë. Mr. Weightman was twenty-six years of age when he died. His successor was Mr. Peter Augustus Smith, whom Charlotte Brontë has made famous in 'Shirley' as Mr. Malone, curate of Briarfield. Mr. Smith was Mr. A. B. Nicholls's predecessor at Haworth. Here is Charlotte Brontë's vigorous treatment of him in a letter to her friend.

TO MISS ELLEN NUSSEY.

'JANUARY 26, 1844.

'DEAR NELL, — We were all very glad to get your letter this morning. *We*, I say, as both papa and Emily were anxious to hear of the safe arrival of yourself and the little *varmint*.[1]

'As you conjecture, Emily and I set to shirt-making the very day after you left, and we have stuck to it pretty closely ever since. We miss your society at least as much as you miss ours, depend upon it. Would that you were within calling distance, that you could as you say burst in upon us in an afternoon, and, being despoiled of your bonnet and shawl, be fixed in the rocking-chair for the evening once or twice every week. I certainly cherished a dream during your stay that such might one day be the case, but the dream is somewhat dissipating. I allude of course to Mr. Smith, to whom you do not allude in your letter, and I think you foolish for the omission. I say the dream is dissipating, because Mr. Smith has not mentioned your name since you left, except once when papa said you were a nice girl, he said, "Yes, she is a nice girl — rather quiet. I suppose she has money," and that is all. I think the words

---

[1] A little dog, called in the next letter 'Flossy, jun.,' which indicates its parentage. Flossy was the little dog given by the Robinsons to Anne.

speak volumes ; they do not prejudice one in favour of Mr. Smith.
I can well believe what papa has often affirmed, and continues to
affirm, *i. e.*, that Mr. Smith is a very fickle man, that if he marries
he will soon get tired of his wife, and consider her as a burden,
also that money will be a principal consideration with him in
marrying.

'Papa has two or three times expressed a fear that since Mr.
Smith paid you so much attention he will perhaps have made an
impression on your mind which will interfere with your comfort.
I tell him I think not, as I believe you to be mistress of yourself
in those matters. Still, he keeps saying that I am to write to you
and dissuade you from thinking of him. I never saw papa make
himself so uneasy about a thing of the kind before ; he is usually
very sarcastic on such subjects.

'Mr. Smith be hanged! I never thought very well of him,
and I am much disposed to think very ill of him at this blessed
minute. I have discussed the subject fully, for where is the use
of being mysterious and constrained — it is not worth while.

'Be sure you write to me and immediately, and tell me
whether you have given up eating and drinking altogether.
I am not surprised at people thinking you looked pale and
thin. I shall expect another letter on Thursday — don't disappoint me.

'My best regards to your mother and sisters. — Yours, somewhat irritated,   C. B.'

TO MISS ELLEN NUSSEY.

'DEAR NELL, — I did not "swear at the postman" when I saw
another letter from you. And I hope you will not "swear" at
me when I tell you that I cannot think of leaving home at
present, even to have the pleasure of joining you at Harrogate,
but I am obliged to you for thinking of me. I have nothing
new about Rev. Lothario Smith. I think I like him a little bit
less every day. Mr. Weightman was worth 200 Mr. Smiths tied
in a bunch. Good-bye. I fear by what you say, "Flossy, jun."
behaves discreditably, and gets his mistress into scrapes.

'C. BRONTË.'

CHARLOTTE BRONTË

TO MISS ELLEN NUSSEY.

'MARCH 16, 1844.

'DEAR ELLEN, — I received your kind note last Saturday, and should have answered it immediately, but in the meantime I had a letter from Mary Taylor, and had to reply to her, and to write sundry letters to Brussels to send by opportunity. My sight will not allow me to write several letters per day, so I was obliged to do it gradually.

'I send you two more circulars because you ask for them, not because I hope their distribution will produce any result. I hope that if a time should come when Emily, Anne, or I shall be able to serve you, we shall not forget that you have done your best to serve us.

'Mr. Smith is gone hence. He is in Ireland at present, and will stay there six weeks. He has left neither a bad nor a good character behind him. Nobody regrets him, because nobody could attach themselves to one who could attach himself to nobody. I thought once he had a regard for you, but I do not think so now. He has never asked after you since you left, nor even mentioned you in my hearing, except to say once when I purposely alluded to you, that you were "not very locomotive." The meaning of the observation I leave you to divine.

'Yet the man is not without points that will be most useful to himself in getting through life. His good qualities, however, are all of the selfish order, but they will make him respected where better and more generous natures would be despised, or at least neglected.

'Mr. Grant fills his shoes at present decently enough — but one cares naught about these sort of individuals, so drop them.

'Mary Taylor is going to leave our hemisphere. To me it is something as if a great planet fell out of the sky. Yet, unless she marries in New Zealand, she will not stay there long.

'Write to me again soon and I promise to write you a regular long letter next time. C. BRONTË.'

The Mr. Grant here described had come to Haworth as master of the small grammar school in which Branwell had

received some portion of his education. He is the Mr.
Donne, curate of Whinbury, in 'Shirley.' Whinbury is Oxenhope, of which village and district Mr. Grant after a time
became incumbent. The district was taken out of Haworth
Chapelry, and Mr. Grant collected the funds to build a
church, schoolhouse, and parsonage. He died at Oxenhope,
many years ago, greatly respected by his parishioners. He
seems to have endured good-naturedly much chaff from Mr.
Brontë and others, who always called him Mr. Donne. It
was the opinion of many of his acquaintances that the satire
of 'Shirley' had improved his disposition.

Mr. Smith left Haworth in 1844, to become curate of the
parish church of Keighley. He became, at a later date,
incumbent of a district church, but, his health failing, he
returned to his native country, where he died.

TO MISS ELLEN NUSSEY.

'OCTOBER 15, 1844.

'DEAR NELL, — I send you two additional circulars, and will
send you two more, if you desire it, when I write again. I have
no news to give you. Mr. Smith leaves in the course of a fortnight. He will spend a few weeks in Ireland previously to
settling at Keighley. He continues just the same: often anxious
and bad-tempered, sometimes rather tolerable — just supportable.
How did your party go off? How are you? Write soon, and
at length, for your letters are a great comfort to me. We
are all pretty well. Remember me kindly to each member of
the household at Brookroyd. — Yours,   C. B.'

The third curate of 'Shirley,' Mr. Sweeting of Nunnely, was
Mr. Richard Bradley, curate of Oakworth, an outlying
district of Keighley parish. He is at this present time vicar
of Haxby, Yorkshire, but far too aged and infirm to have
any memories of those old Haworth days.

Mr. Brontë's one other curate was Mr. De Renzi, who
occupied the position for a little more than a year. During

the period, in fact, of Mr. Brontë's quarrel with Mr. Nicholls for aspiring to become his son-in-law. After he left Haworth, Mr. De Renzi became a curate at Bradford. He has been dead for some years. The story of Mr. Nicholls's curacy belongs to another chapter. It is sufficient testimony to his worth, however, that he was able to win Charlotte Brontë in spite of the fact that his predecessors had inspired in her such hearty contempt. 'I think he must be like all the curates I have seen,' she writes of one; 'they seem to me a self-seeking, vain, empty race.'

CHAPTER XII.

CHARLOTTE BRONTË'S LOVERS.

CHARLOTTE BRONTË was not beautiful, but she must have been singularly fascinating. That she was not beautiful there is abundant evidence. When, as a girl of fifteen, she became a pupil at Roe Head, Mary Taylor once told her to her face that she was ugly. Ugly she was not in later years. All her friends emphasise the soft silky hair, and the beautiful grey eyes which in moments of excitement seemed to glisten with remarkable brilliancy. But she had a sallow complexion, and a large nose slightly on one side. She was small in stature, and, in fact, the casual observer would have thought her a quaint, unobtrusive little body. Mr. Grundy's memory was very defective when he wrote about the Brontës; but, with the exception of the reference to red hair — and all the girls had brown hair — it would seem that he was not very wide of the mark when he wrote of 'the daughters — distant and distrait, large of nose, small of figure, red of hair, prominent of spectacles, showing great intellectual development, but with eyes constantly cast down, very silent, painfully retiring,'

Charlotte was indeed painfully shy. Miss Wheelwright, who saw much of her during her visits to London in the years of her literary success, says that she would never enter a room without sheltering herself under the wing of some taller friend. A resident of Haworth, still alive, remembers the girls passing him frequently on the way down to the shops, and their hands would involuntarily be lifted to the face on the side nearest to him, with a view to avoid observation. This was not affectation; it was absolute timidity. Miss Wheelwright always thought George Richmond's portrait — for which Charlotte sat during a stay at Dr. Wheelwright's in Phillimore Place — entirely flattering. Many of Charlotte's friends were pleased that it should be so, but there can be no doubt that the magnificent expanse of forehead was an exaggeration. Charlotte's forehead was high, but very narrow.

All this is comparatively unimportant. Charlotte certainly was under no illusion; and we who revere her to-day as one of the greatest of Englishwomen need have no illusions. It is sufficient that, if not beautiful, Charlotte possessed a singular charm of manner, and, when interested, an exhilarating flow of conversation which carried intelligent men off their feet. She had at least four offers of marriage. The three lovers she refused have long since gone to their graves, and there can be no harm now in referring to the actual facts as they present themselves in Charlotte's letters. Two of these offers of marriage were made in one year, when she was twenty-three years of age. Her first proposal came from the brother of her friend Ellen Nussey. Henry Nussey was a curate at Bonnington when he asked Charlotte Brontë to be his wife. Two letters on the subject, one of which is partly printed in a mangled form in Mrs. Gaskell's Memoir, speak for themselves.

TO REV. HENRY NUSSEY.

'HAWORTH, March 5, 1839.

'MY DEAR SIR, — Before answering your letter I might have spent a long time in consideration of its subject; but as from the first moment of its reception and perusal I determined on what course to pursue, it seemed to me that delay was wholly unnecessary. You are aware that I have many reasons to feel grateful to your family, that I have peculiar reasons for affection towards one at least of your sisters, and also that I highly esteem yourself — do not therefore accuse me of wrong motives when I say that my answer to your proposal must be a *decided negative*. In forming this decision, I trust I have listened to the dictates of conscience more than to those of inclination. I have no personal repugnance to the idea of a union with you, but I feel convinced that mine is not the sort of disposition calculated to form the happiness of a man like you. It has always been my habit to study the characters of those amongst whom I chance to be thrown, and I think I know yours and can imagine what description of woman would suit you for a wife. The character should not be too marked, ardent, and original, her temper should be mild, her piety undoubted, her spirits even and cheerful, and her *personal attractions* sufficient to please your eyes and gratify your just pride. As for me, you do not know me; I am not the serious, grave, cool-headed individual you suppose; you would think me romantic and eccentric; you would say I was satirical and severe. However, I scorn deceit, and I will never, for the sake of attaining the distinction of matrimony and escaping the stigma of an old maid, take a worthy man whom I am conscious I cannot render happy. Before I conclude, let me thank you warmly for your other proposal regarding the school near Bonnington. It is kind in you to take so much interest about me; but the fact is, I could not at present enter upon such a project because I have not the capital necessary to insure success. It is a pleasure to me to hear that you are so comfortably settled and that your health is so much improved. I trust God will continue His kindness towards you. Let me say also that I admire the good-sense and absence of flattery and cant which your letter displayed. Farewell. I shall always be glad to hear from you as a *friend*. — Believe me, yours truly,   C. Brontë.'

TO MISS ELLEN NUSSEY.

' Haworth, March 12, 1839.

'My dearest Ellen, — When your letter was put into my hands, I said, "She is coming at last, I hope," but when I opened it and found what the contents were, I was vexed to the heart. You need not ask me to go to Brookroyd any more. Once for all, and at the hazard of being called the most stupid little wretch that ever existed, I *won't go* till you have been to Haworth. I don't blame *you*, I believe you would come if you might ; perhaps I ought not to blame others, but I am grieved.

'Anne goes to Blake Hall on the 8th of April, unless some further unseen cause of delay should occur. I've heard nothing more from Mrs. Thos. Brook as yet. Papa wishes me to remain at home a little longer, but I begin to be anxious to set to work again ; and yet it will be *hard work* after the indulgence of so many weeks, to return to that dreary " gin-horse " round.

'You ask me, my dear Ellen, whether I have received a letter from Henry. I have, about a week since. The contents, I confess, did a little surprise me, but I kept them to myself, and unless you had questioned me on the subject, I would never have adverted to it. Henry says he is comfortably settled at Bonnington, that his health is much improved, and that it is his intention to take pupils after Easter. He then intimates that in due time he should want a wife to take care of his pupils, and frankly asks me to be that wife. Altogether the letter is written without cant or flattery, and in a common-sense style, which does credit to his judgment.

'Now, my dear Ellen, there were in this proposal some things which might have proved a strong temptation. I thought if I were to marry Henry Nussey, his sister could live with me, and how happy I should be. But again I asked myself two questions : Do I love him as much as a woman ought to love the man she marries ? Am I the person best qualified to make him happy ? Alas ! Ellen, my conscience answered *no* to both these questions. I felt that though I esteemed, though I had a kindly leaning towards him, because he is an amiable and well-disposed man, yet I had not, and could not have, that intense attachment which would make me willing to die for him ; and, if ever I marry, it must be in that light of adoration that I will regard my husband. Ten to one I shall never have the chance again ; but *n'importe*. Moreover, I was aware that Henry knew so little of me he could hardly be conscious to whom he was writing. Why, it would startle him to see me in my natural home character; he would think I was a wild, romantic enthusiast indeed. I could not sit all day long making a grave face before my husband. I would laugh, and satirise, and say whatever came into my head first. And if he were a clever man, and loved me, the whole world weighed in the balance against his smallest wish should be light as air. Could I, knowing my mind to be such as that, conscientiously say that I would take a grave, quiet young man like Henry ? No, it would have been deceiving him, and deception of that sort is beneath me. So I wrote a long letter back, in which I expressed my refusal as gently as I could, and also candidly avowed my reasons for that refusal. I described to him, too, the sort of character that would suit him for a wife. — Good-bye, my dear Ellen.   C. BRONTË.'

Mr. Nussey was a very good man, with a capacity for making himself generally esteemed, becoming in turn vicar of Earnley, near Chichester, and afterwards of Hathersage, in Derbyshire. It was honourable to his judgment that he had aspired to marry Charlotte Brontë, who, as we know, had neither money nor much personal attraction, and at the time no possible prospect of literary fame. Her common-sense letter in reply to his proposal had the desired effect. He speedily took the proffered advice, and six months later we find her sending him a letter of congratulation upon his engagement to be married.

TO REV HENRY NUSSEY.

'HAWORTH, October 28, 1839.

' DEAR SIR, — I have delayed answering your last communication in the hopes of receiving a letter from Ellen, that I might be able to transmit to you the latest news from Brookroyd ; however, as she does not write, I think I ought to put off my reply no longer lest you should begin to think me negligent. As you rightly conjecture, I had heard a little hint of what you allude to before, and the account gave me pleasure, coupled as it was with the assurance that the object of your regard is a worthy and estimable woman. The step no doubt will by many of your friends be considered scarcely as a prudent one, *since* fortune is not amongst the number of the young lady's advantages. For my own part, I must confess that I esteem you the more for not hunting after wealth if there be strength of mind, firmness of principle, and sweetness of temper to compensate for the absence of that usually all-powerful attraction. The wife who brings riches to her husband sometimes also brings an idea of her own importance and a tenacity about what she conceives to be her rights, little calculated to produce happiness in the married state. Most probably she will wish to control when nature and affection bind her to submit — in this case there cannot, I should think, be much comfort.

' On the other hand, it must be considered that when two persons marry without money, there ought to be moral courage and physical exertion to atone for the deficiency — there should be spirit to scorn dependence, patience to endure privation, and energy to labour for a livelihood. If there be these qualities, I think, with the blessing of God, those who join heart and hand have a right to expect success and a moderate share of happiness, even though they may have departed a step or two from the stern maxims of worldly prudence. The bread earned by honourable toil is sweeter than the bread of idleness ; and mutual love and domestic calm are treasures far preferable to the possessions rust can corrupt and moths consume away.

' I enjoyed my late excursion with Ellen with the greater zest because such pleasures have not often chanced to fall in my way. I will not tell you what I thought of the sea, because I should fall into my besetting sin of enthusiasm. I may, however, say that its glories, changes, its ebbs and flow, the sound of its restless waves, formed a subject for contemplation that never wearied either the eye, the ear, or the mind. Our visit

at Easton was extremely pleasant ; I shall always feel grateful
to Mr. and Mrs. Hudson for their kindness. We saw Agnes
Burton, during our stay, and called on two of your former parishioners — Mrs. Brown and Mrs. Dalton. I was pleased to hear
your name mentioned by them in terms of encomium and sincere
regard. Ellen will have detailed to you all the minutiæ of our
excursion, a recapitulation from me would therefore be tedious.
I am happy to say that her health appeared to be greatly improved
by the change of air and regular exercise. I am still at home,
as I have not yet heard of any situation which meets with the
approbation of my friends. I begin, however, to grow exceedingly
impatient of a prolonged period of inaction. I feel I ought to be
doing something for myself, for my health is now so perfectly
re-established by this long rest that it affords me no further pretext
for indolence. With every wish for your future welfare, and with
the hope that whenever your proposed union takes place it may
contribute in the highest sense to your good and happiness,— Believe me, your sincere friend, C. Brontë.

' P.S.— Remember me to your sister Mercy, who, I understand,
is for the present your companion and housekeeper.'

The correspondence did not end here. Indeed, Charlotte
was so excellent a letter-writer, that it must have been hard
indeed for any one who had had any experience of her in that
capacity to readily forego its continuance.

TO REV. HENRY NUSSEY.

'Haworth, May 26, 1840.

' Dear Sir,— In looking over my papers this morning I found
a letter from you of the date of last February with the mark upon
it unanswered. Your sister Ellen often accuses me of want of
punctuality in answering letters, and I think her accusation is here
justified. However, I give you credit for as much considerateness
as will induce you to excuse a greater fault than this, especially as
I shall hasten directly to repair it.
' The fact is, when the letter came Ellen was staying with

me, and I was so fully occupied in talking to her that I had no
time to think of writing to others. This is no great compliment,
but it is no insult either. You know Ellen's worth, you know
how seldom I see her, you partly know my regard for her; and
from these premises you may easily draw the inference that her
company, when once obtained, is too valuable to be wasted for a
moment. One woman can appreciate the value of another better
than a man can do. Men very often only see the outside gloss
which dazzles in prosperity, women have opportunities for closer
observation, and they learn to value those qualities which are useful in adversity.

' There is much, too, in that mild even temper and that placid
equanimity which keep the domestic hearth always bright and
peaceful — this is better than the ardent nature that changes
twenty times in a day. I have studied Ellen and I think she would
make a good wife — that is, if she had a good husband. If she
married a fool or a tyrant there is spirit enough in her composition
to withstand the dictates of either insolence or weakness, though
even then I doubt not her sense would teach her to make the best
of a bad bargain.

' You will see my letters are all didactic. They contain no news,
because I know of none which I think it would interest you to
hear repeated. I am still at home, in very good health and spirits,
and uneasy only because I cannot yet hear of a situation.

' I shall always be glad to have a letter from you, and I promise
when you write again to be less dilatory in answering. I trust
your prospects of happiness still continue fair; and from what
you say of your future partner I doubt not she will be one who
will help you to get cheerfully through the difficulties of this
world and to obtain a permanent rest in the next, at least I hope
such may be the case. You do right to conduct the matter with
due deliberation, for on the step you are about to take depends the
happiness of your whole lifetime.

' You must not again ask me to write in a regular literary way
to you on some particular topic. I cannot do it at all. Do
you think I am a blue-stocking? I feel half inclined to laugh
at you for the idea, but perhaps you would be angry. What was

the topic to be? Chemistry? or astronomy? or mechanics? or conchology? or entomology? or what other ology? I know nothing at all about any of these. I am not scientific; I am not a linguist. You think me far more learned than I am. If I told you all my ignorance, I am afraid you would be shocked; however, as I wish still to retain a little corner in your good opinion, I will hold my tongue.— Believe me, yours respectfully,

'C. BRONTË.'

TO REV. HENRY NUSSEY.

'JANUARY 11, 1841.

'DEAR SIR, — It is time I should reply to your last, as I shall fail in fulfilling my promise of not being so dilatory as on a former occasion.

'I shall be glad to receive the poetry which you offer to send me. You ask me to return the gift in kind. How do you know that I have it in my power to comply with that request? Once indeed I was very poetical, when I was sixteen, seventeen, eighteen, and nineteen years old, but I am now twenty-four, approaching twenty-five, and the intermediate years are those which begin to rob life of some of its superfluous colouring. At this age it is time that the imagination should be pruned and trimmed, that the judgment should be cultivated, and a *few*, at least, of the countless illusions of early youth should be cleared away. I have not written poetry for a long while.

'You will excuse the dulness, morality, and monotony of this epistle, and — Believe me, with all good wishes for your welfare here and hereafter, your sincere friend, 'C. BRONTË.'

This letter closes the correspondence; but, as we have seen, Charlotte spent three pleasant weeks in Mr. Nussey's home with his sister Ellen when that gentleman became vicar of Hathersage, in Derbyshire. She thus congratulates her friend when Mr. Nussey is appointed to the latter living.

TO MISS ELLEN NUSSEY.

'JULY 29, 1844.

'DEAR NELL, — I am very glad to hear of Henry's good fortune. It proves to me what an excellent thing perseverance is for getting

301

on in the world. Calm self-confidence (not impudence, for that
is vulgar and repulsive) is an admirable quality; but how are
those not naturally gifted with it to attain it? We all here get on
much as usual. Papa wishes he could hear of a curate, that Mr.
Smith may be at liberty to go. Good-bye, dear Ellen. I wish to
you and yours happiness, health, and prosperity.

'Write again before you go to Burlington. My best love to
Mary. C. Brontë.'

Meanwhile, as I have said, a second lover appeared on the
field in this same year, 1839, and the quickness of his wooing
is a remarkable testimony to the peculiar fascination which
Miss Brontë must have exercised.

TO MISS ELLEN NUSSEY.

'August 4, 1839.

'My dearest Ellen, — I have an odd circumstance to relate to
you — prepare for a hearty laugh! The other day Mr. Hodgson,
papa's former curate, now a vicar, came over to spend the day
with us, bringing with him his own curate. The latter gentleman,
by name Mr. Price, is a young Irish clergyman, fresh from Dublin
University. It was the first time we had any of us seen him,
but, however, after the manner of his countrymen, he soon made
himself at home. His character quickly appeared in his conversation: witty, lively, ardent, clever too, but deficient in the
dignity and discretion of an Englishman. At home, you know,
Ellen, I talk with ease, and am never shy, never weighed down
and oppressed by that miserable *mauvaise honte* which torments
and constrains me elsewhere. So I conversed with this Irishman
and laughed at his jests, and though I saw faults in his character, excused them because of the amusement his originality
afforded. I cooled a little, indeed, and drew in towards the
latter part of the evening, because he began to season his conversation with something of Hibernian flattery, which I did
not quite relish. However, they went away, and no more was
thought about them. A few days after I got a letter, the direc-

302

tion of which puzzled me, it being in a hand I was not accustomed to see. Evidently, it was neither from you nor Mary Taylor, my only correspondents. Having opened and read it, it proved to be a declaration of attachment and proposal of matrimony, expressed in the ardent language of the sapient young Irishman! Well! thought I, I have heard of love at first sight, but this beats all. I leave you to guess what my answer would be, convinced that you will not do me the injustice of guessing wrong. When we meet I'll show you the letter. I hope you are laughing heartily. This is not like one of my adventures, is it? It more nearly resembles Martha Taylor's. I am certainly doomed to be an old maid. Never mind, I made up my mind to that fate ever since I was twelve years old. Write soon.

'C. Brontë.'

It was not many months after this that we hear the last of poor Mr. Price.

TO MISS ELLEN NUSSEY.

'January 24, 1840.

'My dear Ellen, — Mr. Price is dead. He had fallen into a state of delicate health for some time, and the rupture of a blood-vessel carried him off. He was a strong, athletic-looking man when I saw him, and that is scarcely six months ago. Though I knew so little of him, and of course could not be deeply or permanently interested in what concerned him, I confess, when I suddenly heard he was dead, I felt both shocked and saddened: it was no shame to feel so, was it? I scold you, Ellen, for writing illegibly and badly, but I think you may repay the compliment with cent per cent interest. I am not in the humour for writing a long letter, so good-bye. God bless you.   C. B.'

There are many thoughts on marriage scattered through Charlotte's correspondence. It was a subject upon which she never wearied of asking questions, and of finding her own answers. 'I believe it is better to marry *to* love than to marry *for* love,' she says on one occasion. And in reference to the somewhat uncertain attitude of the admirer of one of her friends, she thus expresses herself to Miss Nussey:

TO MISS ELLEN NUSSEY.

'NOVEMBER 20, 1840.

' MY DEAREST NELL, — That last letter of thine treated of matters so high and important I cannot delay answering it for a day. Now I am about to write thee a discourse, and a piece of advice which thou must take as if it came from thy grandmother. But in the first place, before I begin with thee, I have a word to whisper in the ear of Mr. Vincent, and I wish it could reach him. In the name of St. Chrysostom, St. Simon, and St. Jude, why does not that amiable young gentleman come forward like a man and say all that he has to say personally, instead of trifling with kinsmen and kinswomen ? " Mr. Vincent," I say, " go personally, and say : ' Miss ———, I want to speak to you.' Miss ——— will of course civilly answer, 'I am at your service, Mr. Vincent.' And then, when the room is cleared of all but yourself and herself, just take a chair nearer. Insist upon her laying down that silly . . . work, and listening to you. Then begin, in a clear, distinct, deferential, but determined voice : ' Miss ———, I have a question to put to you — a very important question, Will you take me as your husband, for better, for worse. I am not a rich man, but I have sufficient to support us. I am not a great man, but I love you honestly and truly. Miss ———, if you knew the world better you would see that this is an offer not to be despised — a kind attached heart and a moderate competency.' Do this, Mr. Vincent, and you may succeed. Go on writing sentimental and love-sick letters to ———, and I would not give sixpence for your suit." So much for Mr. Vincent. Now Miss ———'s turn comes to swallow the black bolus, called a friend's advice. Say to her : "Is the man a fool? is he a knave? a humbug, a hypocrite, a ninny, a noodle? If he is any or all of these, of course there is no sense in trifling with him. Cut him short at once — blast his hopes with lightning rapidity and keenness. Is he something better than this? has he at least common sense, a good disposition, a manageable temper? Then consider the matter." Say further: "You feel a disgust towards him now — an utter repugnance. Very likely, but be so good as to remember you don't know him; you have only had three or four days' acquaintance with him. Longer and closer intimacy might reconcile you to a wonderful extent. And now I'll tell you a word of truth, at which you may be offended or not as you like." Say to her: "From what I know of your character, and I think I know it pretty well, I should say you will never love before marriage. After that ceremony is over, and after you have had some months to settle down, and to get accustomed to the creature you have taken for your worse half, you will probably make a most affectionate and happy wife; even if the individual should not prove all you could wish, you will be indulgent towards his little follies and foibles, and will not feel much annoyance at them. This will especially be the case if he should have sense sufficient to allow you to guide him in important matters." Say also: "I hope you will not have the romantic folly to wait for what the French call 'une grande passion.' My good girl, 'une grande passion' is 'une grande folie.' Mediocrity in all things is wisdom; mediocrity in the sensations is superlative wisdom." Say to her: "When you are as old as I am (I am sixty at least, being your grandmother), you will find that the majority of those worldly precepts, whose seeming coldness shocks and repels us in youth, are founded in wisdom."

'No girl should fall in love till the offer is actually made. This maxim is just. I will even extend and confirm it: No young lady should fall in love till the offer has been made, accepted, the marriage ceremony performed, and the first half-year of wedded life has passed away. A woman may then begin to love, but with great precaution, very coolly, very moderately, very rationally. If she ever loves so much that a harsh word or a cold look cuts her to the heart she is a fool. If she ever loves so much that her husband's will is her law, and that she has got into a habit of watching his looks in order that she may anticipate his wishes, she will soon be a neglected fool.

'I have two studies: you are my study for the success, the credit, and the respectability of a quiet, tranquil character; Mary is my study for the contempt, the remorse, the misconstruction which follow the development of feelings in themselves noble, warm, generous, devoted, and profound, but which, being too freely revealed, too frankly bestowed, are not estimated at their real value. I never hope to see in this world a character more truly noble. She would die willingly for one she loved. Her intellect and her attainments are of the very highest standard. Yet I doubt whether Mary will ever marry. Mr. Weightman expresses himself very strongly on young ladies saying " No," when they mean " Yes." He assures me he means nothing personal. I hope not. Assuredly I quite agree with him in his disapprobation of such a senseless course. It is folly indeed for the tongue to stammer a negative when the heart is proclaiming an affirmative. Or rather, it is an act of heroic self-denial, of which *I* for one confess myself wholly incapable. *I would not tell such a lie* to gain a thousand pounds. Write to me again soon. What made you say I admired Hippocrates? It is a confounded " fib." I tried to find something admirable in him, and failed.'

'He is perhaps only like the majority of men' (she says of an acquaintance). 'Certainly those men who lead a gay life in their youth, and arrive at middle-age with feelings blunted and passions exhausted, can have but one aim in marriage — the selfish advancement of their interest. Hard to think that such men take as wives — as second-selves — women young, modest, sincere, pure in heart and life, with feelings all fresh and emotions all unworn, and bind such virtue and vitality to their own withered existence, such sincerity to their own hollowness, such disinterestedness to their own haggard avarice — to think this, troubles the soul to its inmost depths. Nature and justice forbid the banns of such wedlock.'

TO MISS ELLEN NUSSEY.

'AUGUST 9, 1846.

'DEAR NELL, — Anne and I both thank you for your kind invitation. And our thanks are not mere words of course — they are very sincere, both as addressed to yourself and your mother and sisters. But we cannot accept it; and I *think* even *you* will consider our motives for declining valid this time.

'In a fortnight I hope to go with papa to Manchester to have his eyes couched. Emily and I made a pilgrimage there a week ago to search out an operator, and we found one in the person of Mr. Wilson. He could not tell from the description whether the eyes were ready for an operation. Papa must therefore necessarily take a journey to Manchester to consult him. If he judges the cataract ripe, we shall remain; if, on the contrary, he thinks it not yet sufficiently hardened, we shall have to return — and papa must remain in darkness a while longer.

'There is a defect in your reasoning about the feelings a wife ought to experience. Who holds the purse will wish to be master, Ellen, depend on it, whether man or woman. Who provided the cash will now and then value himself, or herself, upon it, and even in the case of ordinary minds, reproach the less wealthy partner. Besides, no husband ought to be an object of charity to his wife, as no wife to her husband. No, dear Ellen; it is doubtless pleasant to marry *well*, as they say, but with all pleasures are mixed bitters. I do not wish for my friend a very rich husband. I should not like her to be regarded by any man ever as "a sweet object of charity." Give my sincere love to all.—
Yours, C. BRONTË.'

Many years were to elapse before Charlotte Brontë received her third offer of marriage. These were the years of Brussels life, and the year during which she lost her sisters. It came in the period of her early literary fame, and indeed was the outcome of it. Mr. James Taylor was in the employment of Smith & Elder. He was associated with the literary department, and next in command to Mr. W. S. Williams as adviser to the firm. Mr. Williams appears to have written to Miss Brontë suggesting that Mr. Taylor should come to Haworth in person for the manuscript of her new novel, 'Shirley,' and here is Charlotte's reply.

TO W. S. WILLIAMS.

'August 24, 1849.

'My dear Sir, — I think the best title for the book would be "Shirley," without any explanation or addition — the simpler and briefer, the better.

'If Mr. Taylor calls here on his return to town he might take charge of the MS.; I would rather intrust it to him than send it by the ordinary conveyance. Did I see Mr. Taylor when I was in London? I cannot remember him.

'I would with pleasure offer him the homely hospitalities of the Parsonage for a few days, if I could at the same time offer him the company of a brother, or if my father were young enough and strong enough to walk with him on the moors and show him the neighbourhood, or if the peculiar retirement of papa's habits were not such as to render it irksome to him to give much of his society to a stranger, even in the house. Without being in the least misanthropical or sour-natured, papa habitually prefers solitude to society, and custom is a tyrant whose fetters it would now be impossible for him to break. Were it not for difficulties of this sort, I believe I should ere this have asked you to come down to Yorkshire. Papa, I know, would receive any friend of Mr. Smith's with perfect kindness and good-will, but I likewise know that, unless greatly put out of his way, he could not give a guest much of his company, and that, consequently, his entertainment would be but dull.

'You will see the force of these considerations, and understand why I only ask Mr. Taylor to come for a day instead of requesting the pleasure of his company for a longer period; you will believe me also, and so will he, when I say I shall be most happy to see him. He will find Haworth a strange uncivilised little place, such as, I daresay, he never saw before.

It is twenty miles distant from Leeds; he will have to come by rail to Keighley (there are trains every two hours I believe). He must remember that at a station called Shipley the carriages are changed, otherwise they will take him on to Skipton or Colne, or I know not where. When he reaches Keighley, he will yet have four miles to travel; a conveyance may be hired at the Devonshire Arms — there is no coach or other regular communication.

'I should like to hear from him before he comes, and to know on what day to expect him, that I may have the MS. ready; if it is not quite finished I might send the concluding chapter or two by post.

'I advise you to send this letter to Mr. Taylor — it will save you the trouble of much explanation, and will serve to apprise him of what lies before him; he can then weigh well with himself whether it would suit him to take so much trouble for so slight an end. — Believe me, my dear sir, yours sincerely,

'C. BRONTË.'

TO JAMES TAYLOR, Cornhill.

'September 3, 1849.

'My dear Sir, — It will be quite convenient to my father and myself to secure your visit on Saturday the 8th inst.

'The MS. is now complete, and ready for you.

'Trusting that you have enjoyed your holiday and derived from your excursion both pleasure and profit, — I am, dear sir, yours sincerely, C. BRONTË.'

Mr. Taylor was small and red-haired. There are two portraits of him before me. They indicate a determined, capable man, thick-set, well bearded: on the whole a vigorous and interesting personality. In any case, Mr. Taylor lost his heart to Charlotte, and was much more persistent than earlier lovers. He had also the advantage of Mr. Brontë's good-will. This is all there is to add to the letters themselves.

CHARLOTTE BRONTË

TO MISS ELLEN NUSSEY.

'SEPTEMBER 14, 1850.

'DEAR ELLEN, — I found after sealing my last note to you that I had forgotten after all to inclose Amelia's letter; however, it appears it does not signify. While I think of it I must refer to an act of petty larceny committed by me when I was last at Brookroyd. Do you remember lending me a parasol, which I should have left with you when we parted at Leeds? I unconsciously carried it away in my hand. You shall have it when you next come to Haworth.

'I wish, dear Ellen, you would tell me what is the "twaddle about my marrying, etc.," which you hear. If I knew the details I should have a better chance of guessing the quarter from which such gossip comes — as it is, I am quite at a loss. Whom am I to marry? I think I have scarcely seen a single man with whom such a union would be possible since I left London. Doubtless there are men whom, if I chose to encourage, I might marry ; but no matrimonial lot is even remotely offered me which seems to me truly desirable. And even if that were the case, there would be many obstacles. The least allusion to such a thing is most offensive to papa.

'An article entitled "Currer Bell" has lately appeared in the "Palladium," a new periodical published in Edinburgh. It is an eloquent production, and one of such warm sympathy and high appreciation as I had never expected to see. It makes mistakes about authorships, etc., but these I hope one day to set right. Mr. Taylor (the little man) first informed me of this article. I was somewhat surprised to receive his letter, having concluded nine months ago that there would be no more correspondence from that quarter. I inclose you a note from him received subsequently, in answer to my acknowledgment. Read it and tell me exactly how it impresses you regarding the writer's character, etc. His little newspaper disappeared for some weeks, and I thought it was gone to the tomb of the Capulets ; however, it has reappeared, with an explanation that he had feared its regular transmission might rather annoy than gratify.

310

I told him this was a mistake — that I was well enough pleased to receive it, but hoped he would not make a task of sending it. For the rest, I cannot consider myself placed under any personal obligation by accepting this newspaper, for it belongs to the establishment of Smith & Elder. This little Taylor is deficient neither in spirit nor sense.

'The report about my having published again is, of course, an arrant lie.

'Give my kind regards to all, and — Believe me, yours faithfully,   C. B.'

Her friend's reference to 'Jupiter' is to another suggested lover, and the kindly allusion to the 'little man' may be taken to imply that had he persevered, or not gone off to India, whither he was sent to open a branch establishment in Bombay for Smith & Elder, Mr. Taylor might possibly have been successful in the long run.

TO MISS ELLEN NUSSEY.

'JANUARY 30, 1851.

'DEAR NELL,— I am very sorry to hear that Amelia is again far from well ; but I think both she and I should try and not be too anxious. Even if matters do not prosper this time, all may go as well some future day. I think it is not these *early* mishaps that break the constitution, but those which occur in a much later stage. She must take heart — there may yet be a round dozen of little Joe Taylors to look after — run after — to sort and switch and train up in the way they should go — that is, with a generous use of pickled birch. From whom do you think I have received a couple of notes lately? From Alice. They are returned from the Continent, it seems, and are now at Torquay. The first note touched me a little by what I thought its subdued tone ; I trusted her character might be greatly improved. There were, indeed, traces of the "old Adam," but such as I was willing to overlook. I answered her soon and kindly. In reply I received to-day a longish letter, full of clap-trap sentiment and humbugging attempts at fine writing. In each production the old trading spirit peeps out; she asks for autographs. It seems she had read in some paper that I was staying with Miss Martineau, thereupon she applies for specimens of her handwriting, and Wordsworth's, and Southey's, and my own. The account of her health, if given by any one else, would grieve and alarm me. She talks of fearing that her constitution is almost broken by repeated trials, and intimates a doubt as to whether she shall live long: but, remembering her of old, I have good hopes that this may be a mistake. Her "beloved papa and mama" and her "precious sister," she says, are living, and "gradely." (That last is my word. I don't know whether they use it in Birstall as they do here — it means in a middling way.)

'You are to say no more about "Jupiter" and "Venus"— what do you mean by such heathen trash? The fact is, no fallacy can be wilder, and I won't have it hinted at even in jest, because my common sense laughs it to scorn. The idea of the "little man" shocks me less — it would be a more likely match if "matches" were at all in question, which *they are not*. He still sends his little newspaper; and the other day there came a letter of a bulk, volume, pith, judgment, and knowledge, worthy to have been the product of a giant. You may laugh as much and as wickedly as you please; but the fact is, there is a quiet constancy about this, my diminutive and red-haired friend, which adds a foot to his stature, turns his sandy locks dark, and altogether dignifies him a good deal in my estimation. However, I am not bothered by much vehement ardour — there is the nicest distance and respect preserved now, which makes matters very comfortable.

'This is all nonsense, Nell, and so you will understand it. — Yours very faithfully,   C. B.

'The name of Miss Martineau's coadjutor is Atkinson. She often writes to me with exceeding cordiality.'

TO JAMES TAYLOR, CORNHILL.

'MARCH 22, 1851.

'MY DEAR SIR, — Yesterday I despatched a box of books to Cornhill, including the number of the "North British Review" which you kindly lent me. The article to which you particularly directed my attention was read with pleasure and interest, and if I do not now discuss it more at length, it is because I am well aware how completely your attention must be at present engrossed, since, if I rightly understood a brief paragraph in Mr. Smith's last note, you are now on the eve of quitting England for India.

'I will limit myself, then, to the expression of a sincere wish for your welfare and prosperity in this undertaking, and to the hope that the great change of climate will bring with it no corresponding risk to health. I should think you will be missed in Cornhill, but doubtless "business" is a Moloch which demands such sacrifices.

'I do not know when you go, nor whether your absence is likely to be permanent or only for a time; whichever it be, accept my best wishes for your happiness, and my farewell, if I should not again have the opportunity of addressing you. — Believe me, sincerely yours,   C. BRONTË.'

TO JAMES TAYLOR, CORNHILL.

'MARCH 24, 1851.

'MY DEAR SIR, — I had written briefly to you before I received yours, but I fear the note would not reach you in time. I will now only say that both my father and myself will have pleasure in seeing you on your return from Scotland — a pleasure tinged with sadness certainly, as all partings are, but still a pleasure.

'I do most entirely agree with you in what you say about Miss Martineau's and Mr. Atkinson's book. I deeply regret its publication for the lady's sake, it gives a death-blow to her future usefulness. Who can trust the word, or rely on the judgment of an avowed atheist?

'May your decision in the crisis through which you have gone result in the best effect on your happiness and welfare; and indeed, guided as you are by the wish to do right and a high sense of duty, I trust it cannot be otherwise. The change of climate is all I fear; but Providence will over-rule this too

CHARLOTTE BRONTË

for the best — in Him you can believe and on Him rely. You will want, therefore, neither solace nor support, though your lot be cast as a stranger in a strange land. — I am, yours sincerely,

'C. BRONTË.

'When you shall have definitely fixed the time of your return southward, write me a line to say on what day I may expect you at Haworth. C. B.'

TO MISS ELLEN NUSSEY.

'APRIL 5, 1851.

DEAR ELLEN, — Mr. Taylor has been and is gone; things are just as they were. I only know in addition to the slight information I possessed before, that this Indian undertaking is necessary to the continued prosperity of the firm of Smith, Elder & Co., and that he, Taylor, alone was pronounced to possess the power and means to carry it out successfully — that mercantile honour combined with his own sense of duty, obliged him to accept the post of honour and of danger to which he has been appointed, that he goes with great personal reluctance, and that he contemplates an absence of five years.

'He looked much thinner and older. I saw him very near, and once through my glass; the resemblance to Branwell struck me forcibly — it is marked. He is not ugly, but very peculiar; the lines in his face show an inflexibility, and I must add, a hardness of character which do not attract. As he stood near me, as he looked at me in his keen way, it was all I could do to stand my ground tranquilly and steadily, and not to recoil as before. It is no use saying anything if I am not candid. I avow then, that on this occasion, predisposed as I was to regard him very favourably, his manners and his personal presence scarcely pleased me more than at the first interview. He gave me a book at parting, requesting in his brief way that I would keep it for his sake, and adding hastily, "I shall hope to hear from you in India — your letters *have* been and *will* be a greater refreshment than you can think or I can tell."

'And so he is gone; and stern and abrupt little man as he
314

is — too often jarring as are his manners — his absence and the exclusion of his idea from my mind leave me certainly with less support and in deeper solitude than before.

'You see, dear Nell, though we are still precisely on the same level — *you* are not isolated. I feel that there is a certain mystery about this transaction yet, and whether it will ever be cleared up to me I do not know; however, my plain duty is to wean my mind from the subject, and if possible to avoid pondering over it. In his conversation he seemed studiously to avoid reference to Mr. Smith individually, speaking always of the "house" — the "firm." He seemed throughout quite as excited and nervous as when I first saw him. I feel that in his way he has a regard for me — a regard which I cannot bring myself entirely to reciprocate in kind, and yet its withdrawal leaves a painful blank.'

TO MISS ELLEN NUSSEY.

'APRIL 9, 1851.

'DEAR NELL, — Thank you for your kind note; it was just like you to write it *though* it was your school-day. I never knew you to let a slight impediment stand in the way of a friendly action.

'Certainly I shall not soon forget last Friday, and *never*, I think, the evening and night succeeding that morning and afternoon. Evils seldom come singly. And soon after Mr. Taylor was gone, papa, who had been better, grew much worse. He went to bed early, and was very sick and ill for an hour; and when at last he began to doze, and I left him, I came down to the dining-room with a sense of weight, fear, and desolation hard to express and harder to endure. A wish that you were with me *did* cross my mind, but I repulsed it as a most selfish wish; indeed, it was only short-lived: my natural tendency in moments of this sort is to get through the struggle alone — to think that one is burdening and racking others makes all worse.

'You speak to me in soft consoling accents, but I hold far sterner language to myself, dear Nell.

315

CHARLOTTE BRONTË

'An absence of five years — a dividing expanse of three oceans — the wide difference between a man's active career and a woman's passive existence — these things are almost equivalent to an eternal separation. But there is another thing which forms a barrier more difficult to pass than any of these. Would Mr. Taylor and I ever suit? Could I ever feel for him enough love to accept him as a husband? Friendship — gratitude — esteem I have, but each moment he came near me, and that I could see his eyes fastened on me, my veins ran ice. Now that he is away I feel far more gently towards him; it is only close by that I grow rigid — stiffening with a strange mixture of apprehension and anger, which nothing softens but his retreat and a perfect subduing of his manner. I did not want to be proud, nor intend to be proud, but I was forced to be so.

'Most true it is that we are over-ruled by one above us — that in His hands our very will is as clay in the hands of the potter.

'Papa continues very far from well, though yesterday, and I hope this morning, he is a little better. How is your mother? Give my love to her and your sister. How are you? Have you suffered from tic since you returned home? Did they think you improved in looks?

'Write again soon. — Yours faithfully,   C. BRONTË.'

TO MISS ELLEN NUSSEY.

'APRIL 23, 1851.

'MY DEAR ELLEN, — I have heard from Mr. Taylor to-day — a quiet little note. He returned to London a week since on Saturday; he has since kindly chosen and sent me a parcel of books. He leaves England May 20th. His note concludes with asking whether he has any chance of seeing me in London before that time. I must tell him that I have already fixed June for my visit, and therefore, in all human probability, we shall see each other no more.

'There is still a want of plain mutual understanding in this business, and there is sadness and pain in more ways than one. My conscience, I can truly say, does not *now* accuse me of having treated Mr. Taylor with injustice or unkindness. What I once did wrong in this way, I have endeavoured to remedy both to himself and in speaking of him to others — Mr. Smith to wit, though I more than doubt whether that last opinion will ever reach him. I am sure he has estimable and sterling qualities; but with every disposition and with every wish, with every intention even to look on him in the most favourable point of view at his last visit, it was impossible to me in my inward heart to think of him as one that might one day be acceptable as a husband. It would sound harsh were I to tell even *you* of the estimate I felt compelled to form respecting him. Dear Nell, I looked for something of the gentleman — something I mean of the *natural* gentleman ; you know I can dispense with acquired polish, and for looks, I know myself too well to think that I have any right to be exacting on that point. I could not find one gleam, I could not see one passing glimpse of true good-breeding. It is hard to say, but it is true. In mind too, though clever, he is second-rate — thoroughly second-rate. One does not like to say these things, but one had better be honest. Were I to marry him my heart would bleed in pain and humiliation ; I could not, *could* not look up to him. No ; if Mr. Taylor be the only husband fate offers to me, single I must always remain. But yet, at times I grieve for him, and perhaps it is superfluous, for I cannot think he will suffer much : a hard nature, occupation, and change of scene will befriend him.

'With kind regards to all, — I am, dear Nell, your middle-aged friend,   C. BRONTË.

'Write soon.'

TO MISS ELLEN NUSSEY.

'MAY 5, 1851.

'MY DEAR ELLEN, — I have had a long kind letter from Miss Martineau lately. She says she is well and happy. Also, I have had a very long letter from Mr. Williams. He speaks with much respect of Mr. Taylor. I discovered with some surprise, papa has taken a decided liking to Mr. Taylor. The

marked kindness of his manner when he bid him good-bye,
exhorting him to be " true to himself, his country, and his
God," and wishing him all good wishes, struck me with some
astonishment. Whenever he has alluded to him since, it has
been with significant eulogy. When I alluded that he was no
gentleman, he seemed out of patience with me for the objection.
You say papa has penetration. On this subject I believe he
has indeed. I have told him nothing, yet he seems to be
au fait to the whole business. I could think at some moments
his guesses go farther than mine. I believe he thinks a
prospective union, deferred for five years, with such a decorous
reliable personage, would be a very proper and advisable
affair.

' How has your tic been lately ? I had one fiery night when
this same dragon " tic " held me for some hours with pestilent
violence. It still comes at intervals with abated fury. Owing
to this and broken sleep, I am looking singularly charming,
one of my true London looks — starved out and worn down.
Write soon, dear Nell. — Yours faithfully, C. BRONTË.'

TO MISS ELLEN NUSSEY.

'112 GLOUCESTER PLACE,
'HYDE PARK, June 2, 1851.

' DEAR ELLEN, — Mr. Taylor has gone some weeks since. I
hear more open complaints now about his temper. Of Mr.
Williams's society I have enjoyed one evening's allowance, and
liked it and him as usual. On such occasions his good qualities
of ease, kindliness, and intelligence are seen, and his little
faults and foibles hidden. Mr. Smith is somewhat changed in
appearance. He looks a little older, darker, and more careworn ;
his ordinary manner is graver, but in the evening his spirits
flow back to him. Things and circumstances seem here to be
as usual, but I fancy there has been some crisis in which his
energy and filial affection have sustained them all. This I judge
from the fact that his mother and sisters are more peculiarly
bound to him than ever, and that his slightest wish is an un-
questioned law. — Faithfully yours, C. BRONTË.'

TO MISS ELLEN NUSSEY.

'November 4, 1851.

'Dear Ellen, — Papa, Tabby, and Martha are at present all better, yet none of them well. Martha at present looks feeble. I wish she had a better constitution. As it is, one is always afraid of giving her too much to do; and yet there are many things I cannot undertake myself, and we do not like to change when we have had her so long. How are you getting on in the matter of servants? The other day I received a long letter from Mr. Taylor. I told you I did not expect to hear thence, nor did I. The letter is long but it is worth your while to read it. In its way it has merit, that cannot be denied; abundance of information, talent of a certain kind, alloyed (I think) here and there with errors of taste. He might have spared many of the details of the bath scene, which, for the rest, tallies exactly with Mr. Thackeray's account of the same process. This little man with all his long letters remains as much a conundrum to me as ever. Your account of the domestic joys at Hunsworth amused me much. The good folks seem very happy — long may they continue so! It somewhat cheers me to know that such happiness *does* exist on the earth. Return Mr. Taylor's letter when you have read it. With love to your mother, — I am, dear Nell, sincerely yours, C. B.'

TO JAMES TAYLOR, Bombay.

'Haworth, November 15, 1851.

'My dear Sir, — Both your communications reached me safely — the note of the 17th September and the letter of the 2nd October. You do yourself less than justice when you stigmatise the latter as "ill-written." I found it quite legible, nor did I lose a word, though the lines and letters were so close. I should have been sorry if such had not been the case, as it appeared to me throughout highly interesting. It is observable that the very same information which we have previously collected, perhaps with rather languid attention, from printed books, when placed before us in familiar manuscript, and comprising the actual expe-

319

rience of a person with whom we are acquainted, acquires a new and vital interest : when we know the narrator we seem to realise the tale.

'The bath scene amused me much. Your account of that operation tallies in every point with Mr. Thackeray's description in the "Journey from Cornhill to Grand Cairo." The usage seems a little rough, and I cannot help thinking that equal benefit might be obtained through less violent means ; but I suppose without the previous fatigue the after-sensation would not be so enjoyable, and no doubt it is that indolent after-sensation which the self-indulgent Mahometans chiefly cultivate. I think you did right to disdain it.

'It would seem to me a matter of great regret that the society at Bombay should be so deficient in all intellectual attraction. Perhaps, however, your occupations will so far absorb your thoughts as to prevent them from dwelling painfully on this circumstance. No doubt there will be moments when you will look back to London and Scotland, and the friends you have left there, with some yearning ; but I suppose business has its own excitement. The new country, the new scenes too, must have their interest ; and as you will not lack books to fill your leisure, you will probably soon become reconciled to a change which, for some minds, would too closely resemble exile.

'I fear the climate — such as you describe it — must be very trying to an European constitution. In your first letter, you mentioned October as the month of danger ; it is now over. Whether you have passed its ordeal safely, must yet for some weeks remain unknown to your friends in England — they can but *wish* that such may be the case. You will not expect me to write a letter that shall form a parallel with your own either in quantity or quality ; what I write must be brief, and what I communicate must be commonplace and of trivial interest.

'My father, I am thankful to say, continues in pretty good health. I read portions of your letter to him and he was interested in hearing them. He charged me when I wrote to convey his very kind remembrances.

'I had myself ceased to expect a letter from you. On taking leave at Haworth you said something about writing from India, but I doubted at the time whether it was not one of those forms of speech which politeness dictates; and as time passed, and I did not hear from you, I became confirmed in this view of the subject. With every good wish for your welfare, — I am, yours sincerely,   C. Brontë.'

TO MISS ELLEN NUSSEY.

'NOVEMBER 19, 1851.

'DEAR ELLEN, — All here is much as usual, and I was thinking of writing to you this morning when I received your note. I am glad to hear your mother bears this severe weather tolerably, as papa does also. I had a cold, chiefly in the throat and chest, but I applied cold water which relieved me, I think, far better than hot applications would have done. The only events in my life consist in that little change occasional letters bring. I have had two from Miss Wooler since she left Haworth which touched me much. She seems to think so much of a little congenial company. She says she has not for many days known such enjoyment as she experienced' during the ten days she stayed here. Yet you know what Haworth is — dull enough.

'How could you imagine your last letter offended me? I only disagreed with you on *one point*. The little man's disdain of the sensual pleasure of a Turkish bath had, I must own, my approval. Before answering his epistle I got up my courage to write to Mr. Williams, through whose hands or those of Mr. Smith I knew the Indian letter had come, and beg him to give me an impartial judgment of Mr. Taylor's character and disposition, owning that I was very much in the dark. I did not like to continue correspondence without further information. I got the answer, which I inclose. You say nothing about the Hunsworth Turtle-doves — how are they? and how is the branch of promise? I hope doing well. — Yours faithfully,
                                                                'C. Brontë.'

CHARLOTTE BRONTË

TO W. S. WILLIAMS.

'JANUARY 1, 1852.

'MY DEAR SIR, — I am glad of the opportunity of writing to you, for I have long wished to send you a little note, and was only deterred from doing so by the conviction that the period preceding Christmas must be a very busy one to you.

'I have wished to thank you for your last, which gave me very genuine pleasure. You ascribe to Mr. Taylor an excellent character; such a man's friendship, at any rate, should not be disregarded; and if the principles and disposition be what you say, faults of manner and even of temper ought to weigh light in the balance. I always believed in his judgment and good-sense, but what I doubted was his kindness — he seemed to me a little too harsh, rigid, and unsympathising. Now, judgment, sense, principle are invaluable and quite indispensable points, but one would be thankful for a *little* feeling, a *little* indulgence in addition — without these, poor fallible human nature shrinks under the domination of the sterner qualities. I answered Mr. Taylor's letter by the mail of the 19th November, sending it direct, for, on reflection, I did not see why I should trouble you with it.

'Did your son Frank call on Mrs. Gaskell? and how did he like her?

'My health has not been very satisfactory lately, but I think, though I vary almost daily, I am much better than I was a fortnight ago. All the winter the fact of my never being able to stoop over a desk without bringing on pain and oppression in the chest has been a great affliction to me, and the want of tranquil rest at night has tried me much, but I hope for the better times. The doctors say that there is no organic mischief.

'Wishing a happy New Year to you,   C. BRONTË.'

TO MISS ELLEN NUSSEY.

'MARCH 7, 1852.

'DEAR ELLEN, — I hope both your mother's cold and yours are quite well ere this. Papa has got something of his spring attack of bronchitis, but so far it is in a greatly ameliorated form, very different to what it has been for three years past. I do trust it may pass off thus mildly. I continue better.

'Dear Nell, I told you from the beginning that my going to Sussex was a most improbable event; I tell you now that unless want of health should absolutely compel me to give up work and leave home (which I trust and hope will not be the case) I *certainly shall not think of going*. It is better to be decided, and decided I must be. You can never want me less than when in Sussex surrounded by amusement and friends. I do not know that I shall go to Scarboro', but it might be possible to spare a fortnight to go there (for the sake of a sad duty rather than pleasure), when I could not give a month to a longer excursion. I have not a word of news to tell you. Many mails have come from India since I was at Brookroyd. Expectation would at times be on the alert, but disappointment knocked her down. I have not heard a syllable, and cannot think of making inquiries at Cornhill. Well, long suspense in any matter usually proves somewhat cankering, but God orders all things for us, and to His Will we must submit. Be sure to keep a calm mind ; expect nothing. — Yours faithfully,

'C. BRONTË.'

When Mr. Taylor returned to England in 1856 Charlotte Brontë was dead. His after-life was more successful than happy. He did not, it is true, succeed in Bombay with the firm of Smith, Taylor & Co. That would seem to have collapsed. But he made friends in Bombay and returned there in 1863 as editor of the 'Bombay Gazette' and the Bombay 'Quarterly Review.' A little later he became editor of the Bombay 'Saturday Review,' which had not, however, a long career. Mr. Taylor's successes were not journalistic but mercantile. As Secretary of the Bombay Chamber of Commerce, which appointment he obtained in 1865, he obtained much real distinction. To this post he added that of Registrar of the University of Bombay and many other offices. He was elected Sheriff in 1874, in which year he died. An imposing funeral ceremony took place

CHARLOTTE BRONTË AND HER CIRCLE

in the Cathedral, and he was buried in the Bombay cemetery, where his tomb may be found to the left of the entrance
gates, inscribed —

JAMES TAYLOR. DIED APRIL 29, 1874, AGED 57.

He married during his visit to England, but the marriage
was not a happy one. That does not belong to the present
story. Here, however, is a cutting from the 'Times' marriage record in 1863 : —

'On the 23rd inst., at the Church of St. John the Evangelist,
St. Pancras, by the Rev. James Moorhouse, M.A., James Taylor,
Esq., of Furnival's-inn, and Bombay, to Annie, widow of Adolph
Ritter, of Vienna, and stepdaughter of Thos. Harrison, Esq., of
Birchanger Place, Essex.'

324

CHAPTER XIII.

LITERARY AMBITIONS.

WE have seen how Charlotte Brontë and her sisters wrote from their earliest years those little books which embodied their vague aspirations after literary fame. Now and again the effort is admirable, notably in ' The Adventures of Ernest Alembert,' but on the whole it amounts to as little as did the juvenile productions of Shelley. That poet, it will be remembered, wrote ' Zastrozzi' at nineteen, and much else that was bad, some of which he printed. Charlotte Brontë was mercifully restrained by a well-nigh empty purse from this ill-considered rashness. It was not till the death of their aunt had added to their slender resources that the Brontë girls conceived the idea of actually publishing a book at their own expense. They communicated with the now extinct firm of Aylott & Jones of Paternoster Row, and Charlotte appears to have written many letters to the firm,[1] only two or three of which are printed by Mrs. Gaskell. The correspondence is comparatively insignificant, but as the practical beginning of Charlotte's literary career, the hitherto unpublished letters which have been preserved are perhaps worth reproducing here.

[1] The originals are in the possession of Mr. Alfred Morrison of Carlton House Terrace, London.

CHARLOTTE BRONTË

TO AYLOTT & JONES.

'JANUARY 28, 1846.

'GENTLEMEN, — May I request to be informed whether you would undertake the publication of a collection of short poems in one volume, 8vo.

'If you object to publishing the work at your own risk, would you undertake it on the author's account? — I am, gentlemen, your obedient humble servant,   C. BRONTË.

'Address — Rev. P. Brontë, Haworth, Bradford, Yorkshire.'

TO AYLOTT & JONES.

'MARCH 3, 1846.

'GENTLEMEN, — I send a draft for £31, 10s., being the amount of your estimate.

'I suppose there is nothing now to prevent your immediately commencing the printing of the work.

'When you acknowledge the receipt of the draft, will you state how soon it will be completed. — I am, gentlemen, yours truly,   C. BRONTË.'

TO AYLOTT & JONES.

'MARCH 11, 1846.

'GENTLEMEN, — I have received the proof-sheet, and return it corrected. If there is any doubt at all about the printer's competency to correct errors, I would prefer submitting each sheet to the inspection of the authors, because such a mistake, for instance, as *tumbling* stars, instead of *trembling*, would suffice to throw an air of absurdity over a whole poem; but if you know from experience that he is to be relied on, I would trust to your assurance on the subject, and leave the task of correction to him, as I know that a considerable saving both of time and trouble would be thus effected.

'The printing and paper appear to me satisfactory. Of course I wish to have the work out as soon as possible, but I am still more anxious that it should be got up in a manner creditable to the publishers and agreeable to the authors. — I am, gentlemen, yours truly,   C. BRONTË.'

TO AYLOTT & JONES.

'MARCH 13, 1846.

'GENTLEMEN, — I return you the second proof. The authors have finally decided that they would prefer having all the proofs sent to them in turn, but you need not inclose the MS., as they can correct the errors from memory. — I am, gentlemen, yours truly, C. BRONTË.'

TO AYLOTT & JONES.

'MARCH 23, 1846.

'GENTLEMEN, — As the proofs have hitherto come safe to hand under the direction of C. Brontë, *Esq.*, I have not thought it necessary to request you to change it, but a little mistake having occurred yesterday, I think it will be better to send them to me in future under my *real* address, which is Miss Brontë, Rev. P. Brontë, etc. — I am, gentlemen, yours truly, C. BRONTË.'

TO AYLOTT & JONES.

'APRIL 6, 1846.

'GENTLEMEN, — C., E., and A. Bell, are now preparing for the press a work of fiction, consisting of three distinct and unconnected tales, which may be published either together, as a work of three volumes, of the ordinary novel size, or separately as single volumes, as shall be deemed most advisable.

'It is not their intention to publish these tales on their own account. They direct me to ask you whether you would be disposed to undertake the work, after having, of course, by due inspection of the MS., ascertained that its contents are such as to warrant an expectation of success.

'An early answer will oblige, as, in case of your negativing the proposal, inquiry must be made of other publishers. — I am, gentlemen, yours truly, C. BRONTË.'

TO AYLOTT & JONES.

'APRIL 15, 1846.

'GENTLEMEN, — I have to thank you for your obliging answer to my last. The information you give is of value to us,

327

and when the MS. is completed your suggestions shall be acted on.

'There will be no preface to the poems. The blank leaf may be filled up by a table of contents, which I suppose the printer will prepare. It appears the volume will be a thinner one than was calculated on. — I am, gentlemen, yours truly,

'C. BRONTË.'

TO AYLOTT & JONES.

'MAY 11, 1846.

'GENTLEMEN, — The books may be done up in the style of Moxon's duodecimo edition of Wordsworth.

'The price may be fixed at 5s., or if you think that too much for the size of the volume, say 4s.

'I think the periodicals I mentioned in my last will be sufficient for advertising in at present, and I should not wish you to lay out a larger sum than £2, especially as the estimate is increased by nearly £5, in consequence, it appears, of a mistake. I should think the success of a work depends more on the notice it receives from periodicals, than on the quantity of advertisements.

'If you do not object, the additional amount of the estimate can be remitted when you send in your account at the end of the first six months.

'I should be obliged to you if you could let me know how soon copies can be sent to the editors of the magazines and newspapers specified. — I am, gentlemen, yours truly,

'C. BRONTË.'

TO AYLOTT & JONES.

'MAY 25, 1846.

'GENTLEMEN, — I received yours of the 22nd this morning. I now transmit £5, being the additional sum necessary to defray the entire expense of paper and printing. It will leave a small surplus of 11s. 9d., which you can place to my account.

'I am glad you have sent copies to the newspapers you mention, and in case of a notice favourable or otherwise appearing in them, or in any of the other periodicals to which copies have been sent, I should be obliged to you if you would send me down the numbers ; otherwise, I have not the opportunity of seeing these publications regularly. I might miss it, and should the poems be remarked upon favourably, it is my intention to appropriate a further sum to advertisements. If, on the other hand, they should pass unnoticed or be condemned, I consider it would be quite useless to advertise, as there is nothing, either in the title of the work or the names of the authors to attract attention from a single individual. — I am, gentlemen, yours truly, C. Brontë.'

TO AYLOTT & JONES.

'July 10, 1846.

' Gentlemen,— I am directed by the Messrs. Bell to acknowledge the receipt of the " Critic " and the " Athenæum " containing notices of the poems.

' They now think that a further sum of £10 may be devoted to advertisements, leaving it to you to select such channels as you deem most advisable.

' They would wish the following extract from the " Critic " to be appended to each advertisement : —

' " They in whose hearts are chords strung by Nature to sympathise with the beautiful and the true, will recognise in these compositions the presence of more genius than it was supposed this utilitarian age had devoted to the loftier exercises of the intellect."

' They likewise request you to send copies of the poems to " Fraser's Magazine," " Chambers' Edinburgh Journal," the " Globe," and " Examiner." — I am, gentlemen, yours truly, C. Brontë.'

To an appreciative editor Currer Bell wrote as follows :

TO THE EDITOR OF THE ' DUBLIN UNIVERSITY MAGAZINE.'

'October 6, 1846.

' Sir, — I thank you in my own name and that of my brothers, Ellis and Acton, for the indulgent notice that appeared in your

CHARLOTTE BRONTË

last number of our first humble efforts in literature; but I thank
you far more for the essay on modern poetry which preceded
that notice — an essay in which seems to me to be condensed
the very spirit of truth and beauty. If all or half your other
readers shall have derived from its perusal the delight it afforded
to myself and my brothers, your labours have produced a rich
result.

'After such criticism an author may indeed be smitten at first
by a sense of his own insignificance — as we were — but on a
second and a third perusal he finds a power and beauty therein
which stirs him to a desire to do more and better things. It
fulfils the right end of criticism: without absolutely crushing,
it corrects and rouses. I again thank you heartily, and beg to
subscribe myself, — Your constant and grateful reader,

'CURRER BELL.'

The reception which it met with from the public may be
gathered from the following letter which accompanied De
Quincey's copy.[1]

TO THOMAS DE QUINCEY.

'JUNE 16, 1847.

'SIR, — My relatives, Ellis and Acton Bell, and myself, heedless of the repeated warnings of various respectable publishers,
have committed the rash act of printing a volume of poems.

'The consequences predicted have, of course, overtaken us:
our book is found to be a drug; no man needs it or heeds it.
In the space of a year our publisher has disposed but of two
copies, and by what painful efforts he succeeded in getting rid of
these two, himself only knows.

'Before transferring the edition to the trunkmakers, we have
decided on distributing as presents a few copies of what we cannot sell; and we beg to offer you one in acknowledgment of the
pleasure and profit we have often and long derived from your
works. — I am, sir, yours very respectfully,   CURRER BELL.'

[1] 'De Quincey Memorials,' by Alexander H. Japp. 2 vols. 1891. William
Heinemann.

Charlotte Brontë could not have carried out the project of distribution to any appreciable extent, as a considerable 'remainder' appear to have been bound up with a new title-page by Smith & Elder. With this Smith & Elder title-page, the book is not uncommon, whereas, with the Aylott & Jones title-page it is exceedingly rare. Perhaps there were a dozen review copies and a dozen presentation copies, in addition to the two that were sold, but only three or four seem to have survived for the pleasure of the latter-day bibliophile.

Here is the title-page in question:

POEMS

BY

CURRER, ELLIS

AND

ACTON BELL

LONDON
AYLOTT & JONES, 8 PATERNOSTER ROW
1846.

We see by the letter to Aylott & Jones, the first announcement of 'Wuthering Heights,' 'Agnes Grey,' and 'The Professor.' It would not seem that there was much, or indeed any, difficulty in disposing of 'Wuthering Heights' and 'Agnes Grey.' They bear the imprint of Newby of Mortimer Street, and they appeared in three uniform volumes, the two first being taken up by 'Wuthering Heights,' and the third by 'Agnes Grey,'[1] which is quaintly marked as if it were a three volumed novel in itself, having 'Volume III' on title-page and binding. I have said that there were no travels before the manuscripts of Emily and Anne. That is not quite certain. Mrs. Gaskell implies that there were; but, at any rate, there is no definite information on the subject. Newby, it is clear, did not publish them until all the world was discussing 'Jane Eyre.' 'The Professor,' by Currer Bell, had, however, travel enough! It was offered to six publishers in succession before it came into the hands of Mr. W. S. Williams, the 'reader' for Smith & Elder. The circumstance of its courteous refusal by that firm, and the suggestion that a three-volumed novel would be gladly considered, are within the knowledge of all Charlotte Brontë's admirers. [2]

One cannot but admire the fearless and uncompromising honesty with which Charlotte Brontë sent the MSS. round with all its previous journeys frankly indicated.

It is not easy at this time of day to understand why Mr. Williams refused 'The Professor.' The story is incomparably superior to the average novel, and, indeed, contains touches which are equal to anything that Currer Bell ever wrote. It seems to me possible that Charlotte Brontë rewrote the story after its rejection, but the manuscript does not bear out that impression.[3]

Charlotte Brontë's method of writing was to take a piece

1 'Agnes Grey,' a novel, by Acton Bell. Vol. III. London, Thomas Cantley Newby, publisher, 72 Mortimer Street, Cavendish Square.

2 And yet the error not infrequently occurs, and was recently made by Professor Saintsbury ('Nineteenth Century Literature'), of assuming that it was 'Jane Eyre' which met with many refusals.

3 Mr. Nicholls assures me that the manuscript was not rewritten after his marriage, although I had thought it possible, not only on account of its intrinsic merits, which have not been sufficiently acknowledged, but on account of the singular fact that Mlle. Henri, the charming heroine, is married in a white muslin dress, and that her going away dress was of lilac silk. These were the actual wedding dresses of Mrs. Nicholls.

of cardboard — the broken cover of a book, in fact — and a few sheets of note-paper, and write her first form of a story upon these sheets in a tiny handwriting in pencil. She would afterwards copy the whole out upon quarto paper very neatly in ink. None of the original pencilled MSS. of her greater novels have been preserved. The extant manuscripts of 'Jane Eyre' and 'The Professor' are in ink.

'Jane Eyre' was written, then, under Mr. Williams's kind encouragement, and immediately accepted. It was published in the first week of October 1847.

The following letters were received by Mr. Williams while the book was beginning its course.

TO W. S. WILLIAMS.

'OCTOBER 4, 1847.

'DEAR SIR,— I thank you sincerely for your last letter. It is valuable to me because it furnishes me with a sound opinion on points respecting which I desired to be advised ; be assured I shall do what I can to profit by your wise and good counsel.

'Permit me, however, sir, to caution you against forming too favourable an idea of my powers, or too sanguine an expectation of what they can achieve. I am myself sensible both of deficiencies of capacity and disadvantages of circumstance which will, I fear, render it somewhat difficult for me to attain popularity as an author. The eminent writers you mention — Mr. Thackeray, Mr. Dickens, Mrs. Marsh,[1] etc., doubtless enjoyed facilities for observation such as I have not ; certainly they possess a knowledge of the world, whether intuitive or acquired, such as I can lay no claim to, and this gives their writings

---

[1] Anne Marsh (1791–1874), a daughter of James Caldwell, J.P., of Linley Wood, Staffordshire, married a son of the senior partner in the London banking firm of Marsh, Stacey, & Graham. Her first volume appeared in 1834, and contained, under the title of 'Two Old Men's Tales,' two stories, 'The Admiral's Daughter' and 'The Deformed,' which won considerable popularity. 'Emilia Wyndham,' 'Time,' 'The Avenger,' 'Mount Sorel,' and 'Castle Avon,' are perhaps the best of her many subsequent novels.

an importance and a variety greatly beyond what I can offer the public.

'Still, if health be spared and time vouchsafed me, I mean to do my best; and should a moderate success crown my efforts, its value will be greatly enhanced by the proof it will seem to give that your kind counsel and encouragement have not been bestowed on one quite unworthy. — Yours respectfully,

'C. BELL.'

TO W. S. WILLIAMS.

'OCTOBER 9, 1847.

'DEAR SIR,— I do not know whether the "Dublin University Magazine" is included in the list of periodicals to which Messrs. Smith & Elder are accustomed to send copies of new publications, but as a former work, the joint production of myself and my two relatives, Ellis and Acton Bell, received a somewhat favourable notice in that magazine, it appears to me that if the editor's attention were drawn to "Jane Eyre" he might possibly bestow on it also a few words of remark.

'The "Critic" and the "Athenæum" also gave comments on the work I allude to. The review in the first-mentioned paper was unexpectedly and generously eulogistic, that in the "Athenæum" more qualified, but still not discouraging. I mention these circumstances and leave it to you to judge whether any advantage is derivable from them.

'You dispensed me from the duty of answering your last letter, but my sense of the justness of the views it expresses will not permit me to neglect this opportunity both of acknowledging it and thanking you for it.— Yours sincerely,

'C. BRONTË.'

TO W. S. WILLIAMS.

'HAWORTH, December 13, 1847.

'DEAR SIR, — Your advice merits and shall have my most serious attention. I feel the force of your reasoning. It is my wish to do my best in the career on which I have entered.

So I shall study and strive; and by dint of time, thought, and effort, I hope yet to deserve in part the encouragement you and others have so generously accorded me. But *time* will be necessary — that I feel more than ever. In case of "Jane Eyre" reaching a second edition, I should wish some few corrections to be made, and will prepare an errata. How would the accompanying preface do? I thought it better to be brief.

'The "Observer" has just reached me. I always compel myself to read the analysis in every newspaper-notice. It is a just punishment, a due though severe humiliation for faults of plan and construction. I wonder if the analysis of other fictions read as absurdly as that of "Jane Eyre" always does. — I am, dear sir, yours respectfully, C. BELL.'

The following letter is interesting because it discusses the rejected novel, and refers to the project of recasting it, which ended in the writing of 'Villette.'[1]

TO W. S. WILLIAMS.

'DECEMBER 14, 1847.

'DEAR SIR, — I have just received your kind and welcome letter of the 11th. I shall proceed at once to discuss the principal subject of it.

'Of course a second work has occupied my thoughts much. I think it would be premature in me to undertake a serial now — I am not yet qualified for the task: I have neither gained a sufficiently firm footing with the public, nor do I possess sufficient confidence in myself, nor can I boast those unflagging animal spirits, that even command of the faculty of composition, which as you say and I am persuaded, most justly, is an indispensable requisite to success in serial literature. I decidedly feel that ere I change my ground I had better make another venture in the three volume novel form.

[1] 'The Professor' was published, with a brief note by Mr. Nicholls, two years after the death of its author. 'The Professor,' a Tale, by Currer Bell. in two volumes. Smith, Elder & Co., 65 Cornhill, 1857.

CHARLOTTE BRONTË

'Respecting the plan of such a work, I have pondered it, but as yet with very unsatisfactory results. Three commencements have I essayed, but all three displease me. A few days since I looked over "The Professor." I found the beginning very feeble, the whole narrative deficient in incident and in general attractiveness.. Yet the middle and latter portion of the work, all that relates to Brussels, the Belgian school, etc., is as good as I can write : it contains more pith, more substance, more reality, in my judgment, than much of "Jane Eyre." It gives, I think, a new view of a grade, an occupation, and a class of characters — all very commonplace, very insignificant in themselves, but not more so than the materials composing that portion of "Jane Eyre" which seems to please most generally.

'My wish is to recast "The Professor," add as well as I can what is deficient, retrench some parts, develop others, and make of it a three volume work — no easy task, I know, yet I trust not an impracticable one.

'I have not forgotten that "The Professor" was set aside in my agreement with Messrs. Smith & Elder, therefore before I take any step to execute the plan I have sketched, I should wish to have your judgment on its wisdom. You read or looked over the MS. — what impression have you now respecting its worth? and what confidence have you that I can make it better than it is?

'Feeling certain that from business reasons as well as from natural integrity you will be quite candid with me, I esteem it a privilege to be able thus to consult you. — Believe me, dear sir, yours respectfully,   C. Bell.

' "Wuthering Heights" is, I suppose, at length published, at least Mr. Newby has sent the authors their six copies. I wonder how it will be received. I should say it merits the epithets of "vigorous" and "original" much more decidedly than "Jane Eyre" did. "Agnes Grey" should please such critics as Mr. Lewes, for it is "true" and "unexaggerated" enough. The books are not well got up — they abound in errors of the press. On a former occasion I expressed myself with perhaps too little reserve regarding Mr. Newby, yet I cannot but feel, and feel painfully, that Ellis and Acton have not had the justice at his hands that I have had at those of Messrs. Smith & Elder.'

TO W. S. WILLIAMS.

'DECEMBER 31, 1847.

'DEAR SIR, — I think, for the reasons you mention, it is better to substitute *author* for *editor*. I should not be ashamed to be considered the author of " Wuthering Heights " and " Agnes Grey," but, possessing no real claim to that honour, I would rather not have it attributed to me, thereby depriving the true authors of their just meed.

'You do very rightly and very kindly to tell me the objections made against " Jane Eyre " — they are more essential than the praises. I feel a sort of heart-ache when I hear the book called " godless " and " pernicious " by good and earnest-minded men ; but I know that heart-ache will be salutary — at least I trust so.

'What is meant by the charges of *trickery* and *artifice* I have yet to comprehend. It was no art in me to write a tale — it was no trick in Messrs. Smith & Elder to publish it. Where do the trickery and artifice lie ?

'I have received the " Scotsman," and was greatly amused to see Jane Eyre likened to Rebecca Sharp — the resemblance would hardly have occurred to me.

'I wish to send this note by to-day's post, and must therefore conclude in haste. — I am, dear sir, yours respectfully,

'C. BELL.'

TO. W. S WILLIAMS.

'HAWORTH, January 4, 1848.

'DEAR SIR, — Your letter made me ashamed of myself that I should ever have uttered a murmur, or expressed by any sign that I was sensible of pain from the unfavourable opinions of

337

some misjudging but well-meaning people. But, indeed, let me assure you, I am not ungrateful for the kindness which has been given me in such abundant measure. I can discriminate the proportions in which blame and praise have been awarded to my efforts : I see well that I have had less of the former and more of the latter than I merit. I am not therefore crushed, though I may be momentarily saddened by the frown, even of the good.

'It would take a great deal to crush me, because I know, in the first place, that my own intentions were correct, that I feel in my heart a deep reverence for religion, that impiety is very abhorrent to me ; and in the second, I place firm reliance on the judgment of some who have encouraged me. You and Mr. Lewes are quite as good authorities, in my estimation, as Mr. Dilke or the editor of the "Spectator," and I would not under any circumstances, or for any opprobrium, regard with shame what my friends had approved — none but a coward would let the detraction of an enemy outweigh the encouragement of a friend. You must not, therefore, fulfil your threat of being less communicative in future ; you must kindly tell me all.

'Miss Kavanagh's view of the maniac coincides with Leigh Hunt's. I agree with them that the character is shocking, but I know that it is but too natural. There is a phase of insanity which may be called moral madness, in which all that is good or even human seems to disappear from the mind, and a fiend-nature replaces it. The sole aim and desire of the being thus possessed is to exasperate, to molest, to destroy, and preter-natural ingenuity and energy are often exercised to that dreadful end. The aspect, in such cases, assimilates with the disposition — all seem demonised. It is true that profound pity ought to be the only sentiment elicited by the view of such degradation, and equally true is it that I have not sufficiently dwelt on that feeling : I have erred in making *horror* too predominant. Mrs. Rochester, indeed, lived a sinful life before she was insane, but sin is itself a species of insanity — the truly good behold and compassionate it as such.

'"Jane Eyre" has got down into Yorkshire, a copy has even

penetrated into this neighbourhood. I saw an elderly clergy-man reading it the other day, and had the satisfaction of hearing him exclaim, " Why, they have got —— School, and Mr. —— here, I declare ! and Miss —— " (naming the originals of Lowood, Mr. Brocklehurst and Miss Temple). He had known them all. I wondered whether he would recognise the portraits, and was gratified to find that he did, and that, moreover, he pronounced them faithful and just. He said, too, that Mr. —— (Brockle-hurst) " deserved the chastisement he had got."

'He did not recognise Currer Bell. What author would be without the advantage of being able to walk invisible ? One is thereby enabled to keep such a quiet mind. I make this small observation in confidence.

'What makes you say that the notice in the "Westminster Review" is not by Mr. Lewes ? It expresses precisely his opinions, and he said he would perhaps insert a few lines in that periodical.

'I have sometimes thought that I ought to have written to Mr. Lewes to thank him for his review in "Fraser ;" and, indeed, I did write a note, but then it occurred to me that he did not require the author's thanks, and I feared it would be superfluous to send it, therefore I refrained ; however, though I have not *expressed* gratitude I have *felt* it.

'I wish you, too, *many, many* happy new years, and prosperity and success to you and yours. — Believe me, etc.,

'CURRER BELL.

'I have received the "Courier" and the "Oxford Chronicle." '

TO W. S. WILLIAMS.

'JANUARY 22, 1848.

' DEAR SIR, — I have received the "Morning Herald," and was much pleased with the notice, chiefly on account of the reference made to that portion of the preface which concerns Messrs. Smith & Elder. If my tribute of thanks can benefit my publishers, it is desirable that it should have as much publicity as possible.

CHARLOTTE BRONTË

'I do not know if the part which relates to Mr. Thackeray is likely to be as well received but whether generally approved of and understood or not, I shall not regret having written it, for I am convinced of its truth.

'I see I was mistaken in my idea that the "Athenæum" and others wished to ascribe the authorship of " Wuthering Heights " to Currer Bell; the contrary is the case, "Jane Eyre" is given to Ellis Bell; and Mr. Newby, it appears, thinks it expedient so to frame his advertisements as to favour the misapprehension. If Mr. Newby had much sagacity he would see that Ellis Bell is strong enough to stand without being propped by Currer Bell, and would have disdained what Ellis himself of all things disdains — recourse to trickery. However, Ellis, Acton, and Currer care nothing for the matter personally; the public and the critics are welcome to confuse our identities as much as they choose; my only fear is lest Messrs. Smith & Elder should in some way be annoyed by it.

'I was much interested in your account of Miss Kavanagh. The character you sketch belongs to a class I peculiarly esteem: one in which endurance combines with exertion, talent with goodness; where genius is found unmarred by extravagance, self-reliance unalloyed by self-complacency. It is a character which is, I believe, rarely found except where there has been toil to undergo and adversity to struggle against: it will only grow to perfection in a poor soil and in the shade; if the soil be too indigent, the shade too dank and thick, of course it dies where it sprung. But I trust this will not be the case with Miss Kavanagh. I trust she will struggle ere long into the sunshine. In you she has a kind friend to direct her, and I hope her mother will live to see the daughter, who yields to her such childlike duty, both happy and successful.

'You asked me if I should like any copies of the second edition of "Jane Eyre," and I said — no. It is true I do not want any for myself or my acquaintances, but if the request be not unusual, I should much like one to be given to Miss Kavanagh. If you would have the goodness, you might write on the fly-leaf that the book is presented with the author's best wishes for her welfare here and hereafter. My reason for wishing that she should have a copy is because she said the book had been to her a *suggestive* one, and I know that suggestive books are valuable to authors.

'I am truly sorry to hear that Mr. Smith has had an attack of the prevalent complaint, but I trust his recovery is by this time complete. I cannot boast entire exemption from its ravages, as I now write under its depressing influence. Hoping that you have been more fortunate, — I am, dear sir, yours faithfully,

'C. BELL.'

TO W. S. WILLIAMS.

'MARCH 3, 1848.

'MY DEAR SIR, — I have received the "Christian Remembrancer," and read the review. It is written with some ability; but to do justice was evidently not the critic's main object, therefore he excuses himself from performing that duty.

'I daresay the reviewer imagines that Currer Bell ought to be extremely afflicted, very much cut up, by some smart things he says — this however is not the case. C. Bell is on the whole rather encouraged than dispirited by the review: the hard-wrung praise extorted reluctantly from a foe is the most precious praise of all — you are sure that this, at least, has no admixture of flattery. I fear he has too high an opinion of my abilities and of what I can do; but that is his own fault. In other respects, he aims his shafts in the dark, and the success, or rather, ill-success of his hits makes me laugh rather than cry. His shafts of sarcasm are nicely polished, keenly pointed; he should not have wasted them in shooting at a mark he cannot see.

'I hope such reviews will not make much difference with me, and that if the spirit moves me in future to say anything about priests, etc., I shall say it with the same freedom as heretofore. I hope also that their anger will not make *me* angry. As a body, I had no ill-will against them to begin with, and I feel it would be an error to let opposition engender such ill-will. A few individuals may possibly be called upon to sit for their portraits some time, if their brethren in general dislike the resemblance and abuse the artist — *tant pis!* — Believe me, my dear sir, yours sincerely, C. BELL.'

It seems that Mr. Williams had hinted that Charlotte might like to emulate Thackeray by illustrating her own books.

TO W. S. WILLIAMS.

'MARCH 11, 1848.

'DEAR SIR, — I have just received the copy of the second edition, and will look over it, and send the corrections as soon as possible; I will also, since you think it advisable, avail myself of the opportunity of a third edition to correct the mistake respecting the authorship of " Wuthering Heights " and " Agnes Grey."

'As to your second suggestion, it is, one can see at a glance, a very judicious and happy one; but I cannot adopt it, because I have not the skill you attribute to me. It is not enough to have the artist's eye, one must also have the artist's hand to turn the first gift to practical account. I have, in my day, wasted a certain quantity of Bristol board and drawing-paper, crayons and cakes of colour, but when I examine the contents of my portfolio now it seems as if during the years it has been lying closed some fairy had changed what I once thought sterling coin into dry leaves, and I feel much inclined to consign the whole collection of drawings to the fire; I see they have no value. If, then, "Jane Eyre " is ever to be illustrated, it must be by some other hand than that of its author. But I hope no one will be at the trouble to make portraits of my characters. Bulwer and Byron heroes and heroines are very well, they are all of them handsome; but my personages are mostly unattractive in look, and therefore ill-adapted to figure in ideal portraits. At the best, I have always thought such representations futile. You will not easily find a second Thackeray. How he can render with a few black lines and dots, shades of expression so fine, so real; traits of character so minute, so subtle, so difficult to seize and fix, I cannot tell — I can only wonder and admire. Thackeray may not be a painter, but he is a wizard of a draughtsman; touched with his pencil, paper lives. And then his drawing is so refreshing; after the wooden limbs one is accustomed to see pourtrayed by common-place illustrators, his shapes of bone and muscle clothed with flesh, correct in proportion and anatomy, are a real relief. All is true in Thackeray. If Truth were again a goddess, Thackeray should be her high priest.

'I read my preface over with some pain — I did not like it. I wrote it when I was a little enthusiastic, like you about the French Revolution. I wish I had written it in a cool moment ; I should have said the same things, but in a different manner. One may be as enthusiastic as one likes about an author who has been dead a century or two, but I see it is a fault to bore the public with enthusiasm about a living author. I promise myself to take better care in future. *Still* I will *think* as I please.

'Are the London republicans and *you* amongst the number cooled down yet ? I suppose not, because your French brethren are acting very nobly. The abolition of slavery, and of the punishment of death for political offences are two glorious deeds, but how will they get over the question of the organisation of labour ! Such theories will be the sand-bank on which their vessel will run aground if they don't mind. Lamartine, there is not doubt, would make an excellent legislator for a nation of Lamartines — but where is that nation ? I hope these observations are sceptical and cool enough. — Believe me, my dear sir, yours sincerely,   C. BELL.'

TO W. S. WILLIAMS.

'NOVEMBER 16, 1848.

' MY DEAR SIR, — I have already acknowledged in a note to Mr. Smith the receipt of the parcel of books, and in my thanks for this well-timed attention, I am sure I ought to include you; your taste, I thought, was recognisable in the choice of some of the volumes and a better selection it would have been difficult to make.

CHARLOTTE BRONTË

'To-day I have received the " Spectator " and the " Revue des deux Mondes." The " Spectator" consistently maintains the tone it first assumed regarding the Bells. I have little to object to its opinion as far as Currer Bell's portion of the volume is concerned. It is true the critic sees only the faults, but for these his perception is tolerably accurate. Blind is he as any bat, insensate as any stone to the merits of Ellis. He cannot feel or will not acknowledge that the very finish and *labor limae* which Currer wants, Ellis has; he is not aware that the "true essence of poetry" pervades his compositions. Because Ellis's poems are short and abstract, the critics think them comparatively insignificant and dull. They are mistaken.

'The notice in the "Revue des deux Mondes" is one of the most able, the most acceptable to the author of any that has yet appeared. Eugene Forcade understood and enjoyed "Jane Eyre." I cannot say that of all who have professed to criticise it. The censures are as well-founded as the commendations. The specimens of the translation given are on the whole good; now and then the meaning of the original has been misapprehended, but generally it is well rendered.

'Every cup given us to taste in this life is mixed. Once it would have seemed to me that an evidence of success like that contained in the "Revue" would have excited an almost exultant feeling in my mind. It comes, however, at a time when counteracting circumstances keep the balance of the emotions even — when my sister's continued illness darkens the present and dims the future. That will seem to me a happy day when I can announce to you that Emily is better. Her symptoms continue to be those of slow inflammation of the lungs, tight cough, difficulty of breathing, pain in the chest, and fever. We watch anxiously for a change for the better — may it soon come. — I am, my dear sir, yours sincerely,   C. Brontë.

'As I was about to seal this I received your kind letter. Truly glad am I to hear that Fanny is taking the path which pleases her parents. I trust she may persevere in it. She may be sure that a contrary one will never lead to happiness; and I

344

should think that the reward of seeing you and her mother pleased must be so sweet that she will be careful not to run the risk of forfeiting it.

'It is somewhat singular that I had already observed to my sisters, I did not doubt it was Mr. Lewes who had shown you the " Revue." '

The many other letters referring to Emily's last illness have already been printed. When the following letters were written, Emily and Anne were both in their graves.

TO JAMES TAYLOR, Cornhill.

'March 1, 1849.

'My dear Sir, — The parcel arrived on Saturday evening. Permit me to express my sense of the judgment and kindness which have dictated the selection of its contents. They appear to be all good books, and good books are, we know, the best substitute for good society ; if circumstances debar me from the latter privilege, the kind attention of my friends supply me with ample measure of the former.

'Thank you for your remarks on "Shirley." Some of your strictures tally with some by Mr. Williams. You both complain of the want of distinctness and impressiveness in my heroes. Probably you are right. In delineating male character I labour under disadvantages : intuition and theory will not always adequately supply the place of observation and experience. When I write about women I am sure of my ground — in the other case, I am not so sure.

'Here, then, each of you has laid the critical finger on a point that by its shrinking confesses its vulnerability ; whether the disapprobation you intimate respecting the Briarchapel scenes, the curates, etc., be equally merited, time will show. I am well aware what will be the author's present meed for these passages : I anticipate general blame and no praise. And were my motive-principle in writing a thirst for popularity, or were the chief check on my pen a dread of censure, I should withdraw these scenes — or rather, I should never have written them. I will not say whether the considerations that really govern me are sound, or whether my convictions are just; but such as they are, to their influence I must yield submission. They forbid me to sacrifice truth to the fear of blame. I accept their prohibition.

'With the sincere expression of my esteem for the candour by which your critique is distinguished, — I am, my dear sir, yours sincerely,   C. BRONTË.'

TO W. S. WILLIAMS.

'AUGUST 16, 1849.

'MY DEAR SIR, — Since I last wrote to you I have been getting on with my book as well as I can, and I think I may now venture to say that in a few weeks I hope to have the pleasure of placing the MS. in the hands of Mr. Smith.

'The "North British Review" duly reached me. I read attentively all it says about E. Wyndham, "Jane Eyre," and F. Hervey. Much of the article is clever, and yet there are remarks which — for me — rob it of importance.

'To value praise or stand in awe of blame we must respect the source whence the praise and blame proceed, and I do not respect an inconsistent critic. He says, "if 'Jane Eyre' be the production of a woman, she must be a woman unsexed."

'In that case the book is an unredeemed error and should be unreservedly condemned. "Jane Eyre" is a woman's autobiography, by a woman it is professedly written. If it is written as no woman would write, condemn it with spirit and decision — say it is bad, but do not eulogise and then detract. I am reminded of the "Economist." The literary critic of that paper praised the book if written by a man, and pronounced it "odious" if the work of a woman.

'To such critics I would say, "To you I am neither man nor woman — I come before you as an author only. It is the sole standard by which you have a right to judge me — the sole ground on which I accept your judgment."

'There is a weak comment, having no pretence either to justice or discrimination, on the works of Ellis and Acton Bell. The critic did not know that those writers had passed from time and life. I have read no review since either of my sisters died which I could have wished *them* to read — none even which did not render the thought of their departure more tolerable to me. To hear myself praised beyond them was cruel, to hear qualities ascribed to them so strangely the reverse of their real characteristics was scarce supportable. It is sad even now; but they are so remote from earth, so safe from its turmoils, I can bear it better.

'But on one point do I now feel vulnerable: I should grieve to see my father's peace of mind perturbed on my account; for which reason I keep my author's existence as much as possible out of his way. I have always given him a carefully diluted and modified account of the success of "Jane Eyre"—just what would please without startling him. The book is not mentioned between us once a month. The "Quarterly" I kept to myself — it would have worried papa. To that same "Quarterly" I must speak in the introduction to my present work —just one little word. You once, I remember, said that review was written by a lady — Miss Rigby. Are you sure of this?

'Give no hint of my intention of discoursing a little with the "Quarterly." It would look too important to speak of it before-hand. All plans are best conceived and executed without noise.— Believe me, yours sincerely,   C. B.'

TO W. S. WILLIAMS.

'AUGUST 21, 1849.

'MY DEAR SIR,— I can only write very briefly at present — first to thank you for your interesting letter and the graphic description it contained of the neighbourhood where you have been staying, and then to decide about the title of the book.

'If I remember rightly, my Cornhill critics objected to "Hollow's Mill," nor do I now find it appropriate. It might rather be called "Fieldhead," though I think "Shirley" would perhaps be

347

the best title. "Shirley," I fancy, has turned out the most prominent and peculiar character in the work.

' Cornhill may decide between "Fieldhead" and "Shirley."—Believe me, yours sincerely,   C. BRONTË.'

The famous 'Quarterly Review' article by Miss Rigby, afterwards Lady Eastlake,[1] appeared in December 1848, under the title of '" Vanity Fair," "Jane Eyre," and Governesses.' It was a review of two novels and a treatise on schools, and but for one or two offensive passages might have been pronounced fairly complimentary. To have coupled 'Jane Eyre' with Thackeray's great book, at a time when Thackeray had already reached to heroic proportions in the literary world, was in itself a compliment. It is small wonder that the speculation was hazarded that J. G. Lockhart, the editor of the 'Quarterly,' had himself supplied the venom. He could display it on occasion. It is quite clear now, however, that that was not the case. Miss Rigby was the reviewer who thought it within a critic's province to suggest that the writer might be a woman ' who had forfeited the society of her sex.' Lockhart must have read the review hastily, as editors will on occasion. He writes to his contributor on November 13, 1848, before the article had appeared : —

' About three years ago I received a small volume of " Poems by Currer, Acton, and Ellis Bell," and a queer little note by Currer, who said the book had been published a year, and just two copies sold, so they were to burn the rest, but distributed a few copies, mine being one. I find, what seems rather a fair review of that tiny tome in the "Spectator" of this week ; pray look at it.

' I think the poems of Currer much better than those of Acton and Ellis, and believe his novel is vastly better than those which they have more recently put forth.

[1] Lady Eastlake died in 1893.

'I know nothing of the writers, but the common rumour is that they are brothers of the weaving order in some Lancashire town. At first it was generally said Currer was a lady, and Mayfair circumstantialised by making her the *chère amie* of Mr. Thackeray. But your skill in "dress" settles the question of sex. I think, however, some woman must have assisted in the school scenes of "Jane Eyre," which have a striking air of truthfulness to me — an ignoramus, I allow, on such points.

'I should say you might as well glance at the novels by Acton and Ellis Bell — "Wuthering Heights" is one of them. If you have any friend about Manchester, it would, I suppose, be easy to learn accurately as to the position of these men.'[1]

This was written in November, and it was not till December that the article appeared. Apart from the offensive imputations upon the morals of the author of 'Jane Eyre,' which reduces itself to smart impertinence when it is understood that Miss Rigby fully believed that the author was a man, the review is not without its compensations for a new writer. The 'equal popularity' of 'Jane Eyre' and 'Vanity Fair' is referred to. 'A very remarkable book,' the reviewer continues; 'we have no remembrance of another containing such undoubted power with such horrid taste.' There is droll irony, when Charlotte Brontë's strong conservative sentiments and church environment are considered, in the following : —

'We do not hesitate to say that the tone of mind and thought which has overthrown authority, and violated every code, human and divine, abroad, and fostered chartism and rebellion at home, is the same which has also written "Jane Eyre."'

In another passage Miss Rigby, musing upon the mascu-

[1] 'Letters and Journals' of Lady Eastlake, edited by her nephew, Charles Eastlake Smith, vol. i. pp. 221, 222 (John Murray).

linity of the author, finally clinches her arguments by proofs of a kind.

'No woman *trusses game*, and garnishes dessert dishes with the same hands, or talks of so doing in the same breath. Above all, no woman attires another in such fancy dresses as Jane's ladies assume. Miss Ingram coming down irresistible in a *morning* robe of sky-blue crape, a gauze azure scarf twisted in her hair!! No lady, we understand, when suddenly roused in the night, would think of hurrying on "a frock." They have garments more convenient for such occasions, and more becoming too.'

'Wuthering Heights' is described as 'too odiously and abominably pagan to be palatable to the most vitiated class of English readers.' This no doubt was Miss Rigby's interpolation in the proofs in reply to her editor's suggestion that she should 'glance at the novels by Acton and Ellis Bell.' It is a little difficult to understand the 'Quarterly' editor's method, or, indeed, the letter to Miss Rigby which I have quoted, as he had formed a very different estimate of the book many months before. 'I have finished the adventures of Miss Jane Eyre,' he writes to Mrs. Hope (Dec. 29th, 1847), 'and think her far the cleverest that has written since Austen and Edgeworth were in their prime, worth fifty Trollopes and Martineaus rolled into one counterpane, with fifty Dickenses and Bulwers to keep them company — but rather a brasen Miss.'[1]

When the 'Quarterly Review' appeared, Charlotte Brontë, as we have seen, was in dire domestic distress, and it was not till many months later, when a new edition of 'Jane Eyre' was projected, that she discussed with her publishers the desirability of an effective reply, which was not however to disclose her sex and environment. A first preface called

[1] 'Life of J. G. Lockhart,' by Andrew Lang. Published by John Nimmo. Mr. Lang has courteously permitted me to copy this letter from his proof-sheets.

A Word to the "Quarterly"' was cancelled, and after some debate, the preface which we now have took its place. The 'book' is of course 'Shirley.'

TO W. S. WILLIAMS.

'AUGUST 29, 1849.

'DEAR SIR, — The book is now finished (thank God) and ready for Mr. Taylor, but I have not yet heard from him. I thought I should be able to tell whether it was equal to "Jane Eyre" or not, but I find I cannot — it may be better, it may be worse. I shall be curious to hear your opinion, my own is of no value. I send the Preface or "Word to the 'Quarterly'" for your perusal.

'Whatever now becomes of the work, the occupation of writing it has been a boon to me. It took me out of dark and desolate reality into an unreal but happier region. The worst of it is my eyes are grown somewhat weak and my head somewhat weary and prone to ache with close work. You can write nothing of value unless you give yourself wholly to the theme, and when you so give yourself, you lose appetite and sleep — it cannot be helped.

'At what time does Mr. Smith intend to bring the book out. It is his now. I hand it and all the trouble and care and anxiety over to him — a good riddance, only I wish he fairly had it. — Yours sincerely, C. BRONTË.'

TO W. S. WILLIAMS.

'AUGUST 31, 1849.

'MY DEAR SIR, — I cannot change my preface. I can shed no tears before the public, nor utter any groan in the public ear. The deep, real tragedy of our domestic experience is yet terribly fresh in my mind and memory. It is not a time to be talked about to the indifferent; it is not a topic for allusion to in print.

'No righteous indignation can I lavish on the "Quarterly." I can condescend but to touch it with the lightest satire. Believe me, my dear sir, " C. Brontë" must not here appear; what she feels or has felt is not the question — it is "Currer Bell" who was insulted — he must reply. Let Mr. Smith fearlessly print the preface I have sent — let him depend upon me this once ; even if I prove a broken reed, his fall cannot be dangerous : a preface is a short distance, it is not three volumes.

'I have always felt certain that it is a deplorable error in an author to assume the tragic tone in addressing the public about his own wrongs or griefs. What does the public care about him as an individual ? His wrongs are its sport ; his griefs would be a bore. What we deeply feel is our own — we must keep it to ourselves. Ellis and Acton Bell were, for me, Emily and Anne ; my sisters — to me intimately near, tenderly dear — to the public they were nothing → worse than nothing — beings speculated upon, misunderstood, misrepresented. If I live, the hour may come when the spirit will move me to speak of them, but it is not come yet. — I am, my dear sir, yours sincerely,

'C. Brontë.'

TO W. S. WILLIAMS.

'September 17, 1849.

'My dear Sir, — Your letter gave me great pleasure. An author who has showed his book to none, held no consultation about plan, subject, characters, or incidents, asked and had no opinion from one living being, but fabricated it darkly in the silent workshop of his own brain — such an author awaits with a singular feeling the report of the first impression produced by his creation in a quarter where he places confidence, and truly glad he is when the report proves favourable.

'Do you think this book will tend to strengthen the idea that Currer Bell is a woman, or will it favour a contrary opinion ?

'I return the proof-sheets. Will they print all the French phrases in italics ? I hope not, it makes them look somehow obtrusively conspicuous.

'I have no time to add more lest I should be too late for the post. — Yours sincerely, C. Brontë.'

TO W. S. WILLIAMS.

'September 19, 1849.

'Dear Sir, — I have made the alteration; but I have made it to please Cornhill, not the public nor the critics.

'I am sorry to say Newby does know my real name. I wish he did not, but that cannot be helped. Meantime, though I earnestly wish to preserve my incognito, I live under no slavish fear of discovery. I am ashamed of nothing I have written — not a line.

'The envelope containing the first proof and your letter had been received open at the General Post Office and resealed there. Perhaps it was accident, but I think it better to inform you of the circumstance. — Yours sincerely, C. Brontë.'

TO W. S. WILLIAMS.

'September 10, 1849.

'Dear Sir, — Your advice is very good, and yet I cannot follow it: I *cannot* alter now. It sounds absurd, but so it is.

'The circumstances of Shirley's being nervous on such a matter may appear incongruous because I fear it is not well managed, otherwise it is perfectly natural. In such minds, such odd points, such queer unexpected inconsistent weaknesses *are* found — perhaps there never was an ardent poetic temperament, however healthy, quite without them; but they never communicate them unless forced, they have a suspicion that the terror is absurd, and keep it hidden. Still the thing is badly managed, and I bend my head and expect in resignation what, *here*, I know I deserve — the lash of criticism. I shall wince when it falls, but not scream.

'You are right about Goethe, you are very right — he is clear, deep, but very cold. I acknowledge him great, but cannot feel him genial.

'You mention the literary coteries. To speak the truth, I recoil from them, though I long to see some of the truly

353

great literary characters. However, this is not to be yet —
I cannot sacrifice my incognito. And let me be content with
seclusion — it has its advantages. In general, indeed, I am
tranquil, it is only now and then that a struggle disturbs me —
that I wish for a wider world than Haworth. When it is past,
Reason tells me how unfit I am for anything very different.
Yours sincerely,   C. Brontë.'

TO W. S. WILLIAMS.

'September 15, 1849.

'My dear Sir, — You observed that the French of "Shirley"
might be cavilled at. There is a long paragraph written in the
French language in that chapter entitled "Le cheval dompté."
I forget the number. I fear it will have a pretentious air. If
you deem it advisable, and will return the chapter, I will efface,
and substitute something else in English. — Yours sincerely,

'C. Brontë.'

TO JAMES TAYLOR, Cornhill.

'September 20, 1849.

'My dear Sir, — It is time I answered the note which I
received from you last Thursday; I should have replied to it
before had I not been kept more than usually engaged by the
presence of a clergyman in the house, and the indisposition of
one of our servants.

'As you may conjecture, it cheered and pleased me much to
learn that the opinion of my friends in Cornhill was favourable to
"Shirley" — that, on the whole, it was considered no falling off
from "Jane Eyre." I am trying, however, not to encourage too
sanguine an expectation of a favourable reception by the public:
the seeds of prejudice have been sown, and I suppose the produce
will have to be reaped — but we shall see.

'I read with pleasure "Friends in Council," and with very great
pleasure "The Thoughts and Opinions of a Statesman." It is the
record of what may with truth be termed a beautiful mind —
serene, harmonious, elevated, and pure; it bespeaks, too, a heart
full of kindness and sympathy. I like it much.

'Papa has been pretty well during the past week, he begs to join me in kind remembrances to yourself. — Believe me, my dear sir, yours very sincerely,   C. Brontë.'

TO W. S. WILLIAMS.

'October 1, 1849.

'My dear Sir, — I am chagrined about the envelope being opened : I see it is the work of prying curiosity, and now it would be useless to make a stir — what mischief is to be apprehended is already done. It was not done at Haworth. I know the people of the post-office there, and am sure they would not venture on such a step — besides, the Haworth people have long since set me down as bookish and quiet, and trouble themselves no farther about me. But the gossiping inquisitiveness of small towns is rife at Keighley ; there they are sadly puzzled to guess why I never visit, encourage no overtures to acquaintance, and always stay at home. Those packets passing backwards and forwards by the post have doubtless aggravated their curiosity. Well, I am sorry, but I shall try to wait patiently and not vex myself too much, come what will.

'I am glad you like the English substitute for the French *devoir*.

'The parcel of books came on Saturday. I write to Mr. Taylor by this post to acknowledge its receipt. His opinion of "Shirley" seems in a great measure to coincide with yours, only he expresses it rather differently to you, owing to the difference in your casts of mind. Are you not different on some points ? — Yours sincerely,   'C. Brontë.'

TO W. S. WILLIAMS.

'November 1, 1849.

'My dear Sir, — I reached home yesterday, and found your letter and one from Mr. Lewes, and one from the Peace Congress Committee awaiting my arrival. The last document it is now too late to answer, for it was an invitation to Currer Bell to appear on the platform at their meeting at Exeter Hall last Tuesday ! A wonderful figure Mr. Currer Bell would have cut under such circumstances! Should the "Peace Congress" chance to read "Shirley" they will wash their hands of its author.

'I am glad to hear that Mr. Thackeray is better, but I did not know he had been seriously ill, I thought it was only a literary indisposition. You must tell me what he thinks of "Shirley" if he gives you any opinion on the subject.

'I am also glad to hear that Mr. Smith is pleased with the commercial prospects of the work. I try not to be anxious about its literary fate; and if I cannot be quite stoical, I think I am still tolerably resigned.

'Mr. Lewes does not like the opening chapter, wherein he resembles you.

'I have permitted myself the treat of spending the last week with my friend Ellen. Her residence is in a far more populous and stirring neighbourhood than this. Whenever I go there I am unavoidably forced into society — clerical society chiefly.

'During my late visit I have too often had reason, sometimes in a pleasant, sometimes in a painful form, to fear that I no longer walk invisible. "Jane Eyre," it appears, has been read all over the district — a fact of which I never dreamt — a circumstance of which the possibility never occurred to me. I met sometimes with new deference, with augmented kindness: old schoolfellows and old teachers, too, greeted me with generous warmth. And again, ecclesiastical brows lowered thunder at me. When I confronted one or two large-made priests, I longed for the battle to come on. I wish they would speak out plainly. You must not understand that my schoolfellows and teachers were of the Clergy Daughters School — in fact, I was never there but for one little year as a very little girl. I am certain I have long been forgotten; though for myself, I remember all and everything clearly: early impressions are ineffaceable.

'I have just received the "Daily News." Let me speak the truth — when I read it my heart sickened over it. It is not a good review, it is unutterably false. If "Shirley" strikes all readers as it has struck that one, but — I shall not say what follows.

'On the whole I am glad a decidedly bad notice has come first — a notice whose inexpressible ignorance first stuns and then stirs me. Are there no such men as the Helstones and Yorkes?

'Yes, there are.

'Is the first chapter disgusting or vulgar?

'*It is not, it is real.*

'As for the praise of such a critic, I find it silly and nauseous, and I scorn it.

'Were my sisters now alive they and I would laugh over this notice; but they sleep, they will wake no more for me, and I am a fool to be so moved by what is not worth a sigh. — Believe me, yours sincerely.   C. B.

'You must spare me if I seem hasty, I fear I really am not so firm as I used to be, nor so patient. Whenever any shock comes, I feel that almost all supports have been withdrawn.'

TO W. S. WILLIAMS.

'NOVEMBER 5, 1849.

'MY DEAR SIR, — I did not receive the parcel of copies till Saturday evening. Everything sent by Bradford is long in reaching me. It is, I think, better to direct, Keighley. I was very much pleased with the appearance and getting up of the book, it looks well.

'I have got the "Examiner" and your letter. You are very good not to be angry with me, for I wrote in indignation and grief. The critic of the "Daily News" struck me as to the last degree incompetent, ignorant, and flippant. A thrill of mutiny went all through me when I read his small effusion. To be judged by such a one revolted me. I ought, however, to have controlled myself, and I did not. I am willing to be judged by the "Examiner" — I like the "Examiner." Fonblanque has power, he has discernment — I bend to his censorship, I am grateful for his praise; his blame deserves consideration; when he approves, I permit myself a moderate emotion of pride. Am I wrong in supposing that critique to be written by Mr. Fonblanque? But whether it is by him or Forster, I am thankful.

'In reading the critiques of the other papers — when I get them — I will try to follow your advice and preserve my equa-

357

nimity. But I cannot be sure of doing this, for I had good resolutions and intentions before, and, you see, I failed.

'You ask me if I am related to Nelson. No, I never heard that I was. The rumour must have originated in our name resembling his title. I wonder who that former schoolfellow of mine was that told Mr. Lewes, or how she had been enabled to identify Currer Bell with C. Brontë. She could not have been a Cowan Bridge girl, none of them can possibly remember me. They might remember my eldest sister, Maria; her prematurely-developed and remarkable intellect, as well as the mildness, wisdom, and fortitude of her character *might* have left an indelible impression on some observant mind amongst her companions. My second sister, Elizabeth, too, may perhaps be remembered, but I cannot conceive that I left a trace behind me. My career was a very quiet one. I was plodding and industrious, perhaps I was very grave, for I suffered to see my sisters perishing, but I think I was remarkable for nothing. — Believe me, my dear sir, yours sincerely, C. BRONTË.'

TO W. S. WILLIAMS.

'NOVEMBER 15, 1849.

'MY DEAR SIR, — I have received since I wrote last the "Globe," "Standard of Freedom," "Britannia," "Economist," and "Weekly Chronicle."

'How is "Shirley" getting on, and what is now the general feeling respecting the work?

'As far as I can judge from the tone of the newspapers, it seems that those who were most charmed with "Jane Eyre" are the least pleased with "Shirley;" they are disappointed at not finding the same excitement, interest, stimulus; while those who spoke disparagingly of "Jane Eyre" like "Shirley" a little better than her predecessor. I suppose its dryer matter suits their dryer minds. But I feel that the fiat for which I wait does not depend on newspapers, except, indeed, such newspapers as the "Examiner." The monthlies and quarterlies will pronounce it, I suppose. Mere novel-readers, it is evident, think "Shirley" something of a failure. Still, the majority of the notices have on the whole been favourable. That in the " Standard of Freedom" was very kindly expressed; and coming from a dissenter, William Howitt, I wonder thereat.

'Are you satisfied at Cornhill, or the contrary? I have read part of the " Caxtons," and, when I have finished, will tell you what I think of it; meantime, I should very much like to hear opinion. Perhaps I shall keep mine till I see you, whenever that may be.

'I am trying by degrees to inure myself to the thought of some day stepping over to Keighley, taking the train to Leeds, thence to London, and once more venturing to set foot in the strange, busy whirl of the Strand and Cornhill. I want to talk to you a little and to hear by word of mouth how matters are progressing. Whenever I come, I must come quietly and but for a short time — I should be unhappy to leave papa longer than a fortnight. — Believe me, yours sincerely,   C. Brontë.'

TO W. S. WILLIAMS.

'November 22, 1849.

'My dear Sir,— If it is discouraging to an author to see his work mouthed over by the entirely ignorant and incompetent, it is equally reviving to hear what you have written discussed and analysed by a critic who is master of his subject — by one whose heart feels, whose powers grasp the matter he undertakes to handle. Such refreshment Eugene Forcade has given me. Were I to see that man, my impulse would be to say, " Monsieur, you know me, I shall deem it an honour to know you."

'I do not find that Forcade detects any coarseness in the work — it is for the smaller critics to find that out. The master in the art — the subtle-thoughted, keen-eyed, quick-feeling Frenchman, knows the true nature of the ingredients which went to the composition of the creation he analyses — he knows the true nature of things, and he gives them their right name.

'Yours of yesterday has just reached me. Let me, in the first place, express my sincere sympathy with your anxiety on Mrs. Williams's account. I know how sad it is when pain and suffering attack those we love, when that mournful guest sickness comes and

359

takes a place in the household circle. That the shadow may soon leave your home is my earnest hope.

'Thank you for Sir J. Herschel's note. I am happy to hear Mr. Taylor is convalescent. It may, perhaps, be some weeks yet before his hand is well, but that his general health is in the way of re-establishment is a matter of thankfulness.

'One of the letters you sent to-day addressed "Currer Bell" has almost startled me. The writer first describes his family, and then proceeds to give a particular account of himself in colours the most candid, if not, to my ideas, the most attractive. He runs on in a strain of wild enthusiasm about "Shirley," and concludes by announcing a fixed, deliberate resolution to institute a search after Currer Bell, and sooner or later to find him out. There is power in the letter — talent; it is at times eloquently expressed. The writer somewhat boastfully intimates that he is acknowledged the possessor of high intellectual attainments, but, if I mistake not, he betrays a temper to be shunned, habits to be mistrusted. While laying claim to the character of being affectionate, warm-hearted, and adhesive, there is but a single member of his own family of whom he speaks with kindness. He confesses himself indolent and wilful, but asserts that he is studious and, to some influences, docile. This letter would have struck me no more than the others rather like it have done, but for its rash power, and the disagreeable resolve it announces to seek and find Currer Bell. It almost makes me feel like a wizard who has raised a spirit he may find it difficult to lay. But I shall not think about it. This sort of fervour often foams itself away in words.

'Trusting that the serenity of your home is by this time restored with your wife's health,— I am, yours sincerely,

'C. Brontë.'

TO MISS ELLEN NUSSEY.

'February 16, 1850.

'Dear Nell,— Yesterday, just after dinner, I heard a loud bustling voice in the kitchen demanding to see Mr. Brontë. Somebody was shown into the parlour. Shortly after, wine was rung for. "Who is it, Martha?" I asked. "Some mak of a tradesman," said she. "He's not a gentleman, I'm sure." The personage stayed about an hour, talking in a loud vulgar key all the time. At tea-time I asked papa who it was. "Why," said he, "no other than the vicar of B——!"[1] Papa had invited him to take some refreshment, but the creature had ordered his dinner at the Black Bull, and was quite urgent with papa to go down there and join him, offering by way of inducement a bottle, or, if papa liked, "two or three bottles of the best wine Haworth could afford!" He said he was come from Bradford just to look at the place, and reckoned to be in raptures with the wild scenery! He warmly pressed papa to come and see him, and to bring his daughter with him!!! Does he know anything about the books, do you think; he made no allusion to them. I did not see him, not so much as the tail of his coat. Martha said he looked no more like a parson than she did. Papa described him as rather shabby-looking, but said he was wondrous cordial and friendly. Papa, in his usual fashion, put him through a regular catechism of questions : what his living was worth, etc., etc. In answer to inquiries respecting his age he affirmed himself to be thirty-seven — is not this a lie? He must be more. Papa asked him if he were married. He said no, he had no thoughts of being married, he did not like the trouble of a wife. He described himself as "living in style, and keeping a very hospitable house."

'Dear Nell, I have written you a long letter; write me a long one in answer. C. B.'

TO W. S. WILLIAMS.

'APRIL 3, 1850.

'MY DEAR SIR, — I have received the "Dublin Review," and your letter inclosing the Indian Notices. I hope these reviews will do good; they are all favourable, and one of them (the "Dublin") is very able. I have read no critique so discriminating since that in the "Revue des deux Mondes." It offers a curious contrast to Lewes's in the "Edinburgh," where forced praise, given

---

[1] Name of place is erased in original.

by jerks, and obviously without real and cordial liking, and
censure, crude, conceited, and ignorant, were mixed in random
lumps — forming a very loose and inconsistent whole.

'Are you aware whether there are any grounds for that conjecture in the "Bengal Harkara," that the critique in the "Times"
was from the pen of Mr. Thackeray? I should much like to
know this. If such were the case (and I feel as if it were by
no means impossible), the circumstance would open a most
curious and novel glimpse of a very peculiar disposition. Do you
think it likely to be true?

'The account you give of Mrs. Williams's health is not cheering, but I should think her indisposition is partly owing to the
variable weather; at least, if you have had the same keen frost
and cold east winds in London, from which we have lately
suffered in Yorkshire. I trust the milder temperature we are
now enjoying may quickly confirm her convalescence. With
kind regards to Mrs. Williams, — Believe me, my dear sir, yours
sincerely,   C. BRONTË.'

TO W. S. WILLIAMS.

'APRIL 25, 1850.

'MY DEAR SIR, — I cannot let the post go without thanking
Mr. Smith through you for the kind reply to Greenwood's
application; and, I am sure, both you and he would feel true
pleasure could you see the delight and hope with which these
liberal terms have inspired a good and intelligent though poor
man. He thinks he now sees a prospect of getting his livelihood by a method which will suit him better than wool-combing
work has hitherto done, exercising more of his faculties and
sparing his health. He will do his best I am sure to extend the
sale of the cheap edition of "Jane Eyre;" and whatever twinges
I may still feel at the thought of that work being in the
possession of all the worthy folk of Haworth and Keighley,
such scruples are more than counterbalanced by the attendant
good. I mean, by the assistance it will give a man who deserves
assistance. I wish he could permanently establish a little
bookselling business in Haworth: it would benefit the place
as well as himself.

'Thank you for the "Leader," which I read with pleasure. The notice of Newman's work in a late number was very good.— Believe me, my dear sir, in haste, yours sincerely,

'C. BRONTË.'

TO W. S. WILLIAMS.

'MAY 6, 1850.

'MY DEAR SIR, — I have received the copy of "Jane Eyre." To me the printing and paper seem very tolerable. Will not the public in general be of the same opinion? And are you not making yourselves causelessly uneasy on the subject?

'I imagine few will discover the defects of typography unless they are pointed out. There are, no doubt, technical faults and perfections in the art of printing to which printers and publishers ascribe a greater importance than the majority of readers.

'I will mention Mr. Smith's proposal respecting the cheap publications to Greenwood. I believe him to be a man on whom encouragement is not likely to be thrown away, and who, if fortune should not prove quite adverse, will contrive to effect something by dint of intelligence and perseverance.

'I am sorry to say my father has been far from well lately — the cold weather has tried him severely ; and, till I see him better, my intended journey to town must be deferred. With sincere regards to yourself and other Cornhill friends, — I am, my dear sir, yours faithfully,   C. BRONTË.'

TO W. S. WILLIAMS.

'SEPTEMBER 5, 1850.

'MY DEAR SIR, — I trust your suggestion for Miss Kavanagh's benefit will have all success. It seems to me truly felicitous and excellent, and, I doubt not, she will think so too. The last class of female character will be difficult to manage: there will be nice points in it — yet, well-managed, both an attractive and instructive book might result therefrom. One thing may be depended upon in the execution of this plan. Miss Kavanagh will commit no error, either of taste, judgment, or principle ; and even when she deals with the feelings, I would rather follow the calm course of her quiet pen than the flourishes of a more redundant one where there is not strength to restrain as well as ardour to impel.

'I fear I seemed to you to speak coolly of the beauty of the Lake scenery. The truth is, it was, as scenery, exquisite — far beyond anything I saw in Scotland; but it did not give me half so much pleasure, because I saw it under less congenial auspices. Mr. Smith and Sir J. K. Shuttleworth are two different people with whom to travel. I need say nothing of the former — you know him. The latter offers me his friendship, and I do my best to be grateful for the gift; but his is a nature with which it is difficult to assimilate — and where there is no assimilation how can there be real regard? Nine parts out of ten in him are utilitarian — the tenth is artistic. This tithe of his nature seems to me at war with all the rest — it is just enough to incline him restlessly towards the artist class, and far too little to make him one of them. The consequent inability to *do* things which he *admires*, embitters him I think — it makes him doubt perfections and dwell on faults. Then his notice or presence scarcely tend to set one at ease or make one happy : he is worldly and formal. But I must stop — have I already said too much? I think not, for you will feel it is said in confidence and will not repeat it.

'The article in the "Palladium" is indeed such as to atone for a hundred unfavourable or imbecile reviews. I have expressed what I think of it to Mr. Taylor, who kindly wrote me a letter on the subject. I thank you also for the newspaper notices, and for some you sent me a few weeks ago.

'I should much like to carry out your suggestions respecting a reprint of "Wuthering Heights" and "Agnes Grey" in one volume, with a prefatory and explanatory notice of the authors; but the question occurs, would Newby claim it? I could not bear to commit it to any other hands than those of Mr. Smith. "Wildfell Hall," it hardly appears to me desirable to preserve. The choice of subject in that work is a mistake : it was too little consonant with the character, tastes, and ideas of the gentle, retiring, inexperienced writer. She wrote it under

a strange, conscientious, half-ascetic notion of accomplishing a painful penance and a severe duty. Blameless in deed and almost in
thought, there was from her very childhood a tinge of religious
melancholy in her mind. This I ever suspected, and I have found
amongst her papers mournful proofs that such was the case. As to
additional compositions, I think there would be none, as I would
not offer a line, to the publication of which my sisters themselves
would have objected.

'I must conclude or I shall be too late for the post. — Believe
me, yours sincerely,   C. Brontë.'

TO W. S. WILLIAMS.

'September 13, 1850.

'My dear Sir, — Mr. Newby undertook first to print 350
copies of "Wuthering Heights," but he afterwards declared he had
only printed 250. I doubt whether he could be induced to
return the £50 without a good deal of trouble — much more
than I should feel justified in delegating to Mr. Smith. For my
own part, the conclusion I drew from the whole of Mr. Newby's
conduct to my sisters was that he is a man with whom it is
desirable to have little to do. I think he must be needy as well
as tricky — and if he is, one would not distress him, even for one's
rights.

'If Mr. Smith thinks right to reprint "Wuthering Heights" and
"Agnes Grey," I would prepare a preface comprising a brief and
simple notice of the authors, such as might set at rest all erroneous
conjectures respecting their identity — and adding a few poetical
remains of each.

'In case this arrangement is approved, you will kindly let me
know, and I will commence the task (a sad, but, I believe, a
necessary one), and send it when finished. — I am, my dear sir,
yours sincerely,   C. Brontë.'

TO W. S. WILLIAMS.

'October 16, 1850.

'My dear Sir, — On the whole it is perhaps as well that the
last paragraph of the Preface should be omitted, for I believe it

was not expressed with the best grace in the world. You must
not, however, apologise for your suggestion — it was kindly meant
and, believe me, kindly taken; it was not *you* I misunderstood —
not for a moment, I never misunderstand you — I was thinking of
the critics and the public, who are always crying for a moral like the
Pharisees for a sign. Does this assurance quite satisfy you?

'I forgot to say that I had already heard, first from Miss Martineau, and subsequently through an intimate friend of Sydney
Yendy's (whose real name is Mr. Dobell) that it was to the author
of the "Roman" we are indebted for that eloquent article in the
"Palladium." I am glad you are going to send his poem, for I
much wished to see it.

'May I trouble you to look at a sentence in the Preface which I
have erased, because on reading it over I was not quite sure about
the scientific correctness of the expressions used. Metal, I know,
will burn in vivid-coloured flame, exposed to galvanic action, but
whether it is consumed, I am not sure. Perhaps you or Mr. Taylor
can tell me whether there is any blunder in the term employed —
if not, it might stand. — I am, yours sincerely,

'C. BRONTË.'

Miss Brontë would seem to have corresponded with Mr.
George Smith, and not with Mr. Williams, over her third
novel, 'Villette,' and that correspondence is to be found in
Mrs. Gaskell's biography.

TO W. S. WILLIAMS.

'FEBRUARY 1, 1851.

'MY DEAR SIR, — I cannot lose any time in telling you that
your letter, after all, gave me heart-felt satisfaction, and such a
feeling of relief as it would be difficult to express in words. The
fact is, what goads and tortures me is not any anxiety of my
own to publish another book, to have my name before the
public, to get cash, etc., but a haunting fear that my dilatori-
ness disappoints others. Now the "others" whose wish on the
subject I really care for, reduces itself to my father and
Cornhill, and since Cornhill ungrudgingly counsels me to take

my own time, I think I can pacify such impatience as my dear father naturally feels. Indeed, your kind and friendly letter will greatly help me.

'Since writing the above, I have read your letter to papa. Your arguments had weight with him : he approves, and I am content. I now only regret the necessity of disappointing the " Palladium," but that cannot be helped. — Good-bye, my dear sir, yours very sincerely,   C. BRONTË.'

TO MISS ELLEN NUSSEY.

'TUESDAY MORNING.

' DEAR ELLEN, — The rather dark view you seem inclined to take of the general opinion about " Villette," surprises me the less, dear Nell, as only the more unfavourable reviews seem to have come in your way. Some reports reach me of a different tendency ; but no matter, time will shew. As to the character of Lucy Snow, my intention from the first was that she should not occupy the pedestal to which Jane Eyre was raised by some injudicious admirers. She is where I meant her to be, and where no charge of self-laudation can touch her.

' I cannot accept your kind invitation. I must be at home at Easter, on two or three accounts connected with sermons to be preached, parsons to be entertained, Mechanics' Institute meetings and tea-drinkings to be solemnised, and ere long I have promised to go and see Mrs. Gaskell ; but till this wintry weather is passed, I would rather eschew visiting anywhere. I trust that bad cold of yours is *quite* well, and that you will take good care of yourself in future. That night work is always perilous. — Yours faithfully,   C. BRONTË.'

TO MISS WOOLER.

'HAWORTH, April 13, 1851.

' MY DEAR MISS WOOLER, — Your last kind letter ought to have been answered long since, and would have been, did I find it practicable to proportion the promptitude of the response to the value I place upon my correspondents and their communications. You will easily understand, however, that the contrary rule often holds good, and that the epistle which importunes often takes precedence of that which interests.

'My publishers express entire satisfaction with the reception which has been accorded to "Villette," and indeed the majority of the reviews has been favourable enough; you will be aware, however, that there is a minority, small in number but influential in character, which views the work with no favourable eye. Currer Bell's remarks on Romanism have drawn down on him the condign displeasure of the High Church party, which displeasure has been unequivocally expressed through their principal organs — the "Guardian," the "English Churchman," and the "Christian Remembrancer." I can well understand that some of the charges launched against me by those publications will tell heavily to my prejudice in the minds of most readers — but this must be borne; and for my part, I can suffer no accusation to oppress me much which is not supported by the inward evidence of conscience and reason.

'"Extremes meet," says the proverb; in proof whereof I would mention that Miss Martineau finds with "Villette" nearly the same fault as the Puseyites. She accuses me with attacking popery "with virulence," of going out of my way to assault it "passionately." In other respects she has shown with reference to the work a spirit so strangely and unexpectedly acrimonious, that I have gathered courage to tell her that the gulf of mutual difference between her and me is so wide and deep, the bridge of union so slight and uncertain, I have come to the conclusion that frequent intercourse would be most perilous and unadvisable, and have begged to adjourn *sine die* my long projected visit to her. Of course she is now very angry, and I know her bitterness will not be short-lived — but it cannot be helped.

'Two or three weeks since I received a long and kind letter from Mr. White, which I answered a short time ago. I believe Mr. White thinks me a much hotter advocate for *change* and what is called "political progress" than I am. However, in my reply, I did not touch on these subjects. He intimated a wish to publish some of his own MSS. I fear he would hardly like the somewhat dissuasive tendency of my answer; but really in these days of headlong competition, it is a great risk to publish. If all be well I purpose going to Manchester next week to spend a few days with Mrs. Gaskell. Ellen's visit to Yarmouth seems for the present given up; and really, all things considered, I think the circumstance is scarcely to be regretted.

'Do you not think, my dear Miss Wooler, that you could come to Haworth before you go to the coast? I am afraid that when you once get settled at the sea-side your stay will not be brief. I must repeat that a visit from you would be anticipated with pleasure, not only by me, but by every inmate of Haworth Parsonage. Papa has given me a general commission to send his respects to you whenever I write — accept them, there-fore and — Believe me, yours affectionately and sincerely,

'C. BRONTË.'

CHAPTER XIV.

WILLIAM SMITH WILLIAMS.

In picturing the circle which surrounded Charlotte Brontë through her brief career, it is of the utmost importance that a word of recognition should be given, and that in no half-hearted manner, to Mr. William Smith Williams, who, in her later years, was Charlotte Brontë's most intimate correspondent. The letters to Mr. Williams are far and away the best that Charlotte wrote, at least of those which have been preserved. They are full of literary enthusiasm and of intellectual interest. They show Charlotte Brontë's sound judgment and good heart more effectually than any other material which has been placed at the disposal of biographers. They are an honour both to writer and receiver, and, in fact, reflect the mind of the one as much as the mind of the other. Charlotte has emphasised the fact that she adapted herself to her correspondents, and in her letters to Mr. Williams we have her at her very best. Mr. Williams occupied for many years the post of 'reader' in the firm of Smith & Elder. That is a position scarcely less honourable and important than authorship itself. In our own days Mr. George Meredith and Mr. John Morley have been 'readers,' and Mr. James Payn has held the same post in the firm which published the Brontë novels.

Mr. Williams, who was born in 1800, and died in 1875, had an interesting career even before he became associated with Smith & Elder. In his younger days he was apprenticed to Taylor & Hessey of Fleet Street; and he used to relate how his boyish ideals of Coleridge were shattered on beholding, for the first time, the bulky and ponderous figure of the great talker. When Keats left England, for an early grave in Rome, it was Mr. Williams who saw him off. Hazlitt, Leigh Hunt, and many other well-known men of letters were friendly with Mr. Williams from his earliest days, and he had for brother-in-law, Wells, the author of 'Joseph and his Brethren.' In his association with Smith & Elder he secured the friendship of Thackeray, of Mrs. Gaskell, and of many other writers. He attracted the notice of Ruskin by a keen enthusiasm for the work of Turner. It was he, in fact, who compiled that most interesting volume of 'Selections from the writings of John Ruskin,' which has long gone out of print in its first form, but is still greatly sought for by the curious. In connection with this volume I may print here a letter written by John Ruskin's father to Mr. Williams, and I do so the more readily, as Mr. Williams's name was withheld from the title-page of the 'Selections.'

TO W. S. WILLIAMS.

'DENMARK HILL, November 25, 1861.

'MY DEAR SIR,— I am requested by Mrs. Ruskin to return her very sincere and grateful thanks for your kind consideration in presenting her with so beautifully bound a copy of the "Selections" from her son's writings; and which she will have great pleasure in seeing by the side of the very magnificent volumes which the liberality of the gentlemen of your house has already enriched our library with.

'Mrs. Ruskin joins me in offering congratulations on the great judgment you have displayed in your "Selections," and sending my own thanks and those of my son for the handsome gift to Mrs. Ruskin,— I am, my dear sir, yours very truly,

'JOHN JAMES RUSKIN.'

CHARLOTTE BRONTË

What Charlotte Brontë thought of Mr. Williams is sufficiently revealed by the multitude of letters which I have the good fortune to print, and that she had a reason to be grateful to him is obvious when we recollect that to him, and to him alone, was due her first recognition. The parcel containing 'The Professor' had wandered from publisher to publisher before it came into the hands of Mr. Williams. It was he who recognised what all of us recognise now, that in spite of faults it is really a most considerable book. I am inclined to think that it was refused by Smith & Elder rather on account of its insufficient length than for any other cause. At any rate it was the length which was assigned to her as a reason for non-acceptance. She was told that another book which would make the accredited three-volume novel, might receive more favourable consideration.

Charlotte Brontë took Mr. Williams's advice. She wrote 'Jane Eyre,' and despatched it quickly to Smith & Elder's house in Cornhill. It was read by Mr. Williams, and read afterwards by Mr. George Smith; and it was published with the success that we know. Charlotte awoke to find herself famous. She became a regular correspondent with Mr. Williams, and not less than a hundred letters were sent to him, most of them treating of interesting literary matters.

One of Mr. Williams's daughters, I may add, married Mr. Lowes Dickenson the portrait painter; his youngest child, a baby when Miss Brontë was alive, is famous in the musical world as Miss Anna Williams. The family has an abundance of literary and artistic association, but the father we know as the friend and correspondent of Charlotte Brontë. He still lives also in the memory of a large circle as a kindly and attractive — a singularly good and upright man.

Comment upon the following letters is in well-nigh every case superfluous.

AND HER CIRCLE

TO W. S. WILLIAMS.

'FEBRUARY 25, 1848.

'MY DEAR SIR, — I thank you for your note; its contents moved me much, though not to unmingled feelings of exultation. Louis Phillippe (unhappy and sordid old man!) and M. Guizot doubtless merit the sharp lesson they are now being taught, because they have both proved themselves men of dishonest hearts. And every struggle any nation makes in the cause of Freedom and Truth has something noble in it — something that makes me wish it success; but I cannot believe that France — or at least Paris — will ever be the battle-ground of true Liberty, or the scene of its real triumphs. I fear she does not know "how genuine glory is put on." Is that strength to be found in her which will not bend "but in magnanimous meekness"? Have not her "unceasing changes" as yet always brought "perpetual emptiness"? Has Paris the materials within her for thorough reform? Mean, dishonest Guizot being discarded, will any better successor be found for him than brilliant, unprincipled Thiers?

'But I damp your enthusiasm, which I would not wish to do, for true enthusiasm is a fine feeling whose flash I admire wherever I see it.

'The little note inclosed in yours is from a French lady, who asks my consent to the translation of "Jane Eyre" into the French language. I thought it better to consult you before I replied. I suppose she is competent to produce a decent translation, though one or two errors of orthography in her note rather afflict the eye; but I know that it is not unusual for what are considered well-educated French women to fail in the point of writing their mother tongue correctly. But whether competent or not, I presume she has a right to translate the book with or without my consent. She gives her address: Mdlle. B——[1] W. Cumming, Esq., 23 North Bank, Regent's Park.

'Shall I reply to her note in the affirmative?

'Waiting your opinion and answer, — I remain, dear sir, yours faithfully, C. BELL.'

[1] Thus in original letter.

CHARLOTTE BRONTË

TO W. S. WILLIAMS.

'FEBRUARY 28, 1848.

'DEAR SIR, — I have done as you advised me respecting Mdlle. B——, thanked her for her courtesy, and explained that I do not wish my consent to be regarded in the light of a formal sanction of the translation.

'From the papers of Saturday I had learnt the abdication of Louis Phillippe, the flight of the royal family, and the proclamation of a republic in France. Rapid movements these, and some of them difficult of comprehension to a remote spectator. What sort of spell has withered Louis Phillippe's strength? Why, after having so long infatuatedly clung to Guizot, did he at once ignobly relinquish him? Was it panic that made him so suddenly quit his throne and abandon his adherents without a struggle to retain one or aid the other?

'Perhaps it might have been partly fear, but I daresay it was still more long-gathering weariness of the dangers and toils of royalty. Few will pity the old monarch in his flight, yet I own he seems to me an object of pity. His sister's death shook him ; years are heavy on him ; the sword of Damocles has long been hanging over his head. One cannot forget that monarchs and ministers are only human, and have only human energies to sustain them ; and often they are sore beset. Party spirit has no mercy ; indignant Freedom seldom shows forbearance in her hour of revolt. I wish you *could* see the aged gentleman trudging down Cornhill with his umbrella and carpet-bag, in good earnest ; he would be safe in England : John Bull might laugh at him but he would do him no harm.

'How strange it appears to see literary and scientific names figuring in the list of members of a Provincial Government! How would it sound if Carlyle and Sir John Herschel and Tennyson and Mr. Thackeray and Douglas Jerrold were selected to manufacture a new constitution for England? Whether do such men sway the public mind most effectually from their quiet studies or from a council-chamber?

'And Thiers is set aside for a time; but won't they be glad of him by-and-by ? Can they set aside entirely anything so clever, so subtle, so accomplished, so aspiring — in a word, so thoroughly French as he is ? Is he not the man to bide his time — to watch while unskilful theorists try their hand at administration and fail; and then to step out and show them how it should be done ?

'One would have thought political disturbance the natural element of a mind like Thiers'; but I know nothing of him except from his writings, and I always think he writes as if the shade of Bonaparte were walking to and fro in the room behind him and dictating every line he pens, sometimes approaching and bending over his shoulder *pour voir de ses yeux* that such an action or event is represented or *mis*represented (as the case may be) exactly as he wishes it. Thiers seems to have contemplated Napoleon's character till he has imbibed some of its nature. Surely he must be an ambitious man, and, if so, surely he will at this juncture struggle to rise.

'You should not apologise for what you call your "crudities." You know I like to hear your opinions and views on whatever subject it interests you to discuss.

'From the little inscription outside your note I conclude you sent me the "Examiner." I thank you therefore for your kind intention and am sorry some unscrupulous person at the Post Office frustrated it, as no paper has reached my hands. I suppose one ought to be thankful that letters are respected, as newspapers are by no means sure of safe conveyance. — I remain, dear sir, yours sincerely,   C. BELL.'

TO W. S. WILLIAMS.

'MAY 12, 1848.

'My DEAR SIR, — I take a large sheet of paper, because I foresee that I am about to write another long letter, and for the same reason as before, viz., that yours interested me.

'I have received the "Morning Chronicle," and was both surprised and pleased to see the passage you speak of in one of its leading articles. An allusion of that sort seems to say more than a regular notice. I *do* trust I may have the power so to write in future as not to disappoint those who have been kind enough to think and speak well of "Jane Eyre;" at any rate, I will take pains. But still, whenever I hear my one book praised, the pleasure I feel is chastened by a mixture of doubt and fear; and, in truth, I hardly wish it to be otherwise: it is much too early for me to feel safe, or to take as my due the commendation bestowed.

'Some remarks in your last letter on teaching commanded my attention. I suppose you never were engaged in tuition yourself; but if you had been, you could not have more exactly hit on the great qualification — I had almost said the *one* great qualification — necessary to the task: the faculty, not merely of *acquiring* but of imparting knowledge — the power of influencing young minds — that natural fondness for, that innate sympathy with, children, which, you say, Mrs. Williams is so happy as to possess. He or she who possesses this faculty, this sympathy — though perhaps not otherwise highly accomplished — need never fear failure in the career of instruction. Children will be docile with them, will improve under them; parents will consequently repose in them confidence. Their task will be comparatively light, their path comparatively smooth. If the faculty be absent, the life of a teacher will be a struggle from beginning to end. No matter how amiable the disposition, how strong the sense of duty, how active the desire to please; no matter how brilliant and varied the accomplishments; if the governess has not the power to win her young charge, the secret to instil gently and surely her own knowledge into the growing mind intrusted to her, she will have a wearing, wasting existence of it. To *educate* a child, as I daresay Mrs, Williams has educated her children, probably with as much pleasure to herself as profit to them, will indeed be impossible to the teacher who lacks this qualification. But, I conceive, should circumstances — as in the case of your daughters — compel a young girl notwithstanding to adopt a governess's profession, she may contrive to *instruct* and even to instruct well. That is, though she cannot form the child's mind, mould its character, influence its disposition, and guide its conduct as she would wish, she may give lessons — even good, clear, clever lessons in the various branches of knowledge. She may earn and doubly earn her scanty salary as a daily governess. As a school-teacher she may succeed; but as a resident governess she will never (except under peculiar and exceptional circumstances) be happy. Her deficiency will harass her not so much in school-time as in play-hours; the moments that would be rest and recreation to the governess who understood and could adapt herself to children, will be almost torture to her who has not that power. Many a time, when her charge turns unruly on her hands, when the responsibility which she would wish to discharge faithfully and perfectly, becomes unmanageable to her, she will wish herself a housemaid or kitchen girl, rather than a baited, trampled, desolate, distracted governess.

'The Governesses' Institution may be an excellent thing in some points of view, but it is both absurd and cruel to attempt to raise still higher the standard of acquirements. Already governesses are not half nor a quarter paid for what they teach, nor in most instances is half or a quarter of their attainments required by their pupils. The young teacher's chief anxiety, when she sets out in life, always is to know a great deal; her chief fear that she should not know enough. Brief experience will, in most instances, show her that this anxiety has been misdirected. She will rarely be found too ignorant for her pupils; the demand on her knowledge will not often be larger than she can answer. But on her patience — on her self-control, the requirement will be enormous; on her animal spirits (and woe be to her if these fail!) the pressure will be immense.

'I have seen an ignorant nursery-maid who could scarcely read or write, by dint of an excellent, serviceable, sanguine, phlegmatic temperament, which made her at once cheerful and unmoveable; of a robust constitution and steady, unimpassionable nerves, which kept her firm under shocks and unharassed under annoyances — manage with comparative ease a large family of spoilt children, while their governess lived amongst them a life of inexpressible misery: tyrannised over, finding her efforts

377

to please and teach utterly vain, chagrined, distressed, worried — so badgered, so trodden on, that she ceased almost at last to know herself, and wondered in what despicable, trembling frame her oppressed mind was prisoned, and could not realise the idea of ever more being treated with respect and regarded with affection — till she finally resigned her situation and went away quite broken in spirit and reduced to the verge of decline in health.

'Those who would urge on governesses more acquirements, do not know the origin of their chief sufferings. It is more physical and mental strength, denser moral impassibility that they require, rather than additional skill in arts or sciences. As to the forcing system, whether applied to teachers or taught, I hold it to be a cruel system.

'It is true the world demands a brilliant list of accomplishments. For £20 per annum, it expects in one woman the attainments of several professors — but the demand is insensate, and I think should rather be resisted than complied with. If I might plead with you in behalf of your daughters, I should say, " Do not let them waste their young lives in trying to attain manifold accomplishments. Let them try rather to possess thoroughly, fully, one or two talents ; then let them endeavour to lay in a stock of health, strength, cheerfulness. Let them labour to attain self-control, endurance, fortitude, firmness ; if possible, let them learn from their mother something of the precious art she possesses — these things, together with sound principles, will be their best supports, their best aids through a governess's life."

'As for that one who, you say, has a nervous horror of exhibition, I need not beg you to be gentle with her ; I am sure you will not be harsh, but she must be firm with herself, or she will repent it in after life. She should begin by degrees to endeavour to overcome her diffidence. Were she destined to enjoy an independent, easy existence, she might respect her natural disposition to seek retirement, and even cherish it as a shade-loving virtue ; but since that is not her lot, since she is fated to make her way in the crowd, and to depend on herself, she should say : I will try and learn the art of self-possession, not that I may display my accomplishments, but that I may have the satisfaction of feeling that I am my own mistress, and can move and speak undaunted by the fear of man. While, however, I pen this piece of advice, I confess that it is much easier to give than to follow. What the sensations of the nervous are under the gaze of publicity none but the nervous know ; and how powerless reason and resolution are to control them would sound incredible except to the actual sufferers.

'The rumours you mention respecting the authorship of "Jane Eyre" amused me inexpressibly. The gossips are, on this subject, just where I should wish them to be, *i.e.*, as far from the truth as possible ; and as they have not a grain of fact to found their fictions upon, they fabricate pure inventions. Judge Erle must, I think, have made up his story expressly for a hoax ; the other *fib* is amazing — so circumstantial ! called on the author, forsooth ! Where did he live, I wonder ? In what purlieu of Cockayne ? Here I must stop, lest if I run on further I should fill another sheet. — Believe me, yours sincerely,

'CURRER BELL.

'P.S. — I must, after all, add a morsel of paper, for I find, on glancing over yours, that I have forgotten to answer a question you ask respecting my next work. I have not therein so far treated of governesses, as I do not wish it to resemble its predecessor. I often wish to say something about the " condition of women" question, but it is one respecting which so much " cant " has been talked, that one feels a sort of repugnance to approach it. It is true enough that the present market for female labour is quite overstocked, but where or how could another be opened ? Many say that the professions now filled only by men should be open to women also ; but are not their present occupants and candidates more than numerous enough to answer every demand ? Is there any room for female lawyers, female doctors, female engravers, for more female artists, more authoresses ? One can see where the evil lies, but who can point out the remedy ? When a woman has a little family to rear and educate and a household to conduct, her hands are full, her vocation is evident; when her destiny isolates her, I suppose she must do what she can, live as she can, complain as little, bear as much, work as well as possible. This is not high theory, but I believe it is sound practice, good to put into execution while philosophers and legislators ponder over the better ordering of the social system. At the same time, I conceive that when patience has done its utmost and industry its best, whether in the case of women or operatives, and when both are baffled, and pain and want triumph, the sufferer is free, is entitled, at last to send up to Heaven any piercing cry for relief, if by that cry he can hope to obtain succour.'

TO W. S. WILLIAMS.

'JUNE 2, 1848.

'MY DEAR SIR, — I snatch a moment to write a hasty line to you, for it makes me uneasy to think that your last kind letter should have remained so long unanswered. A succession of little engagements, much more importunate than important, have quite engrossed my time lately, to the exclusion of more momentous and interesting occupations. Interruption is a sad bore, and I believe there is hardly a spot on earth, certainly not in England, quite secure from its intrusion. The fact is, you cannot live in this world entirely for one aim; you must take along with some single serious purpose a hundred little minor duties, cares, distractions; in short, you must take life as it is, and make the best of it. Summer is decidedly a bad season for application, especially in the country; for the sunshine seems to set all your acquaintances astir, and once bent on amusement, they will come to the ends of the earth in search thereof. I was obliged to you for your suggestion about writing a letter to the " Morning Chronicle," but I did not follow it up. I think I would rather not venture on such a step at present. Opinions I would not hesitate to express to you — because you are indulgent — are not mature or cool enough for the public; Currer Bell is not Carlyle, and must not imitate him.

'Whenever you can write to me without encroaching too much
on your valuable time, remember I shall always be glad to hear
from you. Your last letter interested me fully as much as its two
predecessors; what you said about your family pleased me; I
think details of character always have a charm even when they
relate to people we have never seen, nor expect to see. With
eight children you must have a busy life; but, from the manner
in which you allude to your two eldest daughters, it is evident,
that they at least are a source of satisfaction to their parents;
I hope this will be the case with the whole number, and then
you will never feel as if you had too many. A dozen children
with sense and good conduct may be less burdensome than one
who lacks these qualities. It seems a long time since I heard
from you. I shall be glad to hear from you again. — Believe
me, yours sincerely, C. BELL.'

TO W. S. WILLIAMS.

'HAWORTH, June 15, 1848.

'MY DEAR SIR, — Thank you for your two last letters. In
reading the first I quite realised your May holiday; I enjoyed
it with you. I saw the pretty south-of-England village, so
different from our northern congregations of smoke-dark houses
clustered round their soot-vomiting mills. I saw in your description, fertile, flowery Essex — a contrast indeed to the rough
and rude, the mute and sombre yet well-beloved moors over-
spreading this corner of Yorkshire. I saw the white schoolhouse, the venerable school-master — I even thought I saw you
and your daughters; and in your second letter I see you all
distinctly, for in describing your children, you unconsciously
describe yourself.

'I may well say that your letters are of value to me, for I
seldom receive one but I find something in it which makes me
reflect, and reflect on new themes. Your town life is somewhat
different from any I have known, and your allusions to its advantages, troubles, pleasures, and struggles are often full of
significance to me.

'I have always been accustomed to think that the necessity of
381

earning one's subsistence is not in itself an evil, but I feel it may become a heavy evil if health fails, if employment lacks, if the demand upon our efforts made by the weakness of others dependent upon us becomes greater than our strength suffices to answer. In such a case I can imagine that the married man may wish himself single again, and that the married woman, when she sees her husband over-exerting himself to maintain her and her children, may almost wish — out of the very force of her affection for him — that it had never been her lot to add to the weight of his responsibilities. Most desirable then is it that all, both men and women, should have the power and the will to work for themselves — most advisable that both sons and daughters should early be inured to habits of independence and industry. Birds teach their nestlings to fly as soon as their wings are strong enough, they even oblige them to quit the nest if they seem too unwilling to trust their pinions of their own accord. Do not the swallow and the starling thus give a lesson by which man might profit?

'It seems to me that your kind heart is pained by the thought of what your daughter may suffer if transplanted from a free and indulged home existence to a life of constraint and labour amongst strangers. Suffer she probably will; but take both comfort and courage, my dear sir, try to soothe your anxiety by this thought which is not a fallacious one. Hers will not be a barren suffering; she will gain by it largely; she will "sow in tears to reap in joy." A governess's experience is frequently indeed bitter, but its results are precious: the mind, feeling, temper are there subjected to a discipline equally painful and priceless. I have known many who were unhappy as governesses, but not one who regretted having undergone the ordeal, and scarcely one whose character was not improved — at once strengthened and purified, fortified and softened, made more enduring for her own afflictions, more considerate for the afflictions of others, by passing through it.

'Should your daughter, however, go out as governess, she should first take a firm resolution not to be too soon daunted by difficulties, too soon disgusted by disagreeables; and if she has a high spirit, sensitive feelings, she should tutor the one to submit, the other to endure, *for the sake of those at home.* That is the governess's best talisman of patience, it is the best balm for wounded susceptibility. When tried hard she must say, "I will be patient, not out of servility, but because I love my parents, and wish through my perseverance, diligence, and success, to repay their anxieties and tenderness for me." With this aid the least-deserved insult may often be swallowed quite calmly, like a bitter pill with a draught of fair water.

'I think you speak excellent sense when you say that girls without fortune should be brought up and accustomed to support themselves ; and that if they marry poor men, it should be with a prospect of being able to help their partners. If all parents thought so, girls would not be reared on speculation with a view to their making mercenary marriages ; and, consequently, women would not be so piteously degraded as they now too often are.

'Fortuneless people may certainly marry, provided they previously resolve never to let the consequences of their marriage throw them as burdens on the hands of their relatives. But as life is full of unforeseen contingencies, and as a woman may be so placed that she cannot possibly both "guide the house" and earn her livelihood (what leisure, for instance, could Mrs. Williams have with her eight children ?), young artists and young governesses should think twice before they unite their destinies.

'You speak sense again when you express a wish that Fanny were placed in a position where active duties would engage her attention, where her faculties would be exercised and her mind occupied, and where, I will add, not doubting that my addition merely completes your half-approved idea, the image of the young artist would for the present recede into the background and remain for a few years to come in modest perspective, the finishing point of a vista stretching a considerable distance into futurity. Fanny may feel sure of this : if she intends to be an artist's wife she had better try an apprenticeship with Fortune as a governess first ; she cannot undergo a better preparation for that honourable

(honourable if rightly considered) but certainly not luxurious destiny.

'I should say then — judging as well as I can from the materials for forming an opinion your letter affords, and from what I can thence conjecture of Fanny's actual and prospective position — that you would do well and wisely to put your daughter out. The experiment might do good and could not do harm, because even if she failed at the first trial (which is not unlikely) she would still be in some measure benefited by the effort.

'I duly received "Mirabeau" from Mr. Smith. I must repeat it is really *too* kind. When I have read the book, I will tell you what I think of it — its subject is interesting. One thing a little annoyed me — as I glanced over the pages I fancied I detected a savour of Carlyle's peculiarities of style. Now Carlyle is a great man, but I always wish he would write plain English; and to imitate his Germanisms is, I think, to imitate his faults. Is the author of this work a Manchester man? I must not ask his name I suppose.— Believe me, my dear sir, yours sincerely,   CURRER BELL.'

TO W. S. WILLIAMS.

'JUNE 22, 1848.

'MY DEAR SIR,— After reading a book which has both interested and informed you, you like to be able, on laying it down, to speak of it with unqualified approbation — to praise it cordially; you do not like to stint your panegyric, to counteract its effect with blame.

'For this reason I feel a little difficulty in telling you what I think of "The Life of Mirabeau." It has interested me much, and I have derived from it additional information. In the course of reading it, I have often felt called upon to approve the ability and tact of the writer, to admire the skill with which he conducts the narrative, enchains the reader's attention, and keeps it fixed upon his hero; but I have also been moved frequently to disapprobation. It is not the political principles of the writer with which I find fault, nor is it his talents I feel inclined to disparage; to speak truth, it is his manner of treating Mirabeau's errors that offends — then, I think, he is neither wise nor right — there, I think, he betrays a little of crudeness, a little of presumption, not a little of indiscretion.

'Could you with confidence put this work into the hands of your son, secure that its perusal would not harm him, that it would not leave on his mind some vague impression that there is a grandeur in vice committed on a colossal scale? Whereas, the fact is, that in vice there is no grandeur, that it is, on whichever side you view it, and in whatever accumulation, only a foul, sordid, and degrading thing. The fact is, that this great Mirabeau was a mixture of divinity and dirt; that there was no divinity whatever in his errors, they were all sullying dirt; that they ruined him, brought down his genius to the kennel, deadened his fine nature and generous sentiments, made all his greatness as nothing; that they cut him off in his prime, obviated all his aims, and struck him dead in the hour when France most needed him.

'Mirabeau's life and fate teach, to my perception, the most depressing lesson I have read for years. One would fain have hoped that so many noble qualities *must* have made a noble character and achieved noble ends. No — the mighty genius lived a miserable and degraded life, and died a dog's death, for want of self-control, for want of morality, for lack of religion. One's heart is wrung for Mirabeau after reading his life; and it is not of his greatness we think, when we close the volume, so much as of his hopeless recklessness, and of the sufferings, degradation, and untimely end in which it issued. It appears to me that the biographer errs also in being too solicitous to present his hero always in a striking point of view — too negligent of the exact truth. He eulogises him too much; he subdues all the other characters mentioned and keeps them in the shade that Mirabeau may stand out more conspicuously. This, no doubt, is right in art, and admissible in fiction; but in history (and biography is the history of an individual) it tends to weaken the force of a narrative by weakening your faith in its accuracy.

CHARLOTTE BRONTË

TO W. S. WILLIAMS.

'CHAPTER COFFEE-HOUSE, IVY LANE,
'July 8, 1848.

'MY DEAR SIR, — Your invitation is too welcome not to be at once accepted. I should much like to see Mrs. Williams and her children, and very much like to have a quiet chat with yourself. Would it suit you if we came to-morrow, after dinner — say about seven o'clock, and spent Sunday evening with you?

'We shall be truly glad to see you whenever it is convenient to you to call. — I am, my dear sir, yours faithfully,

'C. BRONTË.'

TO W. S. WILLIAMS.

'HAWORTH, July 13, 1848.

'MY DEAR SIR, — We reached home safely yesterday, and in a day or two I doubt not we shall get the better of the fatigues of our journey.

'It was a somewhat hasty step to hurry up to town as we did, but I do not regret having taken it. In the first place, mystery is irksome, and I was glad to shake it off with you and Mr. Smith, and to show myself to you for what I am, neither more nor less — thus removing any false expectations that may have arisen under the idea that Currer Bell had a just claim to the masculine cognomen he, perhaps somewhat presumptuously, adopted — that he was, in short, of the nobler sex.

'I was glad also to see you and Mr. Smith, and am very happy now to have such pleasant recollections of you both, and of your respective families. My satisfaction would have been complete could I have seen Mrs. Williams. The appearance of your children tallied on the whole accurately with the description you had given of them. Fanny was the one I saw least distinctly; I tried to get a clear view of her countenance, but her position in the room did not favour my efforts.

'I had just read your article in the " John Bull " ; it very clearly and fully explains the cause of the difference obvious between ancient and modern paintings. I wish you had been with us when we went over the Exhibition and the National Gallery, a little explanation from a judge of art would doubtless have enabled us to understand better what we saw ; perhaps, one day, we may have this pleasure.

'Accept my own thanks and my sister's for your kind attention to us while in town, and — Believe me, yours sincerely,

'CHARLOTTE BRONTË.

'I trust Mrs. Williams . is quite recovered from her indisposition.'

TO. W. S. WILLIAMS.

'HAWORTH, July 31, 1848.

'MY DEAR SIR, — I have lately been reading "Modern Painters," and I have derived from the work much genuine pleasure and, I hope, some edification ; at any rate, it made me feel how ignorant I had previously been on the subject which it treats. Hitherto I have only had instinct to guide me in judging of art ; I feel more as if I had been walking blindfold — this book seems to give me eyes. I *do* wish I had pictures within reach by which to test the new sense. Who can read these glowing descriptions of Turner's works without longing to see them ? However eloquent and convincing the language in which another's opinion is placed before you, you still wish to judge for yourself. I like this author's style much : there is both energy and beauty in it ; I like himself too, because he is such a hearty admirer. He does not give Turner half-measure of praise or veneration, he eulogises, he reverences him (or rather his genius) with his whole soul. One can sympathise with that sort of devout, serious admiration (for he is no rhapsodist) — one can respect it ; and yet possibly many people would laugh at it. I am truly obliged to Mr. Smith for giving me this book, not having often met with one that has pleased me more.

'You will have seen some of the notices of "Wildfell Hall." I wish my sister felt the unfavourable ones less keenly. She does not *say* much, for she is of a remarkably taciturn, still, thoughtful nature, reserved even with her nearest of kin, but I cannot avoid seeing that her spirits are depressed sometimes. The fact

387

CHARLOTTE BRONTË

is, neither she nor any of us expected that view to be taken of the
book which has been taken by some critics. That it had faults of
execution, faults of art, was obvious, but faults of intention or
feeling could be suspected by none who knew the writer. For
my own part, I consider the subject unfortunately chosen — it was
one the author was not qualified to handle at once vigorously and
truthfully. The simple and natural — quiet description and simple
pathos are, I think, Acton Bell's forte. I liked "Agnes Grey"
better than the present work.

'Permit me to caution you not to speak of my sisters when
you write to me. I mean, do not use the word in the plural.
Ellis Bell will not endure to be alluded to under any other appellation than the *nom de plume*. I committed a grand error in betray-
ing his identity to you and Mr. Smith. It was inadvertent — the
words, "we are three sisters" escaped me before I was aware. I
regretted the avowal the moment I had made it; I regret it
bitterly now, for I find it is against every feeling and intention of
Ellis Bell.

'I was greatly amused to see in the "Examiner" of this week
one of Newby's little cobwebs neatly swept away by some dexter-
ous brush. If Newby is not too old to profit by experience, such
an exposure ought to teach him that "Honesty is indeed the best
policy."

'Your letter has just been brought to me. I must not pause to
thank you, I should say too much. Our life is, and always has
been, one of few pleasures, as you seem in part to guess, and for
that reason we feel what passages of enjoyment come in our way
very keenly; and I think if you knew *how* pleased I am to get a long
letter from you, you would laugh at me.

'In return, however, I smile at you for the earnestness with
which you urge on us the propriety of seeing something of
London society. There would be an advantage in it — a great
advantage; yet it is one that no power on earth could induce
Ellis Bell, for instance, to avail himself of. And even for Acton
and Currer, the experiment of an introduction to society would be
more formidable than you, probably, can well imagine. An
existence of absolute seclusion and unvarying monotony, such

as we have long — I may say, indeed, ever been habituated to, tends, I fear, to unfit the mind for lively and exciting scenes, to destroy the capacity for social enjoyment.

'The only glimpses of society I have ever had were obtained in my vocation of governess, and some of the most miserable moments I can recall were passed in drawing-rooms full of strange faces. At such times, my animal spirits would ebb gradually till they sank quite away, and when I could endure the sense of exhaustion and solitude no longer, I used to steal off, too glad to find any corner where I could really be alone. Still, I know very well, that though that experiment of seeing the world might give acute pain for the time, it would do good afterwards; and as I have never, that I remember, gained any important good without incurring proportionate suffering, I mean to try to take your advice some day, in part at least — to put off, if possible, that troublesome egotism which is always judging and blaming itself, and to try, country spinster as I am, to get a view of some sphere where civilised humanity is to be contemplated.

'I smile at you again for supposing that I could be annoyed by what you say respecting your religious and philosophical views; that I could blame you for not being able, when you look amongst sects and creeds, to discover any one which you can exclusively and implicitly adopt as yours. I perceive myself that some light falls on earth from Heaven — that some rays from the shrine of truth pierce the darkness of this life and world, but they are few, faint, and scattered, and who without presumption can assert that he has found the *only* true path upwards?

'Yet ignorance, weakness, or indiscretion, must have their creeds and forms; they must have their props — they cannot walk alone. Let them hold by what is purest in doctrine and simplest in ritual; *something*, they *must* have.

'I never read Emerson; but the book which has had so healing an effect on your mind must be a good one. Very enviable is the writer whose words have fallen like a gentle rain on a soil that so needed and merited refreshment, whose influence has come like a genial breeze to lift a spirit which circumstances seem so harshly to have trampled. Emerson, if he has cheered you, has not written in vain.

'May this feeling of self-reconcilement, of inward peace and strength, continue! May you still be lenient with, be just to, yourself! I will not praise nor flatter you, I should hate to pay those enervating compliments which tend to check the exertions of a mind that aspires after excellence; but I must permit myself to remark that if you had not something good and superior in you, something better, whether more *showy* or not, than is often met with, the assurance of your friendship would not make one so happy as it does; nor would the advantage of your correspondence be felt as such a privilege.

'I hope Mrs. Williams's state of health may soon improve and her anxieties lessen. Blamable indeed are those who sow division where there ought to be peace, and especially deserving of the ban of society.

'I thank both you and your family for keeping our secret. It will indeed be a kindness to us to persevere in doing so; and I own I have a certain confidence in the honourable discretion of a household of which you are the head. — Believe me, yours very sincerely,   C. BRONTË.'

TO W. S. WILLIAMS.

'OCTOBER 18, 1848.

'MY DEAR SIR, — Not feeling competent this evening either for study or serious composition, I will console myself with writing to you. My malady, which the doctors call a bilious fever, lingers, or rather it returns with each sudden change of weather, though I am thankful to say that the relapses have hitherto been much milder than the first attack, but they keep me weak and reduced, especially as I am obliged to observe a very low spare diet.

'My book, alas! is laid aside for the present; both head and hand seem to have lost their cunning; imagination is pale, stagnant, mute. This incapacity chagrins me; sometimes I have a feeling of cankering care on the subject, but I combat it as well as I can, it does no good.

'I am afraid I shall not write a cheerful letter to you. A letter, however, of some kind I am determined to write, for I should be sorry to appear a neglectful correspondent to one from whose communications I have derived, and still derive, so much pleasure. Do not talk about not being on a level with Currer Bell, or regard him as "an awful person"; if you saw him now, sitting muffled at the fireside, shrinking before the east wind (which for some days has been blowing wild and keen over our cold hills), and incapable of lifting a pen for any less formidable task than that of writing a few lines to an indulgent friend, you would be sorry not to deem yourself greatly his superior, for you would feel him to be a poor creature.

'You may be sure I read your views on the providence of God and the nature of man with interest. You are already aware that in much of what you say my opinions coincide with those you express, and where they differ I shall not attempt to bias you. Thought and conscience are, or ought to be, free ; and, at any rate, if your views were universally adopted there would be no persecution, no bigotry. But never try to proselytise, the world is not yet fit to receive what you and Emerson say : man, as he now is, can no more do without creeds and forms in religion than he can do without laws and rules in social intercourse. You and Emerson judge others by yourselves ; all mankind are not like you, any more than every Israelite was like Nathaniel.

' "Is there a human being," you ask, "so depraved that an act of kindness will not touch — nay, a word melt him ?" There are hundreds of human beings who trample on acts of kindness and mock at words of affection. I know this though I have seen but little of the world. I suppose I have something harsher in my nature than you have, something which every now and then tells me dreary secrets about my race, and I cannot believe the voice of the Optimist, charm he never so wisely. On the other hand, I feel forced to listen when a Thackeray speaks. I know truth is delivering her oracles by his lips.

' As to the great, good, magnanimous acts which have been

performed by some men, we trace them up to motives and then estimate their value; a few, perhaps, would gain and many lose by this test. The study of motives is a strange one, not to be pursued too far by one fallible human being in reference to his fellows.

'Do not condemn me as uncharitable. I have no wish to urge my convictions on you, but I know that while there are many good, sincere, gentle people in the world, with whom kindness is all-powerful, there are also not a few like that false friend (I had almost written *fiend*) whom you so well and vividly described in one of your late letters, and who, in acting out his part of domestic traitor, must often have turned benefits into weapons wherewith to wound his benefactors. — Believe me, yours sincerely,   C. BRONTË.'

TO W. S. WILLIAMS.

'APRIL 2, 1849.

'MY DEAR SIR, — My critics truly deserve and have my genuine thanks for the friendly candour with which they have declared their opinions on my book. Both Mr. Williams and Mr. Taylor express and support their opinions in a manner calculated to command careful consideration. In my turn I have a word to say. You both of you dwell too much on what you regard as the *artistic* treatment of a subject. Say what you will, gentlemen — say it as ably as you will — truth is better than art. Burns' Songs are better than Bulwer's Epics. Thackeray's rude, careless sketches are preferable to thousands of carefully finished paintings. Ignorant as I am, I dare to hold and maintain that doctrine.

'You must not expect me to give up Malone and Donne too suddenly — the pair are favourites with me; they shine with a chastened and pleasing lustre in that first chapter, and it is a pity you do not take pleasure in their modest twinkle. Neither is that opening scene irrelevant to the rest of the book, there are other touches in store which will harmonise with it.

'No doubt this handling of the surplice will stir up such

publications as the "Christian Remembrancer" and the "Quarterly"— those heavy Goliaths of the periodical press; and if I alone were concerned, this possibility would not trouble me a second. Full welcome would the giants be to stand in their greaves of brass, poising their ponderous spears, cursing their prey by their gods, and thundering invitations to the intended victim to "come forth" and have his flesh given to the fowls of the air and the beasts of the field. Currer Bell, without pretending to be a David, feels no awe of the unwieldy Anakim ; but — comprehend me rightly, gentleman — it would grieve him to involve others in blame : any censure that would really injure and annoy his publishers would wound himself. Therefore believe that he will not act rashly — trust his discretion.

'Mr. Taylor is right about the bad taste of the opening apostrophe — that I had already condemned in my own mind. Enough said of a work in embryo. Permit me to request in conclusion that the MS. may now be returned as soon as convenient.

'The letter you inclosed is from Mary Howitt. It contained a proposal for an engagement as contributor to an American periodical. Of course I have negatived it. When I *can* write, the book I have in hand must claim all my attention. Oh ! if Anne were well, if the void Death has left were a little closed up, if the dreary word *nevermore* would cease sounding in my ears, I think I could yet do something.

'It is a long time since you mentioned your own family affairs. I trust Mrs. Williams continues well, and that Fanny and your other children prosper.— Yours sincerely,   C. BRONTË.'

TO W. S. WILLIAMS.

'JULY 3, 1849.

'MY DEAR SIR,— You do right 'to address 'me on subjects which compel me, in order to give a coherent answer, to quit for a moment my habitual train of thought. The mention of your healthy-living daughters reminds me of the world where other people live — where I lived once. Theirs are cheerful

images as you present them — I have no wish to shut them
out.

'From all you say of Ellen, the eldest, I am inclined to
respect her much. I like practical sense which works to the good
of others. I esteem a dutiful daughter who makes her parents
happy.

'Fanny's character I would take on second hand from nobody,
least of all from her kind father, whose estimate of human nature
in general inclines rather to what *ought* to be than to what *is*. Of
Fanny I would judge for myself, and that not hastily nor on first
impressions.

'I am glad to hear that Louisa has a chance of a presentation
to Queen's College. I hope she will succeed. Do not, my dear
sir, be indifferent — be earnest about it. Come what may afterwards, an education secured is an advantage gained — a priceless
advantage. Come what may, it is a step towards independency,
and one great curse of a single female life is its dependency. It
does credit both to Louisa's heart and head that she herself wishes
to get this presentation. Encourage her in the wish. Your
daughters — no more than your sons — should be a burden on
your hands. Your daughters — as much as your sons — should
aim at making their way honourably through life. Do not wish
to keep them at home. Believe me, teachers may be hard-worked,
ill-paid, and despised, but the girl who stays at home doing nothing
is worse off than the hardest-wrought and worst-paid drudge of a
school. Whenever I have seen, not merely in humble, but in
affluent homes, families of daughters sitting waiting to be married,
I have pitied them from my heart. It is doubtless well — very
well — if Fate decrees them a happy marriage ; but, if otherwise,
give their existence some object, their time some occupation, or the
peevishness of disappointment and the listlessness of idleness
will infallibly degrade their nature.

'Should Louisa eventually go out as a governess, do not be
uneasy respecting her lot. The sketch you give of her character leads me to think she has a better chance of happiness than one in a hundred of her sisterhood. Of pleasing
exterior (that is always an advantage — children like it), good

sense, obliging disposition, cheerful, healthy, possessing a good
average capacity, but no prominent master talent to make her
miserable by its cravings for exercise, by its mutiny under restraint. Louisa thus endowed will find the post of governess
comparatively easy. If she be like her mother — as you say she
is — and if, consequently, she is fond of children, and possesses
tact for managing them, their care is her natural vocation — she
ought to be a governess.

'Your sketch of Braxborne, as it is and as it was, is sadly
pleasing. I remember your first picture of it in a letter written
a year ago — only a year ago. I was in this room — where I now
am — when I received it. I was not alone then. In those days
your letters often served as a text for comment — a theme for
talk ; now, I read them, return them to their covers and put
them away. Johnson, I think, makes mournful mention somewhere of the pleasure that accrues when we are " solitary and
cannot impart it." Thoughts, under such circumstances, cannot
grow to words, impulses fail to ripen to actions.

'Lonely as I am, how should I be if Providence had never
given me courage to adopt a career — perseverance to plead
through two long, weary years with publishers till they admitted
me ? How should I be with youth past, sisters lost, a resident in
a moorland parish where there is not a single educated family ?
In that case I should have no world at all: the raven, weary of
surveying the deluge, and without an ark to return to, would be
my type. As it is, something like a hope and motive sustains
me still. I wish all your daughters — I wish every woman in
England, had also a hope and motive. Alas ! there are many old
maids who have neither. — Believe me, yours sincerely,

'C. BRONTË.'

TO W. S. WILLIAMS.

'JULY 26, 1849.

'MY DEAR SIR, — I must rouse myself to write a line to you,
lest a more protracted silence should seem strange.

'Truly glad was I to hear of your daughter's success. I trust
its results may conduce to the permanent advantage both of herself and her parents.

CHARLOTTE BRONTË

'Of still more importance than your children's education is your wife's health, and therefore it is still more gratifying to learn that your anxiety on that account is likely to be alleviated. For her own sake, no less than for that of others, it is to be hoped that she is now secured from a recurrence of her painful and dangerous attacks. It was pleasing, too, to hear of good qualities being developed in the daughters by the mother's danger. May your girls always so act as to justify their father's kind estimate of their characters; may they never do what might disappoint or grieve him.

'Your suggestion relative to myself is a good one in some respects, but there are two persons whom it would not suit; and not the least incommoded of these would be the young person whom I might request to come and bury herself in the hills of Haworth, to take a church and stony churchyard for her prospect, the dead silence of a village parsonage — in which the tick of the clock is heard all day long — for her atmosphere, and a grave, silent spinster for her companion. I should not like to see youth thus immured. The hush and gloom of our house would be more oppressive to a buoyant than to a subdued spirit. The fact is, my work is my best companion; hereafter I look for no great earthly comfort except what congenial occupation can give. For society, long seclusion has in a great measure unfitted me, I doubt whether I should enjoy it if I might have it. Sometimes I think I should, and I thirst for it; but at other times I doubt my capability of pleasing or deriving pleasure. The prisoner in solitary confinement, the toad in the block of marble, all in time shape themselves to their lot. — Yours sincerely,   C. Brontë.'

TO W. S. WILLIAMS.

'September 13, 1849.

'My dear Sir, — I want to know your opinion of the subject of this proof-sheet. Mr. Taylor censured it; he considers as defective all that portion which relates to Shirley's nervousness — the bite of the dog, etc. How did it strike you on reading it?

'I ask this though I well know it cannot now be altered. I can work indefatigably at the correction of a work before it leaves my hands, but when once I have looked on it as completed and submitted to the inspection of others, it becomes next to impossible to alter or amend. With the heavy suspicion on my mind that all may not be right, I yet feel forced to put up with the inevitably wrong.

'Reading has, of late, been my great solace and recreation. I have read J. C. Hare's "Guesses at Truth," a book containing things that in depth and far-sought wisdom sometimes recall the "Thoughts" of Pascal, only it is as the light of the moon recalls that of the sun.

'I have read with pleasure a little book on "English Social Life" by the wife of Archbishop Whately. Good and intelligent women write well on such subjects. This lady speaks of governesses. I was struck by the contrast offered in her manner of treating the topic to that of Miss Rigby in the "Quarterly." How much finer the feeling — how much truer the feeling — how much more delicate the mind here revealed!

'I have read "David Copperfield"; it seems to me very good — admirable in some parts. You said it had affinity to "Jane Eyre." It has, now and then — only what an advantage has Dickens in his varied knowledge of men and things! I am beginning to read Eckermann's "Goethe" — it promises to be a most interesting work. Honest, simple, single-minded Eckermann! Great, powerful, giant-souled, but also profoundly egotistical, old Johann Wolfgang von Goethe! He *was* a mighty egotist — I see he was: he thought no more of swallowing up poor Eckermann's existence in his own than the whale thought of swallowing Jonah.

'The worst of reading graphic accounts of such men, of seeing graphic pictures of the scenes, the society, in which they moved, is that it excites a too tormenting longing to look on the reality. But does such reality now exist? Amidst all the troubled waters of European society does such a vast, strong, selfish, old Leviathan now roll ponderous! I suppose not. — Believe me, yours sincerely,   C. BRONTË.'

CHARLOTTE BRONTË

TO W. S. WILLIAMS.

'MARCH 19, 1850.

' MY DEAR SIR, — The books came yesterday evening just as I was wishing for them very much. There is much interest for me in opening the Cornhill parcel. I wish there was not pain too — but so it is. As I untie the cords and take out the volumes, I am reminded of those who once on similar occasions looked on eagerly; I miss familiar voices commenting mirthfully and pleasantly; the room seems very still, very empty; but yet there is consolation in remembering that papa will take pleasure in some of the books. Happiness quite unshared can scarcely be called happiness — it has no taste.

' I hope Mrs. Williams continues well, and that she is beginning to regain composure after the shock of her recent bereavement. She has indeed sustained a loss for which there is no substitute. But rich as she still is in objects for her best affections, I trust the void will not be long or severely felt. She must think, not of what she has lost, but of what she possesses. With eight fine children, how can she ever be poor or solitary. — Believe me, dear sir, yours sincerely, C. BRONTË.'

TO W. S. WILLIAMS.

'APRIL 12, 1850.

' MY DEAR SIR, — I own I was glad to receive your assurance that the Calcutta paper's surmise was unfounded.[1] It is said that when we *wish* a thing to be true, we are prone to believe it true; but I think (judging from myself) we adopt with a still prompter credulity the rumour which shocks.

' It is very kind in Dr. Forbes to give me his book. I hope Mr. Smith will have the goodness to convey my thanks for the present. You can keep it to send with the next parcel, or perhaps I may be in London myself before May is over. That invitation I mentioned in a previous letter is still urged upon me, and well as I know what penance its acceptance would entail in some points, I also know the advantage it would bring in others. My conscience tells me it would be

---

[1] That Thackeray had written a certain unfavourable critique of ' Shirley.'

the act of a moral poltroon to let the fear of suffering stand in the way of improvement. But suffer I shall. No matter.

'The perusal of "Southey's Life" has lately afforded me much pleasure. The autobiography with which it commences is deeply interesting, and the letters which follow are scarcely less so, disclosing as they do a character most estimable in its integrity and a nature most amiable in its benevolence, as well as a mind admirable in its talent. Some people assert that genius is inconsistent with domestic happiness, and yet Southey was happy at home and made his home happy; he not only loved his wife and children *though* he was a poet, but he loved them the better *because* he was a poet. He seems to have been without taint of worldliness. London with its pomps and vanities, learned coteries with their dry pedantry, rather scared than attracted him. He found his prime glory in his genius, and his chief felicity in home affections. I like Southey.

'I have likewise read one of Miss Austen's works — "Emma" — read it with interest and with just the degree of admiration which Miss Austen herself would have thought sensible and suitable. Anything like warmth or enthusiasm — anything energetic, poignant, heart-felt is utterly out of place in commending these works : all such demonstration the authoress would have met with a well-bred sneer, would have calmly scorned as outré and extravagant. She does her business of delineating the surface of the lines of genteel English people curiously well. There is a Chinese fidelity, a miniature delicacy in the painting. She ruffles her reader by nothing vehement, disturbs him by nothing profound. The passions are perfectly unknown to her; she rejects even a speaking acquaintance with that stormy sisterhood. Even to the feelings she vouchsafes no more than an occasional graceful but distant recognition — too frequent converse with them would ruffle the smooth elegance of her progress. Her business is not half so much with the human heart as with the human eyes, mouth, hands, and feet. What sees keenly, speaks aptly, moves flexibly, it suits her to study; but what throbs fast and full, though hidden, what the blood rushes through, what is the unseen

CHARLOTTE BRONTË

seat of life and the sentient target of death — this Miss Austen
ignores. She no more, with her mind's eye, beholds the heart
of her race than each man, with bodily vision, sees the heart in
his heaving breast. Jane Austen was a complete and most
sensible lady, but a very incomplete and rather insensible
(*not senseless*) woman. If this is heresy, I cannot help it. If I
said it to some people (Lewes for instance) they would directly
accuse me of advocating exaggerated heroics, but I am not
afraid of your falling into any such vulgar error. — Believe me,
yours sincerely, C. BRONTË.'

TO W. S. WILLIAMS.

'NOVEMBER 9, 1850.

'MY DEAR SIR, — I have read Lord John Russell's letter with
very great zest and relish, and think him a spirited sensible little
man for writing it. He makes no old-womanish outcry of alarm
and expresses no exaggerated wrath. One of the best paragraphs
is that which refers to the Bishop of London and the Puseyites.
Oh! I wish Dr. Arnold were yet living, or that a second Dr.
Arnold could be found! Were there but ten such men amongst
the hierarchs of the Church of England she might bid defiance
to all the scarlet hats and stockings in the Pope's gift. Her
sanctuaries would be purified, her rites reformed, her withered
veins would swell again with vital sap ; but it is not so.

'It is well that *truth* is *indestructible* — that ruin cannot crush
nor fire annihilate her divine essence. While forms change and
institutions perish, "*truth* is great and shall prevail."

'I am truly glad to hear that Miss Kavanagh's health is
improved. You can send her book whenever it is most convenient.
I received from Cornhill the other day a periodical containing a
portrait of Jenny Lind — a sweet, natural, innocent peasant-girl
face, curiously contrasted with an artificial fine-lady dress. I *do*
like and esteem Jenny's character. Yet not long since I heard
her torn to pieces by the tongue of detraction — scarcely a virtue
left — twenty odious defects imputed.

'There was likewise a most faithful portrait of R. H. Horne,
with his imaginative forehead and somewhat foolish-looking
400

mouth and chin, indicating that mixed character which I should think he owns. Mr. Horne writes well. That tragedy on the "Death of Marlowe" reminds me of some of the best of Dumas' dramatic pieces. — Yours very sincerely,   C. Brontë.'

TO MISS ELLEN NUSSEY.

'January, 1851.

'Dear Ellen, — I sent yesterday the "Leader" newspaper, which you must always send to Hunsworth as soon as you have done with it. I will continue to forward it as long as I get it.

'I am trying a little Hydropathic treatment; I like it, and I think it has done me good. Inclosed is a letter received a few days since. I wish you to read it because it gives a very fair notion both of the disposition and mind ; read, return, and tell me what you think of it.

'Thackeray has given dreadful trouble by his want of punctuality. Mr. Williams says if he had not been helped out with the vigour, energy, and method of Mr. Smith, he must have sunk under the day and night labour of the last few weeks.

'Write soon.   C. B.,

TO W. S. WILLIAMS.

'July 21, 1851.

'My dear Sir, — I delayed answering your very interesting letter until the box should have reached me ; and now that it is come I can only acknowledge its arrival : I cannot say at all what I felt as I unpacked its contents. These Cornhill parcels have something of the magic charm of a fairy gift about them, as well as of the less poetical but more substantial pleasure of a box from home received at school. You have sent me this time even more books than usual, and all good.

'What shall I say about the twenty numbers of splendid engravings laid cosily at the bottom? The whole Vernon Gallery brought to one's fireside ! Indeed, indeed I can say nothing, except that I will take care, and keep them clean, and send them back uninjured. — Believe me, yours sincerely,

'C. Brontë.'

CHARLOTTE BRONTË AND HER CIRCLE

TO W. S. WILLIAMS.

'NOVEMBER 6, 1851.

'MY DEAR SIR, — I have true pleasure in inclosing for your son Frank a letter of introduction to Mrs. Gaskell, and earnestly do I trust the acquaintance may tend to his good. To make all sure — for I dislike to go on doubtful grounds — I wrote to ask her if she would permit the introduction. Her frank, kind answer pleased me greatly.

'I have received the books. I hope to write again when I have read "The Fair Carew." The very title augurs well — it has no hackneyed sound. — Believe me, sincerely yours, C. BRONTË.'

TO W. S. WILLIAMS.

'HAWORTH, May 28, 1853.

'MY DEAR SIR, — The box of books arrived safely yesterday evening, and I feel especially obliged for the selection, as it includes several that will be acceptable and interesting to my father.

'I despatch to-day a box of return books. Among them will be found two or three of those just sent, being such as I had read before — i.e., Moore's "Life and Correspondence," 1st and 2nd vols. ; Lamartine's "Restoration of the Monarchy," etc. I have thought of you more than once during the late bright weather, knowing how genial you find warmth and sunshine. I trust it has brought this season its usual cheering and beneficial effect. Remember me kindly to Mrs. Williams and her daughters, and, — Believe me, yours sincerely, C. BRONTË.'

TO W. S. WILLIAMS.

'DECEMBER 6, 1853.

'MY DEAR SIR, — I forwarded last week a box of return books to Cornhill, which I trust arrived safely. To-day I received the " Edinburgh Guardian," [1] for which I thank you.

'Do not trouble yourself to select or send any more books. These courtesies must cease some day, and I would rather give them up than wear them out. — Believe me, yours sincerely,

'C. BRONTË.'

[1] This article was by John Skelton ('Shirley').

402

CHAPTER XV.

WILLIAM MAKEPEACE THACKERAY.

THE devotion of Charlotte Brontë to Thackeray, or rather to Thackeray's genius, is a pleasant episode in literary history. In 1848 he sent Miss Brontë, as we have seen, a copy of 'Vanity Fair.' In 1852 he sent her a copy of 'Esmond,' with the more cordial inscription which came of friendship.

Miss Bronte .

with WMThackerays grateful regards

October 28 : 1852 .

The second edition of 'Jane Eyre' was dedicated to him as possessed of 'an intellect profounder and more unique than his contemporaries have yet recognised,' and as 'the first social regenerator of the day.' And when Currer Bell was dead, it was Thackeray who wrote by far the most eloquent tribute to her memory. When a copy of Lawrence's portrait of Thackeray [1] was sent to Haworth by Mr. George Smith, Charlotte Brontë stood in front of it and, half playfully, half seriously, shook her fist, apostrophising its original as 'Thou Titan!'

With all this hero-worship, it may be imagined that no

---

[1] Now in the possession of Mr. A. B. Nicholls.

favourable criticism gave her more unqualified pleasure than that which came from her 'master,' as she was not indisposed to consider one who was only seven years her senior, and whose best books were practically contemporaneous with her own.

TO W. S. WILLIAMS.

'HAWORTH, October 28, 1847.

'DEAR SIR,— Your last letter was very pleasant to me to read, and is very cheering to reflect on. I feel honoured in being approved by Mr. Thackeray, because I approve Mr. Thackeray. This may sound presumptuous perhaps, but I mean that I have long recognised in his writings genuine talent, such as I admired, such as I wondered at and delighted in. No author seems to distinguish so exquisitely as he does dross from ore, the real from the counterfeit. I believed too he had deep and true feelings under his seeming sternness. Now I am sure he has. One good word from such a man is worth pages of praise from ordinary judges.

'You are right in having faith in the reality of Helen Burns's character; she was real enough. I have exaggerated nothing there. I abstained from recording much that I remember respecting her, lest the narrative should sound incredible. Knowing this, I could not but smile at the quiet self-complacent dogmatism with which one of the journals lays it down that "such creations as Helen Burns are very beautiful but very untrue."

'The plot of "Jane Eyre" may be a hackneyed one. Mr. Thackeray remarks that it is familiar to him. But having read comparatively few novels, I never chanced to meet with it, and I thought it original. The work referred to by the critic of the "Athenæum," I had not had the good fortune to hear of.

'The "Weekly Chronicle" seems inclined to identify me with Mrs. Marsh. I never had the pleasure of perusing a line of Mrs. Marsh's in my life, but I wish very much to read her works, and shall profit by the first opportunity of doing so. I hope I shall not find I have been an unconscious imitator.

'I would still endeavour to keep my expectations low rè-specting the ultimate success of "Jane Eyre." But my desire that it should succeed augments, for you have taken much trouble about the work, and it would grieve me seriously if your active efforts should be baffled and your sanguine hopes disappointed. Excuse me if I again remark that I fear they are rather *too* san-guine; it would be better to moderate them. What will the critics of the monthly reviews and magazines be likely to see in "Jane Eyre" (if indeed they deign to read it), which will win from them even a stinted modicum of approbation? It has no learning, no research, it discusses no subject of public interest. A mere domes-tic novel will, I fear, seem trivial to men of large views and solid attainments.

'Still, efforts so energetic and indefatigable as yours ought to realise a result in some degree favourable, and I trust they will. — I remain, dear sir, yours respectfully,   C. BELL.'

'OCTOBER 28, 1847.

' I have just received the "Tablet" and the "Morning Adver-tiser." Neither paper seems inimical to the book, but I see it pro-duces a very different effect on different natures. I was amused at the analysis in the "Tablet," it is oddly expressed in some parts. I think the critic did not always seize my meaning; he speaks, for instance, of "Jane's inconceivable alarm at Mr. Rochester's repel-ling manner." I do not remember that.'

TO W. S. WILLIAMS.

'DECEMBER 11, 1847.

DEAR SIR,— I have delayed writing to you in the hope that the parcel you sent would reach me ; but after making due in-quiries at the Keighley, Bradford, and Leeds Stations and obtaining no news of it, I must conclude that it has been lost.

' However, I have contrived to get a sight of "Fraser's Maga-zine " from another quarter, so that I have only to regret Mr. Horne's kind present. Will you thank that gentleman for me when you see him, and tell him that the railroad is to blame for my not having acknowledged his courtesy before.

405

CHARLOTTE BRONTË

'Mr. Lewes is very lenient: I anticipated a degree of severity which he has spared me. This notice differs from all the other notices. He must be a man of no ordinary mind: there is a strange sagacity evinced in some of his remarks; yet he is not always right. I am afraid if he knew how much I write from intuition, how little from actual knowledge, he would think me presumptuous ever to have written at all. I am sure such would be his opinion if he knew the narrow bounds of my attainments, the limited scope of my reading.

'There are moments when I can hardly credit that anything I have done should be found worthy to give even transitory pleasure to such men as Mr. Thackeray, Sir John Herschel, Mr. Fonblanque, Leigh Hunt, and Mr. Lewes — that my humble efforts should have had such a result is a noble reward.

'I was glad and proud to get the bank bill Mr. Smith sent me yesterday, but I hardly ever felt delight equal to that which cheered me when I received your letter containing an extract from a note by Mr. Thackeray, in which he expressed himself gratified with the perusal of "Jane Eyre." Mr. Thackeray is a keen ruthless satirist. I had never perused his writings but with blended feelings of admiration and indignation. Critics, it appears to me, do not know what an intellectual boa-constrictor he is. They call him "humorous," "brilliant" — his is a most scalping humour, a most deadly brilliancy: he does not play with his prey, he coils round it and crushes it in his rings. He seems terribly in earnest in his war against the falsehood and follies of "the world." I often wonder what that "world" thinks of him. I should think the faults of such a man would be distrust of anything good in human nature — galling suspicion of bad motives lurking behind good actions. Are these his failings?

'They are, at any rate, the failings of his written sentiments, for he cannot find in his heart to represent either man or woman as at once good and wise. Does he not too much confound benevolence with weakness and wisdom with mere craft?

'But I must not intrude on your time by too long a letter. — Believe me, yours respectfully,   C. BELL.

'I have received the "Sheffield Iris," the "Bradford Observer," the "Guardian," the "Newcastle Guardian," and the "Sunday Times" since you wrote. The contrast between the notices in the two last named papers made me smile. The "Sunday Times" almost denounces "Jane Eyre" as something very reprehensible and obnoxious, whereas the "Newcastle Guardian" seems to think it a mild potion which may be "safely administered to the most delicate invalid." I suppose the public must decide when critics disagree.'

TO W. S. WILLIAMS.

'HAWORTH, December 23, 1847.

'DEAR SIR,—I am glad that you and Messrs. Smith & Elder approve the second preface.

'I send an errata of the first volume, and part of the second. I will send the rest of the corrections as soon as possible.

'Will the inclosed dedication suffice? I have made it brief, because I wished to avoid any appearance of pomposity or pretension.

'The notice in the "Church of England Journal" gratified me much, and chiefly because it *was* the "Church of England Journal." Whatever such critics as he of the "Mirror" may say, I love the Church of England. Her ministers, indeed, I do not regard as infallible personages, I have seen too much of them for that, but to the Establishment, with all her faults—the profane Athanasian creed *ex*cluded—I am sincerely attached.

'Is the forthcoming critique on Mr. Thackeray's writings in the "Edinburgh Review" written by Mr. Lewes? I hope it is. Mr. Lewes, with his penetrating sagacity and fine acumen, ought to be able to do the author of "Vanity Fair" justice. Only he must not bring him down to the level of Fielding—he is far, far above Fielding. It appears to me that Fielding's style is arid, and his views of life and human nature coarse, compared with Thackeray's.

'With many thanks for your kind wishes, and a cordial reciprocation of them,—I remain, dear sir, yours respectfully,
'C. BELL.

CHARLOTTE BRONTË

'On glancing over this scrawl, I find it so illegibly written that I fear you will hardly be able to decipher it; but the cold is partly to blame for this — my fingers are numb.'

The dedication here referred to is that to Thackeray. People had been already suggesting that the book might have been written by Thackeray under a pseudonym, others had implied, knowing that there was 'something about a woman' in Thackeray's life, that it was written by a mistress of the great novelist. Indeed, the 'Quarterly' had half hinted as much. Currer Bell, knowing nothing of the gossip of London, had dedicated her book in single-minded enthusiasm. Her distress was keen when it was revealed to her that the wife of Mr. Thackeray, like the wife of Rochester in 'Jane Eyre,' was of unsound mind. However, a correspondence with him would seem to have ended amicably enough. [1]

TO W. S. WILLIAMS.

'HAWORTH, January 28, 1848.

'DEAR SIR, — I need not tell you that when I saw Mr. Thackeray's letter inclosed under your cover, the sight made me very happy. It was some time before I dared open it, lest my pleasure in receiving it should be mixed with pain on learning its contents — lest, in short, the dedication should have been, in some way, unacceptable to him.

'And, to tell you the truth, I fear this must have been the case; he does not say so, his letter is most friendly in its noble simplicity, but he apprises me, at the commencement, of a circumstance which both surprised and dismayed me.

'I suppose it is no indiscretion to tell you this circumstance,

[1] Thackeray writes to Mr. Brookfield, in October 1848, as follows : — 'Old Dilke of the "Athenæum" vows that Procter and his wife, between them, wrote "Jane Eyre"; and when I protest ignorance, says, "Pooh! you know who wrote it — you are the deepest rogue in England, etc." I wonder whether it can be true? It is just possible. And then what a singular circumstance is the + fire of the two dedications.' ('Jane Eyre' to Thackeray, 'Vanity Fair' to Barry Cornwall.) — 'A Collection of Letters to W. M. Thackeray,' 1847–1855. Smith & Elder.

for you doubtless know it already. It appears that his private
position is in some points similar to that I have ascribed to Mr.
Rochester; that thence arose a report that "Jane Eyre" had been
written by a governess in his family, and that the dedication
coming now has confirmed everybody in the surmise.

'Well may it be said that fact is often stranger than fiction!
The coincidence struck me as equally unfortunate and extraor-
dinary. Of course I knew nothing whatever of Mr. Thackeray's
domestic concerns, he existed for me only as an author.
Of all regarding his personality, station, connections, private
history, I was, and am still in a great measure, totally in
the dark; but I am *very, very* sorry that my inadvertent blunder
should have made his name and affairs a subject for common
gossip.

' The very fact of his not complaining at all and addressing
me with such kindness, notwithstanding the pain and annoyance
I must have caused him, increases my chagrin. I could not half
express my regret to him in my answer, for I was restrained by
the consciousness that that regret was just worth nothing at all
— quite valueless for healing the mischief I had done.

'Can you tell me anything more on this subject? or can you
guess in what degree the unlucky coincidence would affect him
— whether it would pain him much and deeply; for he says so
little himself on the topic, I am at a loss to divine the exact
truth — but I fear.

'Do not think, my dear sir, from my silence respecting the
advice you have, at different times, given me for my future
literary guidance, that I am heedless of, or indifferent to, your
kindness. I keep your letters and not unfrequently refer to
them. Circumstances may render it impracticable for me to act
up to the letter of what you counsel, but I think I comprehend
the spirit of your precepts, and trust I shall be able to profit
thereby. Details, situations which I do not understand and
cannot personally inspect, I would not for the world meddle
with, lest I should make even a more ridiculous mess of the
matter than Mrs. Trollope did in her "Factory Boy." Besides,
not one feeling on any subject, public or private, will I ever

affect that I do not really experience. Yet though I must limit my sympathies; though my observation cannot penetrate where the very deepest political and social truths are to be learnt; though many doors of knowledge which are open for you are for ever shut for me; though I must guess and calculate and grope my way in the dark, and come to uncertain conclusions unaided and alone where such writers as Dickens and Thackeray, having access to the shrine and image of Truth, have only to go into the temple, lift the veil a moment, and come out and say what they have seen, — yet with every disadvantage, I mean still, in my own contracted way, to do my best. Imperfect my best will be, and poor, and compared with the works of the true masters — of that greatest modern master Thackeray in especial (for it is him I at heart reverence with all my strength) it will be trifling, but I trust not affected or counterfeit. — Believe me, my dear sir, yours with regard and respect, CURRER BELL.'

TO W. S. WILLIAMS.

'MARCH 29, 1848.

'MY DEAR SIR, — The notice from the "Church of England Quarterly Review" is not on the whole a bad one. True, it condemns the tendency of "Jane Eyre," and seems to think Mr. Rochester should have been represented as going through the mystic process of "regeneration" before any respectable person could have consented to believe his contrition for his past errors sincere; true, also, that it casts a doubt on Jane's creed, and leaves it doubtful whether she was Hindoo, Mahommedan, or infidel. But notwithstanding these eccentricities, it is a conscientious notice, very unlike that in the "Mirror," for instance, which seemed the result of a feeble sort of spite, whereas this is the critic's real opinion : some of the ethical and theological notions are not according to his system, and he disapproves of them.

'I am glad to hear that Mr. Lewes's new work is soon to appear, and pleased also to learn that Messrs. Smith & Elder are the publishers. Mr. Lewes mentioned in the last note I received from him that he had just finished writing his new novel, and I have been on the look out for the advertisement of its appearance ever since. I shall long to read it, if it were only to get a further insight into the author's character. I read "Ranthorpe" with lively interest — there was much true talent in its pages. Two thirds of it I thought excellent, the latter part seemed more hastily and sketchily written.

'I trust Miss Kavanagh's work will meet with the success that, from your account, I am certain she and it deserve. I think I have met with an outline of the facts on which her tale is founded in some periodical, "Chambers' Journal" I believe. No critic, however rigid, will find fault with "the tendency" of her work, I should think.

'I will tell you why you cannot fully sympathise with the French, or feel any firm confidence in their future movements : because too few of them are Lamartines, too many Ledru Rollins. That, at least, is my reason for watching their proceedings with more dread than hope. With the Germans it is different : to their rational and justifiable efforts for liberty one can heartily wish well.

'It seems, as you say, as if change drew near England too. She is divided by the sea from the lands where it is making thrones rock, but earthquakes roll lower than the ocean, and we know neither the day nor the hour when the tremor and heat, passing beneath our island, may unsettle and dissolve its foundations. Meantime, one thing is certain, all will in the end work together for good.

'You mentioned Thackeray and the last number of "Vanity Fair." The more I read Thackeray's works the more certain I am that he stands alone — alone in his sagacity, alone in his truth, alone in his feeling (his feeling, though he makes no noise about it, is about the most genuine that ever lived on a printed page), alone in his power, alone in his simplicity, alone in his self-control. Thackeray is a Titan, so strong that he can afford to perform with calm the most herculean feats ; there is the charm and majesty of repose in his greatest efforts ; *he* borrows nothing from fever, his is never the energy of delirium — his energy is sane

CHARLOTTE BRONTË

energy, deliberate energy, thoughtful energy. The last number of "Vanity Fair" proves this peculiarly. Forcible, exciting in its force, still more impressive than exciting, carrying on the interest of the narrative in a flow, deep, full, resistless, it is still quiet — as quiet as reflection, as quiet as memory ; and to me there are parts of it that sound as solemn as an oracle. Thackeray is never borne away by his own ardour — he has it under control. His genius obeys him — it is his servant, it works no fantastic changes at its own wild will, it must still achieve the task which reason and sense assign it, and none other. Thackeray is unique. I *can* say no more, I *will* say no less. — Believe me, yours sincerely,

'C. Bell.'

TO W. S. WILLIAMS.

'March 2, 1849.

' Your generous indignation against the "Quarterly" touched me. But do not trouble yourself to be angry on Currer Bell's account ; except where the May-Fair gossip and Mr. Thackeray's name were brought in he was never stung at all, but he certainly thought that passage and one or two others quite unwarrantable. However, slander without a germ of truth is seldom injurious : it resembles a rootless plant and must soon wither away.

' The critic would certainly be a little ashamed of herself if she knew what foolish blunders she had committed, if she were aware how completely Mr. Thackeray and Currer Bell are strangers to each other, that "Jane Eyre" was written before the author had seen one line of "Vanity Fair," or that if C. Bell had known that there existed in Mr. Thackeray's private circumstances the shadow of a reason for fancying personal allusion, so far from dedicating the book to that gentleman, he would have regarded such a step as ill-judged, insolent, and indefensible, and would have shunned it accordingly. — Believe me, my dear sir, yours sincerely, C. Brontë.'

TO W. S. WILLIAMS.

'August 14, 1848.

' My dear Sir, — My sister Anne thanks you, as well as myself, for your just critique on "Wildfell Hall." It appears to me

412

that your observations exactly hit both the strong and weak points of the book, and the advice which accompanies them is worthy of, and shall receive, our most careful attention.

'The first duty of an author is, I conceive, a faithful allegiance to Truth and Nature; his second, such a conscientious study of Art as shall enable him to interpret eloquently and effectively the oracles delivered by those two great deities. The Bells are very sincere in their worship of Truth, and they hope to apply themselves to the consideration of Art, so as to attain one day the power of speaking the language of conviction in the accents of persuasion; though they rather apprehend that whatever pains they take to modify and soften, an abrupt word or vehement tone will now and then occur to startle ears polite, whenever the subject shall chance to be such as moves their spirits within them.

'I have already told you, I believe, that I regard Mr. Thackeray as the first of modern masters, and as the legitimate high priest of Truth; I study him accordingly with reverence. He, I see, keeps the mermaid's tail below water, and only hints at the dead men's bones and noxious slime amidst which it wriggles; *but*, his hint is more vivid than other men's elaborate explanations, and never is his satire whetted to so keen an edge as when with quiet mocking irony he modestly recommends to the approbation of the public his own exemplary discretion and forbearance. The world begins to know Thackeray rather better than it did two years or even a year ago, but as yet it only half knows him. His mind seems to me a fabric as simple and unpretending as it is deep-founded and enduring — there is no meretricious ornament to attract or fix a superficial glance; his great distinction of the genuine is one that can only be fully appreciated with time. There is something, a sort of " still profound," revealed in the concluding part of " Vanity Fair " which the discernment of one generation will not suffice to fathom. A hundred years hence, if he only lives to do justice to himself, he will be better known than he is now. A hundred years hence, some thoughtful critic, standing and looking down on the deep waters, will see shining through them the pearl without price of a purely original mind — such a mind as the Bulwers, etc., his contemporaries have *not*. Not acquirements gained from study, but the thing that came into the world with him — his inherent genius: the thing that made him, I doubt not, different as a child from other children, that caused him, perhaps, peculiar griefs and struggles in life, and that now makes him as a writer unlike other writers. Excuse me for recurring to this theme, I do not wish to bore you.

' You say Mr. Huntingdon reminds you of Mr. Rochester. Does he? Yet there is no likeness between the two; the foundation of each character is entirely different. Huntingdon is a specimen of the naturally selfish, sensual, superficial man, whose one merit of a joyous temperament only avails him while he is young and healthy, whose best days are his earliest, who never profits by experience, who is sure to grow worse the older he grows. Mr. Rochester has a thoughtful nature and a very feeling heart; he is neither selfish nor self-indulgent; he is ill-educated, misguided; errs, when he does err, through rashness and inexperience: he lives for a time as too many other men live, but being radically better than most men, he does not like that degraded life, and is never happy in it. He is taught the severe lessons of experience and has sense to learn wisdom from them. Years improve him; the effervescence of youth foamed away, what is really good in him still remains. His nature is like wine of a good vintage: time cannot sour, but only mellows him. Such at least was the character I meant to pourtray.

' Heathcliffe, again, of " Wuthering Heights " is quite another creation. He exemplifies the effects which a life of continued injustice and hard usage may produce on a naturally perverse, vindictive, and inexorable disposition. Carefully trained and kindly treated, the black gipsy-cub might possibly have been reared into a human being, but tyranny and ignorance made of him a mere demon. The worst of it is, some of his spirit seems breathed through the whole narrative in which he figures: it haunts every moor and glen, and beckons in every fir-tree of the Heights.

' I must not forget to thank you for the " Examiner " and " Atlas " newspapers. Poor Mr. Newby! It is not enough that the "Examiner" nails him by both ears to the pillory, but the "Atlas" brands a token of disgrace on his forehead. This is a deplorable plight, and he makes all matters worse by his foolish little answers to his assailants. It is a pity that he has no kind friend to suggest to him that he had better not bandy words with the "Examiner." His plea about the "printer" was too ludicrous, and his second note is pitiable. I only regret that the names of Ellis and Acton Bell should perforce be mixed up with his proceedings. My sister Anne wishes me to say that should she ever write another work, Mr. Smith will certainly have the first offer of the copyright.

'I hope Mrs. Williams's health is more satisfactory than when you last wrote. With every good wish to yourself and your family, — Believe me, my dear sir, yours sincerely,

'C. Brontë.'

TO W. S. WILLIAMS.

'October 19, 1849.

'My dear Sir, — I am again at home; and after the first sensations consequent on returning to a place more dumb and vacant than it once was, I am beginning to feel settled. I think the contrast with London does not make Haworth more desolate; on the contrary, I have gleaned ideas, images, pleasant feelings, such as may perhaps cheer many a long winter evening.

'You ask my opinion of your daughters. I wish I could give you one worth acceptance. A single evening's acquaintance does not suffice with me to form an *opinion*, it only leaves on my mind an *impression*. They impressed me, then, as pleasing in manners and appearance: Ellen's is a character to which I could soon attach myself, and Fanny and Louisa have each their separate advantages. I can, however, read more in a face like Mrs. Williams's than in the smooth young features of her daughters — time, trial, and exertion write a distinct hand, more legible than smile or dimple. I was told you had once some thoughts of bringing out Fanny as a professional singer, and it was added Fanny did not like the project. I thought to myself, if she does not like it, it can never be successfully executed. It seems to me that to achieve triumph in a career so arduous, the artist's own bent to the course must be inborn, decided, resistless. There should be no urging, no goading; native genius and vigorous will should lend their wings to the aspirant — nothing less can lift her to real fame, and who would rise feebly only to fall ignobly? An inferior artist, I am sure, you would not wish your daughter to be, and if she is to stand in the foremost rank, only her own courage and resolve can place her there; so, at least, the case appears to me. Fanny probably looks on publicity as degrading, and I believe that for a woman it is degrading if it is not glorious. If I could not be a Lind, I would not be a singer.

'Brief as my visit to London was, it must for me be memorable. I sometimes fancied myself in a dream — I could scarcely credit the reality of what passed. For instance, when I walked into the room and put my hand into Miss Martineau's, the action of saluting her and the fact of her presence seemed visionary. Again, when Mr. Thackeray was announced, and I saw him enter, looked up at his tall figure, heard his voice, the whole incident was truly dream-like, I was only certain it was true because I became miserably destitute of self-possession. Amour propre suffers terribly under such circumstances : woe to him that thinks of himself in the presence of intellectual greatness! Had I not been obliged to speak, I could have managed well, but it behoved me to answer when addressed, and the effort was torture — I spoke stupidly.

'As to the band of critics, I cannot say they overawed me much; I enjoyed the spectacle of them greatly. The two contrasts, Forster and Chorley, have each a certain edifying carriage and conversation good to contemplate. I by no means dislike Mr. Forster — quite the contrary, but the distance from his loud swagger to Thackeray's simple port is as the distance from Shakespeare's writing to Macready's acting.

'Mr. Chorley tantalised me. He is a peculiar specimen — one whom you could set yourself to examine, uncertain whether, when you had probed all the small recesses of his character, the result would be utter contempt and aversion, or whether for the sake of latent good you would forgive obvious evil. One could well pardon his unpleasant features, his strange voice, even his very foppery and grimace, if one found these disadvantages connected with living talent and any spark of genuine goodness. If there is nothing more than acquirement, smartness, and the affectation of philanthropy, Chorley is a fine creature.

'Remember me kindly to your wife and daughters, and — Believe me, yours sincerely, C. BRONTË.'

TO MISS ELLEN NUSSEY.

'HAWORTH, December 19, 1849.

'DEAR ELLEN, — Here I am at Haworth once more. I feel as if I had come out of an exciting whirl. Not that the hurry or stimulus would have seemed much to one accustomed to society and change, but to me they were very marked. My strength and spirits too often proved quite insufficient for the demand on their exertions. I used to bear up as well and as long as I possibly could, for, whenever I flagged, I could see Mr. Smith became disturbed; he always thought that something had been said or done to annoy me, which never once happened, for I met with perfect good breeding even from antagonists — men who had done their best or worst to write me down. I explained to him, over and over again, that my occasional silence was only failure of the power to talk, never of the will, but still he always seemed to fear there was another cause underneath.

'Mrs. Smith is rather stern, but she has sense and discrimination; she watched me very narrowly. When surrounded by gentlemen she never took her eye from me. I liked the surveillance, both when it kept guard over me amongst many, or only with her cherished one. She soon, I am convinced, saw in what light I received all, Thackeray included. Her "George" is a very fine specimen of a young English man of business; so I regard him, and I am proud to be one of his props.

'Thackeray is a Titan of mind. His presence and powers impress me deeply in an intellectual sense; I do not see him or know him as a man. All the others are subordinate to these. I have esteem for some, and, I trust, courtesy for all. I do not, of course, know what they thought of me, but I believe most of them expected me to come out in a more marked eccentric, striking light. I believe they desired more to admire and more to blame. I felt sufficiently at my ease with all except Thackeray, and with him I was painfully stupid.

'Now, dear Nell, when can you come to Haworth? Settle, and let me know as soon as you can. Give my best love to all. — Yours, C. B.'

TO W. S. WILLIAMS.

'JANUARY 10, 1850.

'MY DEAR SIR, — Mrs. Ellis has made her "morning call." I rather relished her chat about "Shirley" and "Jane Eyre." She praises reluctantly and blames too often affectedly. But whenever a reviewer betrays that he has been thoroughly influenced and stirred by the work he criticises, it is easy to forgive the rest — hate and personality excepted.

'I have received and perused the "Edinburgh Review" — it is very brutal and savage. I am not angry with Lewes, but I wish in future he would let me alone, and not write again what makes me feel so cold and sick as I am feeling just now.

'Thackeray's Christmas Book at once grieved and pleased me, as most of his writings do. I have come to the conclusion that whenever he writes, Mephistopheles stands on his right hand and Raphael on his left; the great doubter and sneerer usually guides the pen, the Angel, noble and gentle, interlines letters of light here and there. Alas! Thackeray, I wish your strong wings would lift you oftener above the smoke of cities into the pure region nearer heaven!

'Good-bye for the present. — Yours sincerely.

'C. BRONTË.'

AND HER CIRCLE

TO MISS ELLEN NUSSEY.

'JANUARY 25, 1850.

'DEAR ELLEN, — Your indisposition was, I have no doubt, in a great measure owing to the change in the weather from frost to thaw. I had one sick-headachy day ; but, for me, only a slight attack. You must be careful of cold. I have just written to Amelia a brief note thanking her for the cuffs, etc. It was a burning shame I did not write sooner. Herewith are inclosed three letters for your perusal, the first from Mary Taylor. There is also one from Lewes and one from Sir J. K. Shuttleworth, both which peruse and return. I have also, since you went, had a remarkable epistle from Thackeray, long, interesting, characteristic, but it unfortunately concludes with the strict injunction, *show this letter to no one*, adding that if he thought his letters were seen by others, he should either cease to write or write only what was conventional ; but for this circumstance I should have sent it with the others. I answered it at length. Whether my reply will give satisfaction or displeasure remains yet to be ascertained. Thackeray's feelings are not such as can be gauged by ordinary calculation : variable weather is what I should ever expect from that quarter, yet in correspondence as in verbal intercourse, this would torment me. — Yours faithfully,   C. B.'

TO REV. P. BRONTË.

'76 GLOUCESTER TERRACE, HYDE PARK,
'LONDON, Thursday Morning.

'DEAR PAPA, — I write one hasty line just to tell you that I got here quite safely at ten o'clock last night without any damage or smash in tunnels or cuttings. Mr. and Mrs. Smith met me at the station and gave me a kind and cordial welcome. The weather was beautiful the whole way, and warm ; it is the same to-day. I have not yet been out, but this afternoon, if all be well, I shall go to Mr. Thackeray's lecture. I don't know when I shall see the Exhibition, but when I do, I shall write and tell you all about it. I hope you are well, and will continue

419

well and cheerful. Give my kind regards to Tabby and Martha, and — Believe me, your affectionate daughter,   C. BRONTË.'

It cannot be said that Charlotte Brontë and Thackeray gained by personal contact. 'With him I was painfully stupid,' she says. It was the case of Heine and Goethe over again. Heine in the presence of the king of German literature could talk only of the plums in the garden. Charlotte Brontë in the presence of her hero Thackeray could not express herself with the vigour and intelligence which belonged to her correspondence with Mr. Williams. Miss Brontë, again, was hypercritical of the smaller vanities of men, and, as has been pointed out, she emphasised in 'Villette' a trivial piece of not unpleasant egotism on Thackeray's part after a lecture — his asking her if she had liked it. This question, which nine men out of ten would be prone to ask of a woman friend, was 'over-eagerness' and '*naïveté*' in her eyes. Thackeray, on his side, found conversation difficult, if we may judge by a reminiscence by his daughter Mrs. Ritchie : —

'One of the most notable persons who ever came into our bow-windowed drawing-room in Young Street is a guest never to be forgotten by me — a tiny, delicate, little person, whose small hand nevertheless grasped a mighty lever which set all the literary world of that day vibrating. I can still see the scene quite plainly — the hot summer evening, the open windows, the carriage driving to the door as we all sat silent and expectant ; my father, who rarely waited, waiting with us ; our governess and my sister and I all in a row, and prepared for the great event. We saw the carriage stop, and out of it sprang the active well-knit figure of Mr. George Smith, who was bringing Miss Brontë to see our father. My father, who had been walking up and down the room, goes out into the hall to meet his guests, and then, after a moment's delay, the door opens wide, and the two gentlemen come in, leading a tiny, delicate, serious, little lady, pale, with fair straight hair, and steady eyes. She may be a little over thirty; she is dressed in a little *barège* dress, with a pattern of faint green moss. She enters in mittens, in silence, in seriousness; our hearts are beating with wild excitement. This, then, is the authoress, the unknown power whose books have set all London talking, reading, speculating; some people even say our father wrote the books — the wonderful books. To say that we little girls had been given " Jane Eyre " to read scarcely represents the facts of the case; to say that we had taken it without leave, read bits here and read bits there, been carried away by an un-dreamed-of and hitherto unimagined whirlwind into things, times, places, all utterly absorbing, and at the same time absolutely unintelligible to us, would more accurately describe our state of mind on that summer's evening as we look at Jane Eyre — the great Jane Eyre — the tiny little lady. The moment is so breathless that dinner comes as a relief to the solemnity of the occasion, and we all smile as my father stoops to offer his arm; for, though genius she may be, Miss Bronte can barely reach his elbow. My own personal impressions are that she is somewhat grave and stern, especially to forward little girls who wish to chatter. Mr. George Smith has since told me how she afterwards remarked upon my father's wonderful forbearance and gentleness with our uncalled-for incursions into the conversation. She sat gazing at him with kindling eyes of interest, lighting up with a sort of illumination every now and then as she answered him. I can see her bending forward over the table, not eating, but listening to what he said as he carved the dish before him.

' I think it must have been on this very occasion that my father invited some of his friends in the evening to meet Miss Brontë — for everybody was interested and anxious to see her. Mrs. Crowe, the reciter of ghost-stories, was there. Mrs. Brookfield, Mrs. Carlyle, Mr. Carlyle himself was present, so I am told, railing at the appearance of cockneys upon Scotch mountain sides; there were also too many Americans for his taste, "but the Americans were as gods compared to the cockneys," says the philosopher. Besides the Carlyles, there were Mrs. Elliott and Miss Perry, Mrs. Procter and her daughter, most of my father's habitual friends and companions. In the recent life of Lord Houghton I was amused to see a note quoted in which Lord Houghton also was convened. Would that he had been present — perhaps the party would have gone off better. It was a gloomy and a silent evening. Every one waited for the brilliant conversation which never began at all. Miss Brontë retired to the sofa in the study, and murmured a low word now and then to our kind governess, Miss Truelock. The room looked very dark, the lamp began to smoke a little, the conversation grew dimmer and more dim, the ladies sat round still expectant, my father was too much perturbed by the gloom and the silence to be able to cope with it at all. Mrs. Brookfield, who was in the doorway by the study, near the corner in which Miss Brontë was sitting, leant forward with a little commonplace, since brilliance was not to be the order of the evening. "Do you like London, Miss Brontë?" she said; another silence, a pause, then Miss Brontë answers, "Yes and No," very gravely. Mrs. Brookfield has herself reported the conversation. My sister and I were much too young to be bored in those days; alarmed, impressed we might be, but not yet bored. A party was a party, a lioness was a lioness; and — shall I confess it? — at that time an extra dish of biscuits was enough to mark the evening. We felt all the importance of the occasion: tea spread in the dining-room, ladies in the drawing-room. We roamed about inconveniently, no doubt, and excitedly, and in one of my incursions crossing the hall, after Miss Brontë had left, I was surprised to see my father opening the front door with his hat on. He put his fingers to his lips, walked out into the darkness, and shut the door quietly behind him. When I went back to the drawing-room again, the ladies asked me where he was. I vaguely answered that I thought he was coming back. I was puzzled at the time, nor was it all made clear to me till long years afterwards, when one day Mrs. Procter asked me if I knew what had happened once when my father had invited a party to meet Jane Eyre at his house. It was one of the

dullest evenings she had ever spent in her life, she said. And
then with a good deal of humour she described the situation —
the ladies who had all come expecting so much delightful conversation, and the gloom and the constraint, and how, finally,
overwhelmed by the situation, my father had quietly left the
room, left the house, and gone off to his club. The ladies
waited, wondered, and finally departed also; and as we were
going up to bed with our candles after everybody was gone,
I remember two pretty Miss L——s, in shiny silk dresses,
arriving, full of expectation. . . . We still said we thought our
father would soon be back, but the Miss L——s declined to
wait upon the chance, laughed, and drove away again almost
immediately.'[1]

TO REV. P. BRONTË.

'MAY 28, 1851.

'DEAR PAPA, — I must write another line to you to tell you
how I am getting on. I have seen a great many things since I
left home about which I hope to talk to you at future tea-times
at home. I have been to the theatre and seen Macready in
Macbeth. I have seen the pictures in the National Gallery.
I have seen a beautiful exhibition of Turner's paintings, and
yesterday I saw Mr. Thackeray. He dined here with some
other gentlemen. He is a very tall man — about six feet high,
with a peculiar face — not handsome, very ugly indeed, generally
somewhat stern and satirical in expression, but capable also of a
kind look. He was not told who I was, he was not introduced
to me, but I soon saw him looking at me through his spectacles;
and when we all rose to go down to dinner he just stepped
quietly up and said, "Shake hands"; so I shook hands. He
spoke very few words to me, but when he went away he shook
hands again in a very kind way. It is better, I should think, to
have him for a friend than an enemy, for he is a most formidable-
looking personage. I listened to him as he conversed with the

[1] 'Chapters from Some Memories,' by Anne Thackeray Ritchie. Macmillan & Co. Mrs. Ritchie and her publishers kindly permit me to incor-
porate her interesting reminiscence in this chapter.

other gentlemen. All he says is most simple, but often cynical, harsh, and contradictory. I got on quietly. Most people know me I think, but they are far too well bred to show that they know me, so that there is none of that bustle or that sense of publicity I dislike.

'I hope you continue pretty well; be sure to take care of yourself. The weather here is exceedingly changeful, and often damp and misty, so that it is necessary to guard against taking cold. I do not mean to stay in London above a week longer, but I shall write again two or three days before I return. You need not give yourself the trouble of answering this letter unless you have something particular to say. Remember me to Tabby and Martha. — I remain, dear papa, your affectionate daughter,

'C. BRONTË.'

TO REV. P. BRONTË.

'76 GLOUCESTER TERRACE,
'HYDE PARK, LONDON, May 30, 1851.

'DEAR PAPA, — I have now heard one of Mr. Thackeray's lectures and seen the great Exhibition. On Thursday afternoon I went to hear the lecture. It was delivered in a large and splendid kind of saloon — that in which the great balls of Almacks are given. The walls were all painted and gilded, the benches were sofas stuffed and cushioned and covered with blue damask. The audience was composed of the *élite* of London society. Duchesses were there by the score, and amongst them the great and beautiful Duchess of Sutherland, the Queen's Mistress of the Robes. Amidst all this Thackeray just got up and spoke with as much simplicity and ease as if he had been speaking to a few friends by his own fireside. The lecture was truly good: he had taken pains with the composition. It was finished without being in the least studied; a quiet humour and graphic force enlivened it throughout. He saw me as I entered the room, and came straight up and spoke very kindly. He then took me to his mother, a fine, handsome old lady, and introduced me to her. After the lecture somebody came behind me, leaned over the bench, and said, "Will you permit me, as a Yorkshireman,

424

to introduce myself to you?" I turned round, was puzzled at first by the strange face I met, but in a minute I recognised the features. "You are the Earl of Carlisle," I said. He smiled and assented. He went on to talk for some time in a courteous, kind fashion. He asked after you, recalled the platform electioneering scene at Haworth, and begged to be remembered to you. Dr. Forbes came up afterwards, and Mr. Monckton Milnes, a Yorkshire Member of Parliament, who introduced himself on the same plea as Lord Carlisle.

'Yesterday we went to the Crystal Palace. The exterior has a strange and elegant but somewhat unsubstantial effect. The interior is like a mighty Vanity Fair. The brightest colours blaze on all sides; and ware of all kinds, from diamonds to spinning jennies and printing presses, are there to be seen. It was very fine, gorgeous, animated, bewildering, but I liked Thackeray's lecture better.

'I hope, dear papa, that you are keeping well. With kind regards to Tabby and Martha, and hopes that they are well too, — I am, your affectionate daughter, C. BRONTË.'

TO REV. P. BRONTË,

'112 GLOUCESTER TERRACE,
'HYDE PARK, June 7, 1851.

'DEAR PAPA, — I was very glad to hear that you continued in pretty good health, and that Mr. Cartman came to help you on Sunday. I fear you will not have had a very comfortable week in the dining-room; but by this time I suppose the parlour reformation will be nearly completed, and you will soon be able to return to your old quarters. The letter you sent me this morning was from Mary Taylor. She continues well and happy in New Zealand, and her shop seems to answer well. The French newspaper duly arrived. Yesterday I went for the second time to the Crystal Palace. We remained in it about three hours, and I must say I was more struck with it on this occasion than at my first visit. It is a wonderful place — vast, strange, new, and impossible to describe. Its grandeur does not consist in *one* thing, but in the unique assemblage of *all* things.

Whatever human industry has created, you find there, from the
great compartments filled with railway engines and boilers,
with mill-machinery in full work, with splendid carriages of all
kinds, with harness of every description — to the glass-covered
and velvet-spread stands loaded with the most gorgeous work
of the goldsmith and silvermith, and the carefully guarded
caskets full of real diamonds and pearls worth hundreds of
thousands of pounds. It may be called a bazaar or a fair,
but it is such a bazaar or fair as Eastern genii might have
created. It seems as if magic only could have gathered this
mass of wealth from all the ends of the earth — as if none but
supernatural hands could have arranged it thus, with such a
blaze and contrast of colours and marvellous power of effect.
The multitude filling the great aisles seems ruled and subdued by
some invisible influence. Amongst the thirty thousand souls that
peopled it the day I was there, not one loud noise was to be heard,
not one irregular movement seen — the living tide rolls on quietly,
with a deep hum like the sea heard from the distance.

'Mr. Thackeray is in high spirits about the success of his
lectures. It is likely to add largely both to his fame and purse.
He has, however, deferred this week's lecture till next Thursday,
at the earnest petition of the duchesses and marchionesses, who,
on the day it should have been delivered, were necessitated to
go down with the Queen and Court to Ascot Races. I told him
I thought he did wrong to put it off on their account — and I
think so still. The amateur performance of Bulwer's play for
the Guild of Literature has likewise been deferred on account
of the races. I hope, dear papa, that you, Mr. Nicholls, and all
at home continue well. Tell Martha to take her scrubbing
and cleaning in moderation and not overwork herself. With
kind regards to her and Tabby, — I am, your affectionate daughter,
'C. BRONTË.'

TO REV. P. BRONTË.

'112 GLOUCESTER TERRACE,
'HYDE PARK, June 14, 1851.

'DEAR PAPA, — If all be well, and if Martha can get the
cleaning, etc., done by that time, I think I shall be coming

home about the end of next week or the beginning of the week after. I have been pretty well in London, only somewhat troubled with headaches, owing, I suppose, to the closeness and oppression of the air. The weather has not been so favourable as when I was last here, and in wet and dark days this great Babylon is not so cheerful. All the other sights seem to give way to the great Exhibition, into which thousands and tens of thousands continue to pour every day. I was in it again yesterday afternoon, and saw the ex-royal family of France — the old Queen, the Duchess of Orleans, and her two sons, etc., pass down the transept. I almost wonder the Londoners don't tire a little of this vast Vanity Fair — and, indeed, a new toy has somewhat diverted the attention of the grandees lately, viz., a fancy ball given last night by the Queen. The great lords and ladies have been quite wrapt up in preparations for this momentous event. Their pet and darling, Mr. Thackeray, of course sympathises with them. He was here yesterday to dinner, and left very early in the evening, in order that he might visit respectively the Duchess of Norfolk, the Marchioness of Londonderry, Ladies Chesterfield and Clanricarde, and see them all in their fancy costumes of the reign of Charles ii. before they set out for the Palace! His lectures, it appears, are a triumphant success. He says they will enable him to make a provision for his daughters; and Mr. Smith believes he will not get less than four thousand pounds by them. He is going to give two courses, and then go to Edinburgh and perhaps America, but *not* under the auspices of Barnum. Amongst others, the Lord Chancellor attended his last lecture, and Mr. Thackeray says he expects a place from him; but in this I think he was joking. Of course Mr. T. is a good deal spoiled by all this, and indeed it cannot be otherwise. He has offered two or three times to introduce me to some of his great friends, and says he knows many great ladies who would receive me with open arms if I would go to their houses; but, seriously, I cannot see that this sort of society produces so good an effect on him as to tempt me in the least to try the same experiment, so I remain obscure.

CHARLOTTE BRONTË AND HER CIRCLE

'Hoping you are well, dear papa, and with kind regards to Mr. Nicholls, Tabby, and Martha, also poor old Keeper and Flossy, — I am, your affectionate daughter,   C. Brontë.

'P.S.— I am glad the parlour is done and that you have got safely settled, but am quite shocked to hear of the piano being dragged up into the bedroom — there it must necessarily be absurd, and in the parlour it looked so well, besides being convenient for your books.   I wonder why you don't like it.'

There are many pleasant references to Thackeray to be found in Mrs. Gaskell's book, including a letter to Mr. George Smith, thanking him for the gift of the novelist's portrait. 'He looks superb in his beautiful, tasteful, gilded gibbet,' she says.   A few years later, and Thackeray was to write the eloquent tribute to his admirer, which is familiar to his readers : 'I fancied an austere little Joan of Arc marching in upon us and rebuking our easy lives, our easy morals.' 'She gave me,' he tells us, 'the impression of being a very pure, and lofty, and high-minded person. A great and holy reverence of right and truth seemed to be with her always. Who that has known her books has not admired the artist's noble English, the burning love of truth, the bravery, the simplicity, the indignation at wrong, the eager sympathy, the pious love and reverence, the passionate honour, so to speak, of the woman? What a story is that of the family of poets in their solitude yonder on the gloomy Yorkshire moors!'

CHAPTER XVI.

LITERARY FRIENDSHIPS.

THERE is a letter, printed by Mrs. Gaskell, from Charlotte Brontë to Ellen Nussey, in which Miss Brontë, when a girl of seventeen, discusses the best books to read, and expresses a particular devotion to Sir Walter Scott. During those early years she was an indefatigable student of literature. She read all that her father's study and the Keighley library could provide. When the years brought literary fame and its accompanying friendships, she was able to hold her own with the many men and women of letters whom she was destined to meet. Her staunchest friend was undoubtedly Mr. Williams, who sent her, as we have seen, all the newest books from London, and who appears to have discussed them with her as well. Next to Mr. Williams we must place his chief at Cornhill, Mr. George Smith, and Mr. Smith's mother. Mr. Smith happily still lives to reign over the famous house which introduced Thackeray, John Ruskin, and Charlotte Brontë to the world. What Charlotte thought of him may be gathered from her frank acknowledgment that he was the original of Dr. John in 'Villette,' as his mother was the original of Mrs. Bretton — perhaps the two most entirely charming characters in Charlotte Brontë's novels. Mrs. Smith and her son lived, at the beginning of the friendship, at Westbourne Place, but afterwards removed to Gloucester Terrace, and Charlotte stayed with them at both houses. It was from the former that this first letter was addressed.

CHARLOTTE BRONTË

TO MISS ELLEN NUSSEY.

'4 Westbourne Place,
'Bishop's Road, London.

'Dear Ellen, — I have just remembered that as you do not know my address you cannot write to me till you get it; it is as above. I came to this big Babylon last Thursday, and have been in what seems to me a sort of whirl ever since; for changes, scenes, and stimulus which would be a trifle to others, are much to me. I found when I mentioned to Mr. Smith my plan of going to Dr. Wheelwright's it would not do at all — he would have been seriously hurt. He made his mother write to me, and thus I was persuaded to make my principal stay at his house. I have found no reason to regret this decision. Mrs. Smith received me at first like one who had received the strictest orders to be scrupulously attentive. I had fires in my bedroom evening and morning, wax candles, etc., etc. Mrs. Smith and her daughters seemed to look upon me with a mixture of respect and alarm. But all this is changed — that is to say, the attention and politeness continues as great as ever, but the alarm and estrangement are quite gone. She treats me as if she liked me, and I begin to like her much; kindness is a potent heart-winner. I had not judged too favourably of her son on a first impression; he pleases me much. I like him better even as a son and brother than as a man of business. Mr. Williams, too, is really most gentlemanly and well-informed. His weak points he certainly has, but these are not seen in society. Mr. Taylor — the little man — has again shown his parts; in fact, I suspect he is of the Helstone order of men — rigid, despotic, and self-willed. He tries to be very kind and even to express sympathy sometimes, but he does not manage it. He has a determined, dreadful nose in the middle of his face, which, when poked into my countenance, cuts into my soul like iron. Still, he is horribly intelligent, quick, searching, sagacious, and with a memory of relentless tenacity. To turn to Mr. Williams after him, or to Mr. Smith himself, is to turn from granite to easy down or warm fur. I have seen Thackeray.   C. Brontë.'

430

TO JAMES TAYLOR, Cornhill.

'My dear Sir,—I am afraid Mr. Williams told you I was sadly "put out" about the "Daily News," and I believe it is to that circumstance I owe your letters. But I have now made good resolutions, which were tried this morning by another notice in the same style in the "Observer." The praise of such critics mortifies more than their blame; an author who becomes the object of it cannot help momentarily wishing he had never written. And, speaking of the press, they were still ignorant of my being a woman. Why can they not be content to take Currer Bell for a man?

'I imagined, mistakenly it now appears, that "Shirley" bore fewer traces of a female hand than "Jane Eyre"; that I have misjudged disappoints me a little, though I cannot exactly see where the error lies. You keep to your point about the curates. Since you think me to blame, you do right to tell me so. I rather fancy I shall be left in a minority of one on that subject.

'I was indeed very much interested in the books you sent. Eckermann's "Conversations with Goethe," "Guesses at Truth," "Friends in Council," and the little work on English social life pleased me particularly, and the last not least. We sometimes take a partiality to books as to characters, not on account of any brilliant intellect or striking peculiarity they boast, but for the sake of something good, delicate, and genuine. I thought that small book the production of a lady, and an amiable, sensible woman, and I like it.

'You must not think of selecting any more works for me yet, my stock is still far from exhausted.

'I accept your offer respecting the "Athenæum"; it is a paper I should like much to see, providing you can send it without trouble. It shall be punctually returned.

'Papa's health has, I am thankful to say, been very satisfactory of late. The other day he walked to Keighley and back, and was very little fatigued. I am myself pretty well.

CHARLOTTE BRONTË

'With thanks for your kind letter and good wishes, — Believe me, yours sincerely, C. BRONTË,'

Mrs. Gaskell has much to say of Miss Brontë's relations with George Henry Lewes.[1] He was a critic with whom she had much correspondence and not a few differences. It will be remembered that Charlotte describes him as bearing a resemblance to Emily — a curious circumstance by the light of the fact that Lewes was always adjudged among his acquaintances as a peculiarly ugly man. Here is a portion of a letter upon which Mrs. Gaskell practised considerable excisions, and of which she prints the remainder: —

TO MISS ELLEN NUSSEY.

'JUNE 12, 1850.

'I have seen Lewes. He is a man with both weakness and sins, but unless I err greatly, the foundation of his nature is not bad; and were he almost a fiend in character I could not feel otherwise to him than half-sadly, half-tenderly. A queer word that last, but I use it because the aspect of Lewes's face almost moves me to tears, it is so wonderfully like Emily — her eyes, her features, the very nose, the somewhat prominent mouth, the forehead — even, at moments, the expression. Whatever Lewes does or says, I believe I cannot hate him. Another likeness I have seen, too, that touched me sorrowfully. You remember my speaking of a Miss Kavanagh, a young authoress, who supported her mother by her writings. Hearing from Mr. Williams that she had a longing to see me, I called on her yesterday. I found a little, almost dwarfish figure, to which even I had to look down; not deformed — that is, not hunch-backed, but long-armed and with a large head, and (at first sight) a strange face. She met me half-frankly, half-tremblingly; we sat down together, and when I had talked with her five minutes,

[1] George Henry Lewes (1817–1878). Published 'Biographical History of Philosophy,' 1845–46; 'Ranthorpe,' 1847; 'Rose, Blanche, and Violet,' 1848; 'Life of Goethe,' 1855. Editor of the 'Fortnightly Review,' 1865–66. 'Problems of Life and Mind,' 1873–79; and many other works.

her face was no longer strange, but mournfully familiar — it was Martha Taylor on every lineament. I shall try to find a moment to see her again. She lives in a poor but clean and neat little lodging. Her mother seems a somewhat weak-minded woman, who can be no companion to her. Her father has quite deserted his wife and child, and this poor little, feeble, intelligent, cordial thing wastes her brains to gain a living. She is twenty-five years old. I do not intend to stay here, at the furthest, more than a week longer; but at the end of that time I cannot go home, for the house at Haworth is just now unroofed; repairs were become necessary.

'I should like to go for a week or two to the sea-side, in which case I wonder whether it would be possible for you to join me. Meantime, with regards to all — Believe me, yours faithfully,   C. B.'

But her acquaintance with Lewes had apparently begun three years earlier.

TO W. S. WILLIAMS.
'November 6, 1847.

'Dear Sir, — I should be obliged to you if you will direct the inclosed to be posted in London as I wish to avoid giving any clue to my place of residence, publicity not being my ambition.

'It is an answer to the letter I received yesterday, favoured by you. This letter bore the signature G. H. Lewes, and the writer informs me that it is his intention to write a critique on "Jane Eyre" for the December number of "Fraser's Magazine," and possibly also, he intimates, a brief notice to the "Westminster Review." Upon the whole he seems favourably inclined to the work, though he hints disapprobation of the melodramatic portions.

'Can you give me any information respecting Mr. Lewes? what station he occupies in the literary world and what works he has written? He styles himself "a fellow novelist." There is something in the candid tone of his letter which inclines me to think well of him.

CHARLOTTE BRONTË

'I duly received your letter containing the notices from the "Critic," and the two magazines, and also the "Morning Post." I hope all these notices will work together for good ; they must at any rate give the book a certain publicity. — Yours sincerely,

'C. BRONTË.'

Mr. R. H. Horne [1] sent her his 'Orion.'

TO R. H. HORNE.

'DECEMBER 15, 1847.

'DEAR SIR, — You will have thought me strangely tardy in acknowledging your courteous present, but the fact is it never reached me till yesterday ; the parcel containing it was missent — consequently it lingered a fortnight on its route.

'I have to thank you, not merely for the gift of a little book of 137 pages, but for that of a *poem*. Very real, very sweet is the poetry of "Orion" ; there are passages I shall recur to again and yet again — passages instinct both with power and beauty. All through it is genuine — pure from one flaw of affectation, rich in noble imagery. How far the applause of critics has rewarded the author of "Orion" I do not know, but I think the pleasure he enjoyed in its composition must have been a bounteous meed in itself. You could not, I imagine, have written that epic without at times deriving deep happiness from your work.

'With sincere thanks for the pleasure its perusal has afforded me, — I remain, dear sir, yours faithfully,   C. BELL.'

TO W. S. WILLIAMS.

'HAWORTH, December 15, 1847.

'DEAR SIR, — I write a line in haste to apprise you that I have got the parcel. It was sent, through the carelessness of the railroad people, to Bingley, where it lay a fortnight, till a Haworth carrier happening to pass that way brought it on to me.

---

[1] Richard Hengist Horne (1803–1884). Published 'Cosmo de Medici,' 1837 ; 'Orion,' an epic poem in ten books, passed through six editions in 1843, the first three editions being issued at a farthing; 'A New Spirit of the Age,' 1844 ; 'Letters of E. B. Browning to R. H. Horne,' 1877.

434

'I was much pleased to find that you had been kind enough to forward the "Mirror" along with "Fraser." The article on "the last new novel" is in substance similar to the notice in the "Sunday Times." One passage only excited much interest in me, it was that where allusion is made to some former work which the author of "Jane Eyre" is supposed to have published — there, I own, my curiosity was a little stimulated. The reviewer cannot mean the little book of rhymes to which Currer Bell contributed a third; but as that, and "Jane Eyre," and a brief translation of some French verses sent anonymously to a magazine, are the sole productions of mine that have ever appeared in print, I am puzzled to know to what else he can refer.

'The reviewer is mistaken, as he is in perverting my meaning, in attributing to me designs I know not, principles I disown.

'I have been greatly pleased with Mr. R. H. Horne's poem of "Orion." Will you have the kindness to forward to him the inclosed note, and to correct the address if it is not accurate. — Believe me, dear sir, yours respectfully,   C. Bell.'

The following elaborate criticism of one of Mr. Lewes's now forgotten novels is almost pathetic; it may give a modern critic pause in his serious treatment of the abundant literary ephemera of which we hear so much from day to day.

TO W. S. WILLIAMS.

'May 1, 1848.

'My dear Sir, — I am glad you sent me your letter just as you had written it — without revisal, without retrenching or softening touch, because I cannot doubt that I am a gainer by the omission.

'It would be useless to attempt opposition to your opinions, since, in fact, to read them was to recognise, almost point for point, a clear definition of objections I had already felt, but had found neither the power nor the will to express. Not the power, because I find it very difficult to analyse closely, or to criticise in appropriate words; and not the will because I was afraid of doing Mr. Lewes injustice. I preferred overrating to under-rating the merits of his work.

'Mr. Lewes's sincerity, energy, and talent assuredly command the reader's respect, but on what points he depends to win his attachment I know not. I do not think he cares to excite the pleasant feelings which incline the taught to the teacher as much in friendship as in reverence. The display of his acquire-ments, to which almost every page bears testimony — citations from Greek, Latin, Italian, Spanish, French, and German authors covering as with embroidery the texture of his English — awes and astonishes the plain reader; but if, in addition, you permit yourself to require the refining charm of delicacy, the elevating one of imagination — if you permit yourself to be as fastidious and exacting in these matters as, by your own con-fession, it appears *you* are, then Mr. Lewes must necessarily inform you that he does not deal in the article; probably he will add that *therefore* it must be non-essential. I should fear he might even stigmatise imagination as a figment, and delicacy as an affectation.

'An honest rough heartiness Mr. Lewes will give you; yet in case you have the misfortune to remark that the heartiness might be quite as honest if it were less rough, would you not run the risk of being termed a sentimentalist or a dreamer?

'Were I privileged to address Mr. Lewes, and were it wise or becoming to say to him exactly what one thinks, I should utter words to this effect —

'"You have a sound, clear judgment as far as it goes, but I conceive it to be limited; your standard of talent is high, but I cannot acknowledge it to be the highest; you are deserving of all attention when you lay down the law on principles, but you are to be resisted when you dogmatise on feelings.

'"To a certain point, Mr. Lewes, you can go, but no farther. Be as sceptical as you please on whatever lies beyond a certain intellectual limit; the mystery will never be cleared up to you, for that limit you will never overpass. Not all your learning, not all your reading, not all your sagacity, not all your perseverance can help you over one viewless line — one boundary as impassable as it is invisible. To enter that sphere a man must be born within it; and untaught peasants have there drawn their first breath, while learned philosophers have striven hard till old age to reach it, and have never succeeded." I should not dare, nor would it be right, to say this to Mr. Lewes, but I cannot help thinking it both of him and many others who have a great name in the world.

'Hester Mason's character, career, and fate appeared to me so strange, grovelling, and miserable, that I never for a moment doubted the whole dreary picture was from the life. I thought in describing the "rustic poetess," in giving the details of her vulgar provincial and disreputable metropolitan notoriety, and especially in touching on the ghastly catastrophe of her fate, he was faithfully recording facts — thus, however repulsively, yet conscientiously "pointing a moral," if not "adorning a tale;" but if Hester be the daughter of Lewes's imagination, and if her experience and her doom be inventions of his fancy, I wish him better, and higher, and truer taste next time he writes a novel.

'Julius's exploit with the side of bacon is not defensible; he might certainly, for the fee of a shilling or sixpence, have got a boy to carry it for him.

'Captain Heath, too, must have cut a deplorable figure behind the post-chaise.

'Mrs. Vyner strikes one as a portrait from the life; and it equally strikes one that the artist hated his original model with a personal hatred. She is made so bad that one cannot in the least degree sympathise with any of those who love her; one can only despise them. She is a fiend, and therefore not like Mr. Thackeray's Rebecca, where neither vanity, heartlessness, nor falsehood have been spared by the vigorous and skilful hand which pourtrays them, but where the human being has been preserved nevertheless, and where, consequently, the lesson given is infinitely more impressive. We can learn little from the strange fantasies or demons — we are not of their kind; but the vices of the deceitful, selfish man or woman humble and warn us. In your re-

437

marks on the good girls I concur to the letter ; and I must add that I think Blanche, amiable as she is represented, could never have loved her husband after she had discovered that he was utterly despicable. Love is stronger than Cruelty, stronger than Death, but perishes under Meanness ; Pity may take its place, but Pity is not Love.

'So far, then, I not only agree with you, but I marvel at the nice perception with which you have discriminated, and at the accuracy with which you have marked each coarse, cold, improbable, unseemly defect. But now I am going to take another side : I am going to differ from you, and it is about Cecil Chamberlayne.

'You say that no man who had intellect enough to paint a picture, or write a comic opera, could act as he did ; you say that men of genius and talent may have egregious faults, but they cannot descend to brutality or meanness. Would that the case were so ! Would that intellect could preserve from low vice ! But, alas ! it cannot. No, the whole character of Cecil is painted with but too faithful a hand ; it is very masterly, because it is very true. Lewes is nobly right when he says that intellect is *not* the highest faculty of man, though it may be the most brilliant ; when he declares that the *moral* nature of his kind is more sacred than the *intellectual* nature ; when he prefers " goodness, lovingness, and quiet self-sacrifice to all the talents in the world."

'There is something divine in the thought that genius preserves from degradation, were it but true ; but Savage tells us it was not true for him ; Sheridan confirms the avowal, and Byron seals it with terrible proof.

'You never probably knew a Cecil Chamberlayne. If you had known such a one you would feel that Lewes has rather subdued the picture than overcharged it ; you would know that mental gifts without moral firmness, without a clear sense of right and wrong, without the honourable principle which makes a man rather proud than ashamed of honest labour, are no guarantee from even deepest baseness.

'I have received the "Dublin University Magazine." The notice is more favourable than I had anticipated; indeed, I had for a long time ceased to anticipate any from that quarter; but the critic does not strike one as too bright. Poor Mr. James is severely handled; *you*, likewise, are hard upon him. He always strikes me as a miracle of productiveness.

'I must conclude by thanking you for your last letter, which both pleased and instructed me. You are quite right in thinking it exhibits the writer's character. Yes, it exhibits it *unmistakeably* (as Lewes would say). And whenever it shall be my lot to submit another MS. to your inspection, I shall crave the full benefit of certain points in that character: I shall ever entreat my *first critic* to be as impartial as he is friendly; what he feels to be out of taste in my writings, I hope he will unsparingly condemn. In the excitement of composition, one is apt to fall into errors that one regrets afterwards, and we never feel our own faults so keenly as when we see them exaggerated in others.

'I conclude in haste, for I have written too long a letter; but it is because there was much to answer in yours. It interested me. I could not help wishing to tell you how nearly I agreed with you. — Believe me, yours sincerely,   C. BELL.'

TO W. S. WILLIAMS.

'APRIL 5, 1849.

'MY DEAR SIR, — Your note was very welcome. I purposely impose on myself the restraint of writing to you seldom now, because I know but too well my letters cannot be cheering. Yet I confess I am glad when the post brings me a letter: it reminds me that if the sun of action and life does not shine on us, it yet beams full on other parts of the world — and I like the recollection.

'I am not going to complain. Anne has indeed suffered much at intervals since I last wrote to you — frost and east wind have had their effect. She has passed nights of sleeplessness and pain, and days of depression and languor which nothing could cheer — but still, with the return of genial weather she revives. I cannot perceive that she is feebler now than she was a month ago, though

CHARLOTTE BRONTË

that is not saying much. It proves, however, that no rapid process
of destruction is going on in her frame, and keeps alive a hope that
with the renovating aid of summer she may yet be spared a long
time.

'What you tell me of Mr. Lewes seems to me highly characteristic. How sanguine, versatile, and self-confident must that man
be who can with ease exchange the quiet sphere of the author
for the bustling one of the actor! I heartily wish him success; and, in happier times, there are few things I should have
relished more than an opportunity of seeing him in his new
character.

'The Cornhill books are still our welcome and congenial resource when Anne is well enough to enjoy reading. Carlyle's
"Miscellanies" interest me greatly. We have read "The Emigrant Family." The characters in the work are good, full of quiet
truth and nature, and the local colouring is excellent; yet I
can hardly call it a good novel. Reflective, truth-loving, and
even elevated as is Alexander Harris's mind, I should say he
scarcely possesses the creative faculty in sufficient vigour to excel
as a writer of fiction. He *creates* nothing — he only copies. His
characters are portraits — servilely accurate; whatever is at all
ideal is not original. "The Testimony to the Truth" is a better
book than any tale he can write will ever be. Am I too dogmati-
cal in saying this?

'Anne thanks you sincerely for the kind interest you take in her
welfare, and both she and I beg to express our sense of Mrs. Williams's good wishes, which you mentioned in a former letter. We
are grateful, too, to Mr. Smith and to all who offer us the sympathy of friendship.

'Whenever you can write with pleasure to yourself, remember
Currer Bell is glad to hear from you, and he will make his letters
as little dreary as he can in reply. — Yours sincerely,
                                                      'C. BRONTË.'

It was always a great trouble to Miss Wheelwright, whose
friendship, it will be remembered, she had made in Brussels,
that Charlotte was monopolised by the Smiths on her

rare visits to London, but she frequently came to call at Lower Phillimore Place.

TO MISS LÆTITIA WHEELWRIGHT.

'HAWORTH, KEIGHLEY, December 17, 1849.

' MY DEAR LÆTITIA, — I have just time to save the post by writing a brief note. I reached home safely on Saturday afternoon, and, I am thankful to say, found papa quite well.

' The evening after I left you passed better than I expected. Thanks to my substantial lunch and cheering cup of coffee, I was able to wait the eight o'clock dinner with complete resignation, and to endure its length quite courageously, nor was I too much exhausted to converse; and of this I was glad, for otherwise I know my kind host and hostess would have been much disappointed. There were only seven gentlemen at dinner besides Mr. Smith, but of these, five were critics — a formidable band, including the literary Rhadamanthi of the "Times," the " Athenæum," the " Examiner," the " Spectator," and the " Atlas " : men more dreaded in the world of letters than you can conceive. I did not know how much their presence and conversation had excited me till they were gone, and then reaction commenced. When I had retired for the night I wished to sleep ; the effort to do so was vain — I could not close my eyes. Night passed, morning came, and I rose without having known a moment's slumber. So utterly worn out was I when I got to Derby, that I was obliged to stay there all night.

' The post is going. Give my affectionate love to your mamma, Emily, Fanny, and Sarah Anne. Remember me respectfully to your papa, and — Believe me, dear Lætitia, yours faithfully,

C. BRONTË'.

Miss Wheelwright's other sisters well remember certain episodes in connection with these London visits. They recall Charlotte's anxiety and trepidation at the prospect of meeting Thackeray. They recollect her simple, dainty dress, her shy demeanour, her absolutely unspoiled character. They tell me it was in the ' Illustrated London News,' about

the time of the publication of 'Shirley,' that they first
learnt that Currer Bell and Charlotte Brontë were one.
They would, however, have known that 'Shirley' was by
a Brussels pupil, they declared, from the absolute resemblance of Hortense Moore to one of their governesses—
Mlle. Hausse.

At the end of 1849 Miss Brontë and Miss Martineau
became acquainted. Charlotte's admiration for her more
strong-minded sister writer was at first profound.

TO JAMES TAYLOR.

'JANUARY 1, 1850.

'MY DEAR SIR,—I am sorry there should have occurred
an irregularity in the transmission of the papers; it has been
owing to my absence from home. I trust the interruption has
occasioned no inconvenience. Your last letter evinced such a
sincere and discriminating admiration for Dr. Arnold, that perhaps you will not be wholly uninterested in hearing that during
my late visit to Miss Martineau I saw much more of Fox How
and its inmates, and daily admired in the widow and children of
one of the greatest and best men of his time, the possession of
qualities the most estimable and endearing. Of my kind hostess
herself I cannot speak in terms too high. Without being able
to share all her opinions, philosophical, political, or religious,
without adopting her theories, I yet find a worth and greatness in herself, and a consistency, benevolence, perseverance in
her practice such as wins the sincerest esteem and affection.
She is not a person to be judged by her writings alone, but
rather by her own deeds and life—than which nothing can be
more exemplary or nobler. She seems to me the benefactress of
Ambleside, yet takes no sort of credit to herself for her active and
indefatigable philanthropy. The government of her household is
admirably administered; all she does is well done, from the writing
of a history down to the quietest female occupation. No sort of
carelessness or neglect is allowed under her rule, and yet she is not
over strict nor too rigidly exacting; her servants and her poor
neighbours love as well as respect her.

442

' I must not, however, fall into the error of talking too much about her, merely because my own mind is just now deeply impressed with what I have seen of her intellectual power and moral worth. Faults she has, but to me they appear very trivial weighed in the balance against her excellencies.

' With every good wish of the season, — I am, my dear sir, yours very sincerely,   C. BRONTË.'

Meanwhile the excitement which 'Shirley' was exciting in Currer Bell's home circle was not confined to the curates. Here is a letter which Canon Heald (Cyril Hall) wrote at this time : —

TO MISS ELLEN NUSSEY.

' BIRSTALL, near LEEDS,
' January 8, 1850.

' DEAR ELLEN, — Fame says you are on a visit with the renowned Currer Bell, the "great unknown" of the present day. The celebrated "Shirley" has just found its way hither. And as one always reads a book with more interest when one has a correct insight into the writer's designs, I write to ask a favour, which I ought not to be regarded presumptuous in saying that I think I have a species of claim to ask, on the ground of a sort of "poetical justice." The interpretation of this enigma is, that the story goes that either I or my father, I do not exactly know which, are part of "Currer Bell's" stock-in-trade, under the title of Mr. Hall. In that Mr. Hall is represented as black, bilious, and of dismal aspect, stooping a trifle, and indulging a little now and then in the indigenous dialect. This seems to sit very well on your humble servant — other traits do better for my good father than myself. However, though I had no idea that I should be made a means to amuse the public, Currer Bell is perfectly welcome to what she can make of so un-promising a subject. But I think *I have a fair claim in return to be let into the secret of the company I have got into.* Some of them are good enough to tell, and need no Œdipus to solve the riddle. I can tabulate, for instance, the Yorke family for the Taylors, Mr. Moore — Mr. Cartwright, and Mr. Helstone is

443

clearly meant for Mr. Robertson, though the authoress has evidently got her idea of his character through an unfavourable medium, and does not understand the full value of one of the most admirable characters I ever knew or expect to know. May thinks she descries Cecilia Crowther and Miss Johnstone (afterwards Mrs. Westerman) in two old maids.

'Now pray get us a full light on all other names and localities that are adumbrated in this said "Shirley." When some of the prominent characters will be recognised by every one who knows our quarters, there can be no harm in letting one know who may be intended by the rest. And, if necessary, I will bear Currer Bell harmless, and not let the world know that I have my intelligence from head-quarters. As I said before, I repeat now, that as I or mine are part of the stock-in-trade, I think I have an equitable claim to this intelligence, by way of my dividend. Mary and Harriet wish also to get at this information; and the latter at all events seems to have her own peculiar claim, as fame says she is "in the book" too. One had need "walk . . . warily in these dangerous days," when, as Burns (is it not he?) says —

> '" A chiel 's amang you takin' notes,
> And, faith, he 'll prent it." —

Yours sincerely,   W. M. HEALD.

'Mary and Harriet unite with me in the best wishes of the season to you and C—— B——. Pray give my best respects to Mr. Brontë also, who may have some slight remembrance of me as a child. I just remember him when at Hartshead.'[1]

TO W. S. WILLIAMS.

'FEBRUARY 2, 1850.

'MY DEAR SIR, — I have despatched to-day a parcel containing " The Caxtons," Macaulay's " Essays," " Humboldt's Letters," and such other of the books as I have read, packed with a picturesque irregularity well calculated to excite the envy and admiration of your skilful functionary in Cornhill. By-the-

[1] Printed by the kind permission of the Rev. C. W. Heald, of Chale, I. W.

bye, he ought to be careful of the few pins stuck in here and there, as he might find them useful at a future day, in case of having more bonnets to pack for the East Indies. Whenever you send me a new supply of books, may I request that you will have the goodness to include one or two of Miss Austen's. I am often asked whether I have read them, and I excite amazement by replying in the negative. I have read none except "Pride and Prejudice." Miss Martineau mentioned "Persuasion" as the best.

'Thank you for your account of the "First Performance." It was cheering and pleasant to read it, for in your animated description I seemed to realise the scene; your criticism also enables me to form some idea of the play. Lewes is a strange being. I always regret that I did not see him when in London. He seems to me clever, sharp, and coarse; I used to think him sagacious, but I believe now he is no more than shrewd, for I have observed once or twice that he brings forward as grand discoveries of his own, information he has casually received from others — true sagacity disdains little tricks of this sort. But though Lewes has many smart and some deserving points about him, he has nothing truly great; and nothing truly great, I should think, will he ever produce. Yet he merits just such successes as the one you describe — triumphs public, brief, and noisy. Notoriety suits Lewes. Fame — were it possible that he could achieve her — would be a thing uncongenial to him: he could not wait for the solemn blast of her trumpet, sounding long, and slowly waxing louder.

'I always like your way of mentioning Mr. Smith, because my own opinion of him concurs with yours; and it is as pleasant to have a favourable impression of character confirmed, as it is painful to see it dispelled. I am sure he possesses a fine nature, and I trust the selfishness of the world and the hard habits of business, though they may and must modify his disposition, will never quite spoil it.

'Can you give me any information respecting Sheridan Knowles? A few lines received from him lately, and a present of his "George Lovel," induce me to ask the question. Of course

445

CHARLOTTE BRONTË

I am aware that he is a dramatic writer of eminence, but do you know anything about him as a man?

'I believe both "Shirley" and "Jane Eyre" are being a good deal read in the North just now; but I only hear fitful rumours from time to time. I ask nothing, and my life of anchorite seclusion shuts out all bearers of tidings. One or two curiosity-hunters have made their way to Haworth Parsonage, but our rude hills and rugged neighbourhood will, I doubt not, form a sufficient barrier to the frequent repetition of such visits. —Believe me, yours sincerely,   C. BRONTË.'

The most permanent friend among the 'curiosity-hunters,' was Sir James Kay-Shuttleworth, [1] who came a month later to Haworth.

TO MISS ELLEN NUSSEY.

'MARCH 1, 1850.

' DEAR ELLEN, — I scribble you a line in haste to tell you of my proceedings. Various folks are beginning to come boring to Haworth, on the wise errand of seeing the scenery described in "Jane Eyre" and "Shirley"; amongst others, Sir J. K. Shuttleworth and Lady S. have persisted in coming; they were here on Friday. The baronet looks in vigorous health; he scarcely appears more than thirty-five, but he says he is forty-four. Lady Shuttleworth is rather handsome, and still young. They were both quite unpretending. When here they again urged me to visit them. Papa took their side at once — would not hear of my refusing. I must go — this left me without plea or defence. I consented to go for three days. They wanted me to return with them in the carriage, but I pleaded off till to-morrow. I wish it was well over.

'If all be well I shall be able to write more about them when

---

[1] Sir James Kay-Shuttleworth (1804–1877). A doctor of medicine, who was made a baronet in 1849, on resigning the secretaryship of the Committee of Council on Education; assumed the name of Shuttleworth on his marriage, in 1842, to Janet, the only child and heiress of Robert Shuttleworth of Gawthorpe Hall, Burnley (died 1872). His son, the present baronet, is the Right Hon. Sir Ughtred James Kay-Shuttleworth.

I come back. Sir J. is very courtly — fine-looking ; I wish he may be as sincere as he is polished.— In haste, yours faithfully,

'C. B.'

TO W. S. WILLIAMS.

'MARCH 16, 1850.

'MY DEAR SIR, — I found your letter with several others awaiting me on my return home from a brief stay in Lancashire. The mourning border alarmed me much. I feared that dread visitant, before whose coming every household trembles, had invaded your hearth and taken from you perhaps a child, perhaps something dearer still. The loss you have actually sustained is painful, but so much *less* painful than what I had anticipated, that to read your letter was to be greatly relieved. Still, I know what Mrs. Williams will feel. We can have but one father, but one mother, and when either is gone, we have lost what can never be replaced. Offer her, under this affliction, my sincere sympathy. I can well imagine the cloud these sad tidings would cast over your young cheerful family. Poor little Dick's exclamation and burst of grief are most naïve and natural ; he felt the sorrow of a child — a keen, but, happily, a transient pang. Time will, I trust, ere long restore your own and your wife's serenity and your children's cheerfulness.

'I mentioned, I think, that we had one or two visitors at Haworth lately ; amongst them were Sir James Kay-Shuttleworth and his lady. Before departing they exacted a promise that I would visit them at Gawthorpe Hall, their residence on the borders of East Lancashire. I went reluctantly, for it is always a difficult and painful thing to me to meet the advances of people whose kindness I am in no position to repay. Sir James is a man of polished manners, with clear intellect and highly culti-vated mind. On the whole, I got on very well with him. His health is just now somewhat broken by his severe official labours ; and the quiet drives to old ruins and old halls situate amongst older hills and woods, the dialogues (perhaps I should rather say monologues, for I listened far more than I talked) by the fireside in his antique oak-panelled drawing-room, while they suited him, did not, too much oppress and exhaust me. The house, too, is very much to my taste, near three centuries old, grey, stately, and picturesque. On the whole, now that the visit is over, I do not regret having paid it. The worst of it is that there is now some menace hanging over my head of an invitation to go to them in London during the season — this, which would doubtless be a great enjoyment to some people, is a perfect terror to me. I should highly prize the advantages to be gained in an extended range of observation, but I tremble at the thought of the price I must necessarily pay in mental distress and physical wear and tear. But you shall have no more of my confessions — to you they will appear folly.— Yours sincerely, C. BRONTË.'

TO MISS ELLEN NUSSEY.

'MARCH 19, 1850.

'DEAR ELLEN, — I have got home again, and now that the visit is over, I am, as usual, glad I have been; not that I could have endured to prolong it: a few days at once, in an utterly strange place, amongst utterly strange faces, is quite enough for me.

'When the train stopped at Burnley, I found Sir James waiting for me. A drive of about three miles brought us to the gates of Gawthorpe, and after passing up a somewhat desolate avenue, there towered the hall — grey, antique, castellated, and stately — before me. It is 250 years old, and, within as without, is a model of old English architecture. The arms and the strange crest of the Shuttleworths are carved on the oak panelling of each room. They are not a parvenu family, but date from the days of Richard III. This part of Lancashire seems rather remarkable for its houses of ancient race. The Townleys, who live near, go back to the Conquest.

'The people, however, were of still more interest to me than the house. Lady Shuttleworth is a little woman, thirty-two years old, with a pretty, smooth, lively face. Of pretension to aristocratic airs she may be entirely acquitted; of frankness, good-humour, and activity she has enough; truth obliges me to add, that, as it seems to me, grace, dignity, fine feeling were

not in the inventory of her qualities. These last are precisely
what her husband possesses. In manner he can be gracious and
dignified; his tastes and feelings are capable of elevation; frank
he is not, but, on the contrary, politic; he calls himself a man
of the world and knows the world's ways; courtly and affable
in some points of view, he is strict and rigorous in others. In
him high mental cultivation is combined with an extended
range of observation, and thoroughly practical views and habits.
His nerves are naturally acutely sensitive, and the present very
critical state of his health has exaggerated sensitiveness into
irritability. His wife is of a temperament precisely suited to
nurse him and wait on him; if her sensations were more delicate and acute she would not do half so well. They get on
perfectly together. The children — there are four of them — are
all fine children in their way. They have a young German lady
as governess — a quiet, well-instructed, interesting girl, whom I
took to at once, and, in my heart, liked better than anything else
in the house. She also instinctively took to me. She is very
well treated for a governess, but wore the usual pale, despondent look of her class. She told me she was homesick, and she
looked so.

'I have received the parcel containing the cushion and all the
etcetera, for which I thank you very much. I suppose I must begin with the group of flowers; I don't know how I shall manage
it, but I shall try. I have a good number of letters to answer
— from Mr. Smith, from Mr. Williams, from Thornton Hunt,
Lætitia Wheelwright, Harriet Dyson — and so I must bid you
good-bye for the present. Write to me soon. The brief absence
from home, though in some respects trying and painful in itself,
has, I think, given me a little better tone of spirit. All
through this month of February I have had a crushing time of
it. I could not escape from or rise above certain most mournful recollections — the last few days, the sufferings, the remembered
words, most sorrowful to me, of those who, Faith assures me, are
now happy. At evening and bed-time such thoughts would haunt
me, bringing a weary heartache. Good-bye, dear Nell. — Yours
faithfully,   C. B.'

CHARLOTTE BRONTË

TO MISS ELLEN NUSSEY.

'MAY 21, 1850.

'DEAR ELLEN, — My visit is again postponed. Sir James Shuttleworth, I am sorry to say, is most seriously ill. Two physicians are in attendance twice a day, and company and conversation, even with his own relatives, are prohibited as too exciting. Notwithstanding this, he has written two notes to me himself, claiming a promise that I will wait till he is better, and not allow any one else " to introduce me," as he says, "into the Oceanic life of London." Sincerely sorry as I was for him, I could not help smiling at this sentence. But I shall willingly promise. I know something of him, and like part at least, of what I do know. I do not feel in the least tempted to change him for another. His sufferings are very great. I trust and hope God will be pleased to spare his mind. I have just got a note informing me that he is something better; but, of course, he will vary. Lady Shuttleworth is much, much to be pitied too; his nights, it seems, are most distressing. — Good-bye, dear Nell. Write soon to   C. B.'

TO MISS ELLEN NUSSEY.

'76 GLOUCESTER TERRACE,
'HYDE PARK GARDENS, June 3, 1850.

'DEAR ELLEN, — I came to London last Thursday. I am staying at Mrs. Smith's, who has changed her residence, as the address will show. A good deal of writing backwards and forwards, persuasion, etc., took place before this step was resolved on ; but at last I explained to Sir James that I had some little matters of business to transact, and that I should stay quietly at my publisher's. He has called twice, and Lady Shuttleworth once ; each of them alone. He is in a fearfully nervous state. To my great horror he talks of my going with them to Hampton Court, Windsor, etc. God knows how I shall get on. I perfectly dread it.

'Here I feel very comfortable. Mrs. Smith treats me with a serene, equable kindness which just suits me. Her son is, as before, genial and kindly. I have seen very few persons, and am not likely to see many, as the agreement was that I was to be very quiet. We have been to the Exhibition of the Royal Academy, to the Opera, and the Zoological Gardens. The weather is splendid. I shall not stay longer than a fortnight in London. The feverishness and exhaustion beset me somewhat, but not quite so badly as before, as indeed I have not yet been so much tried. I hope you will write soon and tell me how you are getting on. Give my regards to all.—Yours faithfully,   C. B.'

TO REV. P. BRONTË.

'76 Gloucester Terrace,
'Hyde Park Gardens, June 4, 1850.

' Dear Papa,— I was very glad to get your letter this morning, and still more glad to learn that your health continues in some degree to improve. I fear you will feel the present weather somewhat debilitating, at least if it is as warm in Yorkshire as in London. I cannot help grudging these fine days on account of the roofing of the house. It is a great pity the workmen were not prepared to begin a week ago.

'Since I wrote I have been to the Opera; to the Exhibition of the Royal Academy, where there were some fine paintings, especially a large one by Landseer of the Duke of Wellington on the field of Waterloo, and a grand, wonderful picture of Martin's from Campbell's poem of the "Last Man," showing the red sun fading out of the sky, and all the soil of the foreground made up of bones and skulls. The secretary of the Zoological Society also sent me an honorary ticket of admission to their gardens, which I wish you could see. There are animals from all parts of the world inclosed in great cages in the open air amongst trees and shrubs — lions, tigers, leopards, elephants, numberless monkeys, camels, five or six camelopards, a young hippopotamus with an Egyptian for its keeper; birds of all kinds — eagles, ostriches, a pair of great condors from the Andes, strange ducks and water-fowl which seem very happy and comfortable, and build their nests amongst the reeds and sedges of the lakes where they are kept. Some of the American birds make inexpressible noises.

' There are also all sorts of living snakes and lizards in cages, some great Ceylon toads not much smaller than Flossy, some large foreign rats nearly as large and fierce as little bull-dogs. The most ferocious and deadly-looking things in the place were these rats, a laughing hyena (which every now and then uttered a hideous peal of laughter such as a score of maniacs might produce) and a cobra-di-capello snake. I think this snake was the worst of all : it had the eyes and face of a fiend, and darted out its barbed tongue sharply and incessantly.

' I am glad to hear that Tabby and Martha are pretty well. Remember me to them, and—Believe me, dear papa, your affectionate daughter,   C. BRONTË.

' I hope you don't care for the notice in "Sharpe's Magazine"; it does not disturb me in the least. Mr. Smith says it is of no consequence whatever in a literary sense. Sharpe, the proprietor, was an apprentice of Mr. Smith's father.'

TO MISS ELLEN NUSSEY.

' 76 GLOUCESTER TERRACE,
'HYDE PARK GARDENS, June 21, 1850.

'DEAR ELLEN,— I am leaving London, if all be well, on Tuesday, and shall be very glad to come to you for a few days, if that arrangement still remains convenient to you. I intend to start at nine o'clock A.M. by the express train, which arrives in Leeds thirty-five minutes past two. I should then be at Batley about four in the afternoon. Would that suit?

' My London visit has much surpassed my expectations this time ; I have suffered less and enjoyed more than before. Rather a trying termination yet remains to me. Mrs. Smith's youngest son is at school in Scotland, and George, her eldest, is going to fetch him home for the vacation. The other evening he announced his intention of taking one of his sisters with him, and proposed that Miss Brontë should go down to Edinburgh and join them there, and see that city and its suburbs. I concluded he was joking, laughed, and declined; however, it seems he was in earnest. The thing appearing to me perfectly

out of the question, I still refused. Mrs. Smith did not favour
it ; you may easily fancy how she helped me to sustain my
opposition, but her worthy son only waxed more determined.
His mother is master of the house, but he is master of his
mother. This morning she came and entreated me to go.
" George wished it so much " ; he had begged her to use her
influence, etc., etc. Now I believe that George and I understand each other very well, and respect each other very sincerely.
We both know the wide breach time has made between us ;
we do not embarrass each other, or very rarely ; my six or eight
years of seniority, to say nothing of lack of all pretension to
beauty, etc., are a perfect safeguard. I should not in the least
fear to go with him to China. I like to see him pleased, I
greatly *dis*like to ruffle and disappoint him, so he shall have his
mind ; and if all be well, I mean to join him in Edinburgh after
I shall have spent a few days with you. With his buoyant
animal spirits and youthful vigour he will make severe demands
on my muscles and nerves, but I daresay I shall get through
somehow, and then perhaps come back to rest a few days with
you before I go home. With kind regards to all at Brookroyd,
your guests included, — I am, dear Ellen, yours faithfully,

'C. Brontë.

'Write by return of post.'

TO MISS LÆTITIA WHEELWRIGHT.

'Haworth, July 30, 1850.

'My dear Lætitia, — I promised to write to you when I
should have returned home. Returned home I am, but you
may conceive that many, many matters solicit attention and
demand arrangement in a house which has lately been turned
topsy-turvy in the operation of unroofing. Drawers and cup-
boards must wait a moment, however, while I fulfil my promise,
though it is imperatively necessary that this fulfilment should
be achieved with brevity.

'My stay in Scotland was short, and what I saw was chiefly
comprised in Edinburgh and the neighbourhood, in Abbotsford
and Melrose, for I was obliged to relinquish my first intention

of going from Glasgow to Oban and thence through a portion of the Highlands. But though the time was brief, and the view of objects limited, I found such a charm of situation, association, and circumstances that I think the enjoyment experienced in that little space equalled in degree and excelled in kind all which London yielded during a month's sojourn. Edinburgh compared to London is like a vivid page of history compared to a huge dull treatise on political economy ; and as to Melrose and Abbotsford, the very names possess music and magic.

'I am thankful to say that on my return home I found papa pretty well. Full often had I thought of him when I was far away ; and deeply sad as it is on many accounts to come back to this old house, yet I was glad to be with him once more.

'You were proposing, I remember, to go into the country, I trust you are there now and enjoying this fine day in some scene where the air will not be tainted, nor the sunshine dimmed, by London smoke. If your papa, mamma, or any of your sisters are within reach, give them my kindest remembrances — if not, save such remembrances till you see them. — Believe me, my dear Lætitia, yours hurriedly but faithfully,

'C. BRONTË.'

TO REV. P. BRONTË.

'AMBLESIDE, August 15, 1850.

'DEAR PAPA, — I think I shall not come home till Thursday. If all be well I shall leave here on Monday and spend a day or two with Ellen Nussey. I have enjoyed my visit exceedingly. Sir J. K. Shuttleworth has called several times and taken me out in his carriage. He seems very truly friendly ; but, I am sorry to say, he looks pale and very much wasted. I greatly fear he will not live very long unless some change for the better soon takes place. Lady S. is ill too, and cannot go out. I have seen a good deal of Dr. Arnold's family, and like them much. As to Miss Martineau, I admire her and wonder at her more than I can say. Her powers of labour, of exercise, and social cheerfulness are beyond my comprehension. In spite of

the unceasing activity of her colossal intellect she enjoys robust
health. She is a taller, larger, and more strongly made woman
than I had imagined from that first interview with her. She is
very kind to me, though she must think I am a very insignificant
person compared to herself. She has just been into the room
to show me a chapter of her history which she is now writing,
relating to the Duke of Wellington's character and his proceedings
in the Peninsula. She wanted an opinion on it, and I was happy
to be able to give a very approving one. She seems to understand
and do him justice.

'You must not direct any more letters here as they will not
reach me after to-day. Hoping, dear papa, that you are well,
and with kind regards to Tabby and Martha, — I am, your
affectionate daughter,   C. BRONTË.'

TO W. S. WILLIAMS.

'OCTOBER 2, 1850.

'MY DEAR SIR, — I have to thank you for the care and kindness with which you have assisted me throughout in correcting
these " Remains."

'Whether, when they are published, they will appear to others
as they do to me, I cannot tell. I hope not. And indeed I suppose what to me is bitter pain will only be soft pathos to the
general public.

'Miss Martineau has several times lately asked me to go and
see her; and though this is a dreary season for travelling north-
ward, I think if papa continues pretty well I shall go in a week
or two. I feel to my deep sorrow, to my humiliation, that it is
not in my power to bear the canker of constant solitude. I had
calculated that when shut out from every enjoyment, from
every stimulus but what could be derived from intellectual
exertion, my mind would rouse itself perforce. It is not so.
Even intellect, even imagination, will not dispense with the ray
of domestic cheerfulness, with the gentle spur of family discussion.
Late in the evenings, and all through the nights, I fall into a
condition of mind which turns entirely to the past — to memory,
and memory is both sad and relentless. This will never do, and

will produce no good. I tell you this that you may check false anticipations. You cannot help me, and must not trouble yourself in any shape to sympathise with me. It is my cup, and I must drink it, as others drink theirs. — Yours sincerely,

'C. Brontë.'

Among Miss Brontë's papers I find the following letter to Miss Martineau, written with a not unnatural resentment after the publication of a severe critique of 'Shirley.'

TO MISS HARRIET MARTINEAU.

'My dear Miss Martineau, — I think I best show my sense of the tone and feeling of your last, by immediate compliance with the wish you express that I should send your letter. I inclose it, and have marked with red ink the passage which struck me dumb. All the rest is fair, right, worthy of you, but I protest against this passage; and were I brought up before the bar of all the critics in England, to such a charge I should respond, "Not guilty."

'I know what *love* is as I understand it; and if man or woman should be ashamed of feeling such love, then is there nothing right, noble, faithful, truthful, unselfish in this earth, as I comprehend rectitude, nobleness, fidelity, truth, and disinterestedness. — Yours sincerely,   C. B.

'To differ from you gives me keen pain.'

TO JAMES TAYLOR, Cornhill.

'November 6, 1850.

'My dear Sir, — Mrs. Arnold seemed an amiable, and must once have been a very pretty, woman; her daughter I liked much. There was present also a son of Chevalier Bunsen, with his wife, or rather bride. I had not then read Dr. Arnold's Life — otherwise, the visit would have interested me even more than it actually did.

'Mr. Williams told me (if I mistake not) that you had recently visited the Lake Country. I trust you enjoyed your excursion, and that our English Lakes did not suffer too much by

comparison in your memory with the Scottish Lochs. — I am, my
dear sir, yours sincerely,   C. BRONTË.'

TO MISS ELLEN NUSSEY.

'AMBLESIDE, December 21, 1850.

'DEAR ELLEN, — I have managed to get off going to Sir J. K.
Shuttleworth's by a promise to come some other time. I
thought I really should like to spend two or three days with you
before going home ; therefore, if it is not inconvenient for you,
I will come on Monday and stay till Thursday. I shall be at
Bradford (D.V.) at ten minutes past two, Monday afternoon, and
can take a cab at the station forward to Birstall. I have truly
enjoyed my visit. I have seen a good many people, and all have
been so marvellously kind ; not the least so the family of
Dr. Arnold. Miss Martineau I relish inexpressibly. Sir James
has been almost every day to take me for a drive. I begin to
admit in my own mind that he is sincerely benignant to me. I
grieve to say he looks to me as if wasting away. Lady Shuttleworth is ill. She cannot go out, and I have not seen her. Till we
meet, good-bye.   C. BRONTË.'

It was during this visit to Ambleside that Charlotte
Brontë and Matthew Arnold met.

'At seven,' writes Mr. Arnold from Fox How (December
21, 1850), 'came Miss Martineau and Miss Brontë (Jane
Eyre); talked to Miss Martineau (who blasphemes fright-
fully) about the prospects of the Church of England, and,
wretched man that I am, promised to go and see her cow-
keeping miracles [1] to-morrow — I, who hardly know a cow
from a sheep. I talked to Miss Brontë (past thirty and
plain, with expressive grey eyes, though) of her curates, of
French novels, and her education in a school at Brussels,
and sent the lions roaring to their dens at half-past nine,
and came to talk to you.' [2]

[1] Some experiments on a farm of two acres.
[2] Letters of Matthew Arnold, collected and arranged by George W. E. Russell.

CHARLOTTE BRONTË

By the light of this 'impression,' it is not a little interesting to see what Miss Brontë, 'past thirty and plain,' thought of Mr. Matthew Arnold!

TO JAMES TAYLOR, Cornhill.

'January 15, 1851.

'My dear Sir, — I fancy the imperfect way in which my last note was expressed must have led you into an error, and that you must have applied to Mrs. Arnold the remarks I intended for Miss Martineau. I remember whilst writing about " my hostess " I was sensible to some obscurity in the term; permit me now to explain that it referred to Miss Martineau.

'Mrs. Arnold is, indeed, as I judge from my own observations no less than from the unanimous testimony of all who really know her, a good and amiable woman, but the intellectual is not her forte, and she has no pretensions to power or completeness of character. The same remark, I think, applies to her daughters. You admire in them the kindliest feeling towards each other and their fellow-creatures, and they offer in their home circle a beautiful example of family unity, and of that refinement which is sure to spring thence; but when the conversation turns on literature or any subject that offers a test for the intellect, you usually felt that their opinions were rather imitative than original, rather sentimental than sound. Those who have only seen Mrs. Arnold once will necessarily, I think, judge of her unfavourably; her manner on introduction disappointed me sensibly, as lacking that genuineness and simplicity one seemed to have a right to expect in the chosen life-companion of Dr. Arnold. On my remarking as much to Mrs. Gaskell and Sir J. K. Shuttleworth, I was told for my consolation it was a "conventional manner," but that it vanished on closer acquaintance; fortunately this last assurance proved true. It is observable that Matthew Arnold, the eldest son, and the author of the volume of poems to which you allude, inherits his mother's defect. Striking and prepossessing in appearance, his manner displeases from its seeming foppery. I own it caused me at first to regard him with regretful surprise; the

458

shade of Dr. Arnold seemed to me to frown on his young representative. I was told, however, that " Mr. Arnold improved upon acquaintance." So it was : ere long a real modesty appeared under his assumed conceit, and some genuine intellectual aspirations, as well as high educational acquirements, displaced superficial affectations. I was given to understand that his theological opinions were very vague and unsettled, and indeed he betrayed as much in the course of conversation. Most unfortunate for him, doubtless, has been the untimely loss of his father.

'My visit to Westmoreland has certainly done me good. Physically, I was not ill before I went there, but my mind had undergone some painful laceration ; in the course of looking over my sister's papers, mementos and memoranda that would have been nothing to others conveyed for me so keen a sting. Near at hand there was no means of lightening or effacing the sad impression by refreshing social intercourse ; from my father, of course, my sole care was to conceal it — age demanding the same forbearance as infancy in the communication of grief. Continuous solitude grew more than I could bear, and, to speak truth, I was glad of a change. You will say that we ought to have power in ourselves either to bear circumstances or to bend them. True, we should do our best to this end, but sometimes our best is unavailing. However, I am better now, and most thankful for the respite.

'The interest you so kindly express in my sister's works touches me home. Thank you for it, especially as I do not believe you would speak otherwise than sincerely. The only notices that I have seen of the new edition of " Wuthering Heights " were those in the " Examiner," the "Leader," and the " Athenæum." That in the " Athenæum " somehow gave me pleasure : it is quiet but respectful — so I thought, at least.

'You asked whether Miss Martineau made me a convert to mesmerism ? Scarcely ; yet I heard miracles of its efficacy and could hardly discredit the whole of what was told me. I even underwent a personal experiment ; and though the result was not absolutely clear, it was inferred that in time I should prove an excellent subject.

CHARLOTTE BRONTË

'The question of mesmerism will be discussed with little reserve, I believe, in a forthcoming work of Miss Martineau's, and I have some painful anticipations of the manner in which other subjects, offering less legitimate ground for speculation, will be handled.

'You mention the "Leader"; what do you think of it? I have been asked to contribute; but though I respect the spirit of fairness and courtesy in which it is on the whole conducted, its principles on some points are such that I have hitherto shrunk from the thought of seeing my name in its columns.

'Thanking you for your good wishes, — I am, my dear sir, yours sincerely,   C. BRONTË.'

TO MISS LÆTITIA WHEELWRIGHT.

'HAWORTH, January 12, 1851.

'DEAR LÆTITIA, — A spare moment must and shall be made for you, no matter how many letters I have to write (and just now there is an influx). In reply to your kind inquiries, I have to say that my stay in London and excursion to Scotland did me good — much good at the time; but my health was again somewhat sharply tried at the close of autumn, and I lost in some days of indisposition the additional flesh and strength I had previously gained. This resulted from the painful task of looking over letters and papers belonging to my sisters. Many little mementos and memoranda conspired to make an impression inexpressibly sad, which solitude deepened and fostered till I grew ill. A brief trip to Westmoreland has, however, I am thankful to say, revived me again, and the circumstance of papa being just now in good health and spirits gives me many causes for gratitude. When we have but one precious thing left we think much of it.

'I have been staying a short time with Miss Martineau. As you may imagine, the visit proved one of no common interest. She is certainly a woman of wonderful endowments, both intellectual and physical, and though I share few of her opinions, and regard her as fallible on certain points of judgment, I must still accord her my sincerest esteem. The manner in which

460

she combines the highest mental culture with the nicest discharge
of feminine duties filled me with admiration, while her affectionate
kindness earned my gratitude.

'Your description of the magician Paxton's Crystal Palace is
quite graphic. Whether I shall see it or not I don't know.
London will be so dreadfully crowded and busy this season, I
feel a dread of going there.

'Compelled to break off, I have only time to offer my kindest
remembrances to your whole circle, and my love to yourself. —
Yours ever,   C. Brontë.'

TO REV. P. BRONTË.

'112 Gloucester Terrace, Hyde Park,
'London, June 17, 1851.

'Dear Papa, — I write a line in haste to tell you that I find
they will not let me leave London till next Tuesday; and as I
have promised to spend a day or two with Mrs. Gaskell on my
way home, it will probably be Friday or Saturday in next week
before I return to Haworth. Martha will thus have a few days
more time, and must not hurry or overwork herself. Yesterday
I saw Cardinal Wiseman and heard him speak. It was at a
meeting for the Roman Catholic Society of St. Vincent de Paul;
the Cardinal presided. He is a big portly man something of
the shape of Mr. Morgan; he has not merely a double but a
treble and quadruple chin; he has a very large mouth with oily
lips, and looks as if he would relish a good dinner with a bottle
of wine after it. He came swimming into the room smiling,
simpering, and bowing like a fat old lady, and sat down very
demure in his chair and looked the picture of a sleek hypocrite.
He was dressed in black like a bishop or dean in plain clothes,
but wore scarlet gloves and a brilliant scarlet waistcoat. A bevy
of inferior priests surrounded him, many of them very dark-
looking and sinister men. The Cardinal spoke in a smooth
whining manner, just like a canting Methodist preacher. The
audience seemed to look up to him as to a god. A spirit of the
hottest zeal pervaded the whole meeting. I was told afterwards
that except myself and the person who accompanied me there

461

CHARLOTTE BRONTË

was not a single Protestant present. All the speeches turned on the necessity of straining every nerve to make converts to popery. It is in such a scene that one feels what the Catholics are doing. Most persevering and enthusiastic are they in their work! Let Protestants look to it. It cheered me much to hear that you continue pretty well. Take every care of yourself. Remember me kindly to Tabby and Martha, also to Mr. Nicholls, and — Believe me, dear papa, your affectionate daughter,

'C. Brontë.'

TO MISS ELLEN NUSSEY.

'June 19, 1851.

'Dear Ellen, — I shall have to stay in London a few days longer than I intended. Sir J. K. Shuttleworth has found out that I am here. I had some trouble in warding off his wish that I should go directly to his house and take up my quarters there, but Mrs. Smith helped me, and I got off with promising to spend a day. I am engaged to spend a day or two with Mrs. Gaskell on my way home, and could not put her off, as she is going away for a portion of the summer. Lady Shuttleworth looks very delicate. Papa is now very desirous I should come home; and when I have as quickly as possible paid my debts of engagements, home I must go. Next Tuesday I go to Manchester for two days. 'C. Brontë.'

TO MISS ELLEN NUSSEY.

'112 Gloucester Terrace,
'Hyde Park, June 24, 1851.

'Dear Ellen, — I cannot now leave London till Friday. To-morrow is Mr. Smith's only holiday. Mr. Taylor's departure leaves him loaded with work. More than once since I came he has been kept in the city till three in the morning. He wants to take us all to Richmond, and I promised last week I would stay and go with him, his mother, and sisters. I go to Mrs. Gaskell's on Friday. — Believe me, yours faithfully,

'C. Brontë.

AND HER CIRCLE

TO REV. P. BRONTË, Haworth, Yorks.

'112 Gloucester Terrace, June 26, 1851.

'Dear Papa, — I have not yet been able to get away from
London, but if all be well I shall go to-morrow, stay two days
with Mrs. Gaskell at Manchester, and return home on Monday
30th *without fail.* During this last week or ten days I have
seen many things, some of them very interesting, and have also
been in much better health than I was during the first fortnight
of my stay in London. Sir James and Lady Shuttleworth have
really been very kind, and most scrupulously attentive. They
desire their regards to you, and send all manner of civil
messages. The Marquis of Westminster and the Earl of
Ellsmere each sent me an order to see their private collection
of pictures, which I enjoyed very much. Mr. Rogers, the
patriarch-poet, now eighty-seven years old, invited me to
breakfast with him. His breakfasts, you must understand, are
celebrated throughout Europe for their peculiar refinement and
taste. He never admits at that meal more than four persons to
his table : himself and three guests. The morning I was there I
met Lord Glenelg and Mrs. Davenport, a relation of Lady
Shuttleworth's, and a very beautiful and fashionable woman.
The visit was very interesting ; I was glad that I had paid it
after it was over. An attention that pleased and surprised me
more I think than any other was the circumstance of Sir David
Brewster, who is one of the first scientific men of his day,
coming to take me over the Crystal Palace and pointing out
and explaining the most remarkable curiosities. You will know,
dear papa, that I do not mention those things to boast of them,
but merely because I think they will give you pleasure.
Nobody, I find, thinks the worse of me for avoiding publicity
and declining to go to large parties, and everybody seems truly
courteous and respectful, a mode of behaviour which makes me
grateful, as it ought to do. Good-bye till Monday. Give my
best regards to Mr. Nicholls, Tabby, and Martha, and — Believe
me, your affectionate daughter,   C. Brontë.'

CHAPTER XVII.

THE REV. ARTHUR BELL NICHOLLS.

WITHOUT the kindly assistance of Mr. Arthur Bell Nicholls, this book could not have been written, and I might therefore be supposed to guide my pen with appalling discretion in treating of the married life of Charlotte Brontë. There are, however, no painful secrets to reveal, no skeletons to lay bare. Mr. Nicholls's story is a very simple one ; and that it is entirely creditable to him, there is abundant evidence. Amid the full discussion to which the lives of the Brontës have necessarily been subjected through their ever-continuous fame, it was perhaps inevitable that a contrary opinion should gain ground. Many of Mr. Nicholls's relatives in his own country have frequently sighed over the perverted statements which have obtained currency. 'It is cruel that your uncle Arthur, the best of men, as we know, should be thus treated,' was the comment of Mr. Nicholls's brother to his daughter after reading an unfriendly article concerning Charlotte's husband. Yet it was not unnatural that such an estimate should get abroad ; and I may frankly admit that until I met Mr. Nicholls I believed that Charlotte Brontë's marriage had been an unhappy one — an opinion gathered partly from Mrs. Gaskell, partly from current tradition in Yorkshire. Mrs. Gaskell, in fact, did not like Mr. Nicholls, and there were those with whom she came in contact while writing Miss Brontë's Life who were eager to fan that feeling in the usually kindly biographer. Mr.

THE REV. ARTHUR BELL NICHOLLS.
From a Portrait taken during his Curacy at Haworth.

Nicholls himself did not work in the direction of concilia-
tion. He was, as we shall see, a Scotchman, and Scottish
taciturnity brought to bear upon the genial and jovial
Yorkshire folk did not make for friendliness. Further, he
would not let Mrs. Gaskell 'edit' and change 'The Professor,'
and here also he did wisely and well. He hated publicity,
and above all things viewed the attempt to pierce the veil of
his married life with almost morbid detestation. Who shall
say that he was not right, and that his retirement for more
than forty years from the whole region of controversy has
not abundantly justified itself? One at least of Miss Brontë's
friends has been known in our day to complain bitterly of
all the trouble to which she has been subjected by the ill-
considered zeal of Brontë enthusiasts. Mr. Nicholls has
escaped all this by a judicious silence. Now that forty years
and more have passed since his wife's death, it cannot be
inopportune to tell the public all that they can fairly ask to
know.

Mr. Nicholls was born in Co. Antrim in 1817, but of
Scottish parents on both sides. He was left at the age of
seven to the charge of an uncle — the Rev. Alan Bell —
who was headmaster of the Royal School at Banagher, in
King's Co. Mr. Nicholls afterwards entered Trinity College,
Dublin, and it was thence that he went to Haworth, his
first curacy. He succeeded a fellow-countryman, Mr. Peter
Augustus Smith, in 1844. The first impression we have of
the new curate in Charlotte's letters is scarcely more favourable than that of his predecessors.

TO MISS ELLEN NUSSEY.

'OCTOBER 9, 1844.

'DEAR ELLEN, — We are getting on here the same as usual,
only that Branwell has been more than ordinarily troublesome
and annoying of late; he leads papa a wretched life. Mr.
Nicholls is returned just the same. I cannot for my life see

those interesting germs of goodness in him you discovered; his narrowness of mind always strikes me chiefly. I fear he is indebted to your imagination for his hidden treasure. — Yours,

'C. B.'

TO MISS ELLEN NUSSEY.

' July 10, 1846.

' Dear Ellen, — Who gravely asked you whether Miss Brontë was not going to be married to her papa's curate? I scarcely need say that never was rumour more unfounded. A cold far-away sort of civility are the only terms on which I have ever been with Mr. Nicholls. I could by no means think of mentioning such a rumour to him even as a joke. It would make me the laughing-stock of himself and his fellow curates for half a year to come. They regard me as an old maid, and I regard them, one and all, as highly uninteresting, narrow, and unattractive specimens of the coarser sex.

' Write to me again soon, whether you have anything particular to say or not. Give my sincere love to your mother and sisters. C. Brontë.'

TO MISS ELLEN NUSSEY.

' November 17, 1846.

' Dear Ellen, — I will just write a brief despatch to say that I received yours and that I was very glad to get it. I do not know when you have been so long without writing to me before. I had begun to imagine you were gone to your brother Joshua's.

' Papa continues to do very well. He read prayers twice in the church last Sunday. Next Sunday he will have to take the whole duty of the three services himself as Mr. Nicholls is in Ireland. Remember me to your mother and sisters. Write as soon as you possibly can after you get to Oundle. Good luck go with you. C. Brontë.'

That Scotch reticence held sway, and told against Mr. Nicholls for many a day to come.

AND HER CIRCLE

TO MISS ELLEN NUSSEY.

'OCTOBER 7, 1847.

'DEAR ELLEN, — I have been expecting you to write to me ; but as you don't do it, and as, moreover, you may possibly think it is my turn, and not yours, though on that point I am far from clear, I shall just send you one of my scrubby notes for the express purpose of eliciting a reply. Anne was very much pleased with your letter ; I presume she has answered it before now. I would fain hope that her health is a little stronger than it was, and her spirits a little better, but she leads much too sedentary a life, and is continually sitting stooping either over a book or over her desk. It is with difficulty we can prevail upon her to take a walk or induce her to converse. I look forward to next summer with the confident intention that she shall, if possible, make at least a brief sojourn at the sea-side.

'I am sorry I inoculated you with fears about the east wind ; I did not feel the last blast so severely as I have often done. My sympathies were much awakened by the touching anecdote. Did you salute your boy-messenger with a box on the ear the next time he came across you ? I think I should have been strongly tempted to have done as much. Mr. Nicholls is not yet returned. I am sorry to say that many of the parishioners express a desire that he should not trouble himself to recross the Channel. This is not the feeling that ought to exist between shepherd and flock. It is not such as is prevalent at Birstall. It is not such as poor Mr. Weightman excited.

'Give my best love to all of them, and — Believe me, yours faithfully,   C. BRONTË.'

The next glimpse is more kindly.

TO MISS ELLEN NUSSEY.

'JANUARY 28, 1850.

'DEAR ELLEN, — I cannot but be concerned to hear of your mother's illness ; write again soon, if it be but a line, to tell me how she gets on. This shadow will, I trust and believe, be but a passing one, but it is a foretaste and warning of what *must come* one day. Let it prepare your mind, dear Ellen, for that great trial

467

which, if you live, it *must* in the course of a few years be your lot
to undergo. That cutting asunder of the ties of nature is the pain
we most dread and which we are most certain to experience. Lewes's
letter made me laugh; I cannot respect him more for it. Sir J. K.
Shuttleworth's letter did not make me laugh; he has written again
since. I have received to-day a note from Miss Alexander, daughter,
she says, of Dr. Alexander. Do you know anything of her? Mary
Taylor seems in good health and spirits, and in the way of doing
well. I shall feel anxious to hear again soon.   C. B.

'P.S. — Mr. Nicholls has finished reading "Shirley"; he is
delighted with it. John Brown's wife seriously thought he had
gone wrong in the head as she heard him giving vent to roars
of laughter as he sat alone, clapping his hands and stamping on
the floor. He would read all the scenes about the curates aloud to
papa. He triumphed in his own character.[1] What Mr. Grant
will say is another thing. No matter.'

TO MISS ELLEN NUSSEY.

'HAWORTH, July 27, 1851.

'DEAR NELL, — I hope you have taken no cold from your
wretched journey home; you see you should have taken my
advice and stayed till Saturday. Didn't I tell you I had a
"presentiment" it would be better for you to do so?

[1] Mr. Nicholls is the Mr. Macarthey of 'Shirley.' Here is the reference
which not unnaturally gratified him : — 'Perhaps I ought to remark that, on
the premature and sudden vanishing of Mr. Malone from the stage of Briarfield parish . . . there came as his successor, another Irish curate, Mr. Macarthey. I am happy to be able to inform you, *with truth*, that this gentleman
did as much credit to his country as Malone had done it discredit; he proved
himself as decent, decorous, and conscientious, as Peter was rampant, boisterous, and — (this last epithet I choose to suppress, because it would let the cat
out of the bag). He laboured faithfully in the parish; the schools, both Sunday and day schools, flourished under his sway like green bay-trees. Being
human, of course he had his faults; these, however, were proper, steady-going,
clerical faults: the circumstance of finding himself invited to tea with a dissenter would unhinge him for a week; the spectacle of a Quaker wearing his
hat in the church, the thought of an unbaptized fellow-creature being interred
with Christian rites — these things could make strange havoc in Mr. Macarthey's physical and mental economy; otherwise he was sane and rational,
diligent and charitable.' — *Shirley*, chap. xxxvii.

'I am glad you found your mother pretty well. Is she disposed to excuse the wretched petrified condition of the bilberry preserve, in consideration of the intent of the donor? It seems they had high company while you were away. You see what you lose by coming to Haworth. No events here since your departure except a long letter from Miss Martineau. (She did not write the article on "Woman" in the "Westminster," by the way, it is the production of a man, and one of the first philosophers and political economists and metaphysicians of the day.[1]) Item, the departure of Mr. Nicholls for Ireland, and his inviting himself on the eve thereof to come and take a farewell tea; good, mild, uncontentious. Item, a note from the stiff-like chap who called about the epitaph for his cousin. I inclose this — a finer gem in its way it would be difficult to conceive. You need not, however, be at the trouble of returning it. How are they at Hunsworth yet? It is no use saying whether I am solitary or not; I drive on very well, and papa continues pretty well. — Yours faithfully, C. BRONTË.'

I print the next letter here because, although it contains no reference to Mr. Nicholls, it has a bearing upon the letter following it. Dr. Wheelwright shared Mr. Brontë's infirmity of defective eyesight.

TO MISS LÆTITIA WHEELWRIGHT.

'HAWORTH, April 12, 1852.

'DEAR LÆTITIA, — Your last letter gave me much concern. I had hoped you were long ere this restored to your usual health, and it both pained and surprised me to hear that you still suffer so much from debility. I cannot help thinking your constitution is naturally sound and healthy. Can it be the air of London which disagrees with you? For myself, I struggled through the winter and the early part of spring often with great difficulty. My friend stayed with me a few days in the early part of January — she could not be spared longer. I was

---

[1] John Stuart Mill, who, however, attributed the authorship of this article to his wife.

better during her visit, but had a relapse soon after she left me, which reduced my strength very much. It cannot be denied that the solitude of my position fearfully aggravated its other evils. Some long, stormy days and nights there were when I felt such a craving for support and companionship as I cannot express. Sleepless, I lay awake night after night; weak and unable to occupy myself I sat in my chair day after day, the saddest memories my only company. It was a time I shall never forget, but God sent it and it must have been for the best.

'I am better now, and very grateful do I feel for the restoration of tolerable health; but, as if there was always to be some affliction, papa, who enjoyed wonderful health during the whole winter, is ailing with his spring attack of bronchitis. I earnestly trust it may pass over in the comparatively ameliorated form in which it has hitherto shown itself.

'Let me not forget to answer your question about the cataract. Tell your papa my father was seventy at the time he underwent an operation; he was most reluctant to try the experiment — could not believe that at his age and with his want of robust strength it would succeed. I was obliged to be very decided in the matter and to act entirely on my own responsibility. Nearly six years have now elapsed since the cataract was extracted (it was not merely depressed). He has never once, during that time, regretted the step, and a day seldom passes that he does not express gratitude and pleasure at the restoration of that inestimable privilege of vision whose loss he once knew.

'I hope the next tidings you hear of your brother Charles will be satisfactory for his parents' and sisters' sake as well as his own. Your poor mamma has had many successive trials, and her uncomplaining resignation seems to offer us all an example worthy to be followed. Remember me kindly to her, to your papa, and all your circle, and — Believe me, with best wishes to yourself, yours sincerely,   C. Brontë.'

AND HER CIRCLE

TO REV. P. BRONTË, HAWORTH, YORKS.

'CLIFF HOUSE, FILEY, June 2, 1852.

'DEAR PAPA, — Thank you for your letter, which I was so glad to get that I think I must answer it by return of post. I had expected one yesterday, and was perhaps a little unreasonably anxious when disappointed, but the weather has been so *very* cold that I feared either you were ill or Martha worse. I hope Martha will take care of herself. I cannot help feeling a little uneasy about her.

'On the whole I get on very well here, but I have not bathed yet as I am told it is much too cold and too early in the season. The sea is very grand. Yesterday it was a somewhat unusually high tide, and I stood about an hour on the cliffs yesterday afternoon watching the tumbling in of great tawny turbid waves, that made the whole shore white with foam and filled the air with a sound hollower and deeper than thunder. There are so very few visitors at Filey yet that I and a few sea-birds and fishing-boats have often the whole expanse of sea, shore, and cliff to ourselves. When the tide is out the sands are wide, long, and smooth, and very pleasant to walk on. When the high tides are in, not a vestige of sand remains. I saw a great dog rush into the sea yesterday, and swim and bear up against the waves like a seal. I wonder what Flossy would say to that.

'On Sunday afternoon I went to a church which I should like Mr. Nicholls to see. It was certainly not more than thrice the length and breadth of our passage, floored with brick, the walls green with mould, the pews painted white, but the paint almost all worn off with time and decay. At one end there is a little gallery for the singers, and when these personages stood up to perform they all turned their backs upon the congregation, and the congregation turned *their* backs on the pulpit and parson. The effect of this manœuvre was so ludicrous, I could hardly help laughing; had Mr. Nicholls been there he certainly would have laughed out. Looking up at the gallery and seeing only the broad backs of the singers presented to their audience was

471

excessively grotesque. There is a well-meaning but utterly in-active clergyman at Filey, and Methodists flourish.

'I cannot help enjoying Mr. Butterfield's defeat; and yet in one sense this is a bad state of things, calculated to make working people both discontented and insubordinate. Give my kind regards, dear papa, to Mr. Nicholls, Tabby, and Martha. Charge Martha to beware of draughts, and to get such help in her cleaning as she shall need. I hope you will continue well. — Believe me, your affectionate daughter,   C. BRONTË.'

TO MISS ELLEN NUSSEY.

'DECEMBER 15, 1852.

'DEAR ELLEN, — I return the note which is highly character-istic, and not, I fear, of good omen for the comfort of your visit. There must be something wrong in herself as well as in her servants. I inclose another note which, taken in conjunction with the incident immediately preceding it, and with a long series of indications whose meaning I scarce ventured hitherto to interpret to myself, much less hint to any other, has left on my mind a feeling of deep concern. This note you will see is from Mr. Nicholls.

'I know not whether you have ever observed him specially when staying here. Your perception is generally quick enough — too quick, I have sometimes thought; yet as you never said anything, I restrained my own dim misgivings, which could not claim the sure guide of vision. What papa has seen or guessed I will not inquire, though I may conjecture. He has minutely noticed all Mr. Nicholls's low spirits, all his threats of expatria-tion, all his symptoms of impaired health — noticed them with little sympathy and much indirect sarcasm. On Monday even-ing Mr. Nicholls was here to tea. I vaguely felt without clearly seeing, as without seeing, I have felt for some time, the mean-ing of his constant looks, and strange, feverish restraint. After tea I withdrew to the dining-room as usual. As usual, Mr. Nicholls sat with papa till between eight and nine o'clock; I then heard him open the parlour door as if going. I expected the clash of the front door. He stopped in the passage; he tapped; like lightning it flashed on me what was coming. He entered; he stood before me. What his words were you can guess; his manner you can hardly realise, nor can I forget it. Shaking from head to foot, looking deadly pale, speaking low, vehemently, yet with difficulty, he made me for the first time feel what it costs a man to declare affection where he doubts response.

'The spectacle of one ordinarily so statue-like thus trembling, stirred, and overcome, gave me a kind of strange shock. He spoke of sufferings he had borne for months, of sufferings he could endure no longer, and craved leave for some hope. I could only entreat him to leave me then and promise a reply on the morrow. I asked him if he had spoken to papa. He said he dared not. I think I half led, half put him out of the room. When he was gone I immediately went to papa, and told him what had taken place. Agitation and anger disproportionate to the occasion ensued; if I had *loved* Mr. Nicholls, and had heard such epithets applied to him as were used, it would have transported me past my patience; as it was, my blood boiled with a sense of injustice. But papa worked himself into a state not to be trifled with : the veins on his temples started up like whip-cord, and his eyes became suddenly bloodshot. I made haste to promise that Mr. Nicholls should on the morrow have a distinct refusal.

'I wrote yesterday and got this note. There is no need to add to this statement any comment. Papa's vehement antipathy to the bare thought of any one thinking of me as a wife, and Mr. Nicholls's distress, both give me pain. Attachment to Mr. Nicholls you are aware I never entertained, but the poignant pity inspired by his state on Monday evening, by the hurried revelation of his sufferings for many months, is something galling and irksome. That he cared something for me, and wanted me to care for him, I have long suspected, but I did not know the degree or strength of his feelings. Dear Nell, good-bye. — Yours faithfully, C. Brontë.

'I have letters from Sir J. K. Shuttleworth and Miss Martineau, but I cannot talk of them now.'

CHARLOTTE BRONTË

With this letter we see the tragedy beginning. Mr. Brontë, with his daughter's fame ringing in his ears, thought she should do better than marry a curate with a hundred pounds per annum. For once, and for the only time in his life there is reason to believe, his passions were thoroughly aroused. It is to the honour of Mr. Nicholls, and says much for his magnanimity, that he has always maintained that Mr. Brontë was perfectly justified in the attitude he adopted. His present feeling for Mr. Brontë is one of unbounded respect and reverence, and the occasional unfriendly references to his father-in-law have pained him perhaps even more than when he has been himself the victim.

'Attachment to Mr. Nicholls you are aware I never entertained.' A good deal has been made of this and other casual references of Charlotte Brontë to her slight affection for her future husband. Martha Brown, the servant, used in her latter days to say that Charlotte would come into the kitchen and ask her if it was right to marry a man one did not entirely love — and Martha Brown's esteem for Mr. Nicholls was very great. But it is possible to make too much of all this. It is a commonplace of psychology to say that a woman's love is of slow growth. It is quite certain that Charlotte Brontë suffered much during this period of alienation and separation ; that she alone secured Mr. Nicholls's return to Haworth, after his temporary estrangement from Mr. Brontë; and finally, that the months of her married life, prior to her last illness, were the happiest she was destined to know.

TO MISS ELLEN NUSSEY.

'HAWORTH, December 18, 1852.

'DEAR NELL, — You may well ask, how is it? for I am sure I don't know. This business would seem to me like a dream, did not my reason tell me it has long been brewing. It puzzles me to comprehend how and whence comes this turbulence of feeling.

'You ask how papa demeans himself to Mr. Nicholls. I only wish you were here to see papa in his present mood : you would know something of him. He just treats him with a hardness not to be bent, and a contempt not to be propitiated. The two have had no interview as yet ; all has been done by letter. Papa wrote, I must say, a most cruel note to Mr. Nicholls on Wednesday. In his state of mind and health (for the poor man is horrifying his landlady, Martha's mother, by entirely rejecting his meals) I felt that the blow must be parried, and I thought it right to accompany the pitiless despatch by a line to the effect that, while Mr. Nicholls must never expect me to reciprocate the feeling he had expressed, yet, at the same time, I wished to disclaim participation in sentiments calculated to give him pain; and I exhorted him to maintain his courage and spirits. On receiving the two letters, he set off from home. Yesterday came the inclosed brief epistle.

' You must understand that a good share of papa's anger arises from the idea, not altogether groundless, that Mr. Nicholls has behaved with disingenuousness in so long concealing his aim. I am afraid also that papa thinks a little too much about his want of money ; he says the match would be a degradation, that I should be throwing myself away, that he expects me, if I marry at all, to do very differently ; in short, his manner of viewing the subject is on the whole far from being one in which I can sympathise. My own objections arise from a sense of incongruity and uncongeniality in feelings, tastes, principles.

' How are you getting on, dear Nell, and how are all at Brookroyd ? Remember me kindly to everybody. — Yours, wishing devoutly that papa would resume his tranquillity, and Mr. Nicholls his beef and pudding. C. BRONTË.

' I am glad to say that the incipient inflammation in papa's eye is disappearing.'

TO MISS ELLEN NUSSEY.

' JANUARY 2, 1853.

'DEAR NELL, — I thought of you on New Year's night, and hope you got well over your formidable tea-making. I trust that Tuesday and Wednesday will also pass pleasantly. I am busy too in my little way preparing to go to London this week, a matter which necessitates some little application to the needle. I find it is quite necessary I should go to superintend the press, as Mr. Smith seems quite determined not to. let the printing get on till I come. I have actually only received three proof-sheets since I was at Brookroyd. Papa wants me to go too, to be out of the way, I suppose; but I am sorry for one other person whom nobody pities but me. Martha is bitter against him; John Brown says, " he should like to shoot him." They don't understand the nature of his feelings, but I see now what they are. He is one of those who attach themselves to very few, whose sensations are close and deep, like an underground stream, running strong, but in a narrow channel. He continues rest-less and ill; he carefully performs the occasional duty, but does not come near the church, procuring a substitute every Sunday. A few days since he wrote to papa requesting permission to withdraw his resignation. Papa answered that he should only do so on condition of giving his written promise never again to broach the obnoxious subject either to him or to me. This he has evaded doing, so the matter remains unsettled. I feel per-suaded the termination will be his departure for Australia. Dear Nell, without loving him, I don't like to think of him suffering in solitude, and wish him anywhere so that he were happier. He and papa have never met or spoken yet. I am very glad to learn that your mother is pretty well, and also that the piece of challenged work is progressing. I hope you will not be called away to Norfolk before I come home : I should like you to pay a visit to Haworth first. Write again soon. — Yours faithfully,   C. BRONTË.'

TO MISS ELLEN NUSSEY.

'MARCH 4, 1853.

'DEAR ELLEN, — We had the parsons to supper as well as to tea. Mr. N. demeaned himself not quite pleasantly. I thought he made no effort to struggle with his dejection but gave way to it in a mannor to draw notice ; the Bishop was obviously puzzled by it. Mr. Nicholls also showed temper once or twice in speaking to papa. Martha was beginning to tell me of certain "flaysome" looks also, but I desired not to hear of them. The fact is, I shall be most thankful when he is well away. I pity him, but I don't like that dark gloom of his. He dogged me up the lane after the evening service in no pleasant manner. He stopped also in the passage after the Bishop and the other clergy were gone into the room, and it was because I drew away and went upstairs that he gave that look which filled Martha's soul with horror. She, it seems, meantime, was making it her business to watch him from the kitchen door. If Mr. Nicholls be a good man at bottom, it is a sad thing that nature has not given him the faculty to put goodness into a more attractive form. Into the bargain of all the rest he managed to get up a most pertinacious and needless dispute with the Inspector, in listening to which all my old unfavourable impressions revived so strongly, I fear my countenance could not but shew them.

'Dear Nell, I consider that on the whole it is a mercy you have been at home and not at Norfolk during the late cold weather. Love to all at Brookroyd. — Yours faithfully, C. BRONTË.'

TO MISS ELLEN NUSSEY.

'MARCH 9, 1853.

'DEAR ELLEN, — I am sure Miss Wooler would enjoy her visit to you, as much as you her company. Dear Nell, I thank you sincerely for your discreet and friendly silence on the point alluded to. I had feared it would be discussed between you two, and had an inexpressible shrinking at the thought ; now less than ever does it seem a matter open to discussion. I hear nothing, and you must quite understand that if I feel any uneasiness it is not that of confirmed and fixed regard, but that anxiety which is inseparable from a state of absolute uncertainty about a somewhat momentous matter. I do not know, I am not sure myself, that any other termination would be better than lasting estrangement and unbroken silence. Yet a good deal of pain has been and must be gone through in that case. However, to each his burden.

'I have not read the papers; D.V. I will send them to-morrow — Yours faithfully,   C. BRONTË.

'Understand that in whatever I have said above, it was not for pity or sympathy. I hardly pity myself. Only I wish that in all matters in this world there was fair and open dealing, and no underhand work.'

TO MISS ELLEN NUSSEY.

HAWORTH, April 6, 1853.

'DEAR ELLEN, — My visit to Manchester is for the present put off by Mr. Morgan having written to say that since papa will not go to Buckingham to see him he will come to Yorkshire to see papa; when, I don't yet know, and I trust in goodness he will not stay long, as papa really cannot bear putting out of his way. I must wait, however, till the infliction is over.

'You ask about Mr. Nicholls. I hear he has got a curacy, but do not yet know where. I trust the news is true. He and papa never speak. He seems to pass a desolate life. He has allowed late circumstances so to act on him as to freeze up his manner and overcast his countenance not only to those immediately concerned but to every one. He sits drearily in his rooms. If Mr. Grant or any other clergyman calls to see, and as they think, to cheer him, he scarcely speaks. I find he tells them nothing, seeks no confidant, rebuffs all attempts to penetrate his mind. I own I respect him for this. He still lets Flossy go to his rooms, and takes him to walk. He still goes over to see Mr. Sowden sometimes, and, poor fellow, that is all. He looks ill and miserable. I think and trust in Heaven that he will be better as soon as he fairly gets away from Haworth. I pity him inexpressibly. We never meet nor speak, nor dare I look at him; silent pity is just all that I can give him, and as he knows nothing about that, it does not comfort. He is now grown so gloomy and reserved that nobody seems to like him. His fellow-curates shun trouble in that shape; the lower orders dislike it. Papa has a perfect antipathy to him, and he, I fear, to papa. Martha hates him. I think he might almost be *dying* and they would not speak a friendly word to or of him. How much of all

478

this he deserves I can't tell ; certainly he never was agreeable or amiable, and is less so now than ever, and alas! I do not know him well enough to be sure that there is truth and true affection, or only rancour and corroding disappointment at the bottom of his chagrin. In this state of things I must be, and I am, *entirely passive*. I may be losing the purest gem, and to me far the most precious, life can give — genuine attachment — or I may be escaping the yoke of a morose temper. In this doubt conscience will not suffer me to take one step in opposition to papa's will, blended as that will is with the most bitter and unreasonable prejudices. So I just leave the matter where we must leave all important matters.

'Remember me kindly to all at Brookroyd, and — Believe me, yours faithfully,   C. BRONTË.'

TO MISS ELLEN NUSSEY.

'MAY 16, 1853.

' DEAR ELLEN, — The east winds about which you inquire have spared me wonderfully till to-day, when I feel somewhat sick physically, and not very blithe mentally. I am not sure that the east winds are entirely to blame for this ailment. Yesterday was a strange sort of day at church. It seems as if I were to be punished for my doubts about the nature and truth of poor Mr. Nicholls's regard. Having ventured on Whit Sunday to stop the sacrament, I got a lesson not to be repeated. He struggled, faltered, then lost command over himself — stood before my eyes and in the sight of all the communicants white, shaking, voiceless. Papa was not there, thank God! Joseph Redman spoke some words to him. He made a great effort, but could only with difficulty whisper and falter through the service. I suppose he thought this would be the last time ; he goes either this week or the next. I heard the women sobbing round, and I could not quite check my own tears. What had happened was reported to papa either by Joseph Redman or John Brown ; it excited only anger, and such expressions as "unmanly driveller." Compassion or relenting is no more to be looked for than sap from firewood.

479

CHARLOTTE BRONTË

'I never saw a battle more sternly fought with the feelings than Mr. Nicholls fights with his, and when he yields momentarily, you are almost sickened by the sense of the strain upon him. However, he is to go, and I cannot speak to him or look at him or comfort him a whit, and I must submit. Providence is over all, that is the only consolation. — Yours faithfully,

'C. BRONTË.'

TO MISS ELLEN NUSSEY.

'MAY 19, 1853.

'DEAR ELLEN, — I cannot help feeling a certain satisfaction in finding that the people here are getting up a subscription to offer a testimonial of respect to Mr. Nicholls on his leaving the place. Many are expressing both their commiseration and esteem for him. The Churchwardens recently put the question to him plainly : Why was he going? Was it Mr. Brontë's fault or his own? "His own," he answered. Did he blame Mr. Brontë? "No ! he did not : if anybody was wrong it was himself." Was he willing to go? "No ! it gave him great pain." Yet he is not always right. I must be just. He shows a curious mixture of honour and obstinacy — feeling and sullenness. Papa addressed him at the school tea-drinking, with *constrained* civility, but still with *civility*. He did not reply civilly ; he cut short further words. This sort of treatment offered in public is what papa never will forget or forgive, it inspires him with a silent bitterness not to be expressed. I am afraid both are unchristian in their mutual feelings. Nor do I know which of them is least accessible to reason or least likely to forgive. It is a dismal state of things.

'The weather is fine now, dear Nell. We will take these sunny days as a good omen for your visit to Yarmouth. With kind regards to all at Brookroyd, and best wishes to yourself, — I am, yours sincerely,   C. BRONTË.'

TO MISS ELLEN NUSSEY.

'HAWORTH, May 27, 1853.

'DEAR ELLEN, — You will want to know about the leave-taking? The whole matter is but a painful subject, but I must treat it briefly. The testimonial was presented in a public meeting. Mr. Taylor and Mr. Grant were there. Papa was not very well and I advised him to stay away, which he did. As to the last Sunday, it was a cruel struggle. Mr. Nicholls ought not to have had to take any duty.

'He left Haworth this morning at six o'clock. Yesterday evening he called to render into papa's hands the deeds of the National School, and to say good-bye. They were busy cleaning — washing the paint, etc., in the dining-room, so he did not find me there. I would not go into the parlour to speak to him in papa's presence. He went out, thinking he was not to see me; and indeed, till the very last moment, I thought it best not. But perceiving that he stayed long before going out at the gate, and remembering his long grief, I took courage and went out, trembling and miserable. I found him leaning against the garden door in a paroxysm of anguish, sobbing as women never sob. Of course I went straight to him. Very few words were interchanged, those few barely articulate. Several things I should have liked to ask him were swept entirely from my memory. Poor fellow! But he wanted such hope and such encouragement as I could not give him. Still, I trust he must know now that I am not cruelly blind and indifferent to his constancy and grief. For a few weeks he goes to the south of England, afterwards he takes a curacy somewhere in Yorkshire, but I don't know where.

'Papa has been far from strong lately. I dare not mention Mr. Nicholls's name to him. He speaks of him quietly and without opprobrium to others, but to me he is implacable on the matter. However, he is gone — gone, and there's an end of it. I see no chance of hearing a word about him in future, unless some stray shred of intelligence comes through Mr. Sowden or some other second-hand source. In all this it is not I who am to be pitied at all, and of course nobody pities me. They all think in Haworth that I have disdainfully refused him. If pity would do Mr. Nicholls any good, he ought to have, and I believe has it. They may abuse me if they will; whether they do or not I can't tell.

Write soon and say how your prospects proceed. I trust they
will daily brighten. — Yours faithfully,   C. BRONTË.'

TO MISS LÆTITIA WHEELWRIGHT.

'HAWORTH, March 18, 1854.

'MY DEAR LÆTITIA, — I was very glad to see your handwriting
again; it is, I believe, a year since I heard from you. Again
and again you have recurred to my thoughts lately, and I was
beginning to have some sad presages as to the cause of your
silence. Your letter happily does away with all these; it
brings, on the whole, good tidings both of your papa, mamma,
your sister, and, last but not least, your dear respected English
self.

'My dear father has borne the severe winter very well, a
circumstance for which I feel the more thankful, as he had many
weeks of very precarious health last summer, following an attack
from which he suffered last June, and which for a few hours
deprived him totally of sight, though neither his mind, speech,
nor even his powers of motion were in the least affected. I can
hardly tell you how thankful I was, dear Lætitia, when, after
that dreary and almost despairing interval of utter darkness,
some gleam of daylight became visible to him once more. I
had feared that paralysis had seized the optic nerve. A
sort of mist remained for a long time, and indeed his vision is
not yet perfectly clear, but he can read, write, and walk
about, and he preaches *twice* every Sunday, the curate only
reading the prayers. *You* can well understand how earnestly I
pray that sight may be spared him to the end; he so dreads the
privation of blindness. His mind is just as strong and active as
ever, and politics interest him as they do *your* papa. The Czar,
the war, the alliance between France and England — into all these
things he throws himself heart and soul. They seem to carry him
back to his comparatively young days, and to renew the excitement of the last great European struggle. Of course, my father's
sympathies, and mine too, are all with justice and Europe against
tyranny and Russia.

'Circumstanced as I have been you will comprehend that I

have neither the leisure nor inclination to go from home much during the past year. I spent a week with Mrs. Gaskell in the spring, and a fortnight with some other friends more recently, and that includes the whole of my visiting since I saw you last. My life is indeed very uniform and retired, more so than is quite healthful either for mind or body; yet I feel reason for often renewed feelings of gratitude in the sort of support which still comes and cheers me from time to time. My health, though not unbroken, is, I sometimes fancy, rather stronger on the whole than it was three years ago; headache and dyspepsia are my worst ailments. Whether I shall come up to town this season for a few days I do not yet know; but if I do I shall hope to call in Phillimore Place. With kindest remembrances to your papa, mamma, and sisters, — I am, dear Lætitia, affectionately yours, C. BRONTË.'

Mr. Nicholls's successor did not prove acceptable to Mr. Brontë. He complained again and again, and one day Charlotte turned upon her father and told him pretty frankly that he was alone to blame — that he had only to let her marry Mr. Nicholls, with whom she corresponded and whom she really loved, and all would be well. A little arrangement, the transfer of Mr. Nicholls's successor, Mr. De Renzi, to a Bradford church, and Mr. Nicholls left his curacy at Kirk-Smeaton and returned once more to Haworth as an accepted lover.

TO MISS ELLEN NUSSEY.

'HAWORTH, March 28, 1854.

'MY DEAR ELLEN, — The inclosure in yours of yesterday puzzled me at first, for I did not immediately recognise my own handwriting; when I did, the sensation was one of consternation and vexation, as the letter ought by all means to have gone on Friday. It was intended to relieve him of great anxiety. However, I trust he will get it to-day; and on the whole, when I think it over, I can only be thankful that the mistake was no worse, and did not throw the letter into the hands of some indifferent and unscrupulous person. I wrote it after some days of indisposition and uneasiness, and when I felt weak and unfit to write. While writing to him, I was at the same time intending to answer your note, which I suppose accounts for the confusion of ideas, shown in the mixed and blundering address.

'I wish you could come about Easter rather than at another time, for this reason : Mr. Nicholls, if not prevented, proposes coming over then. I suppose he will stay at Mr. Grant's as he has done two or three times before, but he will be frequently coming here, which would enliven your visit a little. Perhaps, too, he might take a walk with us occasionally. Altogether it would be a little change, such as, you know, I could not always offer.

'If all be well he will come under different circumstances to any that have attended his visits before ; were it otherwise, I should not ask you to meet him, for when aspects are gloomy and unpropitious, the fewer there are to suffer from the cloud the better.

'He was here in January and was then received, but not pleasantly. I trust it will be a little different now.

'Papa breakfasts in bed and has not yet risen ; his bronchitis is still troublesome. I had a bad week last week, but am greatly better now, for my mind is a little relieved, though very sedate, and rising only to expectations the most moderate.

'Sometime, perhaps in May, I may hope to come to Brook-royd, but, as you will understand from what I have now stated, I could not come before.

'Think it over, dear Nell, and come to Haworth if you can. Write as soon as you can decide. — Yours affectionately,

'C. Brontë.'

TO MISS ELLEN NUSSEY.

'April 1, 1854.

'My dear Ellen, — You certainly were right in your second interpretation of my note. I am too well aware of the dulness of Haworth for any visitor, not to be glad to avail myself of the chance of offering even a slight change. But this morning my little plans have been disarranged by an intimation that Mr. Nicholls is coming on Monday. I thought to put him off, but have not succeeded. As Easter now consequently seems an unfavourable period both from your point of view and mine, we will adjourn it till a better opportunity offers. Meantime, I thank you, dear Ellen, for your kind offer to come in case I wanted you. Papa is still very far from well : his cough very troublesome, and a good deal of inflammatory action in the chest. To-day he seems somewhat better than yesterday, and I earnestly hope the improvement may continue.

'With kind regards to your mother and all at Brookroyd, — I am, dear Ellen, yours affectionately,   C. BRONTË.'

TO MISS ELLEN NUSSEY.

'HAWORTH, April 11, 1854.

'DEAR ELLEN, — Thank you for the collar ; it is very pretty, and I will wear it for the sake of her who made and gave it.

'Mr. Nicholls came on Monday, and was here all last week. Matters have progressed thus since July. He renewed his visit in September, but then matters so fell out that I saw little of him. He continued to write. The correspondence pressed on my mind. I grew very miserable in keeping it from papa. At last sheer pain made me gather courage to break it. I told all. It was very hard and rough work at the time, but the issue after a few days was that I obtained leave to continue the communication. Mr. Nicholls came in January ; he was ten days in the neighbourhood. I saw much of him. I had stipulated with papa for opportunity to become better acquainted. I had it, and all I learnt inclined me to esteem and affection. Still papa was very, very hostile, bitterly unjust.

'I told Mr. Nicholls the great obstacle that lay in his way. He has persevered. The result of this, his last visit, is, that papa's consent is gained, that his respect, I believe, is won, for Mr. Nicholls has in all things proved himself disinterested and forbearing. Certainly, I must respect him, nor can I withhold from him more than mere cool respect. In fact, dear Ellen, I am engaged.

CHARLOTTE BRONTË

'Mr. Nicholls, in the course of a few months, will return to the curacy of Haworth. I stipulated that I would not leave papa; and to papa himself I proposed a plan of residence which should maintain his seclusion and convenience uninvaded, and in a pecuniary sense bring him gain instead of loss. What seemed at one time impossible is now arranged, and papa begins really to take a pleasure in the prospect.

'For myself, dear Ellen, while thankful to One who seems to have guided me through much difficulty, much and deep distress and perplexity of mind, I am still very calm, very inexpectant. What I taste of happiness is of the soberest order. I trust to love my husband. I am grateful for his tender love to me. I believe him to be an affectionate, a conscientious, a high-principled man; and if, with all this, I should yield to regrets that fine talents, congenial tastes and thoughts are not added, it seems to me I should be most presumptuous and thankless.

'Providence offers me this destiny. Doubtless, then, it is the best for me. Nor do I shrink from wishing those dear to me one not less happy.

'It is possible that our marriage may take place in the course of the summer. Mr. Nicholls wishes it to be in July. He spoke of you with great kindness, and said he hoped you would be at our wedding. I said I thought of having no other bridesmaid. Did I say rightly? I mean the marriage to be literally as quiet as possible.

'Do not mention these things just yet. I mean to write to Miss Wooler shortly. Good-bye. There is a strange half-sad feeling in making these announcements. The whole thing is something other than imagination paints it beforehand; cares, fears, come mixed inextricably with hopes. I trust yet to talk the matter over with you. Often last week I wished for your presence and said so to Mr. Nicholls — Arthur, as I now call him, but he said it was the only time and place when he could not have wished to see you. Good-bye. — Yours affectionately,

'C. BRONTË.'

AND HER CIRCLE

TO MISS ELLEN NUSSEY.

'MY OWN DEAR NELL, — I hope to see you somewhere about the second week in May.

'The Manchester visit is still hanging over my head. I have deferred it, and deferred it, but have finally promised to go about the beginning of next month. I shall only stay three days, then I spend two or three days at Hunsworth, then come to Brookroyd. The three visits must be compressed into the space of a fortnight, if possible.

'I suppose I shall have to go to Leeds. My purchases cannot be either expensive or extensive. You must just resolve in your head the bonnets and dresses; something that can be turned to decent use and worn after the wedding-day will be best I think.

'I wrote immediately to Miss Wooler and received a truly kind letter from her this morning. If you think she would like to come to the marriage I will not fail to ask her.

'Papa's mind seems wholly changed about the matter, and he has said both to me and when I was not there, how much happier he feels since he allowed all to be settled. It is a wonderful relief for me to hear him treat the thing rationally, to talk over with him themes on which once I dared not touch. He is rather anxious things should get forward now, and takes quite an interest in the arrangement of preliminaries. His health improves daily, though this east wind still keeps up a slight irritation in the throat and chest.

'The feeling which had been disappointed in papa was ambition, paternal pride — ever a restless feeling, as we all know. Now that this unquiet spirit is exorcised, justice, which was once quite forgotten, is once more listened to, and affection, I hope, resumes some power.

'My hope is that in the end this arrangement will turn out more truly to papa's advantage than any other it was in my power to achieve. Mr. Nicholls in his last letter refers touchingly to his earnest desire to prove his gratitude to papa, by offering support and consolation to his declining age. This will not be mere talk with him — he is no talker, no dealer in professions. — Yours affectionately, C. BRONTË.'

TO MISS ELLEN NUSSEY.

'APRIL 28, 1854.

'MY DEAR ELLEN, — I have delayed writing till I could give you some clear notion of my movements. If all be well, I go to Manchester on the 1st of May. Thence, on Thursday, to Hunsworth till Monday, when (D.V.) I come to Brookroyd. I must be at home by the close of the week. Papa, thank God! continues to improve much. He preached twice on Sunday and again on Wednesday, and was not tired; his mind and mood are different to what they were, so much more cheerful and quiet. I trust the illusions of ambition are quite dissipated, and that he really sees it is better to relieve a suffering and faithful heart, to secure its fidelity, a solid good, than unfeelingly to abandon one who is truly attached to his interest as well as mine, and pursue some vain empty shadow.

'I thank you, dear Ellen, for your kind invitation to Mr. Nicholls. He was asked likewise to Manchester and Hunsworth. I would not have opposed his coming had there been no real obstacle to the arrangement — certain little awkwardnesses of feeling I would have tried to get over for the sake of introducing him to old friends; but it so happens that he cannot leave on account of his rector's absence. Mr. C. will be in town with his family till June, and he always stipulates that his curate shall remain at Kirk-Smeaton while he is away.

'How did you get on at the Oratorio? And what did Miss Wooler say to the proposal of being at the wedding? I have many points to discuss when I see you. I hope your mother and all are well. With kind remembrances to them, and true love to you, — I am, dear Nell, faithfully yours, C. BRONTË.

'When you write, address me at Mrs. Gaskell's, Plymouth Grove, Manchester.'

TO MISS ELLEN NUSSEY.

'MAY 22, 1854.

'DEAR ELLEN, — I wonder how you are, and whether that
488

harassing cough is better. Be scrupulously cautious about undue exposure. Just now, dear Ellen, an hour's inadvertence might cause you to be really ill. So once again, take care. Since I came home I have been very busy stitching. The little new room is got into order, and the green and white curtains are up; they exactly suit the papering, and look neat and clean enough. I had a letter a day or two since announcing that Mr. Nicholls comes to-morrow. I feel anxious about him, more anxious on one point than I dare quite express to myself. It seems he has again been suffering sharply from his rheumatic affection. I hear this not from himself, but from another quarter. He was ill while I was at Manchester and Brookroyd. He uttered no complaint to me, dropped no hint on the subject. Alas! he was hoping he had got the better of it, and I know how this contradiction of his hopes will sadden him. For unselfish reasons he did so earnestly wish this complaint might not become chronic. I fear, I fear. But, however, I mean to stand by him now, whether in weal or woe. This liability to rheumatic pain was one of the strong arguments used against the marriage. It did not weigh somehow. If he is doomed to suffer, it seems that so much the more will he need care and help. And yet the ultimate possibilities of such a case are appalling. You remember your aunt. Well, come what may, God help and strengthen both him and me. I look forward to to-morrow with a mixture of impatience and anxiety. Poor fellow! I want to see with my own eyes how he is.

'It is getting late and dark. Write soon, dear Ellen. Good-night and God bless you. — Yours affectionately,   C. BRONTË.'

TO MISS ELLEN NUSSEY.

'HAWORTH, May 27, 1854.

'DEAR ELLEN, — Your letter was very welcome, and I am glad and thankful to learn you are better. Still, beware of presuming on the improvement — don't let it make you careless. Mr. Nicholls has just left me. Your hopes were not ill-founded about his illness. At first I was thoroughly frightened. However, inquiring gradually relieved me. In short, I soon discovered that my business was, instead of sympathy, to rate soundly. The patient had wholesome treatment while he was at Haworth, and went away singularly better; perfectly unreasonable, however, on some points, as his fallible sex are not ashamed to be.

'Man is, indeed, an amazing piece of mechanism when you see, so to speak, the full weakness of what he calls his strength. There is not a female child above the age of eight but might rebuke him for spoilt petulance of his wilful nonsense. I bought a border for the table-cloth and have put it on.

'Good-bye, dear Ellen. Write again soon, and mind and give a bulletin. — Yours faithfully,   C. BRONTË.'

TO MISS ELLEN NUSSEY.

'JUNE 12, 1854.

'DEAR ELLEN, — Papa preached twice to-day as well and as strongly as ever. It is strange how he varies, how soon he is depressed and how soon revived. It makes me feel so thankful when he is better. I am thankful too that you are stronger, dear Nell. My worthy acquaintance at Kirk-Smeaton refuses to acknowledge himself better yet. I am uneasy about not writing to Miss Wooler. I fear she will think me negligent, while I am only busy and bothered. I want to clear up my needlework a little, and have been sewing against time since I was at Brookroyd. Mr. Nicholls hindered me for a full week.

'I like the card very well, but not the envelope. I should like a perfectly plain envelope with a silver initial.

'I got my dresses from Halifax a day or two since, but have not had time to have them unpacked, so I don't know what they are like.

'Next time I write, I hope to be able to give you clear information, and to beg you to come here without further delay. Good-bye, dear Nell. — Yours faithfully,   C. BRONTË.

'I had almost forgotten to mention about the envelopes. Mr. Nicholls says I have ordered far too few; he thinks sixty will be wanted. Is it too late to remedy this error? There is no end to his string of parson friends. My own list I have not made out.'

Charlotte Brontë's list of friends, to whom wedding-cards were to be sent, is in her own handwriting, and is not without interest.

SEND CARDS TO

The Rev. W. Morgan, Rectory, Hulcott, Aylesbury, Bucks.
Joseph Branwell, Esq., Thamar Terrace, Launceston, Cornwall.
Dr. Wheelwright, 29 Phillimore Place, Kensington, London.
George Smith, Esq., 65 Cornhill, London.
Mrs. and Misses Smith, 65 Cornhill, London.
W. S. Williams, Esq., 65 Cornhill, London.
R. Monckton Milnes, Esq.
Mrs. Gaskell, Plymouth Grove, Manchester.
Francis Bennoch, Esq., Park, Blackheath, London.
George Taylor, Esq., Stanbury.
Mrs. and Miss Taylor.
H. Merrall, Esq., Lea Sykes, Haworth.
E. Merrall, Esq., Ebor House, Haworth.
R. Butterfield, Esq., Woodlands, Haworth.
R. Thomas, Esq., Haworth.
J. Pickles, Esq., Brow Top, Haworth.
Wooler Family.
Brookroyd.[1]

The following was written on her wedding day, June 29th, 1854.

TO MISS ELLEN NUSSEY.

Thursday Evening.

'Dear Ellen, — I scribble one hasty line just to say that after a pleasant enough journey we have got safely to Conway; tho evening is wet and wild, though the day was fair chiefly, with some gleams of sunshine. However, we are sheltered in a comfortable inn. My cold is not worse. If you get this scrawl to-morrow and write by return, direct to me at the post-office, Bangor, and I may get it on Monday. Say how you and Miss

[1] The Nusseys.

491

Wooler got home. Give my kindest and most grateful love to Miss Wooler whenever you write. On Monday, I think, we cross the Channel. No more at present. — Yours faithfully and lovingly, C. B. N.'

TO MISS ELLEN NUSSEY.

'HAWORTH, August 29.

'DEAR ELLEN, —Can you come here on Wednesday week (Sept. 6th)? Try to arrange matters to do so if possible, for it will be better than to delay your visit till the days grow cold and short. I want to see you again, dear Nell, and my husband too will receive you with pleasure; and he is not diffuse of his courtesies or partialities I can assure you. One friendly word from him means as much as twenty from most people.

'We have been busy lately giving a supper and tea-drinking to the singers, ringers, Sunday-school teachers, and all the scholars of the Sunday and National Schools, amounting in all to some 500 souls. It gave satisfaction and went off well.

'Papa, I am thankful to say, is much better; he preached last Sunday. How does your mother bear this hot weather? Write soon, dear Nell, and say you will come. — Yours faithfully,

'C. B. N.'

TO MISS ELLEN NUSSEY.

'HAWORTH, August 9, 1854.

'DEAR ELLEN, — I earnestly hope you are by yourself now, and relieved from the fag of entertaining guests. You do not complain, but I am afraid you have had too much of it.

'Since I came home I have not had an unemployed moment. My life is changed indeed : to be wanted continually, to be constantly called for and occupied seems so strange ; yet it is a marvellously good thing. As yet I don't quite understand how some wives grow so selfish. As far as my experience of matrimony goes, I think it tends to draw you out of, and away from yourself.

'We have had sundry callers this week. Yesterday Mr. Sowden and another gentleman dined here, and Mr. and Mrs. Grant joined them at tea.

'I do not think we shall go to Brookroyd soon, on papa's account. I do not wish again to leave home for a time, but I trust you will ere long come here.

'I really like Mr. Sowden very well. He asked after you. Mr. Nicholls told him we expected you would be coming to stay with us in the course of three or four weeks, and that he should then invite him over again as he wished us to take sundry rather long walks, and as he should have his wife to look after, and she was trouble enough, it would be quite necessary to have a guardian for the other lady. Mr. Sowden seemed perfectly acquiescent.

'Dear Nell, during the last six weeks, the colour of my thoughts is a good deal changed : I know more of the realities of life than I once did. I think many false ideas are propagated, perhaps unintentionally. I think those married women who indiscriminately urge their acquaintance to marry, much to blame. For my part, I can only say with deeper sincerity and fuller significance what I always said in theory, "Wait God's will." Indeed, indeed, Nell, it is a solemn and strange and perilous thing for a woman to become a wife. Man's lot is far, far different. Tell me when you think you can come. Papa is better, but not well. How is your mother? give my love to her. — Yours faithfully, C. B. NICHOLLS.

'Have I told you how much better Mr. Nicholls is? He looks quite strong and hale; he gained 12 lbs. during the four weeks we were in Ireland. To see this improvement in him has been a main source of happiness to me, and to speak truth, a subject of wonder too.'

TO MISS ELLEN NUSSEY.

'HAWORTH, September 7, 1854.

'DEAR ELLEN, — I send a French paper to-day. You would almost think I had given them up, it is so long since one was despatched. The fact is, they had accumulated to quite a pile during my absence. I wished to look them over before sending them off, and as yet I have scarcely found time. That same Time is an article of which I once had a large stock always on hand; where it is all gone now it would be difficult to say, but my moments are very fully occupied. Take warning, Ellen, the married woman can call but a very small portion of each day her own. Not that I complain of this sort of monopoly as yet, and I hope I never shall incline to regard it as a misfortune, but it certainly exists. We were both disappointed that you could not come on the day I mentioned. I have grudged this splendid weather very much. The moors are in glory, I never saw them fuller of purple bloom. I wanted you to see them at their best; they are just turning now, and in another week, I fear, will be faded and sere. As soon as ever you can leave home, be sure to write and let me know.

'Papa continues greatly better. My husband flourishes; he begins indeed to express some slight alarm at the growing improvement in his condition. I think I am decent, better certainly than I was two months ago, but people don't compliment me as they do Arthur — excuse the name, it has grown natural to use it now. I trust, dear Nell, that you are all well at Brookroyd, and that your visiting stirs are pretty nearly over. I compassionate you from my heart for all the trouble to which you must be put, and I am rather ashamed of people coming sponging in that fashion one after another; get away from them and come here. — Yours faithfully,   C. B. NICHOLLS.'

TO MISS ELLEN NUSSEY.

'HAWORTH, November 7, 1854.

'DEAR ELLEN, — Arthur wishes you would burn my letters. He was out when I commenced this letter, but he has just come in. It is not "old friends" he mistrusts, he says, but the chances of war — the accidental passing of letters into hands and under eyes for which they were never written.

'All this seems mighty amusing to me; it is a man's mode of viewing correspondence. Men's letters are proverbially uninteresting and uncommunicative. I never quite knew before why they made them so. They may be right in a sense: strange chances do fall out certainly. As to my own notes, I never thought of attaching importance to them or considering their fate, till Arthur seemed to reflect on both so seriously.

'I will write again next week if all be well to name a day for coming to see you. I am sure you want, or at least ought to have a little rest before you are bothered with more company; but whenever I come, I suppose, dear Nell, under present circumstances, it will be a quiet visit, and that I shall not need to bring more than a plain dress or two. Tell me this when you write.— Believe me faithfully yours,

'C. B. NICHOLLS.'

TO MISS ELLEN NUSSEY.

'HAWORTH, November 14, 1854.

'DEAR ELLEN, — I am only just at liberty to write to you; guests have kept me very busy during the last two or three days. Sir J. Kay-Shuttleworth and a friend of his came here on Saturday afternoon and stayed till after dinner on Monday.

'When I go to Brookroyd, Arthur will take me there and stay one night, but I cannot yet fix the time of my visit. Good-bye for the present, dear Nell. — Yours faithfully,

'C. B. NICHOLLS.'

TO MISS ELLEN NUSSEY.

'HAWORTH, November 21, 1854.

'DEAR ELLEN, — You ask about Mr. Sowden's matter. He walked over here on a wild rainy day. We talked it over. He is quite disposed to entertain the proposal, but of course there must be close inquiry and ripe consideration before either he or the patron decide. Meantime Mr. Sowden [1] is most anxious that the affairs be kept absolutely quiet; in the event of disappointment it would be both painful and injurious to him if it should be rumoured at Hebden Bridge that he has had thoughts of leaving. Arthur says if a whisper gets out these things fly from parson to parson like wildfire. I cannot help somehow wishing

---

[1] The Rev. George Sowden, vicar of Hebden Bridge, Halifax, and honorary canon of Wakefield, is still alive.

that the matter should be arranged, if all on examination is found tolerably satisfactory.

'Papa continues pretty well, I am thankful to say; his deafness is wonderfully relieved. Winter seems to suit him better than summer; besides, he is settled and content, as I perceive with gratitude to God.

'Dear Ellen, I wish you well through every trouble. Arthur is not in just now or he would send a kind message. — Believe me, yours faithfully,   C. B. NICHOLLS.'

TO MISS ELLEN NUSSEY.

'HAWORTH, November 29, 1854.

'DEAR ELLEN, — Arthur somewhat demurs about my going to Brookroyd as yet; fever, you know, is a formidable word. I cannot say I entertain any apprehensions myself further than this, that I should be terribly bothered at the idea of being taken ill from home and causing trouble; and strangers are sometimes more liable to infection than persons living in the house.

'Mr. Sowden has seen Sir J. K. Shuttleworth, but I fancy the matter is very uncertain as yet. It seems the Bishop of Manchester stipulates that the clergyman chosen should, if possible, be from his own diocese, and this, Arthur says, is quite right and just. An exception would have been made in Arthur's favour, but the case is not so clear with Mr. Sowden. However, no harm will have been done if the matter does not take wind, as I trust it will not. Write very soon, dear Nell, and, — Believe me, yours faithfully,   C. B. NICHOLLS.'

TO MISS ELLEN NUSSEY.

'HAWORTH, December 7, 1854.

'DEAR ELLEN, — I shall not get leave to go to Brookroyd before Christmas now, so do not expect me. For my own part I really should have no fear, and if it just depended on me I should come. But these matters are not quite in my power now: another must be consulted; and where his wish and judgment have a decided bias to a particular course, I make no stir, but just adopt it. Arthur is sorry to disappoint both you and me, but it is his fixed wish that a few weeks should be allowed yet to elapse before we meet. Probably he is confirmed in this desire by my having a cold at present. I did not achieve the walk to the waterfall with impunity. Though I changed my wet things immediately on returning home, yet I felt a chill afterwards, and the same night had sore throat and cold; however, I am better now, but not quite well.

'Did I tell you that our poor little Flossy is dead? He drooped for a single day, and died quietly in the night without pain. The loss even of a dog was very saddening, yet perhaps no dog ever had a happier life or an easier death.

'Papa continues pretty well, I am happy to say, and my dear boy flourishes. I do not mean that he continues to grow stouter, which one would not desire, but he keeps in excellent condition.

'You would wonder, I dare say, at the long disappearance of the French paper. I had got such an accumulation of them unread that I thought I would not wait to send the old ones; now you will receive them regularly. I am writing in haste. It is almost inexplicable to me that I seem so often hurried now; but the fact is, whenever Arthur is in I must have occupations in which he can share, or which will not at least divert my attention from him — thus a multitude of little matters get put off till he goes out, and then I am quite busy. Good-bye, dear Ellen, I hope we shall meet soon. — Yours faithfully,

'C. B. NICHOLLS.'

TO MISS ELLEN NUSSEY.

'HAWORTH, December 26, 1854.

'DEAR ELLEN, — I return the letter. It is, as you say, very genuine, truthful, affectionate, maternal — without a taint of sham or exaggeration. Mary will love her child without spoiling it, I think. She does not make an uproar about her happiness either. The longer I live the more I suspect exaggerations. I fancy it is sometimes a sort of fashion for each to vie with the

other in protestations about their wonderful felicity, and sometimes they — FIB. I am truly glad to hear you are all better
at Brookroyd. In the course of three or four weeks more I
expect to get leave to come to you. I certainly long to see
you again. One circumstance reconciles me to this delay — the
weather. I do not know whether it has been as bad with you
as with us, but here for three weeks we have had little else than
a succession of hurricanes.

'In your last you asked about Mr. Sowden and Sir James. I
fear Mr. Sowden has little chance of the living; he had heard
nothing more of it the last time he wrote to Arthur, and in a
note he had from Sir James yesterday the subject is not
mentioned.

'You inquire too after Mrs. Gaskell. She has not been here,
and I think I should not like her to come now till summer. She
is very busy with her story of " North and South."

'I must make this note short that it may not be overweight.
Arthur joins me in sincere good wishes for a happy Christmas,
and many of them to you and yours. He is well, thank God, and
so am I, and he is "my dear boy," certainly dearer now than he
was six months ago. In three days we shall actually have been
married that length of time! Good-bye, dear Nell. — Yours
faithfully,   C. B. NICHOLLS.'

At the beginning of 1855 Mr. and Mrs. Nicholls visited
Sir James Kay-Shuttleworth at Gawthorpe. I know of only
four letters by her, written in this year.

TO MISS ELLEN NUSSEY.

'HAWORTH, January 19, 1855.

'DEAR ELLEN, — Since our return from Gawthorpe we have had
a Mr. Bell, one of Arthur's cousins, staying with us. It was a
great pleasure. I wish you could have seen him and made his
acquaintance; a true gentleman by nature and cultivation is not
after all an everyday thing.

'As to the living of Habergham or Padiham, it appears the

chance is doubtful at present for anybody. The present incumbent wishes to retract his resignation, and declares his intention of appointing a curate for two years. I fear Mr. Sowden hardly produced a favourable impression; a strong wish was expressed that Arthur could come, but that is out of the question.

'I very much wish to come to Brookroyd, and I hope to be able to write with certainty and fix Wednesday, the 31st January, as the day; but the fact is I am not sure whether I shall be well enough to leave home. At present I should be a most tedious visitor. My health has been really very good since my return from Ireland till about ten days ago, when the stomach seemed quite suddenly to lose its tone; indigestion and continual faint sickness have been my portion ever since. Don't conjecture, dear Nell, for it is too soon yet, though I certainly never before felt as I have done lately. But keep the matter wholly to yourself, for I can come to no decided opinion at present. I am rather mortified to lose my good looks and grow thin as I am doing just when I thought of going to Brookroyd. Dear Ellen, I want to see you, and I hope I shall see you well. My love to all. — Yours faithfully,

'C. B. Nicholls.'

There were three more letters, but they were written in pencil from her deathbed. Two of them are printed by Mrs. Gaskell — one to Miss Nussey, the other to Miss Wheelwright. Here is the third and last of all.

TO MISS ELLEN NUSSEY.

'My dear Ellen, — Thank you very much for Mrs. Hewitt's sensible clear letter. Thank her too. In much her case was wonderfully like mine, but I am reduced to greater weakness; the skeleton emaciation is the same. I cannot talk. Even to my dear, patient, constant Arthur I can say but few words at once.

'These last two days I have been somewhat better, and

have taken some beef-tea, a spoonful of wine and water, a mouthful of light pudding at different times.

'Dear Ellen, I realise full well what you have gone through and will have to go through with poor Mercy. Oh, may you continue to be supported and not sink. Sickness here has been terribly rife. Kindest regards to Mr. and Mrs. Clapham, your mother, Mercy. Write when you can. — Yours,

'C. B. NICHOLLS.'

Little remains to be said. This is not a biography but a bundle of correspondence, and I have only to state that Mrs. Nicholls died of an illness incidental to childbirth on March 31st, 1855, and was buried in the Brontë tomb in Haworth church. Her will runs as follows : —

Extracted from the District Probate Registry at York attached to Her Majesty's High Court of Justice.

In the name of God. Amen. I, CHARLOTTE NICHOLLS, of Haworth in the parish of Bradford and county of York, being of sound and disposing mind, memory, and understanding, but mindful of my own mortality, do this seventeenth day of February, in the year of our Lord one thousand eight hundred and fifty-five, make this my last Will and Testament in manner and form following, that is to say : In case I die without issue I give and bequeath to my husband all my property to be his absolutely and entirely, but, In case I leave issue I bequeath to my husband the interest of my property during his lifetime, and at his death I desire that the principal should go to my surviving child or children ; should there be more than one child, share and share alike. And I do hereby make and appoint my said husband, Arthur Bell Nicholls, clerk, sole executor of this my last Will and Testament ; In witness whereof I have to this my last Will and Testament subscribed my hand, the day and year first above written — CHARLOTTE NICHOLLS. Signed and acknowledged by the said testatrix CHARLOTTE NICHOLLS, as and for her last Will and Testament in the presence of us, who, at her request, in her presence and in presence of each other, have at the same time hereunto subscribed our names as witnesses thereto: Patrick Brontë, B.A., Incumbent of Haworth, Yorkshire; Martha Brown.

The eighteenth day of April 1855, the Will of CHARLOTTE NICHOLLS, late of Haworth in the parish of Bradford in the county of York (wife of the Reverend Arthur Bell Nicholls, Clerk in Holy Orders) (having *bona notabilia* within the province of York), deceased, was proved in the prerogative court of York by the oath of the said Arthur Bell Nicholls (the husband), the sole executor to whom administration was granted, he having been first sworn daily to administer.

Testatrix died 31st March 1855.

It is easy as fruitless to mourn over 'unfulfilled renown,' but it is not easy to believe that the future had any great things in store. Miss Brontë's four novels will remain for all time imperishable monuments of her power. She had touched with effect in two of them all that she knew of her home surroundings, and in two others all that was revealed to her of a wider life. More she could not have done with equal effect had she lived to be eighty. Hers was, it is true, a sad life, but such gifts as these rarely bring happiness with them. It was surely something to have tasted the sweets of fame, and a fame so indisputably lasting.

Mr. Nicholls stayed on at Haworth for the six years that followed his wife's death. When Mr. Brontë died he returned to Ireland. Some years later he married again — a cousin, Miss Bell by name. That second marriage has been one of unmixed blessedness. I found him in a home of supreme simplicity and charm, esteemed by all who knew him and idolised in his own household. It was not difficult to understand that Charlotte Brontë had loved him and had fought down parental opposition in his behalf. The qualities of gentleness, sincerity, unaffected piety, and delicacy of mind are his; and he is beautifully jealous, not only for the fair fame of Currer Bell, but — what she would equally have loved — for her father, who also has had much undue detraction in the years that are past. That Mr. Nicholls may long continue to enjoy the kindly calm of his Irish home will be the wish of all who have read of his own continuous devotion to a wife who must ever rank among the greatest of her sex.

INDEX

INDEX

INDEX

INDEX

'North American Review,' 169.

'—— British Review,' 313, 346.

Nussey, Ellen, Chapter VIII. (204–233) ; her pedigree, 206 ; at school, 76, 234, 261, 264; at Haworth, 59, 60, 61, 158, 273, 274, 276, 299; in Sussex, 271, 272; visited by Charlotte, 239, 301 ; help to Mrs. Gaskell, 9–15, 24, 145 ; 'The Story of Charlotte Brontë's Life,' 23, 25 ; recollections of Anne, 203; recollections of Emily, 178–80; recollections of Miss Wooler, 261; Charlotte's admiration for, 300; Mary Taylor on 249, 250; letters from Anne, 182–4; letters from Charlotte, v, 76–86, 89–95, 98, 102, 105–7, 116, 119, 131–2, 134–8, 166, 173, 191, 196, 206–32, 237–8, 240–4, 254, 281–91, 295–7, 302–7, 310–2, 314–9, 321, 322, 360, 367, 401, 417, 419, 429, 430, 432, 443, 446, 448–50, 452, 457, 462, 465–9, 472–500; letter from Emily, 160; letter from Canon Heald, 443; letter from Martha Taylor, 240; letter from Mary Taylor, 256, 258.

—— George, 85, 86, 89.

—— Rev. Henry, 87, 119, 160, 221, 294–301.

—— Mrs. Henry, 220, 222, 223.

—— John, 206.

—— Mrs., 208, 222, 275.

—— Mercy, 89, 94, 141, 222, 226.

—— Richard, 89.

—— Sarah, 89.

OAKWORTH, 291.

'Observer,' 335, 431.

O'Callaghan Castle, 64–6.

O'Prunty, Patrick, 29.

'Orion,' 434, 435.

Orleans, Duchess of, 427.

Outhwaite, Miss, 181, 197.

'Oxford Chronicle,' 339.

PADIHAM, 498.

'Pag.' See Taylor, Mary.

'Palladium,' 310, 364, 366, 367.

Paris, Charlotte and, 96, 153.

Pascal's 'Thoughts,' 397.

Patchet, Miss, 145, 149.

Paxton, Sir Joseph, 54.

Payn, James, 370.

'Pendennis,' 172.

Penzance, 30, 33, 34, 51, 103, 105, 217.

Perry, Miss, 422.

Phillips, George Searle, 142.

Pickles, J., 491.

Poems by the sisters — in manuscript,

68–72; Aylott & Jones's edition, 325–31, 334, 348.

'Poor Relations,' 164.

Port Nicholson, N. Z., 239.

Portraits — of Anne, 181; of Branwell, 138; of Charlotte, 123, 294; of Emily, 123.

Postlethwaite, Mr., 124.

'Prelude,' Wordsworth's, 7.

Price, Rev. Mr., 302–3.

Procter, Mrs., 408, 422.

'Professor, The,' — its inception, 99, 100, 101; where written, 61; the manuscript, 332; seeking a publisher, 331, 332, 372; its publication, 275, 335; Charlotte on, 336; Mrs. Gaskell's proposed recasting of, 465.

Prunty, 157.

Puseyite struggle, 368, 400.

'QUARTERLY REVIEW,' 158, 176, 190, 195, 347, 348, 350, 351, 352, 393, 397, 408, 410, 412.

RAILWAY PANIC, 133.

Rands of Bradford, 41.

'Ranthorpe,' 411, 432.

Rawson, Mr., 42.

Read, Mrs. See Branwell, Elizabeth.

Redhead, Rev. Mr., 17.

Redman, Joseph, 55, 479.

Reform Bill, 121.

Reid, Sir Wemyss, vi, 23, 24.

'Reuter, Mdlle. Zoraide.' See Héger, Madame.

'Revue des deux Mondes,' 344, 345, 361.

Richmond's portrait of Charlotte, 294.

Rigby, Miss. See Eastlake, Lady.

Ringrose, Miss, 135, 225, 227.

Ritchie, Mrs. Richmond, 420–3.

'Rivers, St. John,' 245.

Robertson, Mr. ('Helstone'), 430, 443.

Robinson, Rev. Edmund, 18, 129, 136, 146, 148.

—— Mrs. Edmund, 18, 19, 128, 129, 130, 136, 137, 182.

—— Edmund, jun., 112, 129.

—— Misses, 137, 154, 182, 288.

—— William, of Leeds, 123.

Robinson's 'Emily Brontë,' 121, 122.

'Rochester,' 162, 405, 409, 410, 414.

—— Mrs., 339, 408.

Roe Head, 14, 15, 62, 63, 75, 76, 113, 120, 145, 182, 204, 206, 209, 213, 260, 261, 269, 293.

Rogers, Samuel, 463.

Rouse Mill, 215.

CHARLOTTE BRONTË AND HER CIRCLE